2141

D0475899

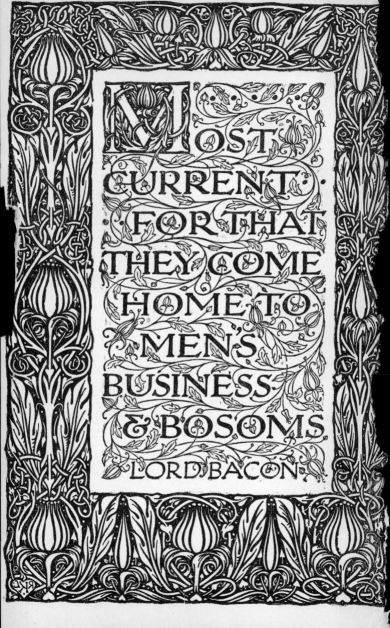

Most current for that they come home to men's business & bosoms.

LORD BACON

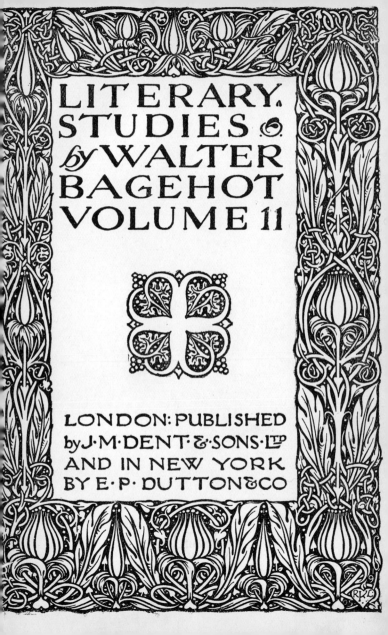

LITERARY.
STUDIES &
by WALTER
BAGEHOT
VOLUME II

LONDON: PUBLISHED
by J·M·DENT·&·SONS·L^{TD}
AND IN NEW YORK
BY E·P·DUTTON&CO

CONTENTS

LITERARY STUDIES

Edward Gibbon*
(1856)

'Papa, I wish I was the Roman Empire;' 'Child, don't talk nonsense;' was a dialogue of the early years of this century. This is the fate of Gibbon; no one does or can separate the historian from his subject. If you ask as to the antiquities of Constantinople, you are told those are the times which are 'in Gibbon.' Mr. Carlyle, who never exaggerates, speaks of Madame de Staël, in youth of course, romping about the knees of the 'Decline and Fall.' He plainly traced a resemblance himself; for he has narrated the events of his own life, 'his progression from London to Buriton and from Buriton to London,' in the same majestic periods which record the downfall of states and empires. What the commonplace parent thought absurd, has in simple reality happened. It may be useful to attempt in a few pages to substitute a notion of the man for the indistinct idea of a huge imperial being.

The diligence of their descendant accumulated many particulars of the remote annals of the Gibbon family; but its real founder was the grandfather of the historian, who lived in the times of the 'South Sea.' He was a capital man of business according to the custom of that age—a dealer in many kinds of merchandise—rivalling probably the 'complete tradesman' of Defoe, who was to understand the price and quality of *all* articles made within the kingdom, and be in consequence a complete master of the inland trade. The peculiar forte, however, of Edward Gibbon, the grandfather, was the article 'shares;' his genius, like that of Mr. Hudson, had a natural

---

* *The History of the Decline and Fall of the Roman Empire.* By Edward Gibbon, Esq. With Notes by Dean Milman and M. Guizot. Edited, with additional Notes, by William Smith, LL.D. In Eight Volumes. London, 1855. Murray.

tendency towards a commerce in the metaphysical and non-
existent; and he was fortunate in the age on which his lot was
thrown. It afforded many opportunities of gratifying that
taste. A great deal has been written and is being written on
panics and manias—a great deal more than with the most
outstretched intellect we are able to follow or conceive; but one
thing seems certain, that at particular times a great many
stupid people have a great deal of stupid money. Many saving
people have only the faculty of saving; they accumulate ably,
and contemplate their accumulations with approbation; but
what to do with them they do not know. Aristotle, who was
not in trade, had a great idea that money is barren; and barren
it certainly is to quiet ladies, rural clergymen, and country
misers. Several excellent economists have plans for prevent-
ing improvident speculation; one would abolish Peel's act, and
substitute one-pound notes; another would retain Peel's act, and
make the calling for one-pound notes a capital crime: but the
only real way is, not to allow any man to have a hundred
pounds who cannot prove to the satisfaction of the Lord
Chancellor that he knows what to do with a hundred pounds.
The want of this obvious and proper precaution allows the
accumulation of wealth in the hands of rectors, sweepers,
grandmothers, and other persons who have no knowledge of
business, and no idea except that their money now produces
nothing, and ought and must be forced immediately to produce
something. 'I wish,' said one of this class, 'for the largest immediate income, and I am therefore naturally disposed to
purchase an *advowson*.' Every now and then, from causes
which are not to the present purpose, the money of people of
this class—the blind capital (as oculists call it) of the country—
happens to be particularly large and craving; it seeks for some
one to devour it, and there is ' plethora '—it finds some one,
and there is 'speculation'—it is devoured, and there is ' panic.'
The age of Mr. Gibbon was one of these. The interest of money
was very low, perhaps under three per cent. The usual consequence followed; able men started wonderful undertakings;
the ablest of all, a company ' for carrying on an undertaking of
great importance, but no one to know what it was.' Mr.
Gibbon was not idle. According to the narrative of his grand-
son, he already filled a considerable position, was worth sixty
thousand pounds, and had great influence both in Parliament

and in the City. He applied himself to the greatest bubble of
all—one so great, that it is spoken of in many books as the
cause and parent of all contemporary bubbles—the great South
Sea Company—the design of which was to reduce the interest
on the national debt, which, oddly enough, it in fact effected,
and to trade exclusively to the South Sea or Spanish America,
where, of course, it hardly did trade. Mr. Gibbon became a
director, sold and bought, traded and prospered; and was considered, no doubt with truth, to have obtained much money.
The bubble was essentially a fashionable one. Public intelligence and the quickness of communication did not then as now
at once spread pecuniary information and misinformation to
secluded districts; but fine ladies, men of fashion—the London
world—ever anxious to make as much of its money as it can,
and then wholly unwise and not now very wise in discovering
how the most *was* to be made of it—'went in' and speculated
largely. Of course all was favourable so long as the shares
were rising; the price was at one time very high, and the
agitation very general; it was, in a word, the railway mania in
the South Sea. All at once the shares 'hesitated,' declined,
and fell; and there was an outcry against everybody concerned
in the matter, very like the outcry against the οἱ περὶ Hudson
in our own time. The results, however, were very different.
Whatever may be said, and, judging from late experience,
a good deal is likely to be said, as to the advantages of civilisation and education, it seems certain that they tend to diminish
a simple-minded energy. The Parliament of 1720 did not, like
the Parliament of 1847, allow itself to be bored and incommoded
by legal minutiæ, nor did they forego the use of plain words. A
committee reported the discovery of ' a train of the deepest
villany and fraud *hell* ever contrived to ruin a nation;' the
directors of the company were arrested, and Mr. Gibbon among
the rest; he was compelled to give in a list of his effects: the
general wish was that a retrospective act should be immediately
passed, which would impose on him penalties something like,
or even more severe than those now enforced on Paul and
Strahan. In the end, however, Mr. Gibbon escaped with a
parliamentary conversation upon his affairs. His estate
amounted to 140,000*l.*; and as this was a great sum, there was
an obvious suspicion that he was a great criminal. The whole
scene must have been very curious. ' Allowances of twenty

pounds or one shilling were facetiously voted. A vague report
that a director had formerly been concerned in another project
by which some unknown persons had lost their money, was
admitted as a proof of his actual guilt. One man was ruined
because he had dropped a foolish speech that his horses should
feed upon gold; another because he was grown so proud, that
one day, at the Treasury, he had refused a civil answer to persons far above him.' The vanity of his descendant is evidently
a little tried by the peculiar severity with which his grandfather
was treated. Out of his one hundred and forty thousand
pounds it was only proposed that he should retain fifteen, and
on an amendment even this was reduced to ten thousand. Yet
there is some ground for believing that the acute energy and
practised pecuniary power which had been successful in obtaining so large a fortune, were likewise applied with science to the
inferior task of retaining some of it. The historian indeed
says, ' On these ruins,' the 10,000l. aforesaid, ' with skill and
credit of which parliament had not been able to deprive him,
my grandfather erected the edifice of a new fortune: the labours
of sixteen years were amply rewarded; and I have reason to
believe that the second structure was not much inferior to the
first.' But this only shows how far a family feeling may bias
a sceptical judgment. The credit of a man in Mr. Gibbon's
position could not be very lucrative; and his skill must have
been enormous to have obtained so much at the end of life, in
such circumstances, in so few years. Had he been an early
Christian, the narrative of his descendant would have contained
an insidious hint, that ' pecuniary property *may* be so secreted
as to defy the awkward approaches of political investigation.'
It was on this property, in whatever way acquired or retained,
that the social position of the Gibbons was established, and
the remnants of it preserved from death the immortal author
of the Decline and Fall.

The son of this great speculator, the historian's father, was
a man to spend a fortune quietly. He is not related to have
indulged in any particular expense, and nothing is more difficult to follow than the pecuniary fortunes of deceased families;
but one thing is certain, that the property which descended to
the historian—putting out of the question all minor and sub-
sidiary modes of diminution, such as daughters, settlements,
legacies, and so forth—was enormously less than 140,000l.;

and if the statistics above quoted are correct, the second
generation of the family must have made itself very happy out
of the savings of the past generation, and without caring for
the poverty of the next. Nothing that is related, indeed, of
the historian's father indicates a strong judgment or an acute
discrimination; and there are some scarcely dubious signs
of a rather weak character.

Edward Gibbon, the historian, was born on the 27th of April
1737. Of his mother we hear scarcely anything; and what we
do hear is not remarkably favourable. It seems that she was a
faint inoffensive woman, of ordinary capacity, who left a very
slight trace of her influence on the character of her son; who
did little, and died early. The real mother, as he is careful to
explain, of his understanding and education was her sister, and
his aunt, *Mrs.* Catherine Posten, according to the speech of
that age, a maiden lady of much vigour and capacity, and for
whom her pupil really seems to have felt as much affection as
was consistent with a rather easy and cool nature. There is a
panegyric on her in the *Memoirs*; and in a long letter upon the
occasion of her death, he deposes: ' To her care I am indebted
in earliest infancy for the preservation of my life and health.
. . . To her instructions I owe the first rudiments of knowledge, the first exercise of reason, and a taste for books, which
is still the pleasure and glory of my life; and though she taught
me neither language nor science, she was certainly the most
useful preceptress I ever had. As I grew up, an intercourse of
thirty years endeared her to me as the faithful friend and the
agreeable companion. You have observed with what freedom
and confidence we lived,' &c. &c. To a less sentimental mind,
which takes a more tranquil view of aunts and relatives, it is
satisfactory to find that he could not write to her. ' I wish,'
he continues, ' I had as much to applaud and as little to
reproach in my conduct to Mrs. Posten since I left England;
and when I reflect that my letter would have soothed and com-
forted her decline, I feel' what an ardent nephew would naturally feel at so unprecedented an event. Leaving his maturer
years out of the question—a possible rhapsody of affectionate
eloquence—she really seems to have been of the greatest use to
him in infancy. His health was very imperfect. We hear
much of rheumatism, and lameness, and weakness; and he was
clearly in general unable to join in work and play with ordinary

boys. On this account, he was moved from one school to another, never staying anywhere very long, and owing what knowledge he obtained rather to a strong retentive understanding than to any external stimulants or instruction. At one place he gained an acquaintance with the Latin elements at the price of ' many tears and some blood.' At last he was consigned to the instruction of an elegant clergyman, the Rev. Philip Francis, who had obtained notoriety by a metrical translation of Horace, the laxity of which is even yet complained of by construing school-boys, and who, having a truly Horatian taste for combining the pleasures of a town with those of a country life, went to London as often as he could, and translated *invisa negotia* as ' boys to beat.'

In school-work, therefore, Gibbon had uncommon difficulties and unusual deficiencies; but these were much more than counterbalanced by a habit which often accompanies a sickly childhood, and is very often the commencement of a studious life—the habit of desultory reading. The instructiveness of this is often not properly comprehended. S. T. Coleridge used to say that he felt a great superiority over those who had not read—and fondly read—fairy tales in their childhood; he thought they wanted a sense which he possessed, the perception, or apperception—we do not know which he used to say it was —of the unity and wholeness of the universe. As to fairy tales, this is a hard saying; but as to desultory reading it is certainly true. Some people have known a time in life when there was no book they could not read. The fact of its being a book went immensely in its favour. In early life there is an opinion that the obvious thing to do with a horse is to ride it; of a cake, to eat it; of sixpence, to spend it: a few boys carry this further, and think the obviously natural thing to do with a book is to read it. There is an argument from design in the subject: if the book was not meant for that purpose, for what purpose was it meant? Of course, of any understanding of the works so perused there is no question or idea. There is a legend of Bentham, when still in long clothes, climbing to the height of a huge stool and sitting there evening after evening with two candles engaged in the perusal of Rapin's history. It might just as well have been any other book. The doctrine of utility had not then dawned on its immortal teacher; *cui bono* was an idea unknown to him. He would have been ready to read about Egypt, about Spain, about the coals in Borneo, the teak-wood in India, the current in the river Mississipi, on natural history or human history, on theology or morals, on the state of the dark ages or the state of the light ages, on Augustulus or Lord Chatham, on the first century or the seventeenth, on the moon, the millennium, or the whole duty of man. Just then, in fact, reading is an end in itself. At that time of life you no more think of a future consequence, of the remote, the very remote possibility of deriving knowledge from the perusal of a book, than you expect so great a result from spinning a peg-top. You spin the top, and you read the book; and then that scene of life is exhausted. In such studies, of all prose perhaps the best is history. One page is so like another; battle No. 1 is so much on a par with battle No. 2. Truth may be, as they say, stranger than fiction, abstractedly and in itself; but in actual books, novels are certainly odder and more astounding than correct history. It will be said, what is the use of this? Why not leave the reading of great books till a great age? Why plague and perplex childhood with complex facts remote from its experience and inapprehensible by its imagination? The reply is, that though in all great and combined facts there is much which childhood cannot thoroughly imagine or comprehend, there is also in very many a great deal which can only be truly apprehended for the first time at that age. Catch an American of thirty;—tell him about the battle of Marathon; what will he be able to comprehend of all that *you* mean by it; of all that halo which early impression and years of remembrance have cast around it? He may add up the killed and wounded, estimate the missing, and take the dimensions of Greece and Athens; but he will not seem to care much. He may say, ' Well, sir, perhaps it was a smart thing in that small country; but it is a long time ago, and in *my* country James K. Burnup' did that which he will at length explain to you. Or try an experiment on yourself. Read the account of a Circassian victory, equal in numbers, in daring, in romance, to the old battle. Will you be able to feel about it at all in the same way? It is impossible. You cannot form a new set of associations; your mind is involved in pressing facts, your memory choked by a thousand details; the liveliness of fancy is gone with the childhood by which it was enlivened. Schamyl will never

seem as great as Leonidas, or Miltiades; Cnokemof, or whoever the Russian is, cannot be so imposing as Xerxes; the un-
pronounceable place cannot strike on your heart like Marathon
of Platæa. Moreover, there is the further advantage which
Coleridge shadowed forth in the remark we cited. Youth
has a principle of consolidation. We begin with the whole.
Small sciences are the labours of our manhood; but the round
universe is the plaything of the boy. His fresh mind shoots
out vaguely and crudely into the infinite and eternal. Nothing
is hid from the depth of it; there are no boundaries to its
vague and wandering vision. Early science, it has been said,
begins in utter nonsense; it would be truer to say that it
starts with boyish fancies. How absurd seem the notions of the
first Greeks! Who could believe now that air or water was
the principle, the pervading substance, the eternal material
of all things? Such affairs will never explain a thick rock;
they scarcely account for pea-soup; and what a white original
for a green and sky-blue world! Yet people disputed in those
ages not whether it was either of those substances, but which
of them it was. And doubtless there was a great deal, at least in
point of quantity, to be said on both sides. Boys are improved;
but some in our own day have asked, ' Mamma, I say, what
did God make the world of?' and several, who did not venture
on speech, have had an idea of some one gray primitive thing,
have felt a difficulty as to how the red came, and wondered
how marble could *ever* have been the same as moonshine. This
is in truth the picture of life. We begin with the infinite and
eternal, which we shall never apprehend; and these form a
framework, a schedule, a set of co-ordinates to which we refer
all which we learn later. At first, like the old Greek, ' we look
up to the whole sky, and are lost in the one and the all;' in
the end we classify and enumerate, learn each star, calculate
distances, draw cramped diagrams on the unbounded sky,
write a paper on α Cygni and a treatise on ε Draconis, map
special facts upon the indefinite void, and engrave precise
details on the infinite and everlasting. So in history; somehow
the whole comes in boyhood; the details later and in manhood.
The wonderful series going far back to the times of old
patriarchs with their flocks and herds, the keen-eyed Greek,
the stately Roman, the watching Jew, the uncouth Goth,
the horrid Hun, the settled picture of the unchanging East,

the restless shifting of the rapid West, the rise of the cold and classical civilisation, its fall, the rough impetuous middle ages, the vague warm picture of ourselves and home,—when did we learn these? Not yesterday nor to-day; but long ago, in the first dawn of reason, in the original flow of fancy. What we learn afterwards are but the accurate littlenesses of the great topic, the dates and tedious facts. Those who begin late learn only these; but the happy first feel the mystic associations and the progress of the whole.

There is no better illustration of all this than Gibbon. Few have begun early with a more desultory reading, and fewer still have described it so skilfully. ' From the ancient I leaped to the modern world; many crude lumps of Speed, Rapin, Mezeray, Davila, Machiavel, Father Paul, Bower, &c., I devoured like so many novels; and I swallowed with the same voracious appetite the descriptions of India and China, of Mexico and Peru. My first introduction to the historic scenes which have since engaged so many years of my life must be ascribed to an accident. In the summer of 1751 I accompanied my father on a visit to Mr. Hoare's, in Wiltshire; but I was less delighted with the beauties of Stourhead than with discovering in the library a common book, the *Continuation of Echard's Roman History*, which is indeed executed with more skill and taste than the previous work. To me the reigns of the successors of Constantine were absolutely new; and I was immersed in the passage of the Goths over the Danube when the summons of the dinner-bell reluctantly dragged me from my intellectual feast. This transient glance served rather to irritate than to appease my curiosity; and as soon as I returned to Bath I procured the second and third volumes of Howel's *History of the World*, which exhibit the Byzantine period on a larger scale. Mahomet and his Saracens soon fixed my attention; and some instinct of criticism directed me to the genuine sources. Simon Ockley, an original in every sense, first opened my eyes; and I was led from one book to another till I had ranged round the circle of Oriental history. Before I was sixteen I had exhausted all that could be learned in English of the Arabs and Persians, the Tartars and Turks; and the same ardour urged me to guess at the French of d'Herbelot, and to construe the barbarous Latin of Pocock's *Abulfaragius*.' To this day the schoolboy student of the Decline and Fall feels the traces of that schoolboy reading. *Once*, he is conscious, the author, like him, felt, and solely felt, the magnificent progress of the great story and the scenic aspect of marvellous events.

A more sudden effect was at hand. However exalted may seem the praises which we have given to loose and unplanned reading, we are not saying that it is the sole ingredient of a good education. Besides this sort of education, which some boys will voluntarily and naturally give themselves, there needs, of course, another and more rigorous kind, which must be impressed upon them from without. The terrible difficulty of early life—the *use* of pastors and masters—really is, that they compel boys to a distinct mastery of that which they do not wish to learn. There is nothing to be said for a preceptor who is not dry. Mr. Carlyle describes with bitter satire the fate of one of his heroes who was obliged to acquire whole systems of information in which he, the hero, saw no use, and which he kept as far as might be in a vacant corner of his mind. And this is the very point—dry language, tedious mathematics, a thumbed grammar, a detested slate, form gradually an interior separate intellect, exact in its information, rigid in its requirements, disciplined in its exercises. The two grow together, the early natural fancy touching the far extremities of the universe, lightly p aying with the scheme of all things; the precise, compacted memory slowly accumulating special facts, exact habits, clear and painful conceptions. At last, as it were in a moment, the cloud breaks up, the division sweeps away; we find that in fact these exercises which puzzled us, these languages which we hated, these details which we despised, are the instruments of true thought, are the very keys and openings, the exclusive access to the knowledge which we loved.

In this second education the childhood of Gibbon had been very defective. He had never been placed under any rigid training. In his first boyhood he disputed with his aunt, ' that were I master of Greek and Latin, I must interpret to myself in English the thoughts of the original, and that such extemporary versions must be inferior to the elaborate translation of professed scholars; a silly sophism,' as he remarks, ' which could not easily be confuted by a person ignorant of any other language than her own.' Ill-health, a not very wise father, an ill-chosen succession of schools and pedagogues, prevented his acquiring exact knowledge in the regular subjects of study. His own description is the best—' erudition that might have puzzled a doctor, and ignorance of which a schoolboy should have been ashamed.' The amiable Mr. Francis, who was to have repaired the deficiency, went to London, and forgot him. On a sudden his father put on his hat, took a resolution, and sent him to Oxford at sixteen.

It is probable that a worse place could not have been found. The University of Oxford was at the very nadir of her history and efficiency. The public professorial training of the middle ages had died away, and the intramural collegiate system of the present time had not begun. The University had ceased to be a teaching body, and had not yet become an examining body. ' The professors,' says Adam Smith, who had studied there, ' have given up almost the pretence of lecturing.' 'The examination,' said a great judge some years later, ' was a farce in my time. I was asked who founded University College; and I said, though the fact is now doubted, that King Alfred founded it; and *that* was the examination.' The colleges, deprived of the superintendence and watchfulness of their natural sovereign, fell, as Gibbon remarks, into ' port and prejudice.' The Fellows were a close corporation; they were chosen from every conceivable motive—because they were respectable men, because they were good fellows, because they were brothers of other fellows, because their fathers had patronage in the church. Men so appointed could not be expected to be very diligent in the instruction of youth; many colleges did not even profess it; that of All Souls has continued down to our own time to deny that it has anything to do with it. Undoubtedly a person who came thither accurately and rigidly drilled in technical scholarship found many means and some motives to pursue it. Some tutorial system probably existed at most colleges. Learning was not wholly useless in the church. The English gentleman has ever loved a nice and classical scholarship. But these advantages were open only to persons who had received a very rigid and peculiar training, and who were voluntarily disposed to discipline themselves still more. To the mass of mankind the University was a ' graduating machine; ' the colleges, monopolist residences,— hotels without bells.

Taking the place as it stood, the lot of Gibbon may be thought rather fortunate. He was placed at Magdalen, whose fascinating walks, so beautiful in the later autumn, still recall the name of Addison, the example of the merits, as Gibbon is of the deficiencies, of Oxford. His first tutor was, in his own opinion, ' one of the best of the tribe.' ' Dr. Waldegrave was a learned and pious man, of a mild disposition, strict morals, and abstemious life, who seldom mingled in the politics or the jollity of the college. But his knowledge of the world was confined to the University; his learning was of the last, rather than of the present age; his temper was indolent; his faculties, which were not of the first rate, had been relaxed by the climate; and he was satisfied, like his fellows, with the slight and superficial discharge of an important trust. As soon as my tutor had sounded the insufficiency of his disciple in school-learning, he proposed that we should read every morning, from ten to eleven, the comedies of Terence. The sum of my improvement in the University of Oxford is confined to three or four Latin plays; and even the study of an elegant classic, which might have been illustrated by a comparison of ancient and modern theatres, was reduced to a dry and literal interpretation of the author's text. During the first weeks I constantly attended these lessons in my tutor's room; but as they appeared equally devoid of profit and pleasure, I was once tempted to try the experiment of a formal apology. The apology was accepted with a smile. I repeated the offence with less ceremony; the excuse was admitted with the same indulgence: the slightest motive of laziness or indisposition, the most trifling avocation at home or abroad, was allowed as a worthy impediment; nor did my tutor appear conscious of my absence or neglect. Had the hour of lecture been constantly filled, a single hour was a small portion of my academic leisure. No plan of study was recommended for my use; no exercises were prescribed for his inspection; and, at the most precious season of youth, whole days and weeks were suffered to elapse without labour or amusement, without advice or account.'

The name of his second tutor is concealed in asterisks, and the sensitive conscience of Dean Milman will not allow him to insert a name ' which *Gibbon* thought proper to suppress.' The account, however, of the anonymous person is sufficiently graphic. ' Dr. **** well remembered that he had a salary to receive, and only forgot that he had a duty to perform. Instead of guiding the studies and watching over the behaviour of his disciple, I was never summoned to attend even the ceremony of a lecture; and excepting one voluntary visit to his rooms, during the eight months of his titular office the tutor and pupil lived in the same college as strangers to each other.' It added to the evils of this neglect, that Gibbon was much younger than most of the students; and that his temper, which was through life reserved, was then very shy. His appearance, too, was odd; ' a thin little figure, with a large head, disputing and arguing with the greatest ability.' Of course he was a joke among undergraduates; he consulted his tutor as to studying Arabic, and was seen buying *La Bibliothèque Orientale d'Herbelot*, and immediately a legend was diffused that he had turned Mahomedan. The random cast was not so far from the mark; cut off by peculiarities from the society of young people; deprived of regular tuition and systematic employment; tumbling about among crude masses of heterogeneous knowledge; alone with the heated brain of youth,—he did what an experienced man would expect— he framed a theory of all things. No doubt it seemed to him the most natural thing in the world. Was he to be the butt of ungenial wine-parties, or spend his lonely hours on shreds of languages? Was he not to know the *truth*? There were the old problems, the everlasting difficulties, the *mœnia mundi*, the Hercules' pillars of the human imagination—' fate, free-will, fore-knowledge absolute.' Surely these should come first; when we had learned the great landmarks, understood the guiding-stars, we might amuse ourselves with small points, and make a plaything of curious information. What particular theory the mind frames in these circumstances is a good deal matter of special accident. The *data* for considering these difficulties are not within its reach. Whether man be or be not born to solve the ' mystery of the knowable,' he certainly is not born to solve it at seventeen, with the first hot rush of the untrained mind. The selection of Gibbon was remarkable: he became a Roman Catholic.

It seems now so natural that an Oxford man should take this step, that one can hardly understand the astonishment it created. Lord Sheffield tells us that the Privy Council

interfered; and with good administrative judgment examined a
London bookseller—some Mr. Lewis—who had no concern in
it. In the manor-house of Buriton it would have probably
created less sensation if 'dear Edward' had announced his
intention of becoming a monkey. The English belief always
is that the Papist is a kind of *creature;* some think that the
Oxford student is its young; and every sound mind would
prefer a beloved child to produce a tail, a hide of hair, and a
taste for nuts, in comparison with transubstantiation, wax-
candles, and a belief in the glories of Mary.

What exact motives impelled Gibbon to this step cannot
now be certainly known; the autobiography casts a mist over
them; but from what appears, his conversion partly much
resembled, and partly altogether differed from, the Oxford
conversions of our own time. We hear nothing of the notes of a
church, or the sin of the Reformation; and Gibbon had not
an opportunity of even rejecting Mr. Sewell's theory that it is
'a holy obligation to acquiesce in the opinions of your grand-
mother.' His memoirs throw a halo of great names over the
occurrence—Bossuet, the *History of Protestant Variations,*
&c. &c.—and he speaks with becoming dignity of falling by a
noble hand. He mentioned also to Lord Sheffield, as having
had a preponderating influence over him, the works of Father
Parsons, who lived in Queen Elizabeth's time. But in all
probability these were secondary persuasions, justifications
after the event. No young man, or hardly any young man of
seventeen, was ever converted by a systematic treatise, especially if written in another age, wearing an obsolete look, speaking a language which scarcely seems that of this world. There
is an unconscious reasoning: 'The world has had this book
before it so long, and has withstood it. There must be something wrong; it seems all right on the surface, but a flaw there
must be.' The mass of the volumes, too, is unfavourable.
'All the treatises in the world,' says the young convert in
Loss and Gain, ' are not equal to giving one a view in a moment.'
What the youthful mind requires is this short decisive argument, this view in a moment, this flash as it were of the
understanding, which settles all, and diffuses a conclusive
light at once and for ever over the whole. It is so much the
pleasanter if the young mind can strike this view out for itself,
from materials which are forced upon it from the controversies

of the day; if it can find a certain solution of pending questions, and show itself wiser even than the wisest of its own, the very last age. So far as appears, this was the fortune of Gibbon. ' It was not long,' he says, ' since Dr. Middleton's *Free Inquiry* had sounded an alarm in the theological world; much ink and much gall had been spent in defence of the primitive miracles; and the two dullest of their champions were crowned with academic honours by the University of Oxford. The name of Middleton was unpopular; and his proscription very naturally led me to peruse his writings and those of his antagonists.' It is not difficult to discover in this work easy and striking arguments which might lead an untaught mind to the communion of Rome. As to the peculiar belief of its author, there has been much controversy, with which we have not here the least concern; but the natural conclusion to which it would lead a simple intellect is, that all miracles are equally certain or equally uncertain.

' It being agreed, then,' says the acute controversialist, ' that in the original promise of these miraculous gifts there is no intimation of any particular period to which their continuance was limited, the next question is, by what sort of evidence the precise time of their duration is to be determined? But to this point one of the writers just referred to excuses himself, as we have seen, from giving any answer; and thinks it sufficient to declare in general that *the earliest fathers unanimously affirm them to have continued down to their times*. Yet he has not told us, as he ought to have done, to what age he limits the character of *the earliest fathers*; whether to the second or to the third century, or, with the generality of our writers, means also to include the fourth. But to whatever age he may restrain it, the difficulty at last will be to assign a reason why we must needs stop there. In the meanwhile, by his appealing thus to the *earliest fathers* only as unanimous on this article, a common reader would be apt to infer that the later fathers are more cold or diffident, or divided upon it; whereas the reverse of this is true, and the more we descend from those earliest fathers the more strong and explicit we find their successors in attesting the perpetual succession and daily exertion of the same miraculous powers in their several ages; so that, if the cause must be determined by *the unanimous consent of fathers*, we shall find as much reason to believe that those powers were continued even to the latest ages as to any other, how early and primitive soever, after the days of the apostles. But the same writer gives us two reasons why he does not choose to say anything upon the subject of their duration; 1st, because *there is not light enough in history to settle it*; 2ndly, because *the thing itself is of no concern to us*. As to his first reason, I am at a loss to conceive what further light a professed advocate of the primitive ages and fathers can possibly require in this case. For as far as the church historians can illustrate or throw light upon anything, there is not a single point in all history so constantly, explicitly, and unanimously affirmed by them all, as the continual succession of these powers through all ages, from the earliest father who first mentions them down to the time of the Reformation. Which same succession is still further deduced by persons of the most eminent character for their probity, learning, and dignity in the Romish church, to this very day. So that the only doubt which can remain with us is, whether the church historians are to be trusted or not; for if any credit be due to them in the present case, it must reach either to all or to none; because the reason of believing them in any one age will be found to be of equal force in all, as far as it depends on the characters of the persons attesting, or the nature of the things attested.'

In *terms* this and the whole of Middleton's argument is so shaped as to avoid including in its scope the miracles of Scripture, which are mentioned throughout with eulogiums and acquiescence, and so as to make you doubt whether the author believed them or not. This is exactly one of the pretences which the young strong mind delights to tear down, which would say, 'This writer evidently *means* that the apostolic miracles have just as much evidence and no more than the popish or the patristic; and how strong '—for Middleton is a master of telling statement—' he shows that evidence to be! I won't give up the apostolic miracles, I cannot; yet I must believe what has so much of historical testimony in its favour. It is no *reductio ad absurdum* that we must go over to the church of Rome; it is the most diffused of Christian creeds, the oldest of Christian churches.' And so the logic of the sceptic becomes, as often since, the most efficient instrument of the all-believing and all-determining church.

The consternation of Gibbon's relatives seems to have been enormous. They cast about what to do. From the experience of Oxford, they perhaps thought that it would be useless to have recourse to the Anglican clergy; they had tried their best, it was perhaps fancied, and had failed. So they took him to Mr. Mallet, a deist, to see if he could do anything; but he did nothing. Their next step was nearly as extraordinary. They placed him at Lausanne in the house of M. Pavilliard, a French Protestant minister. After the easy income, complete independence, and unlimited credit of an English undergraduate, he was thrown into a foreign country, deprived, as he says, by ignorance of the language both of ' speech and hearing,'—in the position of a schoolboy, with a small allowance of pocket-money, and without the Epicurean comforts on which he already set some value. He laments the ' indispensable comfort of a servant,' and the ' sordid and uncleanly table of Madame Pavilliard.' In our own day the watchful sagacity of Cardinal Wiseman would hardly allow a promising convert of expectations and talents to remain unsolaced in so pitiful a situation; we should hear of some soothing offers of flight or succour, of some gentle insinuation of a popish domestic and interesting repasts. But the attention of the Holy See a hundred years ago was very little directed to our English youth, and Gibbon was left to endure his position.

It is curious that he made himself comfortable. Though destitute of external comforts which he did not despise, he found what was the greatest luxury to his disposition, steady study and regular tuition. His tutor was, of course, to convert him if he could; but as they had no language in common, there was the preliminary occupation of teaching French. During five years both tutor and pupil steadily exerted themselves to repair the defects of a neglected and ill-grounded education. We hear of the perusal of Terence, Virgil, Horace, and Tacitus. Cicero was translated into French, and translated back again into Latin. In both languages the pupil's progress was sound and good. From letters of his which still exist, it is clear that he then acquired the exact and steady knowledge of Latin of which he afterwards made so much use. His circumstances compelled him to master French. If his own letters are to be trusted, he would be an example of his own doctrine, that no one is thoroughly master of more than one language at a time; they read like the letters of a Frenchman trying and failing to write English. But perhaps there was some wish to magnify his continental progress, and towards the end of the time some wish to make his friends fear he was forgetting his own language.

Meantime the work of conversion was not forgotten. In some letters which are still extant, M. Pavilliard celebrates the triumph of his logic. '*J'ai renversé*,' says the pastor, '*l'infaillibilité de l'église; j'ai prouvé que jamais St. Pierre n'a été chef des apôtres; que quand il l'aurait été, le pape n'est point son successeur; qu'il est douteux que St. Pierre ait jamais été à Rome, mais supposé qu'il y ait été, il n'a pas été évêque de cette ville; que la transubstantiation est une invention humaine, et peu ancienne dans l'église*,' &c., and so on through the usual list of Protestant arguments. He magnifies perhaps a little Gibbon's strength of conviction, as it makes the success of his own arguments seem more splendid; but states two curious things, first, that Gibbon at least *pretended* to believe in the Pretender, and what is more amazing still—all but incredible—that he fasted. A curious youth for a sceptical and Epicurean historian!

It is probable, however, that the skill of the Swiss pastor was not the really operating cause of the event. Perhaps experience shows that the converts which Rome has made with the threat of unbelief and the weapons of the sceptic have rarely been permanent or advantageous to her. It is at best but a dangerous logic to drive men to the edge and precipice of scepticism, in the hope that they will recoil in horror to the very centre of credulity. It may happen that men may show their courage—that they will vanquish the *argumentum ad terrorem*—they will not find scepticism so terrible. This last was Gibbon's case. A more insidious adversary than the Swiss theology was at hand to sap his Roman Catholic belief. Pavilliard had a fair French library—not ill stored in the recent publications of that age—of which he allowed his pupil the continual use. It was as impossible to open any of them and not come in contact with infidelity, as to come to England and not to see a green field. Scepticism is not so much a part of the French literature of that day as its animating spirit— its essence, its vitality. You can no more cut it out and separate

it, than you can extract from Wordsworth his conception of
nature, or from Swift his common sense. And it is of the subtlest
kind. It has little in common with the rough disputation of
the English deist, or the perplexing learning of the German
theologian; but works with a tool more insinuating than
either. It is, in truth, but the spirit of the world, which does not
argue, but assumes; which does not so much elaborate as
hint; which does not examine, but suggest. With the traditions
of the church it contrasts traditions of its own; its technicalities
are *bon sens, l'usage du monde, le fanatisme, l'enthousiasme*;
to high hopes, noble sacrifices, awful lives, it opposes quiet
ease, skilful comfort, placid calm, polished indifference. Old
as transubstantiation may be, it is not older than Horace and
Lucian. Lord Byron, in the well-known lines, has coupled the
names of the two literary exiles on the Leman Lake. The page
of Voltaire could not but remind Gibbon that the scepticism
from which he had revolted was compatible with literary
eminence and European fame—gave a piquancy to ordinary
writing—was the very expression of caustic caution and
gentlemanly calm.

The grave and erudite habits of Gibbon soon developed
themselves. Independently of these abstruse theological
disputations, he spent many hours daily—rising early and
reading carefully—on classical and secular learning. He was
not, however, wholly thus engrossed. There was in the neighbourhood of Lausanne a certain Mademoiselle Curchod;
a studious and cultivated, it might almost be said a rational
damsel. She showed this peculiar quality in her taste. To
form an attachment to the Roman Empire is a difficult
attainment for any young woman; but Mademoiselle
Curchod went much further than a sentimental appreciation
of the Decline and Fall, she professed to feel real affection for a
grave and lumbering banker—M. Necker, afterwards the Slow
Premier in a quick revolution—the author of various financial
treatises, French sums, and tedious theories, to which this
Genevese beauty, however, devoted much of her attention.
But this was in a later time: Gibbon was, it seems, her first
love;—history on Mondays, finance only on Tuesdays, appears
to have been the rule of that well regulated intellect. The
feelings of Gibbon, it can hardly be supposed, were likely to do
him any harm. However, there was an intimacy, a flirtation, an

engagement—when it suddenly struck one or the other that they neither had any money. That the young lady should procure any seems to have been out of the question; and Gibbon, ' taking ' what Mr. James often terms ' the initiative that becomes a man,' wrote to his father. The reply was unfavourable. Gibbon's mother was dead; Mr. Gibbon senior was married again; and even in other circumstances would have been scarcely ready to encourage a romantic engagement to a lady with nothing. She spoke no English, too, and marriage with a person speaking only French was then regarded as a most unnatural event; forbidden, not indeed by the literal law of the church, but by those higher instinctive principles of our nature, to which the bluntest own obedience. No father could be expected to violate at once pecuniary duties and patriotic principles. Mr. Gibbon senior forbade the match. The young lady does not seem to have been quite ready to relinquish all hope; but she had shown a grave taste, and fixed her affections on a sound and cold mind. ' I sighed,' narrates the historian, ' as a lover; but I obeyed as a son.' ' I have seen,' says M. Suard, ' the letter in which Gibbon communicated to Mademoiselle Curchod the opposition of his father to their marriage. The first pages are tender and melancholy, as might be expected from an unhappy lover; the latter become by degrees calm and reasonable; and the letter concludes with these words: *C'est pourquoi, mademoiselle, j'ai l'honneur d'être votre très-humble et très-obéissant serviteur, Edward Gibbon.*' Her father died soon afterwards, and ' she retired to Geneva, where, by teaching young ladies, she earned a hard subsistence for herself and her mother;' but the tranquil disposition of her historical admirer preserved him from any romantic display of sympathy and fidelity. He continued to study various readings in Cicero, as well as the passage of Hannibal over the Alps; and with these affectionate resources set sentiment at defiance. Yet thirty years later the lady, then the wife of the most conspicuous man in Europe, was able to suggest useful reflections to an aged bachelor, obscurely and slightly dreaming of a superannuated marriage: ' Gardez-vous, monsieur, de former un de ces liens tardifs: le mariage qui rend heureux dans l'age mûr, c'est celui qui fut contracté dans la jeunesse. Alors seulement la réunion est parfaite, les goûts se communiquent, les senti-

mens se répandent, les idées deviennent communes, les facultés
intellectuelles se modèlent mutuellement. Toute la vie est
double, et toute la vie est une prolongation de la jeunesse;
car les impressions de l'âme commandent aux yeux, et la
beauté qui n'est plus conserve encore son empire; mais pour
vous, monsieur, dans toute la vigueur de la pensée, lorsque
toute l'existence est décidée, l'on ne pourroit sans un miracle
trouver une femme digne de vous; et une association d'un
genre imparfait rappelle toujours la statue d'Horace, qui joint
à une belle tête le corps d'un stupide poisson. Vous êtes marié
avec la gloire.' She was then a cultivated and instructed
French lady, giving an account of the reception of the Decline
and Fall at Paris, and expressing rather peculiar ideas on the
style of Tacitus. The world had come round to her side, and
she explains to her old lover rather well her happiness with
M. Necker.

After living nearly five years at Lausanne, Gibbon returned
to England. Continental residence has made a great alteration
in many Englishmen; but few have undergone so complete a
metamorphosis as Edward Gibbon. He left his own country
a hot-brained and ill-taught youth, willing to sacrifice friends
and expectations for a superstitious and half-known creed;
he returned a cold and accomplished man, master of many
accurate ideas, little likely to hazard any coin for any faith;
already, it is probable, inclined in secret to a cautious scepticism; placing thereby, as it were, upon a system the frigid
prudence and unventuring incredulity congenial to his
character. His change of character changed his position among
his relatives. His father, he says, met him as a friend; and they
continued thenceforth on a footing of 'easy intimacy.'
Especially after the little affair of Mademoiselle Curchod, and
the 'very sensible view he took in that instance of the
matrimonial relation,' there can be but little question that
Gibbon was justly regarded as a most safe young man, singularly prone to large books, and a little too fond of French
phrases and French ideas; but yet with a great feeling of
common sense, and a wise preference of permanent money to
transitory sentiment. His father allowed him a moderate, and
but a moderate income, which he husbanded with great
affection, and only voluntarily expended in the purchase and
acquisition of serious volumes. He lived for many years, till

his father's death and afterwards, an externally idle but really studious life, varied by tours in France and Italy; the toils of which, though not in description very formidable, somewhat sorely tried a sedentary habit and somewhat corpulent body. The only English avocation which he engaged in was, oddly enough, war. It does not seem the most likely in this pacific country, nor does he seem exactly the man for *la grande guerre*; but so it was; and the fact is an example of a really Anglican invention. The English have discovered pacific war. We may not be able to kill people as well as the French, or fit out and feed distant armaments as neatly as they do; but we are unrivalled at a quiet armament here at home which never kills anybody, and never wants to be sent anywhere. A ' constitutional militia ' is a beautiful example of the mild efficacy of civilisation, which can convert even the ' great manslaying profession ' (as Carlyle calls it) into a quiet and dining association. Into this force Gibbon was admitted; and immediately, contrary to his anticipations, and very much against his will, was called out for permanent duty. The hero of the *corps* was a certain dining Sir Thomas, who used at the end of each new bottle to announce with increasing joy how much soberer he had become. What his fellow-officers thought of Gibbon's French predilections and large volumes it is not difficult to conjecture; and he complains bitterly of the interruption to his studies. However, his easy composed nature soon made itself at home; his polished tact partially concealed from the ' mess ' his recondite pursuits, and he contrived to make the Hampshire armament of classical utility. ' I read,' he says, ' the Analysis of Cæsar's Campaign in Afrca. Every motion of that great general is laid open with a critical sagacity. A complete military history of his campaigns would do almost as much honour to M. Guichardt as to Cæsar. This finished the *Mémoires*, which gave me a much clearer notion of ancient tactics than I ever had before. Indeed, my own military knowledge was of some service to me, as I am well acquainted with the modern discipline and exercise of a battalion. So that though much inferior to M. Folard and M. Guichardt, who had seen service, I am a much better judge than Salmasius, Casaubon, or Lipsius; mere scholars, who perhaps had never seen a battalion under arms.'

The real occupation of Gibbon, as this quotation might

suggest, was his reading; and this was of a peculiar sort. There are many kinds of readers, and each has a sort of perusal suitable to his kind. There is the voracious reader, like Dr. Johnson, who extracts with grasping appetite the large features, the gross essence of a trembling publication, and rejects the rest with contempt and disregard. There is the subtle reader, who pursues with fine attention the most imperceptible and delicate ramifications of an interesting topic, marks slight traits, notes changing manners, has a keen eye for the character of his author, is minutely attentive to every prejudice and awake to every passion, watches syllables and waits on words, is alive to the light air of nice associations which float about every subject—the motes in the bright sunbeam—the delicate gradations of the passing shadows. There is the stupid reader, who prefers dull books—is generally to be known by his disregard of small books and English books, and likes masses in modern Latin, *Grævius de torpore mirabili; Horrificus de gravitate sapientiæ.* But Gibbon was not of any of these classes. He was what common people would call a matter-of-fact, and philosophers now-a-days a *positive* reader. No disciple of M. Comte could attend more strictly to precise and provable phenomena. His favourite points are those which can be weighed and measured. Like the dull reader, he had perhaps a preference for huge books in unknown tongues; but, on the other hand, he wished those books to contain real and accurate information. He liked the firm earth of positive knowledge. His fancy was not flexible enough for exquisite refinement, his imagination too slow for light and wandering literature; but he felt no love for dullness in itself, and had a prompt acumen for serious eloquence. Thus ' the author of the Adventurer, No. 127 (Mr. Joseph Warton, concealed under the signature of Z), concludes his ingenious parallel of the ancients and moderns by the following remark: "That age will never again return, when a Pericles, after walking with Plato in a portico built by Phidias and painted by Apelles, might repair to hear a pleading of Demosthenes or a tragedy of Sophocles." It will never return, because it never existed. Pericles (who died in the fourth year of the LXXXIXth Olympiad, ant. Ch. 429, Dio. Sic. l. xii. 46) was confes edly the patron of Phidias, and the contemporary of Sophocles; but he could enjoy no very great pleasure in the conversation of Plato, who was

born the same year that he himself died (Diogenes Laertius
in Platone v. Stanley's History of Philosophy, p. 154). The
error is still more extraordinary with regard to Apelles and
Demosthenes, since both the painter and the orator survived
Alexander the Great, whose death is above a century posterior
to that of Pericles (in 323). And indeed, though Athens was
the seat of every liberal art from the days of Themistocles to
those of Demetrius Phalereus, yet no particular era will afford
Mr. Wharton the complete synchronism he seems to wish for;
as tragedy was deprived of her famous triumvirate before the
arts of philosophy and eloquence had attained the perfection
which they soon after received from the hands of Plato, Aristotle, and Demosthenes.'

And wonderful is it for what Mr. Hallam calls ' the languid
students of our present age ' to turn over the journal of his daily
studies. It is true, it seems to have been revised by himself;
and so great a narrator would group facts nicely with which
he was so familiar; but allowing any discount (if we may use
such a mean word about a noble being) for the skilful art of the
impressive historian, there will yet remain in the *Extraits de
mon Journal* a wonderful monument of learned industry. You
may open anywhere. ' *Dissertation on the Medal of Smyrna,* by
M. de Boze: replete with erudition and taste; containing
curious researches on the pre-eminence of the cities of Asia.—
Researches on the Polypus, by Mr. Trembley. A new world:
throwing light on physics, but darkening metaphysics.—
Vegetius's *Institutions.* This writer on tactics has good
general notions; but his particular account of the Roman
discipline is deformed by confusion and anachronisms.' Or,
' I this day began a very considerable task, which was, to
read Cluverius' *Italia Antiqua* in two volumes folio, Leyden
1624, Elzevirs; ' and it appears he did read it as well as begin
it, which is the point where most enterprising men would have
failed. From the time of his residence at Lausanne his Latin
scholarship had been sound and good; and the best part of his
studies was directed to the illustration of the best Roman
authors; but it is curious to find on the 16th of August, 1761,
after his return to England, and when he was twenty-four years
old, the following extract: ' I have at last finished the Iliad.
As I undertook it to improve myself in the Greek language,
which I had totally neglected for some years past, and to which

I never applied myself with a proper attention, I must give a reason why I began with Homer, and that contrary to Le Clerc's advice. I had two: 1st, As Homer is the most ancient Greek author (excepting perhaps Hesiod) who is now extant; and as he was not only the poet, but the lawgiver, the theologian, the historian, and the philosopher, of the ancients, every succeeding writer is full of quotations from, or allusions to, his writings, which it would be difficult to understand without a previous knowledge of them. In this situation, was it not natural to follow the ancients themselves, who always began their studies by the perusal of Homer? 2dly, No writer ever treated such a variety of subjects. As every part of civil, military, or economical life is introduced into his poems, and as the simplicity of his age allowed him to call everything by its proper name, almost the whole compass of the Greek tongue is comprised in Homer. I have so far met with the success I hoped for, that I have acquired a great facility in reading the language, and treasured up a very great stock of words. What I have rather neglected is, the grammatical construction of them, and especially the many various inflexions of the verbs. In order to acquire that dry but necessary branch of knowledge, I propose bestowing some time every morning on the perusal of the *Greek Grammar of Port Royal*, as one of the best extant. I believe that I read nearly one-half of Homer like a mere school-boy, not enough master of the words to elevate myself to the poetry. The remainder I read with a good deal of care and criticism, and made many observations on them. Some I have inserted here; for the rest I shall find a proper place. Upon the whole, I think that Homer's few faults (for some he certainly has) are lost in the variety of his beauties. I expected to have finished him long before. The delay was owing partly to the circumstances of my way of life and avocations, and partly to my own fault; for while every one looks on me as a prodigy of application, I know myself how strong a propensity I have to indolence.' Posterity will confirm the contemporary theory that he was a 'prodigy' of steady study. Those who know what the Greek language is, how much of the Decline and Fall depends on Greek authorities, how few errors the keen criticism of divines and scholars has been able to detect in his use of them, will be best able to appreciate the patient every-day labour which could alone repair the early neglect of so difficult an attainment.

It is odd how little Gibbon wrote, at least for the public, in
early life. More than twenty-two years elapsed from his first
return from Lausanne to the appearance of the first volume of
his great work, and in that long interval his only important
publication, if it can indeed be so called, was a French essay,
Sur l'Etude de la Littérature, which contains some sensible
remarks, and shows much regular reading; but which is on the
whole a ' conceivable treatise,' and would be wholly forgotten
if it had been written by any one else. It was little read in
England, and must have been a serious difficulty to his friends
in the militia; but the Parisians read it, or said they had read
it, which is more in their way, and the fame of being a French
author was a great aid to him in foreign society. It flattered,
indeed, the French *literati* more than any one can now fancy.
The French had then the idea that it was uncivilised to speak
any other language, and the notion of *writing* any other seemed
quite a *bêtise*. By a miserable misfortune you might not know
French, but at least you could conceal it assiduously; white
paper any how might go unsoiled; posterity at least should not
hear of such ignorance. The Parisian was to be the universal
tongue. And it did not seem absurd, especially to those only
slightly acquainted with foreign countries at all, that they
might be in part successful. Political eminence had given
their language a diplomatic supremacy. There was no German
literature at all; Italy had ceased to produce important books.
There was only England left to dispute the literary despotism;
and such an attempt as Gibbon's was a peculiarly acceptable
flattery, for it seemed as if her most cultivated men were beginning to abandon their own tongue, and to write like other
nations in the cosmopolitan *lingua franca*. A few far-seeing
observers, however, even then contemplated the train of
events which at the present day give such a preponderating
influence to our own writers, and make it an arduous matter
even to explain the conceivableness of the French ambition.
Of all men living then or since, David Hume was the most
likely from prejudice and habit to take an unfavourable view
of English literary influence; he had more literary fame than he
deserved in France and less in England; yet his cold and discriminating intellect at once emancipated him from the
sophistries which imposed on those less watchful. He wrote
to Gibbon, ' I have only one objection, derived from the language

in which it is written. Why do you compose in French, and carry faggots into the wood, as Horace says with regard to Romans who wrote in Greek? I grant that you have a like motive to those Romans, and adopt a language much more generally diffused than your native tongue; but have you not remarked the fate of those two ancient languages in the following ages? The Latin, though then less celebrated and confined to more narrow limits, has in some measure outlived the Greek, and is now more generally understood by men of letters. Let the French, therefore, triumph in the present diffusion of their tongue. Our solid and increasing establishments in America, where we need less dread the inundation of barbarians, promise a superior stability and duration to the English language.' The cool sceptic was correct. The great breeding people have gone out and multiplied; colonies in every clime attest our success; French is the *patois* of Europe; English is the language of the world.

Gibbon took the advice of his remarkable friend, and prepared himself for the composition of his great work in English. His studies were destined, however, to undergo an interruption. ' Yesterday morning,' he wrote to a friend, ' about half an hour after seven, as I was destroying an army of barbarians, I heard a double rap at the door, and my friend Mr. Eliot was soon introduced. After some idle conversation, he told me that if I was desirous of being in parliament, he had an independent seat very much at my service.' The borough was Liskeard; and the epithet independent is, of course, ironical, Mr. Eliot being himself the constituency of that place. The offer was accepted, and one of the most learned of members of parliament took his seat.

The political life of Gibbon is briefly described. He was a supporter of Lord North. That well-known statesman was, in the most exact sense, a representative man,—although representative of the class of persons most out of favour with the transcendental thinkers, who invented that name. Germans deny it, but it is true that in every country common opinions are very common. In all lands, both now and of old, there exists the easy and comfortable mass; quiet, sagacious, short-sighted,—such as the Jews whom Rabshakeh tempted by their vine and their fig-tree; such as the English with their snug dining-room and after-dinner nap, domestic happiness and

Bulle coal; sensible, solid, practical men, without stretching irritable reason, but with a placid supine instinct; without originality and without folly; judicious in their dealings, respected in the world; wanting little, sacrificing nothing; good-tempered people in a word, ' caring for nothing until they are themselves hurt.' Lord North was of this class. You could hardly make him angry. ' No doubt,' tapping his fat sides, ' I am that odious thing a minister; and I believe other people wish they were so too.' Profound people look deeply for the maxims of his policy; and it being on the surface, of course they fail to find it. He did not what the mind but what the *body* of the community wanted to have done; he appealed to the real people, the large English commonplace herd. His abilities were great; and with them he did what people with no abilities wished to do, and could not do. Lord Brougham has just published his Letters to the King, showing that which partial extracts had made known before, that he was quite opposed to the war he was carrying on; was convinced it could not succeed; hardly, in fact, wished it might. Why did he carry it on? *Vox populi*, the voice of well-dressed wigs commanded it to be done; and he cheerfully sacrificed American people, who were nothing to him, to English, who were something, and a king, who was much. Gibbon was the very man to support such a ruler. His historical writings have given h m a posthumous eminence; but in his own time he was doubtless thought a sensible safe man, of ordinary thoughts and intelligible actions. To do him justice, he did not pretend to be a hero. ' You know,' he wrote to his friend Deyverdun, ' *que je suis entré au parlement sans patriotisme, sans ambition, et que toutes mes vues se bornoient à la place commode et honnête d'un* lord of trade.' ' Wise in his generation ' was written on his brow. He quietly and gently supported the policy of his time.

Even, however, amid the fatigue of parliamentary attendance,—the fatigue, in fact, of attending a nocturnal and oratorical club, where you met the best people, who could not speak, as well as a few of the worst, who always *would*,—Gibbon's history made much progress. The first volume, a quarto, one-sixth of the whole, was published in the spring of 1776, and at once raised his fame to a high point. Ladies actually read it—read about Bœtica and Tarraconensis, the Roman legions and the tribunitian powers. Grave scholars wrote dreary commendations. 'The first impression,' he writes, ' was exhausted in a few days; a second and a third edition were scarcely adequate to the demand; and my book seller's property was twice invaded by the pirates of Dublin. My book was on every table '—tables must have been rather few in that age—' and almost on every toilette; the historian was crowned by the taste or fashion of the day; nor was the general voice disturbed by the barking of any profound critic.' The noise penetrated deep into the unlearned classes. Mr. Sheridan, who never read anything ' on principle,' said that the crimes of Warren Hastings surpassed anything to be found in the ' correct sentences of Tacitus or the *luminous* page of Gibbon.' Some one seems to have been struck with the jet of learning, and questioned the great wit. ' I said,' he replied, ' *vo*luminous.'

History, it is said, is of no use; at least a great critic, who is understood to have in the press a very elaborate work in that kind, not long since seemed to allege that writings of this sort did not establish a theory of the universe, and were therefore of o avail. But whatever may be the use of this sort of compo- sition in itself and abstractedly, it is certainly of great use relatively and to literary men. Consider the position of a man of that species. He sits beside a library-fire, with nice white paper, a good pen, a capital style, and nothing to describe; of course he is an able man, and of course has an active intellect, beside wonderful culture; but still one cannot always have original ideas. Every day cannot be an era; a train of new speculation very often will not be found; and how dull it is to make it your business to write, to stay by yourself in a room to write, and then to have nothing to say ! It is dreary work mend- ing seven pens, and waiting for a theory to ' turn up.' What a gain if something would happen ! then one could describe it. Something has happened, and that something is history. On this account, since a remarkably grave Greek discovered this plan for a serious immortality, a series of accomplished men have seldom been found wanting to derive a literary capital from their active and barbarous kindred. Perhaps when a Visigoth broke a head, he thought that that was all. Not so; he was making history; Gibbon has written it down.

The manner of writing history is as characteristic of the narrator as the actions are of the persons who are related to

have performed them; often much more so. It may be generally defined as a view of one age taken by another; a picture of
a series of men and women painted by one of another series.
Of course, this definition seems to exclude contemporary history; but if we look into the matter carefully, is there such a
thing? What are all the best and most noted works that claim
the title—memoirs, scraps, materials—composed by men of
like passions with the people they speak of, involved it may be
in the events they speak of, and therefore describing them with
the partiality and narrowness of an eager actor; or even
worse, by men far apart from them in a monkish solitude,
familiar with the lettuces of the convent-garden, but hearing
only faint dim murmurs of the great transactions which they
slowly jot down in the barren chronicle; these are not to be
named in the same short breath, or included in the same narrow
word, with the equable, poised, philosophic narrative of the retrospective historian. In the great histories there are two topics
of interest—the man as a type of the age in which he lives,—
the events and manners of the age he is describing; very often
almost all the interest is the contrast of the two.

You should do everything, said Lord Chesterfield, in minuet
time. It was in that time that Gibbon wrote his history, and
such was the manner of the age. You fancy him in a suit of
flowered velvet, with a bag and sword, wisely smiling, com-
posedly rounding his periods. You seem to see the grave bows,
the formal politeness, the finished deference. You perceive the
minuetic action accompanying the words: 'Give,' it would say,
' Augustus a chair: Zenobia, the humblest of your slaves:
Odoacer, permit me to correct the defect in your attire.' As
the slap-dash sentences of a rushing critic express the hasty
impatience of modern manners, so the deliberate emphasis,
the slow acumen, the steady argument, the impressive narration bring before us what is now a tradition, the picture of the
correct eighteenth-century gentleman, who never failed in a
measured politeness, partly because it was due in propriety
towards others, and partly because from his own dignity it was
due most obviously to himself.

And not only is this true of style, but may be extended to
other things also. There is no one of the many literary works
produced in the eighteenth century more thoroughly characteristic of it than Gibbon's history. The special characteristic of

that age is its clinging to the definite and palpable; it had a taste beyond everything for what it called solid information. In literature the period may be defined as that in which men ceased to write for students, and had not begun to write for women. In the present day no one can take up any book intended for general circulation, without clearly seeing that the writer supposes most of his readers will be ladies or young men; and, in proportion to his judgment, he attends to their taste accordingly. Two or three hundred years ago books were written for professed and systematic students,—the class the fellows of colleges were designed to be, who used to go on studying them all their lives. Between these two, there was a time in which the more marked class of literary consumers were strong-headed practical men. Education had not become so general, or so feminine, as to make the present style—what is called the ' brilliant style '—at all necessary; but there was enough culture to make the demand of common diffused persons more effectual than that of special and secluded scholars. A book-buying public had arisen of sensible men, who would not endure the awful folio style in which the schoolmen wrote. From peculiar causes, too, the business of that age was perhaps more free from the hurry and distraction which disable so many of our practical men at the present time from reading. You accordingly see in the books of the last century what is called a masculine tone; a firm, strong, perspicuous narration of matter of fact, a plain argument, a contempt for everything which distinct definite people cannot entirely and thoroughly comprehend. There is no more solid book in the world than Gibbon's history. Only consider the chronology. It begins before the year ONE and goes down to the year 1453, and is a schedule or series of schedules of important events during that time. Scarcely any fact deeply affecting European civilisation is wholly passed over, and the great majority of facts are elaborately recounted. Laws, dynasties, churches, barbarians, appear and disappear. Everything changes; the old world—the classical civilisation of form and definition—passes away, a new world of free spirit and inward growth emerges; between the two lie a mixed weltering interval of trouble and confusion, when everybody hates everybody, and the historical student leads a life of skirmishes, is oppressed with broils and feuds. All through this long period Gibbon's history goes with steady consistent pace; like a

Roman legion through a troubled country—*hæret pede pes;* up hill and down hill, through marsh and thicket, through Goth or Parthian—the firm defined array passes forward—a type of order and an emblem of civilisation. Whatever may be the defects of Gibbon's history, none can deny him a proud precision and a style in marching order.

Another characteristic of the eighteenth century is its taste for dignified pageantry. What an existence was that of Versailles! How gravely admirable to see the *grand monarque* shaved, and dressed, and powdered; to look on and watch a great man carefully amusing himself with dreary trifles. Or do we not even now possess an invention of that age—the great eighteenth-century footman, still in the costume of his era, with dignity and powder, vast calves and noble mien? What a world it must have been when all men looked like that! Go and gaze with rapture at the footboard of a carriage, and say, Who would not obey a premier with such an air? Grave, tranquil, decorous pageantry is a part, as it were, of the essence of the last age. There is nothing more characteristic of Gibbon. A kind of pomp pervades him. He is never out of livery. He ever selects for narration those themes which look most like a levee: grave chamberlains seem to stand throughout; life is a vast ceremony, the historian at once the dignitary and the scribe.

The very language of Gibbon shows these qualities. Its majestic march has been the admiration—its rather pompous cadence the sport of all perusers. It has the greatest merit of an historical style: it is always going on; you feel no doubt of its continuing in motion. Many narrators of the reflective class, Sir Archibald Alison for example, fail in this: your constant feeling is, 'Ah! he is pulled up; he is going to be profound; he never will go on again.' But, at the same time, the manner of the Decline and Fall is about the last which should be recommended for strict imitation. It is not a style in which you can tell the truth. A monotonous writer is suited only to monotonous matter. Truth is of various kinds—grave, solemn, dignified, petty, low, ordinary; and a historian who has to tell the truth must be able to tell what is vulgar as well as what is great, what is little as well as what is amazing. Gibbon is at fault here. He *cannot* mention Asia *Minor*. The petty order of sublunary matters; the common gross existence of ordinary people; the necessary littlenesses of necessary life, are little suited to his sublime narrative. Men on the *Times* feel this acutely; it is most difficult at first to say many things in the huge imperial manner. And after all you cannot tell everything. ' How, sir,' asked a reviewer of Sydney Smith's life, ' do you say a " good fellow " in print ? ' ' Mr. ——,' replied the editor, ' you should not say it at all.' Gibbon was aware of this rule; he omits what does not suit him; and the consequence is, that though he has selected the most various of historical topics, he scarcely gives you an idea of variety. The ages change, but the varnish of the narration is the same.

It is not unconnected with this fault that Gibbon gives us but an indifferent description of individual character. People seem a good deal alike. The cautious scepticism of his cold intellect, which disinclined him to every extreme, depreciates great virtues and extenuates great vices; and we are left with a tame neutral character, capable of nothing extraordinary,— hateful, as the saying is, ' both to God and to the enemies of God.'

A great point in favour of Gibbon is the existence of his history. Some great historians seem likely to fail here. A good judge was asked which he preferred, Macaulay's *History of England* or Lord Mahon's. ' Why,' he replied, ' you observe Lord Mahon has written his history; and by what I see Macaulay's will be written not only for but *among* posterity.' Practical people have little idea of the practical ability required to write a large book, and especially a large history. Long before you get to the pen, there is an immensity of pure business; heaps of material are strewn everywhere; but they lie in disorder, unread, uncatalogued, unknown. It seems a dreary waste of life to be analysing, indexing, extracting works and passages, in which one per cent. of the contents are interesting, and not half of that percentage will ultimately appear in the flowing narrative. As an accountant takes up a bankrupt's books filled with confused statements of ephemeral events, the disorderly record of unprofitable speculations, and charges this to that head, and that to this,—estimates earnings, specifies expenses, demonstrates failures; so the great narrator, going over the scattered annalists of extinct ages, groups and divides, notes and combines, until from a crude mass of darkened fragments there emerges a clear narrative, a concise account of the result and upshot of the whole. In this art Gibbon was a master. The laborious research of German scholarship, the keen eye of theological zeal, a steady criticism of eighty years, have found few faults of detail. The account has been worked right, the proper authorities consulted, an accurate judgment formed, the most telling incidents selected. Perhaps experience shows that there is something English in this talent. The Germans are more elaborate in single monographs; but they seem to want the business-ability to work out a complicated narrative, to combine a long whole. The French are neat enough, and the style is very quick; but then it is difficult to believe their facts; the account on its face seems too plain, and no true Parisian ever was an antiquary. The great classical histories published in this country in our own time show that the talent is by no means extinct; and they likewise show, what is also evident, that this kind of composition is easier with respect to ancient than with respect to modern times. The barbarians burned the books; and though all the historians abuse them for it, it is quite evident that in their hearts they are greatly rejoiced. If the books had existed, they would have had to read them. Mr. Macaulay has to peruse every book printed with long f's; and it is no use after all; somebody will find some stupid MS., an old account-book of an ' ingenious gentleman,' and with five entries therein destroy a whole hypothesis. But Gibbon was exempt from this; he could count the books the splendid Goths bequeathed; and when he had mastered them he might pause. Still it is no light matter, as any one who looks at the books—awful folios in the grave Bodleian—will most certainly credit and believe. And he did it all himself; he never showed his book to any friend, or asked any one to help him in the accumulating work, not even in the correction of the press. ' Not a sheet,' he says, ' has been seen by any human eyes, excepting those of the author and printer; the faults and the merits are exclusively my own.' And he wrote most of it with one pen, which must certainly have grown erudite towards the end.

The nature of his authorities clearly shows what the nature of Gibbon's work is. History may be roughly divided into universal and particular; the first being the narrative of events affecting the whole human race, at least the main historical nations, the narrative of whose fortunes is the story of civilisa tion; and the latter being the relation of events relating to one or a few particular nations only. Universal history, it is evident, comprises great areas of space and long periods of time; you cannot have a series of events visibly operating on all great nations without time for their gradual operation, and without tracking them in succession through the various regions of their power. There is no instantaneous transmission in historical causation; a long interval is required for universal effects. It follows, that universal history necessarily partakes of the character of a summary. You cannot recount the cumbrous annals of long epochs without condensation, selection, and omission; the narrative, when shortened within the needful limits, becomes concise and general. What it gains in time, according to the mechanical phrase, it loses in power. The particular history, confined within narrow limits, can show us the whole contents of these limits, explain its features of human interest, recount in graphic detail all its interesting transactions, touch the human heart with the power of passion, instruct the mind with patient instances of accurate wisdom. The universal is confined to a dry enumeration of superficial transactions; no action can have all its details; the canvas is so crowded that no figure has room to display itself effectively. From the nature of the subject, Gibbon's history is of the latter class; the sweep of the narrative is so wide; the decline and fall of the Roman Empire being in some sense the most universal event which has ever happened,—being, that is, the historical incident which has most affected all civilised men, and the very existence and form of civilisation itself,—it is evident that we must look rather for a comprehensive generality than a telling minuteness of delineation. The history of a thousand years does not admit the pictorial detail which a Scott or a Macaulay can accumulate on the history of a hundred. Gibbon has done his best to avoid the dryness natural to such an attempt. He inserts as much detail as his limits will permit; selects for more full description striking people and striking transactions; brings together at a single view all that relates to single topics; above all, by a regular advance of narration, never ceases to imply the regular progress of events and the steady course of time. None can deny the magnitude of such an effort. After all, however, these are merits of what is technically termed composition, and are analogous to those excellences in painting or sculpture that are more respected by artists than appreciated by the public at large. The fame of Gibbon is highest among writers; those especially who have studied for years particular periods included in his theme (and how many those are; for in the East and West he has set his mark on all that is great for ten centuries!) acutely feel and admiringly observe how difficult it would be to say so much, and leave so little untouched; to compress so many telling points; to present in so few words so apt and embracing a narrative of the whole. But the mere unsophisticated reader scarcely appreciates this; he is rather awed than delighted; or rather, perhaps, he appreciates it for a little while, then is tired by the roll and glare; then on any chance— the creaking of an organ, or the stirring of a mouse,—in time of temptation he falls away. It has been said, the way to answer all objections to Milton is to take down the book and read him; the way to reverence Gibbon is not to read him at all, but look at him, from outside, in the bookcase, and think how much there is inside; what a course of events, what a muster-roll of names, what a steady solemn sound! You will not like to take the book down; but you will think how much you could be delighted if you would.

It may be well, though it can be only in the most cursory manner, to examine the respective treatment of the various elements in this vast whole. The history of the Decline and Fall may be roughly and imperfectly divided into the picture of the Roman Empire—the narrative of barbarian incursions—the story of Constantinople: and some few words may be hastily said on each.

The picture—for so, from its apparent stability when contrasted with the fluctuating character of the later period, we may call it—which Gibbon has drawn of the united empire has immense merit. The organisation of the imperial system is admirably dwelt on; the manner in which the old republican institutions were apparently retained, but really altered, is compendiously explained; the mode in which the imperial will was transmitted to and carried out in remote provinces is distinctly displayed. But though the mechanism is admirably delineated, the dynamical principle, the original impulse, is not made clear. You never feel you are reading about the Romans. Yet no one denies their character to be most marked. Poets and orators have striven for the expression of it:

' Leave gold and myrrh and jewels,
    Rich table and soft bed,
To them who of man's seed are born,
    Whom woman's milk hath fed.
Thou wast not made for lucre,
    For pleasure, nor for rest,—
Thou that art sprung from the War-god's loins,
    And hast tugged at the she-wolf's breast.

*   *   *   *   *

' Thy nurse will bear no master,
    Thy nurse will bear no load;
And woe to them that shear her,
    And woe to them that goad.

*   *   *   *   *

' And such as is the War-god,
    The author of thy line,
And such as she who suckled thee,
    Even such be thou and thine.

What a refreshment from the cold serenity of the Decline and
Fall, where every man seems a statue, and every institution a
formula!

Mr. Macaulay has been similarly criticised; it has been said,
that notwithstanding his great dramatic power, and wonderful felicity in the selection of events on which to exert it,
he yet never makes us feel that we are reading about Englishmen. The coarse clay of our English nature *cannot* be represented in so fine a style. In the same way, and to a much
greater extent (for this is perhaps an unthankful criticism, if
we compare Macaulay's description of any body with that of
any other historian), Gibbon is chargeable with neither expressing nor feeling the essence of the people concerning whom he
is writing. There was, in truth, in the Roman people a warlike
fanaticism, a puritanical essence, an interior, latent, restrained,
enthusiastic religion, which was utterly alien to the cold scep-
cism of the narrator. Of course he was conscious of it. He
indistinctly felt that at least there was something he did not
like; but he could not realise or sympathise with it without a

change of heart or nature. The old Pagan has a sympathy
with the religion of enthusiasm far above the reach of the
modern Epicurean.

It may indeed be said, on behalf of Gibbon, that the old
Roman character was in its decay, and that only so slight
traces of it were remaining in the age of Augustus and the
Antonines that it is no particular defect in him to leave it unnoticed. Yet though the intensity of its nobler peculiarities
was on the wane, many a vestige would perhaps have been
apparent to so learned an eye, if his temperament and disposition had been prone to seize upon and search for them. Nor
is there any adequate appreciation of the compensating element, of the force which really held society together, of the
fresh air of the Illyrian hills, of that army which, evermore
recruited from northern and rugged populations, doubtless
brought into the very centre of a degraded society the healthy
simplicity of a vital if barbarous religion.

It is no wonder that such a mind should have looked with
displeasure on primitive Christianity. The whole of his treatment of that topic has been discussed by many pens, and
three generations of ecclesiastical scholars have illustrated it with
their emendations. Yet if we turn over this, the latest and
most elaborate edition, containing all the important criticisms
of Milman and of Guizot, we shall be surprised to find how few
instances of definite exact error such a scrutiny has been able
to find out. As Paley, with his strong sagacity, at once remarked, the subtle error rather lies hid in the sinuous folds
than is directly apparent on the surface of the polished style.
Who, said the shrewd archdeacon, can refute a sneer? And yet
even this is scarcely the exact truth. The objection of Gibbon
is, in fact, an objection rather to religion than to Christianity;
as has been said, he did not appreciate, and could not describe,
the most inward form of pagan piety; he objected to Christianity because it was the intensest of religions. We do not
mean by this to charge Gibbon with any denial, any overt
distinct disbelief in the existence of a supernatural Being.
This would be very unjust; his cold composed mind had nothing
in common with the Jacobinical outbreak of the next generation. He was no doubt a theist after the fashion of natural
theology; nor was he devoid of more than scientific feeling;
all constituted authorities struck him with emotion, all ancient

ones with awe. If the Roman Empire had descended to his time, how much he would have reverenced it! He had doubtless a great respect for the ' First Cause; ' it had all the titles to approbation; ' it was not conspicuous,' he would have said, ' but it was potent.' A sensitive decorum revolted from the jar of atheistic disputation. We have already described him *ad nauseam*. A sensible middle age in political life; a bachelor not himself gay, but living with gay men; equable and secular; cautious in his habits, tolerant in his creed, as Porson said, ' never failing in natural feeling except when women were to be ravished and Christians to be martyred.' His writings are in character. The essence of the far-famed fifteenth and sixteenth chapters is, in truth, but a description of unworldly events in the tone of this world, of awful facts in unmoved voice, of truths of the heart in the language of the eyes. The wary sceptic has not even committed himself to definite doubts. These celebrated chapters were in the first manuscript much longer, and were gradually reduced to their present size by excision and compression. Who can doubt that in their first form they were a clear, or comparatively clear expression of exact opinions on the Christian history, and that it was by a subsequent and elaborate process that they were reduced to their present and insidious obscurity? The process has been effectual. ' Divest,' says Dean Milman of the introduction to the fifteenth chapter, ' this whole passage of the latent sarcasm betrayed by the whole of the subsequent dissertation, and it might commence a Christian history, written in the most Christian spirit of candour.'

It is not for us here to go into any disquisition as to the comparative influence of the five earthly causes to whose secondary operation the specious historian ascribes the progress of Christianity. Weariness and disinclination forbid. There can be no question that the polity of the church, and the zeal of the converts, and other such things, did most materially conduce to the progress of the Gospel. But few will now attribute to these much of the effect. The real cause is the heaving of the mind after the truth. Troubled with the perplexities of time, weary with the vexation of ages, the spiritual faculty of man turns to the truth as the child turns to its mother. The thirst of the soul was to be satisfied, the deep torture of the spirit to have rest. There was an appeal to those

> ' High instincts, before which our mortal nature
>   Did tremble like a guilty thing surprised.'

The mind of man has an appetite for the truth.

> ' Hence, in a season of calm weather,
>   Though inland far we be,
>   Our souls have sight of that immortal sea
>   Which brought us hither,—
>   Can in a moment travel thither,
>   And see the children sport upon the shore,
>   And hear the mighty voices rolling evermore.'

All this was not exactly in Gibbon's way, and he does not seem to have been able to conceive that it was in any one else's. Why his chapters had given offence he could hardly make out. It actually seems that he hardly thought that other people believed more than he did. ' We may be well assured,' says he, of a sceptic of antiquity, ' that a writer conversant with the world would never have ventured to expose the gods of his country to public ridicule, had they not been already the objects of secret contempt among the polished and enlightened orders of society.' ' Had I,' he says of himself, ' believed that the majority of English readers were so fondly attached even to the name and shadow, had I foreseen that the pious, the timid, and the prudent would feel, or would affect to feel, with such exquisite sensibility,—I might perhaps have softened the two invidious chapters, which would create many enemies and conciliate few friends.' The state of belief at that time is a very large subject; but it is probable that in the cultivated cosmopolitan classes the continental scepticism was very rife; that among the hard-headed classes the rough spirit of English Deism had made much way. Though the mass of the people doubtless believed much as they now believe, yet it seems that the entire upper class was lazy and corrupt, and that there is truth in the picture of the modern divine: ' The thermometer of the Church of England sunk to its lowest point in the first thirty years of the reign of George III. . . . In their preaching, nineteen clergymen out of twenty carefully abstained from dwelling upon Christian doctrines. Such topics exposed the preacher to the charge of fanaticism. Even the calm and sober Crabbe, who certainly never erred from excess of zeal, was stigmatised in those days as a methodist, because he introduced into his sermons the notion of future reward and punishment. An orthodox clergyman (they said) should be content to show his people the worldly advantage of good conduct, and to leave heaven and hell to the ranters. Nor can we wonder that such should have been the notions of country parsons, when, even by those who passed for the supreme arbiters of orthodoxy and taste, the vapid rhetoric of Blair was thought the highest standard of Christian exhortation.' It is among the excuses for Gibbon that he lived in such a world.

There are slight palliations also in the notions then prevalent of the primitive church. There was the Anglican theory, that it was a *via media*, the most correct of periods, that its belief is to be the standard, its institutions the model, its practice the test of subsequent ages. There was the notion, not formally drawn out, but diffused through and implied in a hundred books of evidence,—a notion in opposition to every probability, and utterly at variance with the New Testament,—that the first converts were sober, hard-headed, cultivated inquirers,— Watsons, Paleys, Priestleys, on a small scale; weighing evidence, analysing facts, suggesting doubts, dwelling on distinctions, cold in their dispositions, moderate in their morals, cautious in their creed. We now know that these were not they of whom the world was not worthy. It is now certain that the times of the first church were times of excitement; that great ideas falling on a mingled world were distorted by an untrained intellect, even in the moment in which they were received by a yearning heart; that strange confused beliefs, Millennarianism, Gnosticism, Ebionitism, were accepted, not merely by outlying obscure heretics, but in a measure, half-and-half, one notion more by one man, another more by his neighbour, confusedly and mixedly by the mass of Christians; that the appeal was not to the questioning thinking understanding, but to unheeding all-venturing emotion; to that lower class ' from whom faiths ascend,' and not to the cultivated and exquisite class by whom they are criticised; that fervid men never embraced a more exclusive creed. In a word, that you can say nothing favourable of the first Christians, except that they *were* Christians. There is no ' form nor comeliness ' in them; no intellectual accomplishments, no caution in action, no discretion in understanding; there is no admirable quality except that, with whatever d stortion, or confusion, or singularity, they at once accepted the great clear outline of belief in which to this day we live, move, and have our being. The offence of Gibbon is his disinclination to this simple essence; his excuse, the historical errors then prevalent as to the primitive Christians, the real defects so natural in their position, the false merits ascribed to them by writers who from one reason or another desired to treat them as ' an authority.'*

* Compare the description of a felicitous and admirable writer: ' When we consider what is implied in such expressions as " not many wise, not many learned were called " to the knowledge of the truth, we can scarcely avoid feeling that there must have been much in the early Church which would have been distasteful to us as men of education, much that must have worn the appearance of excitement and enthusiasm. Is the mean conventicle, looking almost like a private house, more like that first assembly of Christians in the large upper room, or the Catholic Church, arrayed in all the glories of Christian art? Neither of them is altogether like in spirit, perhaps; but in externals the first. Is the dignified hierarchy that occupy the seats around the altar more like the multitude of first believers, or the lowly crowd that kneel upon the pavement? If we try to embody in the mind's eye the forms of the first teachers, and still more of their followers, we cannot help reading the true lesson, however great may be the illusions of poetry and art: Not St. Paul standing on Mars' Hill in the fullness of manly strength, as we have him in the cartoon of Raphael, is the true image, but such a one as he himself would glory in, whose bodily presence was weak and speech feeble, who had an infirmity in his flesh, and bore in his body the marks of the Lord Jesus. And when we look at this picture full in the face, however we might by nature be inclined to turn aside from it, or veil its details in general language, we cannot deny that many things that accompany the religion of the uneducated now must also have accompanied the Gospel preached to the poor. There must have been, humanly speaking, spiritual delusions where men lived so exclusively in the spiritual world; there were scenes which we know took place, such as St. Paul says would make the unbeliever think that they were mad. The best and holiest persons among the poor and ignorant are not entirely free from superstition according to the notions of the educated; at best they are apt to speak of religion in a manner not suited to our taste; they sing with a loud excited voice, they imagine themselves to receive divine oracles even about the humblest cares of life. Is not this, in externals at least, very like the appearance which the disciples must have presented who obeyed the apostle's injunction: " Is any sad? let him pray. Is any merry? let him sing psalms! " Could our nerves have borne to witness " the speaking with tongues," or " the administration of baptism," or "the love-feasts " as they probably existed in the early Church? '—Jowett, *Epistles of St. Paul*, vol. II, p. 199.

On the whole, therefore, it may be said of the first, and in some sense the most important part of Gibbon's work, that though he has given an elaborate outline of the framework of society, and described its detail with pomp and accuracy, yet that he has not comprehended or delineated its nobler essence, Pagan or Christian. Nor perhaps was it to be expected that he should, for he inadequately comprehended the dangers of the time; he thought it the happiest period the world has ever known; he would not have comprehended the remark, ' To see the old world in its worst estate we turn to the age of the satirists and of Tacitus, when all the different streams of evil coming from east, west, north, south, the vices of barbarism and the vices of civilisation, remnants of ancient cults and the latest refinements of luxury and impurity, met and mingled on the banks of the Tiber. What could have been the state of society when Tiberius, Caligula, Nero, Domitian, Heliogabalus, were the rulers of the world? To a good man we should imagine that death itself would be more tolerable than the sight of such things coming upon the earth.' So deep an ethical sensibility was not to be expected in the first century; nor is it strange when, after seventeen hundred years, we do not find it in their historian.

Space has failed us, and we must be unmeaningly brief. The second head of Gibbon's history—the narrative of the barbarian invasions—has been recently criticised, on the ground that he scarcely enough explains the gradual but unceasing and inevitable manner in which the outer barbarians were affected by and assimilated to the civilisation of Rome. Mr. Congreve has well observed, that the impression which Gibbon's narrative is insensibly calculated to convey is, that there was little or no change in the state of the Germanic tribes between the time of Tacitus and the final invasion of the empire—a conclusion which is obviously incredible. To the general reader there will perhaps seem some indistinctness in this part of the work, nor is a free confused barbarism a congenial subject for an imposing and orderly pencil. He succeeds better in the delineation of the riding monarchies, if we may so term them, of the equestrian courts of Attila or Timour, in which the great scale, the concentrated power, the very enormity of the barbarism, give, so to speak, a shape to unshapeliness; impart, that is, a horrid dignity to horse-flesh and mare's milk, an imposing oneness to the vast materials of a crude barbarity. It is needless to say that no one would search Gibbon for an explanation of the reasons or feelings by which the northern tribes were induced to accept Christianity.

It is on the story of Constantinople that the popularity of Gibbon rests. The vast extent of the topic; the many splendid episodes it contains; its epic unity from the moment of its far-seeing selection by Constantine to its last fall; its position as the link between Europe and Asia; its continuous history; the knowledge that through all that time it was, as now, a diadem by the water-side, a lure to be snatched by the wistful barbarian, a marvel to the West, a prize for the North and for the East;—these, and such as these ideas, are congenial advantages to a style of pomp and grandeur. The East seems to require to be treated with a magnificence unsuitable to a colder soil. The nature of the events, too, is suitable to Gibbon's cursory imposing manner. It is the history of a form of civilisation, but without the power thereof; a show of splendour and vigour, but without bold life or interior reality. What an opportunity for an historian who loved the imposing pageantry and disliked the purer essence of existence! There were here neither bluff barbarians nor simple saints; there was nothing admitting of particular accumulated detail; we do not wish to know the interior of the stage; the imposing movements are all which should be seized. Some of the features are curious in relation to those of the historian's life; the clear accounts of the theological controversies, followed out with an appreciative minuteness so rare in a sceptic, are not disconnected with his early conversion to the scholastic church. The brilliancy of the narrative reminds us of his enthusiasm for Arabic and the East; the minutest description of a licentious epoch evinces the habit of a mind which, not being bold enough for the practice of license, took a pleasure in following its theory. There is no subject which combines so much of unity with so much of variety.

It is evident, therefore, where Gibbon's rank as an historian must finally stand. He cannot be numbered among the great painters of human nature, for he has no sympathy with the heart and passions of our race; he has no place among the felicitous describers of detailed life, for his subject was too vast for minute painting, and his style too uniform for a shifting scene.

But he is entitled to a high—perhaps to a first place—among the orderly narrators of great events; the composed expositors of universal history; the tranquil artists who have endeavoured to diffuse a cold polish over the warm passions and desultory fortunes of mankind.

The life of Gibbon after the publication of his great work was not very complicated. During its composition he had withdrawn from Parliament and London to the studious retirement of Lausanne. Much eloquence has been expended on this voluntary exile, and it has been ascribed to the best and most profound motives. It is indeed certain that he liked a lettered solitude, preferred easy continental society, was not quite insensible to the charm of scenery, had a pleasure in returning to the haunts of his youth. Prosaic and pure history, however, must explain that he went abroad to *save*. Lord North had gone out of power. Mr. Burke, the Cobden of that era, had procured the abolition of the Lords of Trade; the private income of Gibbon was not equal to his notion of a bachelor London life. The same sum was, however, a fortune at Lausanne. Most things, he acknowledged, were as dear; but then he had not to buy so many things. Eight hundred a year placed him high in the social scale of the place. The inhabitants were gratified that a man of European reputation had selected their out-of-the-way town for the shrine of his fame; he lived pleasantly and easily among easy pleasant people; a gentle hum of local admiration gradually arose, which yet lingers on the lips of erudite *laquais de place*. He still retains a fame unaccorded to any other historian; they speak of the ' hôtel Gibbon: ' there never was even an *estaminet* Tacitus, or a *café* Thucydides.

This agreeable scene, like many other agreeable scenes, was broken by a great thunderclap. The French revolution has disgusted many people; but perhaps it has never disgusted any one more than Gibbon. He had swept and garnished everything about him. Externally he had made a neat little hermitage in a gentle, social place; internally he had polished up a cold theory of life, sufficient for the guidance of a cold and polished man. Everything seemed to be tranquil with him; the rigid must admit his decorum; the lax would not accuse him of rigour; he was of the world, and an elegant society naturally loved its own. On a sudden the hermitage was disturbed. No place was too calm for that excitement; scarcely any too distant for that uproar. The French war was a war of opinion, entering households, disturbing villages, dividing quiet friends. The Swiss took some of the infection. There was a not unnatural discord between the people of the Pays de Vaud and their masters the people of Berne. The letters of Gibbon are filled with invectives on the 'Gallic barbarians' and panegyrics on Mr. Burke; military details, too, begin to abound—the peace of his retirement was at an end. It was an additional aggravation that the Parisians should do such things. It would not have seemed unnatural that northern barbarians—English, or other uncivilised nations—should break forth in rough riot or cruel license; but that the people of the most civilised of all capitals, speaking the sole dialect of polished life, enlightened with all the enlightenment then known, should be guilty of excesses unparalleled, unwitnessed, unheard of, was a vexing trial to one who had admired them for many years. The internal creed and belief of Gibbon was as much attacked by all this as were his external circumstances. He had spent his time, his life, his energy, in putting a polished gloss on human tumult, a sneering gloss on human piety; on a sudden human passion broke forth—the cold and polished world seemed to meet its end; the thin superfices of civilisation was torn asunder; the fountains of the great deep seemed opened; impiety to meet its end; the foundations of the earth were out of course. We now, after long familiarity and in much ignorance, can hardly read the history of those years without horror: what an effect must they have produced on those whose minds were fresh, and who knew the people killed! 'Never,' he writes to an English nobleman, 'did a revolution affect to such a degree the private existence of such numbers of the first people of a great country. Your examples of misery I could easily match with similar examples in this country and neighbourhood, and our sympathy is the deeper, as we do not possess, like you, the means of alleviating in some measure the misfortunes of the fugitives.' It violently affected his views of English politics: he had a tendency, in consideration of his cosmopolitan cultivation, to treat them as local littlenesses, parish squabbles; but now his interest was keen and eager. 'But,' he says, 'in this rage against slavery, in the numerous petitions against the slave-trade, was there no leaven of new democratical principles? no wild ideas of the rights and natural equality of man? It

is these I fear. Some articles in newspapers, some pamphlets of
the year, the Jockey Club, have fallen into my hands. I do not
infer much from such publications; yet I have never known
them of so black and malignant a cast. I shuddered at Grey's
motion; disliked the half-support of Fox, admired the firmness
of Pitt's declaration, and excused the usual intemperance
of Burke. Surely such men as ——, ——, ——, have talents
for mischief. I see a club of reform which contains some respectable names. Inform me of the professions, the principles,
the plans, the resources of these reformers. Will they heat the
minds of the people? Does the French democracy gain no
ground? Will the bulk of your party stand firm to their own
interest and that of their country? Will you not take some
active measures to declare your sound opinions, and separate
yourselves from your rotten members? If you allow them to
perplex government, if you trifle with this solemn business, if
you do not resist the spirit of innovation in the first attempt, if
you admit the smallest and most specious change in our parliamentary system, you are lost. You will be driven from one
step to another; from principles just in theory to consequences
most pernicious in practice; and your first concessions will be
productive of every subsequent mischief, for which you will be
answerable to your country and to posterity. Do not suffer
yourselves to be lulled into a false security; remember the proud
fabric of the French monarchy. Not four years ago it stood
founded, as it might seem, on the rock of time, force, and
opinion; supported by the triple aristocracy of the church, the
nobility, and the parliaments. They are crumbled into dust;
they are vanished from the earth. If this tremendous warning
has no effect on the men of property in England; if it does not
open every eye, and raise every arm,—you will deserve your
fate. If I am too precipitate, enlighten; if I am too despond-
ing, encourage me. My pen has run into this argument; for,
as much a foreigner as you think me, on this momentous subject
I feel myself an Englishman.'

The truth clearly is, that he had arrived at the conclusion
that he was the sort of person a populace kill. People wonder
a great deal why very many of the victims of the French revolution were particularly selected; the Marquis de Custine,
especially, cannot divine why they executed *his* father. The
historians cannot show that they committed any particular

crimes; the marquises and marchionesses seem very in-offensive. The fact evidently is, that they were killed for being polite. The world felt itself unworthy of them. There were so many bows, such regular smiles, such calm superior condescension,—could a mob be asked to stand it? Have we not all known a precise, formal, patronising, old gentleman—bland, imposing, something like Gibbon? have we not suffered from his dignified attentions? If *we* had been on the Committee of Public Safety, can we doubt what would have been the fate of that man? Just so wrath and envy destroyed in France an upper-class world.

After his return to England, Gibbon did not do much or live long. He completed his *Memoirs*, the most imposing of domestic narratives, the model of dignified detail. As we said before, if the Roman empire *had* written about itself, this was how it would have done so. He planned some other works, but executed none; judiciously observing that building castles in the air was more agreeable than building them on the ground. His career, was, however, drawing to an end. Earthly dignity had its limits, even the dignity of an historian. He had long been stout; and now symptoms of dropsy began to appear. After a short interval, he died on the 16th of January, 1794. We have sketched his character, and have no more to say. After all, what is our criticism worth? It only fulfils his aspiration, ' that a hundred years hence I may still continue to be abused.'

Bishop Butler[*]
(1854)

ABOUT the close of the last century, some one discovered the wife of a country rector in the act of destroying, for culinary purposes, the last remnants of a box of sermons, which seemed to have been written by Joseph Butler. The lady was reproved, but the exculpatory rejoinder was, ' Why, the box was full once, and I thought they were my husband's.' Nevertheless, when we first saw the above announcement of unpublished remains, we hoped her exemplary diligence had not been wholly successful, and that some important writings of Butler had been discovered. In this we have been disappointed. The remains in question are slight and rather trivial; the longest is an additional letter addressed to Dr. Clarke; and in all the rest there is scarcely anything very characteristic, except the remark, ' What a wonderful incongruity it is for a man to see the doubtfulness in which things are involved, and yet be impatient out of action, or vehement in it. Say a man is a sceptic, and add what was said of Brutus, *quicquid vult valde vult*, and you say there is the greatest contrariety between his understanding and temper that can be expressed in words: '—an observation which might be borne in mind by some English writers who panegyrise Julius Cæsar, and the many French ones who panegyrise Napoleon.

The life of Butler is one of those in which the events are few, the transitions simple, and the final result strange. He was the son of a dissenting shopkeeper in Berkshire, was always of a meditative disposition and reading habit—grew

---

[*] *Some Remains (hitherto unpublished) of Joseph Butler, LL.D., some time Lord Bishop of Durham.*
Encyclopædia Britannica, Vol. VI. Part II. *Article, Joseph Butler.* By Henry Rogers, Author of the ' Eclipse of Faith.' Eighth edition.

to manhood—was destined to the Dissenting ministry—began to question the principles of Dissent—entered at Oriel College—made valuable acquaintances there—rose in the Church by means of them—obtained, first the chaplaincy of the Rolls, then a decent living—then the rectory of Stanhope, the ' golden ' rectory, one of the best in the English Church—was recommended by his old friends to Queen Caroline—talked philosophy to her—pleased her (this being her favourite topic)—was made Bishop of Bristol, and thence translated to the richest of Anglican dignities—the prince-bishopric of Durham, and there died.

These are the single steps, and there is none of them which is remote from our ordinary observation. We should not be surprised to see any of them every day. But when we look on the life as a whole, when we see its nature, when we observe the son of a dissenting tradesman, a person of simple and pious disposition, of retiring habits, and scrupulous and investigating mind—in a word, the least worldly of ecclesiastics—attain to the most secular of ecclesiastical dignities, be a prince as well as a bishop, become the great magnate of the North of England, and dispense revenues to be envied by many a foreign potentate, we perceive the singularity of such a man with such beginnings attaining such a fortune. No man would guess from Butler's writings that he ever had the disposal of five pounds; it is odd to think what he did with the mining property and landed property, the royalties and rectories, coal dues and curacies, that he must have heard of from morning till evening.

It is certainly most strange that such a man should ever have been made a bishop. In general we observe that those become most eminent in the sheepfold, who partake most eminently of the qualities of the wolf. Nor is this surprising. The Church is (as the Article defines it) a congregation of men, faithful indeed, but faithful in various degrees. In every corporation or combination of men, no matter for what purpose collected, there are certain secular qualities which attain eminence as surely as oil rises above water. Attorneys are for the world, and the world is for attorneys. Activity, vigour, sharp-sightedness, tact, boldness, watchfulness, and such qualities as these, raise a man in the Church as certainly as in the State; so long as there is wealth and preferment in the one, they will be attained a good deal as wealth and office are in the other. The *prowling* faculties will have their way. Those who hunger and thirst after riches will have riches, and those who hunger not, will not. Still to this there are exceptions, and Butler's case is one of them. We might really fancy the world had determined to give for once an encouraging instance of its sensibility to rectitude, of the real and great influence of real and great virtue.

The period at which Butler's elevation occurred certainly does not diminish the oddness of the phenomenon. We are not indeed of those, mostly disciples of Carlyle or Newman, who speak with untempered contempt of the eighteenth century. Rather, if we might trust our own feelings, we view it with appreciating regard. It was the age of substantial comfort. The grave and placid historian (we speak of Mr. Hallam), going learnedly over the generations of men, is disposed to think that there never was so much happiness before or since. Employment was plentiful; industry remunerative. The advantages of material civilisation were enjoyed, and its penalties scarcely foreseen. The troubles of the seventeenth century had died out; those of the nineteenth had not begun Cares were few; the stir and conflict in which we live had barely commenced. It was not an age to trouble itself with prospective tasks; it had no feverish excitement, nor over-intellectual introspection; it lived on the fat of the land; *quieta non movere*, was its motto. Like most comfortable people, those of that time possessed a sleepy, supine sagacity; they had no fine imaginings, no exquisite fancies; but a coarse sense of what was common, a 'large roundabout common sense' (these are Locke's words), which was their guide in what concerned them. Some may not think this romantic enough to be attractive, and yet it has a beauty of its own. They did not 'look before or after,' nor 'pine for what was not;' they enjoyed what was; a solid homeliness was their mark. Exactly as we like to see a large lazy animal lying in the placid shade, without anxiety for the future and chewing the cud of the past, we like to look back at the age of our great-grandfathers, so solid in its habits and placid in the lapse of years. Nevertheless—and this is what is to our purpose—we must own at once that the very merits of that age are of the earth, earthy; there was no talk then of 'obstinate questionings,' or 'incommunicable dream;' heroism, enthusiasm, the sense of the supernatural, deep feeling, seem in a manner foreign to the very idea of it. This is the point of view in which the Tractarian movement was described as 'tending towards the realisation of something better and nobler than satisfied the last century.' For the clergy, the time was indeed evil. The popular view of the profession seems accurately expressed in a well-known book of memoirs. ' But if this was your opinion, how came you not to let your friend Sherlock,' the well-known bishop, ' into the secret? Why did you not tell him that half the pack, and those you most depended on, were drawn off, and the game escaped and safe, instead of leaving his lordship there to bark and yelp by himself, and make the silly figure he has done?' ' Oh,' said Lord Carteret, ' he talks like a parson, and consequently is so used to talk to people who do not mind him, that I left him to find it out at his leisure, and shall have him again for all this, whenever I want him.'

The fact of Butler's success is to be accounted for, as we have said, by his personal excellence. Mr. Talbot liked him, *Bishop* Talbot liked him, the Queen liked him, the King liked him. He says himself in these Remains, ' Good men surely are not treated in this world as they deserve, yet 'tis seldom, very seldom, their goodness makes them disliked, even in cases where it may seem to be so; but 'tis some behaviour or other which, however excusable, perhaps infinitely overbalanced by their virtues, yet is offensive, possibly wrong, however such, it may be, as would pass off very well in a man of the world.' And he must have been alive to the fact in practice. He had every excuse for making virtue detestable. He was educated a Baptist, and brought up at a dissenting academy. He was born in the vulgarest years of English Puritanism, when it had fallen from its first estate, when it had least influence with the higher classes, when the revival which dates from John Wesley had not begun, and the very memory of gentlemen such as Hutchinson or Hampden had passed away. A certain instinctive refinement, a 'niceness' and gentleness of nature, preserved him not only from the coarser consequences of his position, but even from that angularity of mind which is not often escaped by those early trained to object to what is established.

Of his character the principal point may be described in the words which Arnold so often uses to denote the end and aim of his education, ' moral thoughtfulness.' A certain considerateness is, as it were, diffused over all his sentences. To most men conscience is an occasional, almost an external voice; to Butler it was a daily companion, a close anxiety. In a recent novel this disposition is skilfully delineated and delicately contrasted with its opposite. We may quote the passage, though it is encumbered with some detail. ' But what was a real trouble to Charles,' this is the person whose character is in question, ' it got clearer and clearer to his apprehension, that his intimacy with Sheffield was not quite what it had been. They had indeed passed the vacation together, and saw of each other more than ever; but their sympathies with each other were not as strong, they had not the same likings and dislikings; in short, they had not such congenial minds, as when they were freshmen. There was not so much heart in their conversations, and they more easily endured to miss each other's company. They were both reading for honours, reading hard; but Sheffield's whole heart was in his work, and religion was but a secondary matter with him. He had no doubts, difficulties, anxieties, sorrows, which much affected him. It was not the certainty of faith which made a sunshine in his soul, and dried up the mists of human weakness; rather he had no perceptible need within him of that vision of the unseen, which is the Christian's life. He was unblemished in his character, exemplary in his conduct, but he was content with what the perishable world gave him. Charles's characteristic, perhaps more than anything else, was an habitual sense of the Divine Presence—a sense which, of course, did not insure uninterrupted conformity of thought and deed to itself, but still there it was: the pillar of the cloud before him and guiding him. He felt himself to be God's creature, and responsible to Him; God's possession, not his own.' Again the same character is brought home to us, in a part of Walton's delineation of Hooker, which, indeed, except perhaps for the great quickness attributed to his intellect, might as a whole stand well enough for a description of Butler: ' His complexion (if we may guess by him at the age of forty) was sanguine, with a mixture of choler; and yet his motion was slow even in his youth, and so was his speech, never expressing an earnestness in either of them, but an humble gravity suited to the aged. And it is observed (so far as inquiry is able to look back at this distance of time) that at his being a schoolboy he was an early questionist, quietly inquisitive why this was granted and that denied; this being mixed with a remarkable modesty and a sweet serene quietness of nature. . . . It is observable that he was never known to be . . . . extreme in any of his desires; never heard to repine or dispute with Providence, but, by a quiet gentle submission and resignation of his will to the wisdom of the Creator, bore the burden of the day with patience; . . . . and by this, and a grave behaviour, which is a divine charm, he begot an early reverence for his person even from those that, at other times and in other companies, took a liberty to cast off that strictness of behaviour and discourse that is required in a collegiate life.' Something of this is a result of disposition; yet on the whole it seems mainly the effect of the ' moral thoughtfulness ' which has been mentioned.

The very name of this quality reminds us of a difficulty. We cannot but doubt, with the experience of this age, how far this can be made, or ought to be made, the abiding sentiment of all men; how far such teaching as that of Arnold's tends to introduce a too stiff and anxious habit of mind; how far the perpetual presence of a purpose will interfere with the simple happiness of life, and how far also it *can* be forced on the ' lilies of the field; ' how far the care of anxious minds and active thoughts is to be obtruded on the young, on the cheerful, on the natural. Other questions, too, might be asked, if the inculcation of this temper and habit as a daily, universal obligation, a perpetual and general necessity for all characters, would not, or might not, impair the sanguine energy and masculine activity which are necessary for social action; whether it does not, in matter of fact, even now, ' burn and brand ' into excitable fancies a few stern truths more deeply than a feeble reason will bear or the equilibrium of the world demands? But whatever be the issue of such questions, on which there is perhaps now no decided or established opinion, there can be no question of the charm of such a character in those to whom it is natural. We may admire what we cannot share; reverence what we do not imitate. As those who cannot comprehend a strain of soothing music, look with interest on those who can; as those who cannot feel the gentle glow of a quiet landscape, yet stand aside and seem inferior to those who do; so in character the buoyant and the bold, the harsh and the practical, may, at least for the moment, moralise and look upwards, reverence and do homage, when they come to a close experience of what is gentler and simpler, more anxious and more thoughtful, kinder and more religious, than themselves. At any rate, so thought the contemporaries of Butler. They did, as a Frenchman would say, ' their possible ' for a good man; at least they made him a bishop.

We gather, however, that their kindness was scarcely successful. Butler was very prosperous; but it does not appear that he was at all happy. In the midst of the princely establishment of his rich episcopate, so anxious a nature found time to be rather melancholy. The responsibilities of so cumbrous a position were but little pleasant to an apprehensive disposition; wealth and honour were finery and foolishness to a quiet and shrinking man. A small room in a tranquil college, daily walks and thoughtful talk, a little income and a few friends—these, and these only, suit a still and meditative mind. Such, however, were denied him. He is said to have taken much pleasure in discussion and interchange of mind; but his life was passed in courts and country parsonages—the one too noisy, the last too still, to think or reason. Nor were there many people, whom we know of, that were congenial to him in that age. Scarcely any name of a friend of his has come down to us; one, indeed, there is—that of Bishop Secker, afterwards Archbishop of Canterbury, the author of a treatise on the Catechism, a serious work still used for the purposes of tuition, with which, indeed, the name of the writer is now with some so associated by early habit that it is difficult to fancy even Butler on equal social terms with him; the notion of talking to him seems like being asked to converse familiarly with the Catechism itself.

A not unremarkable circumstance, however, shows that Secker, though he was educated at the same academy, could not have been on any terms of extreme intimacy with Butler. Some time after Butler's death, there was a rumour that he had died a Papist. There is no doubt, in fact, that Butler's opinions, being formed on principles of evidence and reasoning too strict to be extremely popular, were not likely to be agreeable to those about him, and when an Englishman sees anything in religion which he does not like, he always, *prima facie*, imputes it to the Pope. Besides this general and strong argument, there were two particular ones—first, that he had erected a cross in the episcopal chapel at Bristol; secondly, that he was of a melancholy and somewhat of an ascetic turn; reasons which, though doubtless of force in their day and generation, are not likely to be of avail with us, who know so much more about crosses and fasting than they did then. We might have expected that Secker, as Butler's old friend and schoolfellow, would have been able from his personal knowledge to throw a good deal of light upon the question. He was only, however, able to advance ' *presumptive* arguments that Bishop Butler did not die a Papist,' which were no doubt valuable; but yet give no great idea of the intimacy between the writer and the person about whom he was writing. Such arguments may easily be found, and have always convinced every one that there was no truth in this rumour. The only reason for which we wish that Secker had been able to say he had heard Butler talk on the subject, and that he was no Papist, is, that we should then have known to whom Butler talked. There is nothing in Butler's writings at all showing any leaning to the peculiar tenets of Roman Catholicism, and there is much which shows a strong opinion against them; and it was far too extreme a doctrine to be at all agreeable to his very English, moderate, and shrinking mind.

Calumny, however, is commonly instructive. It must be granted, that though there is no trace or tendency in the writings of Butler to the peculiar superstitions advocated by the Pope, there is a strong and prevailing tinge of what may be called the principle of superstition, that is, the religion of fear. Some may doubt, especially at the present day, whether there be any true religion of that kind at all; yet it seems, as Butler would have said, but a proper feeling ' in such creatures as we are, in such a world as the present one.'

We may reflect that there are two kinds of religion, which may for some purposes be called, the one the natural, and the other the supernatural. The former seems to take its rise from mere contemplation of external beauty. We look on the world, and we see that it is good. The Greek of former time, reclining softly in his own bright land, ' looked up to the whole sky and declared that the One was God.' From the blue air and the fair cloud, the green earth and the white sea, a presence streams upon us. It modulates—

> ' With murmurs of the air,
> And motions of the forests and the sea,
> And voice of living beings and woven hymns
> Of night and day, and the deep heart of man.'

But the true home of the idea is in the starlight sky; we instinctively mingle it with an admiration of infinite space, a cold purity is around us, and the clear and steel-like words of the poet justly reflect the doctrine of the clear and steel-like heaven:—

> ' The magic car moved on.
> Earth's distant orb appeared
> The smallest light that twinkles in the heaven;
> Whilst round the chariot's way
> Innumerable systems rolled,
> And countless spheres diffused
> An ever-varying glory.
>   It was a sight of wonder: some
> Were hornèd like the crescent moon;
> Some shed a mild and silver beam
> Like Hesperus across the western sea;
> Some dashed athwart with trains of flame,
> Like worlds to death and ruin driven;
> Some shone like suns, and, as the chariot passed,
> Eclipsed all other light.
>   Spirit of nature! here!
> In this interminable wilderness
> Of worlds, at whose immensity
> Even soaring fancy staggers,
> Here is thy fitting temple.
>   Yet not the lightest leaf
> That quivers to the passing breeze
> Is less instinct with thee:
> Yet not——'

And so on; and so it will be as long as there are poets to look upon the sky, or a sky to be looked at by them. The truth is, that there is a certain expressiveness (if we may so speak) in nature which persons of imagination naturally feel more acutely than others, and which cannot easily be in its full degree brought home to others, except in quotations of their writings, from

which ' smiling of the world,' as it has been called, more than
from any other outward appearance, we infer the existence of
an immaterial and animating spirit. This expressiveness perhaps produces its effect on the mind, by a principle analogous
to, perhaps in a severe analysis identical with, the interpretative
faculty by which we acquire a cognizance of the existence of
other human minds. There appear to be certain natural signs
and tokens from which we (like other animals) instinctively
infer, or rather—for there is no conscious reasoning—in which
we silently *see* life and thought and mind. In this way we
interpret the detail of natural expression—the smile, the glance
of the eye, the common interjections, the universal tokens of
our simplest emotions; those signs and marks and expressions
which we make in our earliest infancy without teaching and by
instinct, we appear also, by instinct and without learning, to
read off, interpret, and comprehend, when used to us by others.
The comprehension of this language is perhaps as much an
instinct as the using of it. There is no occasion, however, for
acute metaphysics; whatever was the origin of this faculty,
such a power of interpreting material phenomena, such a faculty
of *seeing* life, undoubtedly there is;—however we come by the
power, we *can* distinguish living from dead creatures. At any
rate, if, like other living creatures, we take a natural cognizance
of the simple expressions of life and mind, and without tuition
comprehend the language and meaning of natural signs, in like
manner, though less clearly and forcibly, because our attention
is so much less forcibly directed to them, do we interpret the
significance of the beauty and the sublimity of outward
nature. ' In the mountains ' do we ' feel our faith.' We seem
to know there is something behind. There is a perception
of something—

> ' Far more deeply interfused,
> Whose dwelling is the light of setting suns,
> And the round ocean and the living air,
> And the blue sky, and in the mind of man—
> A motion and a spirit that impels
> All thinking things, all objects of all thought,
> And rolls through all things.'

The Greek mythology is one entire and unmixed embodiment of this religion of nature, as we may term it, this poetic

interpretation of the spirit that speaks to us in the signs and symbols within us. Nor can any sensitive or imaginative mind scrutinise itself without being distinctly conscious of its teaching.

Now of the poetic religion there is nothing in Butler. No one could tell from his writings that the universe was beautiful. If the world were a Durham mine or an exact square, if no part of it were more expressive than a gravel-pit or a chalk-quarry, the teaching of Butler would be as true as it is now. A young poet, not a very wise one, once said, ' he did not like the Bible, there was nothing about flowers in it.' He might have said so of Butler with great truth; a most ugly and stupid world one would fancy *his* books were written in. But in return and by way of compensation for this, there is a religion of another sort, a religion the source of which is within the mind, as the other's was found to be in the world without; the religion to which we just now alluded as the religion (by an odd yet expressive way of speaking) of *superstition*. The source of this, as most persons are practically aware, is in the conscience. The moral principle (whatever may be said to the contrary by complacent thinkers) is really and to most men a principle of fear. The delights of a good conscience may be reserved for better things, but few men who know themselves will say that they have often felt them by vivid and actual experience. A sensation of shame, of reproach, of remorse, of sin (to use the word we instinctively shrink from because it expresses the meaning), is what the moral principle really and practically thrusts on most men. Conscience is the condemnation of ourselves. We expect a penalty. As the Greek proverb teaches, ' where there is shame there is fear; ' where there is the deep and intimate anxiety of guilt—the feeling which has driven murderers, and other than murderers, forth to wastes, and rocks, and stones, and tempests—we see, as it were, in a single complex and indivisible sensation, the pain and sense of guilt, and the painful anticipation of its punishment. How to be free from this, is the question. How to get loose from this— how to be rid of the secret tie which binds the strong man and cramps his pride, and makes him angry at the beauty of the universe—which will not let him go forth like a great animal, like the king of the forest, in the glory of his might, but restrains him with an inner fear and a secret foreboding, that if he do but exalt himself he shall be abased; if he do but set forth his own dignity, he will offend ONE who will deprive him of it. This, as has often been pointed out, is the source of the bloody rites of heathendom. You are going to battle, you are going out in the bright sun with dancing plumes and glittering spear; your shield shines, and your feathers wave, and your limbs are glad with the consciousness of strength, and your mind is warm with glory and renown,—with coming glory and unobtained renown,—for who are you, to hope for these—who are *you*, to go forth proudly against the pride of the sun, with your secret sin and your haunting shame, and your real fear? First lie down and abase yourself—strike your back with hard stripes—cut deep with a sharp knife as if you would eradicate the consciousness—cry aloud—put ashes on your head—bruise yourself with stones, then perhaps God may pardon you; or, better still—so runs the incoherent feeling— give Him something—your ox, your ass, whole hecatombs, if you are rich enough; anything, it is but a chance—you do not know what will please Him—at any rate, what you love best yourself—that is, most likely, your first-born son; then, after such gifts and such humiliation, He may be appeased, He may let you off—He may without anger let you go forth Achilles- like in the glory of your shield—He may *not* send you home as He would else, the victim of rout and treachery, with broken arms and foul limbs, in weariness and humiliation.

Of course, it is not this kind of fanaticism that we impute to a prelate of the English Church: human sacrifices are not respectable, and Achilles was not rector of Stanhope. But though the costume and circumstances of life change, the human heart does not; its feelings remain. The same anxiety, the same consciousness of personal sin, which led in barbarous times to what has been described, show themselves in civilised life as well. In this quieter period, their great manifestation s scrupulosity, a care about the ritual of life, an attention to meats and drinks, and cups and washings. Being so unworthy as we are, feeling what we feel, abased as we are abased, who shall say that these are beneath us? In ardent imaginative youth they may seem so, but let a few years come, let them dull the will or contract the heart, or stain the mind—then the consequent feeling will be, as all experience shows, not that a ritual is too mean, too low, too degrading for human nature, but that it is a mercy we have to do no more—that we have only to wash in Jordan—that we have not even to go out into the unknown distance to seek for Abana and Pharpar, rivers of Damascus. We have no right to judge, we cannot decide, we must do what is laid down for us,—we fail daily even in this, we must never cease for a moment in our scrupulous anxiety to omit by no tittle and to exceed by no iota. An accomplished divine of the present day has written a dissertation to show that this sort of piety is that expressed by the Greek word εὐλάβεια, ' piety contemplated on the side on which it is a fear of God,' and which he derives from εὐλαμβάνεσθαι, ' the image underlying the word being that of the careful taking hold, the cautious handling of some precious yet delicate vessel, which with ruder or less anxious handling might be broken,' and he subsequently adds, ' The only three places in the New Testament in which εὐλαβὴς occurs are these:— Luke ii. 25, Acts ii. 5, viii. 2. We have uniformly rendered it " devout," nor could this translation be bettered. It will be observed that on all these occasions it is used to express Jewish, and, as one might say, Old Testament piety. On the first it is applied to Simeon (δίκαιος καὶ εὐλαβὴς); on the second to those Jews who came from distant parts to keep the commanded feasts at Jerusalem; and on the third there can scarcely be a doubt that the ἄνδρες εὐλαβεῖς who carry Stephen to his burial are not, as might at first sight appear, *Christian* brethren, but devout Jews, who showed by this courageous act of theirs, as by their great lamentation over the slaughtered saints, that they abhorred this deed of blood, that they separated themselves in spirit from it, and thus, if it might be, from all the judgments which it would bring down on the city of those murderers. Whether it was also further given them to believe on the Crucified who had such witnesses as Stephen, we are not told; we may well presume that it was. . . . If we keep in mind that in that mingled fear and love which together constitute the piety of man toward God, the Old Testament placed its emphasis on the fear, the New places it on the love (though there was love in the fear of God's saints then, as there must be fear in their love now), it will at once be evident how fitly εὐλοβὴς was chosen to set forth their piety under the old covenant, who, like Zacharias and Elizabeth, were righteous before God, walking in all the commandments and ordinances

of the Lord blameless, and leaving nothing willingly undone
which pertained to the circle of their prescribed duties. For
this sense of accurately and scrupulously performing that which
is prescribed with the consciousness of the danger of slipping
into a negligent performance of God's service, and of the need
therefore of anxiously watching against the adding to or
diminishing from, or in any other way altering, that which is
commanded, lies ever in the words εὐλάβης, εὐλάβεια
when used in their religious signification. Plutarch, in more
than one instructive passage, exalts the εὐλάβεια of the old
Romans in divine matters, as contrasted with the comparative
carelessness of the Greeks. Thus, in his " Coriolanus," after
other instances in proof, he goes on to say, " Of late times also
they did renew and begin a sacrifice thirty times one after
another, because they thought still there fell out one fault or
another in the same; so holy and devout were they to the
gods " (τοιαύτη μὲν εὐλάβεια πρὸς τὸ θεῖον 'Ρωμαίων).
Elsewhere he portrays Æmilius Paulus as eminent for his
εὐλάβεια. The passage is long, and I will only quote a portion
of it, availing myself again of old Sir Thomas North's translation, which, though somewhat loose, is in essentials correct:
" When he did anything belonging to his office of priesthood,
he did it with great experience, judgment, and diligence;
leaving all other thoughts, and without omitting any ancient
ceremony or adding any new; contending oftentimes with
his companions in things which seemed light and of small
moment; declaring to them that, though we do presume the
gods are easy to be pacified and that they readily pardon all
faults and scapes committed by negligence, yet if it were no
more but for respect of the Commonwealth's sake, they should
not slightly or carelessly dissemble or pass over faults committed in those matters." ' *

This is the view suggested by what Butler has happily
called the ' presages of conscience ' by the ' natural fear and
apprehension ' of punishment, ' which restrains from crimes and
is a declaration of nature against them.' The great difficulty
of religious philosophy is, to explain how we know that these
two Beings are the same—from what course and principle of
reasoning it is that we acquire our knowledge that the *curiosus
Deus*, the watchful Deity, who is ever in our secret hearts, who

* Trench, *On the Synonyms of the New Testament* (p. 191).

seeks us out in the fairest scenes, who is apt to terrify our
hearts, whose very eyes seem to shine through nature, is the
same Being that animates the universe with its beauty and its
light, smoothes the heaviness from our brow and the weight
from our hearts, pervades the floating cloud and buoyant
air,—

> 'And from the breezes, whether low or loud,
> And from the rain of every passing cloud,
> And from the singing of the summer birds,
> And from all sounds, all silence,'

—gives hints of joy and hope. This seems the natural dualism
—the singular contrast of the God of imagination and the God
of conscience, the God of beauty and the God of fear. How do
we know that the Being who refreshes is the same as He who
imposes the toil, that the God of anxiety is the same as the
God of help, that the intensely personal Deity of the inward
heart is the same as the almost neutral spirit of external
nature, which seems a thing more than a person, a light and
impalpable vapour just beautifying the universe, and no more?
If we are to offer a suggestion, as we have stated a difficulty, we should hold that the only way of obviating or
explaining the contrast, which is so perplexing to susceptible
minds, is by recurring to the same primary assumption which
is required to satisfy our belief in God's infinity, omnipotence,
or veracity. We cannot *prove* in any way that God is infinite
any more than that space is infinite; nor that God is omnipotent, since we do not know what powers there are in nature—
that He is perfectly true, for we have had no experience or
communication with Him, in which His veracity could be
tested. We assume these propositions, and treat them, moreover, not as hypothetical assumptions or provisional theories
to be discarded if new facts should be discovered, and to be
rejected if more elaborate research should require it, but as
positive and clear certainties, on which we must ever act,
and to which we must reduce and square all new information
that may be brought home to us. In these respects we assume
that God is perfect, and it is only necessary for the solution
of our difficulty to assume that He is perfect in all. We have
in both cases the same amount and description of evidence,
the same inward consciousness, the same speaking and urging

voice, requiring us to believe. In every step of religious argument we require the assumption, the belief, the faith if the word is better, in an absolutely *perfect* Being—in and by whom we are, who is omnipotent as well as most holy, who moves on the face of the whole world and ruleth all things by the word of His power. If we grant this, the difficulty of the opposition between what we have called the natural and the supernatural religion is removed; and without granting it, that difficulty is perhaps insuperable. It follows from the very idea and definition of an infinitely-perfect Being, that He is within us, as well as without us—ruling the clouds of the air, and the fishes of the sea, as well as the fears and thoughts of man—smiling through the smile of nature, as well as warning with the pain of conscience, ' Sine qualitate bonum; sine quantitate magnum; sine indigentiâ creatorem; sine situ præsidentem; sine habitu omnia continentem; sine loco ubique totum; sine tempore sempiternum; sine ullâ sui mutatione mutabilia facientem, nihilque patientem.' If we assume this, life is simple; without this all is dark.

The religion of the imagination is, in its consequences upon the character, free and poetical. No one need trouble himself to set about its defence. Its agreeability sufficiently defends it and its congeniality to a refined and literary age. The religion of the conscience will seem to many of the present day selfish and morbid. And doubtless it may become so if it be allowed to eat into the fibre of the character, and to supersede the manliness by which it should be supported. The whole of religion, of course, is not of this sort, and it is one which only very imperfect beings can have a share in. But so long as men are very imperfect, the sense of great imperfection should cleave to them, and while the consciousness of sin is on the mind, the consequent apprehension of deserved punishment seems in its proper degree to be a reasonable service. However, any more of this discussion is scarcely to our purpose. No attentive reader of Butler's writings will hesitate to say that he, at all events, was an example of the ' anxious and scrupulous worshipper, who makes a conscience of changing anything, of omitting anything, being in all things fearful to offend,'* and most likely it was from this habit and charac-

* Trench, *ubi supra.*

teristic of his mind, that he obtained the unenviable reputation
of living and dying a Papist.

Of Butler's personal habits nothing in the way of detail
has descended to us. He was never married, and there is no
evidence of his ever having spoken to any lady save Queen
Caroline. We hear, however, for certain that he was commonly
present at her Majesty's philosophical parties, at which all
questions, religious and moral, speculative and practical, were
discussed with a freedom that would astonish the present
generation. Less intellectual unbelief existed probably at that
time than there is now, but there was an infinitely freer
expression of what did exist. The French Revolution frightened
the English people. The awful calamities and horrors of that
period were thought to be, as in part they were, the results
and consequences of the irreligious opinions which just before
prevailed. Scepticism became what in the days of Lord Hervey
it was not, an ungentlemanly state of mind. At no meeting
of the higher classes, certainly at none where ladies are present,
is there a tenth part of the plain questioning and *bona fide*
discussion of primary Christian topics, that there was at the
select suppers of Queen Caroline. The effect of these may be
seen in many passages, and even in the whole tendency, of
Butler's writings. No great Christian writer, perhaps, is so
exclusively occupied with elementary topics and philosophical
reasonings. His mind is ever directed towards the first principles of belief, and doubtless this was because, more than any
other, he lived with men who plainly and clearly denied them.
His frequent allusion to the difficulties of such discussions are
likewise suggestive of a familiar personal experience. The whole
list of directions which he gives the clergy of Durham on
religious argument shows a daily familiarity with sceptical
men. ' It is come,' he says, ' I know not how, to be taken for
granted by many persons that Christianity is not so much as a
subject of inquiry, but that it is now at length discovered to
be false. And accordingly they treat it as if this were an agreed
point among all people of discernment, and nothing remained
but to set it up as a principal subject of ridicule, as it were by
way of reprisals for its having so long interrupted the pleasures
of the world.' No one would so describe the tone of talk now,
nor would there be an equal reason for remembering Butler's
general caution against rashly entering the lists with the

questioners. Among gentlemen a clergyman has scarcely the chance. ' Then, again, the general evidence of religion is complex and various. It consists of a long series of things: one preparatory to and confirming another from the beginning of the world till the present time, and it is easy to see how impossible it must be in a cursory conversation to unite all this into one argument, and represent it as it ought; and, could it be done, how utterly indisposed would people be to attend to it. I say, in cursory conversation; whereas unconnected objections are thrown out in a few words, and are easily apprehended without more attention than is usual in common talk, so that, notwithstanding we have the best cause in the world, and though a man were very capable of defending it, yet I know not why he should be forward to undertake it upon so great a disadvantage and to so little good effect, as it must be amid the gaiety and carelessness of common conversation.' It is not likely from these remarks that Butler had much pleasure at the Queen's talking parties.

What his pleasures were, indeed, does not very distinctly appear. In reading we doubt if he took any keen interest. A voracious reader is apt, when he comes to write, to exhibit his reading in casual references and careless innuendoes, which run out insensibly from the fulness of his literary memory. But of this in Butler there is nothing. His writings contain little save a bare and often not a very plain statement of the necessary argument; you cannot perhaps find a purely literary allusion in his writings; none, at all events, which shows he had any favourite books, whose topics were ever present to his mind, and whose well-known words might be a constant resource in moments of weariness and melancholy. There is, too, a philippic in the well-known ' Preface ' against vague and thoughtless reading, which seems as if he felt the evil consequences more than the agreeableness of that sin. Some men find a compensation in the excitement of writing, for all other evils and exclusions; but it is probable that, if Butler hated anything, he hated his pen. Composition is pleasant work for men of ready words, fine ears, and thick-coming illustrations. Wit and eloquence please the writer as much as the reader. There is even some pleasantness in feeling that you have given a precise statement of a strong argument. But Butler, so far from having the pleasures of eloquence, had not even the comfort of perspicuity. He never could feel that he had made an argument tell by his way of wording it; it tells in his writings, if it tells at all, by its own native and inherent force. In some places the mode of statement is even stupid; it seems selected to occasion a difficulty. You often see that writers,—Gibbon, for instance,—believe that their words are good to eat, as well as to read; they had plainly a pleasure in rolling them about in the mouth like sugar-plums, and gradually smoothing off any knots or excrescences; but there is nothing of this in Butler.

The circumstance of so great a thinker being such a poor writer is not only curious in itself, but indicates the class of thinkers to which Butler belongs. Philosophers may be divided into seers on the one hand, and into gropers on the other. Plato, to use a contrast which is often used for other purposes, is the type of the first. On all subjects he seems to have before him a landscape of thought, with clear outline, and pure air, keen rocks and shining leaves, an Attic sky and crystal-flowing river, each detail of which was as present, as distinct, as familiar to his mind as the view from the Acropolis, or the road to Decelea. As were his conceptions so is his style. What Protagoras said and Socrates replied, what Thrasymachus and Polemo, what Gorgias and Callicles, all comes out in distinct sequence and accurate expression; each feature is engraved on the paper; an exact beauty is in every line. What a contrast is the style of Aristotle! He sees nothing—he is like a man groping in the dark about a room which he knows. He hesitates and suggests; proposes first one formula and then another; rejects both, gives a multitude of reasons, and ends at last with an expression which he admits to be incorrect and an apologetic ' let it make no difference.' There are whole passages in his writings—the discussion about Solon and happiness in the ' Ethics,' is an instance—in which he appears like a schoolboy who knows the answer to a sum, but cannot get the figures to come to it.

This awkward and hesitating manner is likewise that of Butler. He seems to have an obscure feeling, an undefined perception, of what the truth is; but his manipulation of words and images is not apt enough to bring it out. Like the miser in the story, he has a shilling *about* him somewhere, if people will only give him time and solitude to make research.

for it. As a person hunting for a word or name he has forgotten, he knows what it is, *only* he cannot say it. The fault is one characteristic of a strong and sound mind wanting in imagination. The visual faculty is deficient. The soundness of such men's understanding ensures a correct report of what comes before them, and its strength is shown in vigorous observations upon it; but they are unable to bring those remarks out, the delineative power is wanting, they have no picture of the particulars in their minds; no instance or illustration occurs to them. Popular, in the large sense of the term, such writers can never be. Influential they may often become. The learned have time for difficulties; the critical mind is pleased with crooked constructions; the detective intellect likes the research for lurking and half-hidden truth. In this way portions of Aristotle have been noted these thousand years, as Chinese puzzles; and without detracting for a moment from Butler's real merit, it may be allowed that some of his influence, especially that which he enjoys in the English universities, is partially due to that obscurity of style, which renders his writings such apt exercises for the critical intellect, which makes the truth when found seem more valuable from the difficulty of finding it, and gives scope for an able lecturer to elucidate, annotate, and expound.

The fame of Butler rests mainly on two remarkable courses of reasoning, one of which is contained in the well-known Sermons, the second in the ' Analogy.' Both seem to be in a great measure suggested by the circumstances and topics of the time. There was a certain naturalness in Butler's mind, which took him straight to the questions on which men differed around him. Generally, it is safer to prove what no one denies, and easier to explain difficulties which no one has ever felt. A quiet reputation is best obtained in the literary *quæstiunculæ* of important subjects. But a simple and straightforward man studies great topics because he feels a want of the knowledge which they contain; and if he has ascertained an apparent solution of any difficulty, he is anxious to impart it to others. He goes straight to the real doubts and fundamental discrepancies; to those on which it is easy to excite odium, and difficult to give satisfaction; he leaves to others the amusing skirmishing and superficial literature accessory to such studies.

Thus there is nothing light in Butler; all is grave, serious, and essential; nothing else would be characteristic of him.

The Sermons of Butler are primarily intended as an answer to that recurring topic of ethical discussion, the Utilitarian Philosophy. He is occasionally spoken of by enthusiastic disciples as having uprooted this for ever. But this is hardly so. The selfish system still lives and flourishes. Nor must any writer on the fundamental differences of human opinion propose to himself such an aim. The source of the great heresies of belief lies in their congeniality to certain types of character frequent in the world, and liable to be reproduced by inevitable and recurring circumstances. We do not mean that the variations of creeds are the native and essential variances of the minds which believe them, for this would render truth a matter of personal character, and make general discussion impossible. We believe that all minds are originally so constituted as to be able to acquire right opinions on all subjects of the first importance to them; but, nevertheless, that the native bent of their character instinctively inclines them to particular views; that one man is naturally prone to one error, and another to its opposite; that this is increased by circumstances, and becomes for practical purposes invincible, unless it be met on the part of every man by early and vigorous resistance. The Epicurean philosophy is an example of these recurring and primary errors, inasmuch as it is congenial to clear, vigorous, and hasty minds, which have no great depth of feeling, and no searching introspection of thought, which prefer a ready solution to an accurate, an easy to an elaborate, a simple to a profound. Draw a slight worldliness—and the events of life will draw it—over such a mind, and you have the best Epicurean. There is a use, however, in discussing topics like these. Nothing would be more perverse than to abstain from proving certain truths, because some men were naturally prone to the opposite errors; rather, on the contrary, should we din them into the ears, and thrust them upon the attention, of mankind; go out into the highways and hedges, and leave as few as possible for invincible ignorance to mislead or to excuse. It is much in every generation to state the ancient truth in the manner which that generation requires; to state the old answer to the old difficulty; to transmit, if not discover; convince, if not invent; to translate into the language of the living, the truths first discovered by the dead. This defence, though suggested by the subject, is not, however, required by Butler. He may claim the higher praise of having explained his subject in a manner essentially more satisfactory than his predecessors.

We are not concerned to follow Butler into the entire range of this ancient and well-discussed topic. We are only called on to make, and we shall only make, two or three remarks on the position which he occupies with respect to it. His grand merit is the simple but important one of having given a less complex and more graphic description of the facts of human consciousness than any one had done before. Before his time the Utilitarians had the advantage of appearing to be the only people who talked about real life and human transactions. The doctrines avowed by their opponents were cloudy, lofty, and impalpable. Platonic philosophy in its simple form is utterly inexplicable to the English mind. A plain man will not soon succeed in making anything of an archetypal idea. If an ordinary sensible Englishman takes up even such a book as Cudworth's ' Immutable Morality,' it is nearly inevitable that he should put it down as mystical fancy. True as a considerable portion of the conclusions of that treatise are or may be, nevertheless the truth is commonly so put as to puzzle an Englishman, and the error so as particularly to offend him. We may open at random. ' Wherefore,' says Cudworth, ' the result of all that we have hitherto said is this, that the intelligible natures and essences of things are neither arbitrary nor fantastical, that is, neither alterable by any will or opinion; and therefore everything is necessarily and immutably to science and knowledge what it is, whether absolutely, or relatively to all minds and intellects in the world. So that if moral good and evil, just and unjust, signify any reality, either absolute or relative, in the things so denominated, as they must have some certain natures, which are the actions or souls of men, they are neither alterable by will or opinion. Upon which ground that wise philosopher, Plato, in his " Minos," determined that Νόμος, a law, is not δόγμα πόλεως, any arbitrary decree of a city or supreme governors; because there may be unjust decrees, which, therefore, are no laws, but the *invention of that which* IS, or what is absolutely or immutably just in its own nature; though it be very true also that the arbitrary constitutions of those that have the lawful authority of commanding when they are not

materially unjust, are laws also in a secondary sense, by virtue
of that natural and immutable justice or law that requires political order to be observed. But I have not taken all this pains
only to confute scepticism or fanaticism, or merely to defend
or corroborate our argument for the immutable nature of the
just and unjust; but also for some other weighty purposes that
are very much conducing to the business we have in hand. And
first of all, that the soul is not a mere *tabula rasa*, a naked and
passive thing, which has no innate furniture or activity of its
own, nor anything at all in it but what was impressed on it
from without; for, if it were so, then there could not possibly
be any such thing as moral good and evil, just and unjust, for-
asmuch as these differences do not arise merely from outward
objects or from the impresses which they make upon us by sense,
there being no such thing in them, in which sense it is truly
affirmed by the author of the "Leviathan" (p. 24), " That there
is no common rule of good and evil to be taken from the nature
of the objects themselves," that is, either considered absolutely
in themselves, or relatively to external sense only, but according
to some other interior analogy which things have to a certain
inward determination in the soul itself from whence the foundation of all this difference must needs arise, as I shall show
afterwards; not that the anticipations of morality spring merely
from intellectual forms and notional ideas of the mind, or from
certain rules or propositions printed on the " soul as on a
book," but from some other more inward and vital principle
in intellectual beings, as such, whereby they have a natural
determination in them to do certain things, and to avoid
others, which could not be, if they were mere naked, passive
things.'

It is instructive to compare Butler's way of stating a doctrine substantially similar:—

' Mankind has various instincts and principles of actions, as
brute creatures have; some leading most directly and immediately to the good of the community, and some most directly
to private good.

' Man has several which brutes have not; particularly reflection or conscience, an approbation of some principles or actions,
and disapprobation of others.

' Brutes obey their instincts or principles of action, according to certain rules; suppose the constitution of their body, and the objects around them.

' The generality of mankind also obey their instincts and principles, all of them; those propensions we call good, as well as the bad, according to the same rules, namely, the constitution of their body, and the external circumstances which they are in.

' Brutes, in acting according to the rules before mentioned, their bodily constitution and circumstances, act suitably to their whole nature.

' Mankind also, in acting thus, would act suitably to their whole nature, if no more were to be said of man's nature than what has been now said; if that, as it is a true, were also a complete, adequate account of our nature.

' But that is not a complete account of man's nature. Somewhat further must be brought in to give us an adequate notion of it, namely, that one of those principles of action, conscience, or reflection, compared with the rest, as they all stand together in the nature of man, plainly bears upon it marks of authority over all the rest, and claims the absolute direction of them all, to allow or forbid their gratification; a disapprobation of reflection being in itself a principle manifestly superior to a mere propension. And the conclusion is, that to allow no more to this superior principle or part of our nature, than to other parts; to let it govern and guide only occasionally in common with the rest, as its turn happens to come, from the temper and circumstances one happens to be in,—this is not to act conformably to the constitution of man. Neither can any human creature be said to act conformably to his constitution of nature, unless he allows to that superior principle the absolute authority which is due to it. And this conclusion is abundantly confirmed from hence, that one may determine what course of action the economy of man's nature requires, without so much as knowing in what degrees of *strength* the several principles prevail, or which of them have actually the greatest influence.

' The practical reason of insisting so much upon this natural authority of the principle of reflection or conscience is, that it seems in a great measure overlooked by many, who are by no means the worst sort of men. It is thought sufficient to abstain from gross wickedness, and to be humane and kind to such as happen to come in their way. Whereas, in reality, the very constitution of our nature requires that we bring our whole conduct before this superior faculty; wait its determination; enforce upon ourselves its authority; and make it the business of our lives, as it is absolutely the whole business of a moral agent, to conform ourselves to it. This is the true meaning of that ancient precept, *Reverence thyself*.'

We do not mean that Cudworth's style is not as good, or better, than the style of Butler; but that the language and illustrations of the latter belong to the same world as that we live in, have a relation to practice, and recall sentiments we remember to have felt and sensations which are familiar to us, while those of Cudworth, on the contrary, seem difficult, and are strange in the ears of the common people.

We do not need to go more deeply into the discussion of Butler's doctrine, for it is familiar to our readers. If there is any incorrectness in the delineation which he has given of conscience, it is in the passages in which he speaks, or seems to speak, of it as an animating or suggesting, than as a criticising or regulative faculty. The error of this representation has been repeatedly pointed out and illustrated in these pages.* It is probable, indeed, that Butler's attention had scarcely been directed with sufficient precision to this portion of the subject. It follows easily, from his favourite principles, that when two impulses—say benevolence and self-love—contend for mastery in the mind, and conscience pronounces that one is a higher and better motive of action than the other, the office of conscience is judicial, and not impulsive. Conscience gives its opinion, and the will obeys or disobeys at its pleasure; the impelling spring of action is the selected impulse on which the will finally decides to act. At the same time, it must be admitted that there are cases when, for practical purposes, conscience is an impelling and goading faculty. We mean when it is opposed by indolence. There is a heavy lassitude of the will, which is certainly spurred, some times effectually, and sometimes in vain, by our conscience. Possibly the correct language may be, that in such cases the desire of ease is opposed by the desire of doing our duty; and that in this case also the office of conscience is simply to say,

* *The Prospective Review.*

that the latter is higher than the former. To us it seems, however, if we may trust our consciousness on points of such exact nicety, that it is more graphically true to speak of the sluggishness of the will being goaded and stimulated by the activity of conscience. There is a native inertness in the voluntary faculty which will not come forth unless great occasion is shown it. At any rate, something like this was perhaps the meaning of Butler, and he, no doubt, would have included in the term conscience the desire to do our duty as such, and because it is such.

Butler has been claimed by Mr. Austin, in his ' Province of Jurisprudence ' (and sometimes since by other writers), as a supporter of the compound Utilitarian scheme, as it has been called, which regards the promotion of general happiness as the single inherent characteristic of virtuous actions, and considers the conscience as a special instinct for directing men in determining what actions are for the general interest and what are not. This theory is, of course, distinct from the common Epicurean scheme, which either denies, like Bentham, the fact of a conscience *in limine*, or, like Mill, professes to explain it away as an effect of illusion and association. The ' Composite theory,' on the other hand, distinctly admits the existence and obligatory authority of conscience, but regards it as a ready, expeditious, and, so to say, telegraphic mode of arriving at results which could otherwise be reached only by toilsome and dubious discussions of general utility. In our judgment, however, the writings of Butler hardly warrant an authoritative ascription to him of this philosophy. He doubtless held that the promotion of general happiness, taking all time and all the world into a complete account, is *one* characteristic and ascertainable property of virtue; but there is nothing to show that he thought it was the only one. On the contrary, we think we could show, with some plausibility, from several passages, that, in his judgment, virtuous actions had besides several essential and appropriate qualities. He was, at all events, the last man to deny that they might have; and his whole reasoning on the subject of moral probation seems to imply that, inasmuch as such a state is, according to every appearance, not at all the readiest or surest means of promoting satisfaction and enjoyment, it cannot have been selected for the cultivation of either satisfaction or enjoyment. It is one thing to hold that, the nature of man being what it is, a virtuous life is the happiest as well as best; and another, that such a life is the best because it is the happiest, and that the nature of man was created in the manner it is in order to produce such happiness. The first is, of course, the doctrine of Butler; the second there does not seem any certain ground for imputing to him.

The religious side of morals is rather indicated and implied, than elaborated or worked out by Butler. Yet, as we formerly said, a constant reference to the ' presages of conscience ' pervades his writings. Although he has nowhere drawn out the course of reasoning fully, or step by step, it is certain that he relied on the moral evidence for a moral Providence; not, indeed, with foolhardy assurance, but with the cautious confidence which was habitual to him. The ideas which are implied in the term justice—the connection between virtue and reward—sin and punishment—a sacred law and holy Ruler, were plainly the trains of reflection most commonly present to his mind.

Persons who give credence to an intuitive conscience are so often taunted with the variations and mutability of human nature, that it is worth noticing how complete is the coincidence, in essential points of feeling, between minds so different as Butler, Kant, and Plato. We can scarcely imagine among thoughtful men a greater diversity of times and characters. The great Athenian in his flowing robes daily conversing in captious Athens—the quiet rector wandering in Durham coalfields—the smoking professor in ungainly Königsberg, would, if the contrast were not too great for art, form a trio worthy of a picture. The whole series of truths and reasonings which we have called the supernatural religion, or that of conscience, is, however, as familiar to one as to the other, and is the most important, if not the most conspicuous, feature in the doctrinal teaching of all three. The very great differences of nomenclature and statement, the entire contrast in the style of expression, do but heighten the wonder of the essential and interior correspondence. The doctrine has certainly shown its capability of co-existing with several forms of civilisation; and at least the simplest explanation of its diffusion is by supposing that it has a real warrant in the nature and consciousness of man.

Such is the doctrine of the Sermons; the argument of the

'Analogy' is of a different and more complicated kind; and, from its refinement, requires to be stated with care and precaution. As the Sermons are in a great measure a reply to the caricaturists of Locke, the 'Analogy' is, in reality, designed as a confutation of Shaftesbury and Bolingbroke. It was the object of those writers, as of others since, to disprove the authority of the Christian and Jewish revelation, by showing that they enjoined on man conduct forbidden by the law of nature, and likewise imputed to the Deity actions of an evil tendency and degrading character. These writers are commonly, and perhaps best, met by a clear denial of the fact; by showing in detail, that Christianity is really open to no such objections, contains no such precepts, and imputes no such actions: the reply of Butler is much more refined and peculiar.

The argument has been thus expounded, and its supposed bearing explained by Professor Rogers in the notice of Butler, —the title of which we have ventured to affix to this Article:—

'Further; we cannot but think that the conclusiveness of Butler's work as against its true object, "The Deist," has often been underrated by many even of its genuine admirers. Thus, Dr. Chalmers, for instance, who gives such glowing proofs of his admiration of the work, and expatiates in a congenial spirit on its merits, affirms that "those overrate the power of analogy who look to it for any very distinct or positive contribution to the Christian argument. To repel objections, in fact, is the great service which analogy has rendered to the cause of Revelation, and it is the *only service* which we seek for at its hands." This, abstractedly, is true; but, *in fact*, considering the *position* of the bulk of the objectors, that they have been invincibly persuaded of the truth of theism, and that their objections to Christianity have been exclusively or chiefly of the kind dealt with in the "Analogy," the work is much more than an *argumentum ad hominem*—it is not simply of negative value. To such *objectors* it logically establishes the truth of Christianity, or it forces them to recede from theism, which the bulk will not do. If a man says, " I am invincibly persuaded of the truth of proposition A, but I cannot receive proposition B, because objections a, β, γ are opposed to it; if these were removed, my objections would cease;" then, if you can show that a, β, γ equally apply to the proposition

A, his reception of which, he says, is based on invincible evidence, you do really compel such a man to believe that not only B *may* be true, but that it *is* true, unless he be willing (which few in the parallel case are) to abandon proposition A as well as B. This is precisely the condition in which the majority of Deists have ever been, if we may judge from their writings. It is usually the *à priori* assumption that certain facts in the history of the Bible, or some portions of its doctrine, are unworthy of the Deity, and incompatible with his character or administration, that has chiefly excited the incredulity of the Deist; far more than any dissatisfaction with the positive evidence which substantiates the Divine origin of Christianity. Neutralise these objections by showing that they are *equally* applicable to what he declares he cannot relinquish —the doctrines of theism; and you show him, if he has a particle of logical sagacity, not only that Christianity may be true, but that it is so; and his only escape is by relapsing into atheism, or resting his opposition on other objections of a very feeble character in comparison, and which, probably, few would ever have been contented with alone; for, *apart* from those objections which Butler repels, the historical evidence for Christianity—the evidence on behalf of the integrity of its records and the honesty and sincerity of its founders—showing that they *could* not have constructed such a system if they *would*, and *would* not, supposing them to be impostors, if they *could*—is stronger than that for any fact in history.

' In consequence of this position of the argument, Butler's book, to large classes of objectors, though practically an *argumentum ad hominem*, not only proves Christianity *may* be true, but in all logical fairness proves it *is* so. This he himself, with his usual judgment, points out. He says: " And objections which are equally applicable to both natural and revealed religion are, properly speaking, answered by its being shown that they are so, *provided the former be admitted to be true.*" '

No one can deny the ingenuity of this line of reasoning, but we can only account for the great assent which it has received, by supposing that the goodness of the cause for which it is commonly brought forward has not unnaturally led to an undue approbation of the argument itself. From the amount of authority in its favour we feel some diffidence, but otherwise we should have said, without hesitation, that it was open to several objections.

In the first place, so far from its being probable that Revelation would have contained the same difficulties as Nature, we should have expected that it would explain those difficulties. The very term Supernatural Revelation implies that previously and by nature man is, to a great extent, in ignorance; that particularly he is unaware of some fact, or series of facts, which God deems it fit that he should know. The instinctive presumption certainly is, that those facts would be most important to us. No doubt it is possible that, for incomprehensible reasons, a special revelation should be made of facts purely indifferent, of the date when London was founded, or the precise circumstances of the invasion by William the Conqueror. But this is in the highest degree improbable. What seems likely (and the whole argument is essentially one of likelihood), according to our mind, is that the Revelation which God would vouchsafe to us would be one affecting our daily life and welfare, would communicate truths either on the one hand conducing to our temporal happiness in the present world, or removing the many doubts and difficulties which surround the general plan of Providence, the entire universe, and our particular destiny. These are the two classes of truths on which we seem to require help, and it is in the first instance more probable that assistance would be given us on those points on which it is most required.

The argument of Butler, of course, relates to our religious difficulties. And, it seems impossible to deny that this is the exact class of difficulty which it is most likely a revelation, if given, would explain. No one who reasons on this subject is likely to doubt that the natural faculties of man are more clearly adequate to our daily and temporal happiness, than to the explanation of the perplexities which have confounded men since the beginning of speculation—of which the mere statement is so vast—which relate to the scheme of the universe and the plan of God. This is the one principle on which the most extreme sceptics, and the most thorough advocates of revelation, meet and agree. The sceptic says, ' Man is not born to resolve the mystery of the universe; but he must nevertheless attempt it, that he may keep within the limits of the knowable: ' which really means that he is to fold his hands and be quiet; to abstain from all religious inquiry; to confine himself to this life, and be industrious and practical within its limits. The advocate of revelation is for ever denying the competency of man's faculties to explain, or puzzle out, what in the large sense most concerns him. There are difficulties celestial, and difficulties terrestrial; but it is certainly more likely that God would interfere miraculously to explain the first than to remove the second.

Let us look at the argument more at length. The supposition and idea of a 'miraculous revelation' rest on the ignorance of man. The scene of nature is stretched out before him; it has rich imagery, and varied colours, and infinite extent; its powers move with a vast sweep; its results are executed with exact precision; it gladdens the eyes, and enriches the imagination; it tells us something of God—something important, yet not enough. For example, difficulties abound; poverty and sin, pain and sorrow, fear and anger, press on us with a heavy weight. On every side our knowledge is confined, and our means of enlarging it small. Of this the outer world takes no heed; nature is 'unfeeling;' her laws roll on; 'beautiful and dumb,' she passes forward and vouchsafes no sign. Indeed, she seems to hide, as one might fancy, the dark mysteries of life which seem to lie beneath; our feeble eyes strain to look forward, but her 'painted veil' hangs over all, like an October mist upon the morning hills. Here, as it seems, revelation intervenes; God will break the spell that is upon us; will meet our need; will break, as it were, through the veil of nature; He will show us of Himself. It is not likely, surely, that He will break the everlasting silence to no end; that, having begun to speak, He will tell us nothing; that He will leave the difficulties of life where He found them; that He will repeat them in His speech; that He will revive them in His word. It seems rather, as if His faintest disclosure, His least word, would shed abundant light on all doubts, would take the weight from our minds, would remove the gnawing anguish from our hearts. Surely, surely, if He speaks He will make an end of speaking, He will show us some good, He will destroy ' the veil that is spread over all nations,' and the ' covering over all people;' He will not ' darken counsel by words without knowledge.'

To this line of argument we know of but one objection; it may be said, that, from the immensity of the universe in which man is, reasons may exist for communicating to him facts of which he cannot appreciate the importance, but a belief in which may nevertheless be most important to his ultimate welfare. Of this kind, according to some divines, is the doctrine of the 'Atonement.' As they think, it is impossible to explain the mode in which the death of Christ conduces to the forgiveness of sin, or why a belief in it should be made, as they think it is, a necessary preliminary to such forgiveness. They consider that this is a revealed matter of fact; part of a system of things which is not known now, which would very likely be above our understanding if it were explained, which, at all events, is not explained. We reply, that the revelation of an inexplicable fact is possible, and that, if adequate evidence could be adduced in its favour, we might be bound to acquiesce in it; but that, on the other hand, such a revelation is extremely improbable: so far as we can see, there was no occasion for it; it helps in nothing, explains to us nothing; it enlarges our knowledge only thus far, that for some unknown reason we are bound to believe something from which certain effects follow in a manner which we cannot understand. Such a revelation is, as has been said, possible; but it is much more likely, *à priori*, that a revelation, if given, would be a revelation of facts suited to our comprehension, and throwing a light on the world in which we are.

The same remark is applicable to a revelation commanding rites and ceremonies which do not come home to the conscience as duties, and of which the reasons are not explained to us by the revelation itself. The Pharisaic code of 'cups and washings' is an obvious instance. It is obviously most improbable that we should be ordered to do these things. The fact may be so; but the evidence of it should be overwhelming, and should be examined with almost suspicious and sceptical care. A revelation of a rule of life which approves itself to the heart, which awakens conscience, which seems to come from God, is the greatest conceivable aid to man, the greatest explanation of our most practical perplexities; a revelation of rites and ordinances is a revelation of new difficulties, telling us nothing of God, imposing an additional taskwork on ourselves.

We are to remember, that the 'Analogy' is, as the Germans would speak, a 'Kritik' of every possible revelation. The first principle of it rests on the inquiry, 'What would it be likely that a revelation, if vouchsafed, would contain?' The whole

Bishop Butler 81

argument is one of preconception, presumption, and probability. It claims to establish a principle, which may be used in defence of any revelation, the Mahomedan as well as the Christian; according to it, as soon as you can show that a difficulty exists in nature, you may immediately expect to find it in revelation. If carried out to its extreme logical development, it would come to this, that if a catalogue were constructed of all the inexplicable arrangements and difficulties of nature, you might confidently anticipate that these very same difficulties in the same degree and in the same points would be found in revelation. Both being from the same Author, it is presumed that each would resemble the other. The principle, even to this length, is enunciated by Mr. Rogers; the difficulties of nature are the α, β, γ of the extract: and he asserts, that if you can show that all of them exist in one system, you have every reason to expect *all* of them in the other. Yet, surely, what can be more monstrous than that a supernatural communication from God should simply enumerate all the difficulties of His natural government and not enlighten us as to any of them —should revive our perplexities without removing them— should not satisfy one doubt or one anxiety, but repeat and proclaim every fact which can give a basis to them both?

The case does not rest here. There is a second ground of objection to the argument of the ' Analogy ' on which we are inclined to lay nearly equal stress. As has been said, it is most likely that a revelation from God would explain at least a part of the religious difficulties of man; and, in matter of fact, all systems purporting to be revelations have in their respective degrees professed to do so. They all deal with what may be called the system of the universe—its moral plan and scheme; the destiny of man therein—the motives from which God created it—and the manner in which He directs it. Throughout the whole range of doctrines, from Mormonism up to Christianity, no one has ever gained any acceptance, has ever, perhaps, been sincerely put forward, which did not deal with this whole range of facts—which did not tell man, according to his view, whence he is, and whither he goes. Revelations, as such, are communications concerning eternity. Now, it seems to us, that so far from its being likely, *à priori*, that a revelation of this sort would contain the same perplexing difficulties which cause so much evil in this world, in the same degree in which they exist here, it would be scarcely possible by any evidence, *à posteriori*, to establish the communication of such a system from the Divine Being. It seems clear on the surface of the subject that, the extent of the unknown world being so enormous in comparison with that which is known, this scene being so petty, and the plan of Providence so vast—earth being little, and space infinite—Time short, and Eternity long—a difficulty, which is of no moment in so contracted a sphere as this, becomes of infinite moment when extended to the sphere of the Almighty. From the smallness of the region which we see— the short time which we live—from the few things which we know—it may well be that there are points which perplex the feebleness of our understanding and puzzle the best feelings of our hearts. We see, as some one expresses it, the universe ' not in plan but in section; ' and we cannot expect to understand very much of it. But when our knowledge increases—when, by a revelation, that plan is unfolded to us—when God vouchsafes to communicate to us the system on which He acts, then it is rational to expect those difficulties would diminish—would gradually disappear as the light dawned upon us—would vanish finally when the dayspring arose on our hearts. If a difficulty of nature be repeated in revelation, it would seem to show that it was not, as we had before supposed, a consequence of our shortsighted views and contracted knowledge, but a real inherent element in the scheme of the universe; not a petty shade on a petty globe, but a pervading inherent stain, extending over all things, destroying the beauty of the universe, impairing the perfectness of all creation. Take, as an instance, the extreme doctrine of Antinomian Calvinism—suppose that the eternal condition of man depended in no degree on his acts, or works, or upon himself in any form, but on an arbitrary act of selection by God, which chose some, independently of any antecedent fitness on their part, for eternal happiness, and consigns all others—irrespective of their guilt or innocence—to eternal ruin. Nothing, of course, can be more shocking than such a doctrine when stated in simple language; and if it really were contained in any document that professes to be a revelation, we should be plainly justified in passing it by as a document which no evidence would prove to have been inspired by God. Yet the doctrine certainly does not want partial analogies in this world. The condition of men here does seem to be in a considerable measure the result not of what they do, or of what their characters are, but of the mere circumstances in which they are placed, over which they have no control, choice, or power. One man is born in a ditch, another in a palace; one with a gloomy and painful, another with a cheerful and happy mind; one to honour, another to dishonour. We invent words—fortune, luck, chance—to express in a subtle way the notion that some seem the favourites of circumstance, others the scapegoats. So far as it goes, this is a distinct 'election' on the part of God of some to misery, of others to felicity, irrespective of their personal qualities. Accordingly, it may be argued, why should we not expect to find the same in the world of revelation, which is from the hand of the same Creator? But this will scarcely impose on any one. A certain indignation arises within us—conscience uplifts her voice, and we reply, 'It may well be that for a short time God may afflict His people without their own fault, but that He should do so for ever—that He should make no end of injustice—that He favours one without a reason, and condemns another without a fault—this, come what may, we will not believe—we would sooner cast ourselves at large on the waste of uncertainty;—pass on with your teaching, and ask God, if so be that He will pardon you for attributing such things to Him.' We need not further enlarge on this.

Again, and in the practical conduct of the argument this is a very material consideration. All revelations impute *intentions* to God. Acts are done, observances enjoined, a providential plan pursued, for reasons which are explained. The cause of this is evident from our previous reasoning. As we have seen, all revelations profess to vindicate the ways of God to man; and it is impossible to do so effectually without declaring to us at least some of His motives and designs. It is most important to observe, that no analogy from nature can justify us in judging of these except by the standard of right or wrong which God has implanted within us. From external observation we learn almost nothing of God's intentions. The scheme is too large; the universe too unbounded. One phenomenon follows another; but, except in a few cases, and then very dubiously, we cannot tell which was created for which—which was the design—which the means—which the determining object—and which the subservient purpose. Even in the few cases in which we do impute such intentions, we do so because they seem to be in harmony with God's moral character; they are not strictly proved, they are mere conjectures; and we should reject at once any that might seem ethically unworthy. But the case is different with a revelation which, from its own nature, unfolds ends and instruments in their due measure and their actual subordination, which develops an orderly system, and communicates hidden motives and unforeseen designs. A recent writer, for example, thus defends certain apparent cruelties of the Old Testament by stating those of nature: ' God,' he says, ' sends His pestilence, and produces horrors on which imagination dare not dwell; horrors not only physical, but indirectly moral; often transforming man into something like the fiend so many say he can never become. He sends His famine, and thousands perish—men and women, and ' the child that knows not its right hand from its left '—in prolonged and frightful agonies. He opens the mouths of volcanoes and lakes; boils and fries the population of a whole city in torrents of burning lava, &c. &c.'*—with much else to the same purpose. But this must not be adduced in extenuation of anything of which the reasons are narrated; on the contrary, these last must be judged of by the moral faculties which are among God's highest gifts. To the infliction of pain, with an express view to what conscience tells us to be an unworthy object, outward nature does and can afford no parallel. She has no avowals; it is but from conjecture that we conceive her motives; her laws pass forward; the crush of her forces is upon us; like a child in a railway, we know not anything. The incomprehensible has no analogy to the explained; the mysterious none to that on which the oracle has intelligibly spoken.

Lastly, for a similar reason, it is impossible that there should be any analogy in nature for a precept from God opposed to the law of conscience. External nature gives no precept; our knowledge of our duty comes from within; the physical world is subordinate to our inward teaching; it is silent on points of morality. On the other hand, a revelation, supposing satisfactory means of attesting it were found, might possibly contain

* Professor Rogers's *Defence of the ' Eclipse of Faith,'* p. 43. It is to be observed, we are not at all speaking of the facts of the Old Testament; we are but limiting the considerations on which the above writer has rested its defence. These refined reasonings but weaken the case they are brought to support. ' I did not know,' said George the Third, ' that the Bible needed an apology.'

such a precept. It is very painful to put such suppositions before the mind; but the pain is inherent in the nature of the subject. The topic of the difficulties and perplexities of man cannot, by any artifice of rhetoric, be rendered pleasing. In such a case, supposing there to be no difficulty of evidence in the case, our duty might be to obey God even against conscience, from that assurance of His essential perfection which is the most certain attestation of conscience. But the existence of such a difficulty is in the highest degree improbable; it is one which ought only to be admitted on the completest proof and after the most rigid straining of evidence: it is, from the nature of the case, without a parallel in the common and unrevealed world.

To all these considerable objections, we believe the argument of the 'Analogy' is properly subject. We think in general that, according to every reasonable presumption, a revelation would not repeat the same difficulties as are to be found in nature, but would remove and explain some of them; that difficulties, which are of small importance in the natural world, on account of the smallness of its sphere and the brevity of its duration, become of insuperable magnitude when extended to infinity and eternity, when alleged to be co-extensive with the universe, and to be inherent in its scheme and structure; and that,—what is of less universal scope, but still of essential importance,—nature offers no analogy to the ascription by any professed revelation of an unworthy intention to God, or the inculcation through it of an immoral precept on man.

It is impossible, then, by any such argument as this, to remove from moral criticism the entire contents of any revelation. According to the more natural view, the unimpeachable morality of those contents is a most essential part of the evidence on which our belief must rest; and this seems to remain so, notwithstanding these refinements. On the other hand, we do not contend that the reasoning of the 'Analogy' is wholly worthless. If Butler's* argument had only been adduced to this extent; if it had only been argued that, though a revelation might be expected to explain some difficulties, it could not be expected to explain all; that a certain number

---

*We doubt, however, if Butler would at all have accepted Mr. Rogers's statement of his view, though it is perhaps the most common interpretation of him. Probably, he really meant no more than what we contend for, though his language is not always so limited in terms.

would, from our ignorance and unworthiness, still remain; and these residuary difficulties would be of the same order, class, and kind, to which we were accustomed; that the style of Providence, if one may so say, would be the same in the newly-communicated phenomena as we had observed it to be in those we were familiar with before,—there could be little question of the soundness of the principle. No one would expect that there would be new difficulties introduced by a revelation; what difficulties were found in it we should expect to be identical with those observed before in nature; or, at least, to be similar to them, and likely to be explained in the same way by a more adequate knowledge of God's purposes. We should particularly expect the difficulties of revelation to be *like* those of nature, limited in time and range, not extending to the entire scheme of Providence, not diffused through infinity and eternity, not imputing evil intentions to God, not inculcating immoral precepts on man. We can hardly be said to *expect* to find difficulties in revelation at all; the utmost that seems probable, *à priori*, is, that it should leave unnoticed some of those of nature. Nevertheless, there is no violent, no overwhelming improbability in the fact of some perplexing points being contained in a communication from God; we are so weak, that it may be we cannot entirely understand the smallest intimation from the Infinite Being. And if difficulties are found there, they are, of course, less perplexing, when resembling those which we knew before, than if they be wholly distinct and new in kind. But this principle is, on the face of it, very different from the admission of an antecedent probability, that all the difficulties discoverable in nature would be daguerreotyped in a revelation.

The difference is seen very clearly by looking at the argument which Butler's reasoning is intended to confute. Suppose a professed revelation to be laid before a person who was before unacquainted with it, and that he finds in it several perplexing points. According to Butler's principle, or what is supposed by Mr. Rogers to be Butler's principle, it is enough to reply: You have those same difficulties in nature before; you cannot consistently object to them now; they have not prevented your ascribing nature to a Divine Author; they should not prevent you from ascribing to Him this revelation. Nature is so full of difficulties that almost every doctrine that has ever been attributed to revelation may be provided with a parallel more or less apt. Consequently, it would be almost needless to criticise the contents of any alleged revelation, when we may be met so easily by such a reply. No careful reasoner would attempt that criticism. According to the doctrine which we have reiterated, we should deem it a difficulty that these perplexing points should be found in a revelation; but that difficulty would not amount to much, would not counterbalance strong evidence, if it could be shown that the system claiming to be revealed, although leaving these points unexplained, threw ample light on others; that what gave cause for perplexity was quite subordinate to what removed perplexity; that no immoral actions were enjoined on man; no unworthy motives imputed to God; no vice attributed to the whole scheme and plan of the Creator. There would therefore remain the largest scope for internal criticism on all systems claiming to be messages from God: on the very face they must seem worthy of Him: in their very essence they must seem good.

This is plainly the obvious view. The natural opinion certainly is that the moral and religious faculties would be those on which we should primarily depend, in judging of an alleged communication from heaven; in deciding whether it have a valid claim to that character or no. These faculties are those which, antecedently to revelation, determine our belief in all other moral and religious questions, and it is therefore natural to look to them as the best judges of the authenticity of an alleged revelation. Many divines, however, struggle to deny this. Thus, in the memoir of Butler we are now reviewing, Mr. Rogers observes,—

' The immortal " Analogy " has probably done more to silence the objections of infidelity than any other ever written from the earliest " apologies " downwards. It not only most critically met the spirit of unbelief in the author's own day, but is equally adapted to meet that which *chiefly* prevails in all time. In every age, some of the principal, perhaps *the* principal, objections to the Christian Revelation have been those which men's *preconceptions* of the Divine character and administration—of what God *must* be, and of what God *must* do—have suggested against certain facts in the sacred history, or certain doctrines it reveals. To show the objector, then (supposing him to be a theist, as nine-tenths of all such objectors have been), that the very same or similar difficulties are found in the structure of the universe and the divine administration of it, is to wrest every *such* weapon completely from his hands, if he be a fair reasoner and remain a theist at all. He is bound, by strict logical obligation, either to show that the parallel difficulties do *not* exist, or to show how he can solve them, while he *cannot* solve those of the Bible. In default of doing either of these things, he ought either to renounce all *such* objections to Christianity, or abandon theism altogether. It is true, therefore, that though Butler leaves the alternative of atheism open, he hardly leaves any other alternative to nine-tenths of the theists who have objected to Christianity.'

And there is a perpetual reiteration in the ' Eclipse of Faith ' of the same reasoning. In fact, so far as the latter work has a distinct principle, this argument may be said to be that principle. The answer is, that the proof of all ' revelation ' itself rests on a ' preconception ' respecting the Divine character, and that, if we assume the truth of that one ' preconception,' we must not reject any others which may be found to have the same evidence. We refer, of course, to the assumption of God's veracity; which can only be proved by arguments that, if admitted, would likewise justify our attributing to Him all other perfect virtues. It is evident that a doubt as to this attribute is not only impious in itself, but quite destructive of all confidence in any communication which may be received from Him. And yet, on what evidence does its acceptance rest ? It cannot be said to be demonstrated by what scientific men call ' natural theology.' Competent and careful persons examine the material world, the structure of animals and plants, the courses of the planets, the muscles of man, and they find there a great preponderance of benevolence. They show, with great labour and great merit, that the Being who arranged this universe is, on the whole, a benevolent Being; but does it follow that He will tell the truth ? ' In crossing a heath,' says Paley, ' suppose I pitched my foot against a stone, and were asked how the stone came to be there, I might possibly answer that, for anything I knew to the contrary, it had lain there for ever; nor would it, perhaps, be very easy to show the absurdity of this answer; but, suppose I had found a *watch* on the ground, and it should be inquired how the watch came to be in that place, I should hardly think of the answer I had before given, that, for anything I knew, it had been always there.' And he shows, with his usual power, that this watch was, in all likelihood, made by a watchmaker. There is nothing cleverer, perhaps, in argumentative writing, than the way in which that argument is stated and pointed. But what evidence is there that the watchmaker was *veracious*? The amplest examination of the most refined designs, the minutest scrutiny of the most complex contrivances, do not go one hair's breadth to establish any such conclusion. Nor can it be shown that the virtue of veracity is identical with, or consequent on, the virtue of simple benevolence. We know well in common life that there are such things as pleasing falsehoods, and that such things exist as disagreeable truths. A person (what we ordinarily call a good-natured person) whose only motive is simple benevolence, will constantly assert the first and deny the second. In its application to religion this tendency cannot be illustrated without suppositions which it is painful even to make; but yet they must be made for a moment, or the necessary argument must be left incomplete. Suppose, what is doubtless true, that the belief in a 'future state,' even if false, contributes to the temporal happiness of man in this world; that it does more to enlarge his hopes, stimulate his imagination, and alleviate his sorrows, than any one other consideration; that it contributes to the order of society and the progress of civilisation; that it is, as some one says, 'the last restraint of the powerful, and the last hope of the wretched.' Indisputably, a Being whose only motive was benevolence, who admitted no higher consideration, who looked steadily and solely to our mere happiness, would endeavour to instil that belief although it were quite untrue, would not think that *that* had anything to do with the question, would not hesitate to make a false revelation to confirm men in a belief so pleasant, so advantageous, so consolatory. Perhaps this supposition drives the argument home. We see that it is necessary for us to admit a 'preconception' as to the character of God before we can even begin to prove the truth of a revelation; that we *must* reason of 'what God *must* be and God *must* do,' before we show that there is even a presumption in favour of any facts, or any doctrines, which are revealed in the 'sacred history.'

We have hinted, in an earlier part of this essay, that this doctrine of God's veracity seems to us to rest on the general assumption of the existence of a ' perfect ' Being, who rules and controls all things. It is, perhaps, the Divine attribute of which it is most difficult to find a trace in nature. Of His omnipotence, justice, benevolence, we cannot, indeed, find absolute proof; for we believe that those attributes are infinite, and we can only prove them strictly with respect to the finite and very circumscribed world which we see and know. Yet, at the same time, we discern indications and strong probabilities, that the Ruler of the world possesses these attributes; we can hardly be said to be able to do this with His veracity. The speechlessness of nature, if we may again so speak, deprives us of any such evidence. All Theism is of the nature of faith. We can never *prove* from experience any being to be infinite, for our experience itself is essentially small and finite. We can often, however, as in the instance of the attributes of God above enumerated, and of others which might be added, establish by observation that the qualities in question exist in a certain degree, and we have only to rely on the principle of faith for our belief that these qualities exist in a perfect and supreme degree. In the case of the Divine veracity, it should seem that we believe it to exist in a perfect and infinite degree, without, from the peculiarity of our circumstances, being able to fortify it by any test or trial from experience.

Present controversies show that there should be a distinct understanding as to this matter. Such writers as the author of the ' Eclipse of Faith ' perpetually strive to justify what they think the difficulties of revelation, by insinuating—we might say inculcating—a scepticism as to the religious faculties and conscience of man. These faculties are at one time said to be ' depraved; ' once they were trustworthy, but man is fallen from that high estate; he can only now believe what is announced to him externally. But how can we then rely on those ' depraved ' faculties for our belief in the truthfulness of the Being who announces these things? At another time all the horrid superstitions, all the immoral rites, all the wretched aberrations of savage and licentious nations, are enumerated, displayed, inculcated, in order to convince us that these faculties give no certain information. We will not quote the passages. We do not like to read hard attacks even on the worst side of human nature; we cannot, like some, gloat upon such details. The argument is plain without any painful accuracy. How can you believe in the 'intuition' of the Divine justice, when the Hindoo says this? How in that of his Holiness, when the Papuan accepts that impurity? But this is no defence for any revelation. The writers who exult in such errors because they think they can use them in their logic, are really cutting away the substratum of evidentiary argument from under them. The veracity of God has not been accepted by all nations any more than His justice. In many times and countries He has been thought to inspire falsehoods, to put a 'lying spirit' in the mouths of men, to deceive them to their destruction. Agamemnon's dream is but the type of a whole class of legends imputing untrue revelations to the gods. If we liked such work, we might prove, perhaps, that there is no man on the earth whose ancestors have not believed the like. And what then? Why, we can only answer that, debased, depraved, imperfect as they may be, these faculties are our all. It is on them that we depend for life, and breath, and all things. We must believe our heart and conscience, or we shall believe nothing. We *must* believe that God cannot lie, or we must renounce all that our highest and innermost nature most cleaves to; but if we go so far, we must go further —we cannot believe in God's veracity and deny the intuition of His justice—we know that He is pure on the same ground that we know that He is true. If an alleged revelation contradict this justice or this purity, we must at once deny that it can have proceeded from Him.

Even admitting, as we think it must be admitted, that Butler did not firmly hold the principle which Mr. Rogers and others ascribe to him, some may find a difficulty in so great a thinker having even a tendency towards that tenet. On examination, however, the very error seems characteristic of him.

A mind such as Butler's was in a previous page described to be, is very apt to be prone to over refinement. A thinker of what was there called the picturesque order has a vision, a picture of the natural view of the subject. Those certainties and conclusions, those doubts and difficulties, which occur on the surface, strike him at once; he sees with his mind's eye some conspicuous instance in which all such certainties are realised, and by which all such doubts are suggested. Some great typical fact remains delineated before his mind, and is a perpetual answer to all hypotheses which strive to be over-subtle. But an unimaginative thinker has no such assistance; he has no pictures or instances in his mind; he works by a process like an accountant, and like an accountant he is dependent on the correctness with which he works. He begins with a principle and reasons from it; and if any error have crept into the deduction or into the principle, he has not any means of detecting it. His mind does not yield, as with more fertile fancies, a stock of instances on which to verify his elaborate conclusions. Accordingly he is apt to say he has explained a difficulty, when in reality he has but refined it away.

Again, there is likewise a deeper sense in which the argument of the 'Analogy' is, even in its least valuable portions, characteristic of Butler. On topics so peculiar, the minds most likely to hold right opinions are exactly those most likely to advance wrong arguments in support of them. The opinions themselves are suggested and supported by deep and strong feelings, which it is painful to analyse, and not easy to describe. The real and decisive arguments for those opinions are little save a rational analysis and acute delineation of those feelings. It will necessarily follow that the mind most prone to delineate and analyse that part of itself will be most likely to succeed in the argumentative exposition of these topics; and this is not likely to be the mind which feels those emotions with the greatest intensity. The very keenness of these feelings makes them painful to touch; their depth, difficult to find: constancy, too, is liable to disguise them. The mind which always feels them will, so to speak, be less conscious of them than one which is only visited by them at long and rare intervals. Those who know a place or a person best are not those most likely to describe it best; their knowledge is so familiar that they cannot bring it out in words. A deep, steady under-current of strong feeling is precisely what affects men's highest opinions most, and exactly what prevents men from being able adequately to describe them. In the absence of the delineative faculty, without the power to state their true reasons, minds of this deep and steadfast class are apt to put up with reasons which lie on the surface. They are caught by an appearance of fairness, affect a dry and intellectual tone, endeavour to establish their conclusions without the premises which are necessary,—without mention of the grounds on which, in their own minds, they really rest. The very heartfelt confidence of Butler in Christianity was perhaps the cause of his seeming in part to support it with considerations which appear to be erroneous.

It seems odd to say, and yet it is true, that the power of the 'Analogy' is in its rhetoric. The ancient writers on that art made a distinction between the modes of persuasion which lay in the illustrative and argumentative efficacy of what was said, and a yet more subtle kind which seemed to reside in the manner and disposition of the speaker himself. In the first class, as has been before remarked, no writer of equal eminence is so defective as Butler; his thoughts, if you take each one singly, seem to lose a good deal from the feeble and hesitating manner in which they are stated. And yet, if you read any considerable portion of his writings, you become sensible of a strong disinclination to disagree with him. A strong anxiety first to find the truth, and next to impart it—an evident wish not to push arguments too far—a clear desire not to convince men except by reasonable arguments of true opinions, characterise every feeble word and halting sentence. Nothing is laid down to dazzle or arouse. It is assumed that the reader wants to know what is true, as much as the writer does to tell it. Very possibly this may not be the highest species of religious author. The vehement temperament, the bold assertion, the ecstatic energy of men like St. Augustine or St. Paul, burn, so to speak, into the minds and memories of men, and remain there at once and for ever. Such men excel in the broad statement of great truths which flash at once with vivid evidence on the minds which receive them. The very words seem to glow with life; and even the sceptical reader is half awakened by them to a kindred and similar warmth. Such are the men who move the creeds of mankind, and stamp a likeness of themselves on ages that succeed them. But there is likewise room for a quieter class, who partially state arguments, elaborate theories, appreciate difficulties, solve doubts; who do not expect to gain a hearing from the many—who do not cry in the streets or lift their voice from the hill of Mars— who address quiet and lonely thinkers like themselves, and are well satisfied if a single sentence in all their writings remove one doubt from the mind of any man. Of these was Butler. *Requiescat in pace*, for it was peace that he loved.

Sterne and Thackeray*
(1864)

MR. PERCY FITZGERALD has expressed his surprise that no one
before him has narrated the life of Sterne in two volumes. We
are much more surprised that he has done so. The life of
Sterne was of the very simplest sort. He was a Yorkshire
clergyman, and lived for the most part a sentimental, questionable, jovial life in the country. He was a queer parson, according to our notions; but in those days there were many queer
parsons. Late in life he wrote a book or two, which gave him
access to London society; and then he led a still more questionable and unclerical life at the edge of the great world. After
that he died in something like distress, and leaving his family
in something like misery. A simpler life, as far as facts go,
never was known; and simple as it is, the story has been well
told by Sir Walter Scott, and has been well commented on by
Mr. Thackeray. It should have occurred to Mr. Fitzgerald that
a subject may only have been briefly treated because it is a
limited and simple subject, which suggests but few remarks,
and does not require an elaborate and copious description.

There are but few materials, too, for a long life of Sterne.
Mr. Fitzgerald has stuffed his volumes with needless facts about
Sterne's distant relations, his great uncles and ninth cousins,
in which no one now can take the least interest. Sterne's
daughter, who was left ill-off, did indeed publish two little
volumes of odd letters, which no clergyman's daughter would
certainly have published now. But even these are too small
in size and thin in matter to be spun into a copious narrative.

* *The Life of Laurence Sterne.* By Percy Fitzgerald, M.A., M.R.I.A.
In two volumes. Chapman and Hall.
  Thackeray the Humourist and the Man of Letters. By Theodore
Taylor, Esq. London: John Camden Hotten.

We should in this Review have hardly given even a brief
sketch of Sterne's life, if we did not think that his artistic
character presented one fundamental resemblance and many
superficial contrasts to that of a great man whom we have
lately lost. We wish to point these out; and a few interspersed
remarks on the life of Sterne will enable us to enliven the
tedium of criticism with a little interest from human life.

Sterne's father was a shiftless roving Irish officer in the
early part of the last century. He served in Marlborough's
wars, and was cast adrift, like many greater people, by the
caprice of Queen Anne and the sudden peace of Utrecht. Of
him only one anecdote remains. He was, his son tells us, 'a
little smart man, somewhat rapid and hasty' in his temper;
and during some fighting at Gibraltar he got into a squabble
with another young officer, a Captain Phillips. The subject, it
seems, was a goose; but that is not now material. It ended
in a duel, which was fought with swords in a room. Captain
Phillips pinned Ensign Sterne to a plaster-wall behind; upon
which he quietly asked, or is said to have asked, ' *Do* wipe the
plaster off your sword before you pull it out of me,' which, if
true, showed at least presence of mind. Mr. Fitzgerald, in his
famine of matter, discusses who this Captain Phillips was; but
into this we shall not follow him.

A smart, humorous, shiftless father of this sort is not perhaps
a bad father for a novelist. Sterne was dragged here and there,
through scenes of life where no correct and thriving parent
would ever have taken him. Years afterwards, with all their
harshness softened and half their pains dissembled, Sterne
dashed them upon pages which will live for ever. Of money
and respectability Sterne inherited from his father little or
none; but he inherited two main elements of his intellectual
capital—a great store of odd scenes, and the sensitive Irish
nature which appreciates odd scenes.

Sterne was born in the year 1713, the year of the peace of
Utrecht, which cast his father adrift upon the world. Of his
mother we know nothing. Years afterwards it was said that he
behaved ill to her; at least neglected her in misery when he
had the means of placing her in comfort. His enemies neatly
said that he preferred ' whining over a dead ass to relieving a
living mother.' But these accusations have never been proved.
Sterne was not remarkable for active benevolence, and certainly

may have neglected an old and uninteresting woman, even though that woman was his mother; he was a bad hand at dull duties, and did not like elderly females; but we must not condemn him on simple probabilities, or upon a neat epigram and loose tradition. ' The regiment,' says Sterne, ' in which my father served being broke, he left Ireland as soon as I was able to be carried, and came to the family seat at Elvington, near York, where his mother lived.' After this he was carried about for some years, as his father led the rambling life of a poor ensign, who was one of very many engaged during a very great war, and discarded at a hasty peace. Then, perhaps luckily, his father died, and ' my cousin Sterne of Elvington,' as he calls him, took charge of him, and sent him to school and college. At neither of these was he very eminent. He told one story late in life which may be true, but seems very unlike the usual school-life. ' My schoolmaster,' he says, ' had the ceiling of the schoolroom new whitewashed: the ladder remained there. I one unlucky day mounted it, and wrote with a brush in large capitals LAU. STERNE, for which the usher severely punished me. My master was much hurt at this, and said before me that never should that name be effaced, for I was a boy of genius, and he was sure I should come to preferment.' But ' genius ' is rarely popular in places of education; and it is, to say the least, remarkable that so sentimental a man as Sterne should have chanced upon so sentimental an instructor. It is wise to be suspicious of aged reminiscents; they are like persons entrusted with ' untold gold; ' there is no check on what they tell us.

Sterne went to Cambridge, and though he did not acquire elaborate learning, he thoroughly learned a gentlemanly stock of elementary knowledge. There is even something scholarlike about his style. It bears the indefinable traces which an exact study of words will always leave upon the use of words. He was accused of stealing learning, and it is likely enough that a great many needless quotations which were stuck into *Tristram Shandy* were abstracted from secondhand storehouses where such things are to be found. But what he stole was worth very little, and his theft may now at least be pardoned, for it injures the popularity of his works. Our present novel-readers do not at all care for an elaborate caricature of the scholastic learning; it is so obsolete that we do not care to have it mimicked. Much of *Tristram Shandy* is a sort of antediluvian fun, in which un-couth Saurian jokes play idly in an unintelligible world.

When he left college, Sterne had a piece of good fortune which in fact ruined him. He had an uncle with much influence in the church, and he was thereby seduced to enter the church. There could not have been a greater error. He had no special vice; he was notorious for no wild dissipation or unpardonable folly; he had done nothing which even in this more discreet age would be considered imprudent. He had even a refinement which must save him from gross vice, and a nicety of nature which must save him from coarse associations. But for all that he was as little fit for a Christian priest as if he had been a drunkard and a profligate. Perhaps he was less fit.

There are certain persons whom taste guides, much as morality and conscience guide ordinary persons. They are 'gentlemen.' They revolt from what is coarse; are sickened by that which is gross; hate what is ugly. They have no temptation to what we may call ordinary vices; they have no inclination for such raw food; on the contrary, they are repelled by it, and loathe it. The law in their members does *not* war against the law of their mind; on the contrary, the *taste* of their bodily nature is mainly in harmony with what conscience would prescribe or religion direct. They may not have heard the saying that the 'beautiful is higher than the good, for it includes the good.' But when they do hear it, it comes upon them as a revelation of their instinctive creed, of the guidance under which they have been living all their lives. They are pure because it is ugly to be impure; innocent because it is out of taste to be otherwise; they live within the hedge-rows of polished society; they do not wish to go beyond them into the great deep of human life; they have a horror of that 'impious ocean,' yet not of the impiety, but of the miscellaneous noise, the disordered confusion of the whole. These are the men whom it is hardest to make Christian,—for the simplest reason; paganism is sufficient for them. Their pride of the eye is a good pride; their love of the flesh is a delicate and directing love. They keep 'within the pathways' because they dislike the gross, the uncultured, and the untrodden. Thus they reject the primitive precept which comes before Christianity. Repent! repent! says a voice in the wilderness; but the delicate pagan feels superior to the voice in the wilderness. Why should he attend to this uncouth person? He has nice clothes and well-chosen food, the treasures of exact knowledge, the delicate results of the highest civilisation. Is he to be directed by a person of savage habits, with a distorted countenance, who lives on wild honey, who does not wear decent clothes? To the pure worshipper of beauty, to the naturally refined pagan, conscience and the religion of conscience are not merely intruders, but barbarous intruders. At least so it is in youth, when life is simple and temptations if strong are distinct. Years afterwards, probably, the purest pagan will be taught by a constant accession of indistinct temptations, and by a gradual declension of his nature, that taste at the best, and sentiment of the very purest, are insufficient guides in the perplexing labyrinth of the world.

Sterne was a pagan. He went into the Church; but Mr. Thackeray, no bad judge, said most justly that his sermons 'have not a single Christian sentiment.' They are well expressed, vigorous, moral essays; but they are no more. Much more was not expected by many congregations in the last age. The secular feeling of the English people, though always strong, —though strong in Chaucer's time, and though strong now,— was never so all-powerful as in the last century. It was in those days that the poet Crabbe was remonstrated with for introducing heaven and hell into his sermons; such extravagances, he was told, were very well for the Methodists, but a *clergyman* should confine himself to sober matters of this world, and show the prudence and the reasonableness of virtue during this life. There is not much of heaven and hell in Sterne's sermons, and what there is seems a rhetorical emphasis which is not essential to the argument, and which might perhaps as well be left out. Auguste Comte might have admitted most of these sermons; they are healthy statements of earthly truths, but they would be just as true if there was no religion at all. Religion helps the argument, because foolish people might be perplexed with this world, and they yield readily to another; religion enables you—such is the real doctrine of these divines, when you examine it—to coax and persuade those whom you cannot rationally convince; but it does not alter the matter in hand—it does not affect that of which you wish to persuade men, for you are but inculcating a course of conduct *in this life*. Sterne's sermons would be just as true if the secularists should succeed in their argument, and the 'valuable illusion' of a deity were omitted from the belief of mankind.

However, in fact, Sterne took orders, and by the aid of his uncle, who was a church politician, and who knew the powers that were, he obtained several small livings. Being a pluralist was a trifle in those easy times; nobody then thought that the parishioners of a parson had a right to his daily presence; if some provision were made for the performance of a Sunday service, he had done his duty, and he could spend the surplus income where he liked. He might perhaps be bound to reside, if health permitted, on one of his livings, but the law allowed him to have many, and he could not be compelled to reside on them all. Sterne preached well-written sermons on Sundays, and led an easy pagan life on other days, and no one blamed him.

He fell in love too, and after he was dead, his daughter found two or three of his love-letters to her mother, which she rashly published. They have been the unfeeling sport of persons not in love up to the present time. Years ago Mr. Thackeray used to make audiences laugh till they cried by reading one or two of them, and contrasting them with certain other letters also about his wife, but written many years later. This is the sort of thing:—

' Yes! I will steal from the world, and not a babbling tongue shall tell where I am—Echo shall not so much as whisper my hiding-place—suffer thy imagination to paint it as a little sun-gilt cottage, on the side of a romantic hill—dost thou think I will leave love and friendship behind me? No! they shall be my companions in solitude, for they will sit down and rise up with me in the amiable form of my L.—We will be as merry and as innocent as our first parents in Paradise, before the arch fiend entered that undescribable scene.

' The kindest affections will have room to shoot and expand in our retirement, and produce such fruit as madness, and envy, and ambition have always killed in the bud.—Let the human tempest and hurricane rage at a distance, the desolation is beyond the horizon of peace. My L. has seen a polyanthus blow in December—some friendly wall has sheltered it from the biting wind. No planetary influence shall reach us, but that which presides and cherishes the sweetest flowers—God preserve us ! how delightful this prospect in idea ! We will build, and we will plant, in our own way—simplicity shall not be tortured by art—we will learn of nature how to live—she shall be our alchymist, to mingle all the good of life into one salubrious draught.—The gloomy family of care and distrust shall be banished from our dwelling guarded by thy kind and tutelar deity—we will sing our choral songs of gratitude, and rejoice to the end of our pilgrimage.

'Adieu, my L. Return to one who languishes for thy society.   L. STERNE.'

The beautiful language with which young ladies were wooed a century ago is a characteristic of that extinct age; at least, we fear that no such beautiful English will be discovered when our secret repositories are ransacked. The age of ridicule has come in, and the age of good words has gone out.

There is no reason to doubt, however, that Sterne was really in love with Mrs. Sterne. People have doubted it because of these beautiful words; but, in fact, Sterne was just the sort of man to be subject to this kind of feeling. He took—and to this he owes his fame—the *sensitive* view of life. He regarded it not from the point of view of intellect, or conscience, or religion, but in the plain way in which natural feeling impresses, and will always impress, a natural person. He is a great author; certainly not because of great thoughts, for there is scarcely a sentence in his writings which can be called a thought; nor from sublime conceptions which enlarge the limits of our imagination, for he never leaves the sensuous,—but because of his wonderful sympathy with, and wonderful power of representing, simple human nature. The best passages in Sterne are those which every one knows, like this:

'Thou hast left this matter short, said my uncle Toby to the corporal, as he was putting him to bed,——and I will tell thee in what, Trim.——In the first place, when thou madest an offer of my services to Le Fever,—as sickness and travelling are both expensive, and thou knowest he was but a poor lieutenant, with a son to subsist as well as himself, out of his pay,—that thou didst not make an offer to him of my purse; because, had he stood in need, thou knowest, Trim, he had been as welcome to it as myself.——Your honour knows, said the corporal, I had no orders; ——True, quoth my uncle Toby,—thou didst very right, Trim, as a soldier, but certainly very wrong as a man.

' In the second place, for which, indeed, thou hast the same excuse, continued my uncle Toby,——when thou offeredst him whatever was in my house,—thou shouldst have offered him my house too :——A sick brother officer should have the best quarters, Trim, and if we had him with us,—we could tend and look to him :——Thou art an excellent nurse thyself, Trim,—and what with thy care of him, and the old woman's, and his boy's, and mine together, we might recruit him again at once, and set him upon his legs.——

'——In a fortnight or three weeks, added my uncle Toby, smiling,—he might march.——He will never march, an' please your honour, in this world, said the corporal :—— He will march, said my uncle Toby, rising up from the side of the bed, with one shoe off :——An' please your honour, said the corporal, he will never march, but to his grave :—— He shall march, cried my uncle Toby, marching the foot which had a shoe on, though without advancing an inch,— he shall march to his regiment.——He cannot stand it, said the corporal :——He shall be supported, said my uncle Toby : ——He'll drop at last, said the corporal, and what will become of his boy ?——He shall not drop, said my uncle Toby, firmly.——A-well-o'day,—do what we can for him, said Trim, maintaining his point,—the poor soul will die :——He shall not die, by G—! cried my uncle Toby.

'—The ACCUSING SPIRIT, which flew up to heaven's chancery with the oath, blush'd as he gave it in ;—and the RECORDING ANGEL, as he wrote it down, dropp'd a tear upon the word, and blotted it out for ever.

'—My uncle Toby went to his bureau,—put his purse into his breeches pocket, and having ordered the corporal to go early in the morning for a physician,—he went to bed, and fell asleep.

' The sun looked bright the morning after, to every eye in the village but Le Fever's and his afflicted son's ; the hand of death pressed heavy upon his eye-lids,——and hardly could the wheel at the cistern turn round its circle,—when my uncle Toby, who had rose up an hour before his wonted time, entered the lieutenant's room, and without preface or apology, sat himself down upon the chair by the bed-side, and independently of all modes and customs, opened the curtain in the manner an old friend and brother officer would have done it, and asked him how he did,—how he had rested in the night,—what was his complaint,—where was his pain,—and what he could do to help him;——and without giving him time to answer any one of the inquiries, went on and told him of the little plan which he had been concerting with the corporal the night before for him.——

'——You shall go home directly, Le Fever, said my uncle Toby, to my house,—and we'll send for a doctor to see what's the matter,—and we'll have an apothecary,—and the corporal shall be your nurse;——and I'll be your servant, Le Fever.

' There was a frankness in my uncle Toby,—not the *effect* of familiarity,—but the *cause* of it,—which let you at once into his soul, and showed you the goodness of his nature; to this, there was something in his looks, and voice, and manner, super-added, which eternally beckoned to the unfortunate to come and take shelter under him; so that before my uncle Toby had half finished the kind offers he was making to the father, had the son insensibly pressed up close to his knees, and had taken hold of the breast of his coat, and was pulling it towards him.——The blood and spirits of Le Fever, which were waxing cold and slow within him, and were retreating to their last citadel, the heart,—rallied back,—the film forsook his eyes for a moment,—he looked up wishfully in my uncle Toby's face,—then cast a look upon his boy,——and that *ligament*, fine as it was,—was never broken.————

' Nature instantly ebb'd again,—the film returned to its place,——the pulse fluttered——stopp'd——went on————throbb'd——stopp'd again——moved——stopp'd——shall I go on?——No.'

In one of the ' Roundabout Papers ' Mr. Thackeray introduces a literary man complaining of his ' sensibility.' ' Ah,' he replies, ' my good friend, your sensibility is your livelihood: if you did not feel the events and occurrences of life more acutely than others, you could not describe them better; and it is the excellence of your description by which you live.' This is precisely true of Sterne. He is a great author because he felt acutely. He is the most pathetic of writers because he had —when writing, at least—the most pity. He was, too, we believe, pretty sharply in love with Mrs. Sterne, because he was sensitive to that sort of feeling likewise.

The difficulty of this sort of character is the difficulty of keeping it. It does not last. There is a certain bloom of sensibility and feeling about it which, in the course of nature, is apt to fade soon, and which, when it has faded, there is nothing to replace. A character with the binding elements—with a firm will, a masculine understanding, and a persistent conscience—may retain, and perhaps improve, the early and original freshness. But a loose-set though pure character the moment it is thrown into temptation sacrifices its purity, loses its gloss, and gets, so to speak, out of form entirely.

We do not know with great accuracy what Sterne's temptations were; but there was one, which we can trace with some degree of precision, which has left ineffaceable traces on his works,—which probably left some traces upon his character and conduct. There was in that part of Yorkshire a certain John Hall Stevenson, a country gentleman of some fortune, and possessed of a castle, which he called Crazy Castle. Thence he wrote tales, which he named 'Crazy Tales,' but which certainly are not entitled to any such innocent name. The license of that age was unquestionably wonderful. A man of good property could write any evil. There was no legal check, or ecclesiastical check, and hardly any check of public opinion. These 'Crazy Tales' have license without humour, and vice without amusement. They are the writing of a man with some wit, but only enough wit for light conversation, which becomes overworked and dull when it is reduced to regular composition and made to write long tales. The author, feeling his wit jaded, perpetually becomes immoral, in the vain hope that he will cease to be dull. He has attained his reward; he will be remembered for nauseous tiresomeness by all who have read him.

But though the 'Crazy Tales' are now tedious, Crazy Castle was a pleasant place, at least to men like Sterne. He was an idle young parson, with much sensibility, much love of life and variety, and not a bit of grave goodness. The dull duties of a country parson, as we now understand them, would never have been to his taste; and the sinecure idleness then permitted to parsons left him open to every temptation. The frail texture of merely natural purity, the soft fibre of the instinctive pagan, yield to the first casualty. Exactly what sort of life they led at

Crazy Castle we do not know, but vaguely we do know, and we may be sure *Mrs.* Sterne was against it.

One part of Crazy Castle has had effects which will last as long as English literature. It had a library richly stored in old folio learning, and also in the amatory reading of other days. Every page of *Tristram Shandy* bears traces of both elements. Sterne, when he wrote it, had filled his head and his mind, not with the literature of his own age, but with the literature of past ages. He was thinking of Rabelais rather than of Fielding; of forgotten romances rather than of Richardson. He wrote, indeed, of his own times and of men he had seen, because his sensitive vivid nature would only endure to write of present things. But the *mode* in which he wrote was largely coloured by literary habits and literary fashions that had long passed away. The oddity of the book was a kind of advertisement to its genius, and that oddity consisted in the use of old manners upon new things. No analysis or account of *Tristram Shandy* could be given which would suit the present generation; being, indeed, a book without plan or order, it is in every generation unfit for analysis. This age would not endure a statement of the most telling points, as the writer thought them, and no age would like an elaborate plan of a book in which there is no plan, in which the detached remarks and separate scenes were really meant to be the whole. The notion that ' a plot was to hang plums upon ' was Sterne's notion exactly.

The real excellence of Sterne is single and simple; the defects are numberless and complicated. He excels, perhaps, all other writers in mere simple description of common sensitive human action. He places before you in their simplest form the elemental facts of human life; he does not view them through the intellect, he scarcely views them through the imagination; he does but reflect the unimpaired impression which the facts of life, which does not change from age to age, make on the deep basis of human feeling, which changes as little though years go on. The example we quoted just now is as good as any other, though not better than any other. Our readers should go back to it again, or our praise may seem overcharged. It is the portrait-painting of the heart. It is as pure a reflection of mere natural feeling as literature has ever given, or will ever give. The delineation is nearly perfect. Sterne's feeling in his higher moments so much overpowered his intellect, and so directed his imagination, that no intrusive thought blemishes, no distorting fancy mars, the perfection of the representation. The disenchanting facts which deface, the low circumstances which debase the simpler feelings oftener than any other feelings, his art excludes. The feeling which would probably be coarse in the reality is refined in the picture. The unconscious tact of the nice artist heightens and chastens reality, but yet it is reality still. His mind was like a pure lake of delicate water: it reflects the ordinary landscape, the rugged hills, the loose pebbles, the knotted and the distorted firs perfectly and as they are, yet with a charm and fascination that they have not in themselves. This is the highest attainment of art, to be at the same time nature and something more than nature.

But here the great excellence of Sterne ends as well as begins. In *Tristram Shandy* especially there are several defects which, while we are reading it, tease and disgust so much that we are scarcely willing even to admire as we ought to admire the nice pictures of human emotion. The first of these, and perhaps the worst, is the fantastic disorder of the form. It is an imperative law of the writing-art that a book should go straight on. A great writer should be able to tell a great meaning as coherently as a small writer tells a small meaning. The magnitude of the thought to be conveyed, the delicacy of the emotion to be painted, render the introductory touches of consummate art not of less importance, but of more importance. A great writer should train the mind of the reader for his greatest things; that is, by first strokes and fitting preliminaries he should form and prepare his mind for the due appreciation and the perfect enjoyment of high creations. He should not blunder upon a beauty, nor, after a great imaginative creation, should he at once fall back to bare prose. The high-wrought feeling which a poet excites should not be turned out at once and without warning into the discomposing world. It is one of the greatest merits of the greatest living writer of fiction,—of the authoress of *Adam Bede*,—that she never brings you to anything without preparing you for it; she has no loose lumps of beauty; she puts in nothing at random; after her greatest scenes, too, a natural sequence of subordinate realities again tones down the mind to this sublunary world. Her logical style —the most logical, probably, which a woman ever wrote—aids

E 2

in this matter her natural sense of due proportion. There is not a space of incoherency—not a gap. It is not natural to begin with the point of a story, and she does not begin with it. When some great marvel has been told, we all wish to know what came of it, and she tells us. Her natural way, as it seems to those who do not know its rarity, of telling what happened produces the consummate effect of gradual enchantment and as gradual disenchantment. But Sterne's style is *un*natural. He never begins at the beginning and goes straight through to the end. He shies-in a beauty suddenly; and just when you are affected he turns round and grins at it. ' Ah,' he says, ' is it not fine ? ' And then he makes jokes which at that place and that time are out of place, or passes away into scholastic or other irrelevant matter, which simply disgusts and disheartens those whom he has just delighted. People excuse all this irregularity of form by saying that it was imitated from Rabelais. But this is nonsense. Rabelais, perhaps, could not in his day venture to tell his meaning straight out; at any rate, he did not tell it. Sterne should not have chosen a model so monstrous. Incoherency is not less a defect because an imperfect foreign writer once made use of it. ' You may have, sir, a reason,' said Dr. Johnson, ' for saying that two and two make five, but they will still make four.' Just so a writer may have a reason for selecting the defect of incoherency, but it is a defect still. Sterne's best things read best out of his books,—in Enfield's *Speaker* and other places,—and you can say no worse of any one as a continuous artist.

Another most palpable defect—especially palpable nowadays —in *Tristram Shandy* is its indecency. It is quite true that the customary conventions of writing are much altered during the last century, and much which would formerly have been deemed blameless would now be censured and disliked. The audience has changed; and decency is of course in part dependent on who is within hearing. A divorce case may be talked over across a club-table with a plainness of speech and development of expression which would be indecent in a mixed party, and scandalous before young ladies. Now, a large part of old novels may very fairly be called club-books; they speak out plainly and simply the notorious facts of the world, as men speak of them to men. Much excellent and proper masculine conversation is wholly unfit for repetition to young girls; and just in the same way books written—as was almost all old literature, for men only, or nearly only,—seem coarse enough when contrasted with novels written by young ladies upon the subjects and in the tone of the drawing-room. The change is inevitable; as soon as works of fiction are addressed to boys and girls, they must be fit for boys and girls; they must deal with a life which is real so far as it goes, but which is yet most limited; which deals with the most passionate part of life, and yet omits the errors of the passions; which aim at describing men in their relations to women, and yet omits an all but universal influence which more or less distorts and modifies all these relations.

As we have said, the change cannot be helped. A young ladies' literature must be a limited and truncated literature. The indiscriminate study of human life is not desirable for them, either in fiction or in reality. But the habitual formation of a scheme of thought and a code of morality upon incomplete materials is a very serious evil. The readers for whose sake the omissions are made cannot fancy what is left out. Many a girl of the present day reads novels, and nothing but novels; she forms her mind by them, as far as she forms it by reading at all; even if she reads a few dull books, she soon forgets all about them, and remembers the novels only; she is more influenced by them than by sermons. They form her idea of the world, they define her taste, and modify her morality; not so much in explicit thought and direct act as unconsciously and in her floating fancy. How is it possible to convince such a girl, especially if she is clever, that on most points she is all wrong? She has been reading most excellent descriptions of mere society; she comprehends those descriptions perfectly, for her own experience elucidates and confirms them. She has a vivid picture of a *patch* of life. Even if she admits in words that there is something beyond, something of which she has no idea, she will not admit it really and in practice. What she has mastered and realised will incurably and inevitably overpower the unknown something of which she knows nothing, can imagine nothing, and can make nothing. 'I am not sure,' said an old lady, ' but I think it's the novels that make my girls so *heady*.' It is the novels. A very intelligent acquaintance with limited life makes them think that the world is far simpler than it is, that men are easy to understand, ' that mamma is *so* foolish.'

The novels of the last age have certainly not this fault.
They do not err on the side of reticence. A girl may learn from
them more than it is desirable for her to know. But, as we
have explained, they were meant for men and not for girls; and
if *Tristram Shandy* had simply given a plain exposition of
necessary facts—necessary, that is, to the development of the
writer's view of the world, and to the telling of the story in
hand,—we should not have complained; we should have regarded it as the natural product of a now extinct society. But
there are most unmistakable traces of ' Crazy Castle ' in *Tristram Shandy*. There is indecency for indecency's sake. It is
made a sort of recurring and even permeating joke to mention
things which are not generally mentioned. Sterne himself made
a sort of defence, or rather denial, of this. He once asked a lady
if she had read *Tristram*. ' I have not, Mr. Sterne,' was the
answer; ' and, to be plain with you, I am informed it is not
proper for female perusal.' ' My dear good lady,' said Sterne,
' do not be gulled by such stories; the book is like your young
heir there ' (pointing to a child of three years old who was
rolling on the carpet in white tunics): ' he shows at times a
good deal that is usually concealed, but it is all in perfect
innocence.' But a perusal of *Tristram* would not make good
the plea. The unusual publicity of what is ordinarily imperceptible is not the thoughtless accident of amusing play; it is
deliberately sought after as a nice joke; it is treated as a good
in itself.

The indecency of *Tristram Shandy*—at least of the early
part, which was written before Sterne had been to France—is
especially an offence against taste, because of its ugliness.
Moral indecency is always disgusting. There certainly is a sort
of writing which cannot be called decent, and which describes a
society to the core immoral, which nevertheless is no offence
against art; it violates a higher code than that of taste, but it
does not violate the code of taste. The *Mémoires de Grammont*
—hundreds of French memoirs about France—are of this kind,
more or less. They describe the refined, witty, elegant immorality of an idle aristocracy. They describe a life ' unsuitable
to such a being as man in such a world as the present one,' in
which there are no high aims, no severe duties, where some
precepts of morals seem not so much to be sometimes broken
as to be generally suspended and forgotten; such a life, in short,

as God has never suffered men to lead on this earth long, which
He has always crushed out by calamity and revolution. This
life, though an offence in morals, was not an offence in taste.
It was an elegant, a *pretty* thing while it lasted. Especially in
enhancing description, where the alloy of life may be omitted,
where nothing vulgar need be noticed, where everything elegant
may be neatly painted,—such a world is elegant enough.
Morals and policy must decide how far such delineations are
permissible or expedient; but the art of beauty,—but criticism
has no objection to them. They are pretty paintings of pretty
objects, and that is all it has to say. They may very easily do
harm; if generally read among the young of the middle class,
they would be sure to do harm: they would teach not a few
to aim at a sort of refinement denied them by circumstances,
and to neglect the duties allotted them; it would make shopmen
'bad imitations of polished ungodliness,' and also bad shopmen. But still, though it would in such places be noxious
literature, in itself it would be pretty literature. The critic
must praise it, though the moralist must condemn it, and perhaps the politicians forbid it.

But *Tristram Shandy's* indecency is the very opposite to
this refined sort. It consists in allusions to certain inseparable
accompaniments of actual life which are not beautiful, which
can never be made interesting, which would, *if* they were
decent, be dull and uninteresting. There is, it appears, a
certain excitement in putting such matters into a book: there
is a minor exhilaration even in petty crime. At first such
things look so odd in print that you go on reading them to see
what they look like; but you soon give up. What is disenchanting or even disgusting in reality does not become enchant-
ing or endurable in delineation. You are more angry at it
in literature than in life; there is much which is barbarous and
animal in reality that we could wish away; we endure it because we cannot help it, because we did not make it and cannot
alter it, because it is an inseparable part of this inexplicable
world. But why we should put this coarse alloy, this dross of
life, into the *optional* world of literature, which we can make
as we please, it is impossible to say. The needless introduction of accessory ugliness is always a sin in art, and is not at all
less so when such ugliness is disgusting and improper. *Tristram Shandy* is incurably tainted with a pervading vice; it

dwells at length on, it seeks after, it returns to, it gloats over, the most unattractive part of the world.

There is another defect in *Tristram Shandy* which would of itself remove it from the list of first-rate books, even if those which we have mentioned did not do so. It contains eccentric characters only. Some part of this defect may be perhaps explained by one peculiarity of its origin. Sterne was so sensitive to the picturesque parts of life, that he wished to paint the picturesque parts of the people he hated. Country-towns in those days abounded in odd characters. They were out of the way of the great opinion of the world, and shaped themselves to little opinions of their own. They regarded the customs which the place had inherited as the customs which were proper for it, and which it would be foolish, if not wicked, to try to change. This gave English country life a motley picturesqueness then, which it wants now, when London ideas shoot out every morning, and carry on the wings of the railway a uniform creed to each cranny of the kingdom, north and south, east and west. These little public opinions of little places wanted, too, the crushing power of the great public opinion of our own day; at the worst, a man could escape from them into some different place which had customs and doctrines that suited him better. We now may fly into another ' city,' but it is all the same Roman empire; the same uniform justice, the one code of heavy laws presses us down and makes us—the sensible part of us at least—as like other people as we can make ourselves. The public opinion of county-towns yielded soon to individual exceptions; it had not the confidence in itself which the opinion of each place now receives from the accordant and simultaneous echo of a hundred places. If a man chose to be queer, he was bullied for a year or two, then it was settled that he was ' queer; ' that was the fact about him, and must be accepted. In a year or so he became an ' institution ' of the place, and the local pride would have been grieved if he had amended the oddity which suggested their legends and added a flavour to their life. Of course, if a man was rich and influential, he might soon disregard the mere opinion of the petty locality. Every place has wonderful traditions of old rich men who did exactly as they pleased, because they could set at naught the opinions of the neighbours, by whom they were feared, and who did not, as now, dread the unanimous conscience which does not fear even a squire of 2000*l.* a year, or a banker of 800*l.*, because it is backed by the wealth of London and the magnitude of all the country. There is little oddity in county towns now; they are detached scraps of great places; but in Sterne's time there was much, and he used it unsparingly.

Much of the delineation is of the highest merit. Sterne knew how to describe eccentricity, for he showed its relation to our common human nature: he showed how we were related to it, how in some sort and in some circumstances we might ourselves become it. He reduced the abnormal formation to the normal rules. Except upon this condition, eccentricity is no fit subject for literary art. Every one must have known characters which, if they were put down in books, barely and as he sees them, would seem monstrous and disproportioned,—which would disgust all readers,—which every critic would term unnatural. While characters are monstrous, they should be kept out of books; they are ugly unintelligibilities, foreign to the realm of true art. But as soon as they can be explained to us, as soon as they are shown in their union with, in their outgrowth from common human nature, they are the best subjects for great art—for they are new subjects. They teach us, not the old lesson which our fathers knew, but a new lesson which will please us and make us better than them. Hamlet is an eccentric character, one of the most eccentric in literature; but because, by the art of the poet, we are made to understand that he is a possible, a *vividly* possible man, he enlarges our conceptions of human nature; he takes us out of the bounds of commonplace. He 'instructs us by means of delight.' Sterne does this too. Mr. Shandy, Uncle Toby, Corporal Trim, Mrs. Shandy,—for in strictness she too is eccentric from her abnormal commonplaceness,—are beings of which the possibility is brought home to us, which we feel we could under circumstances and by influences become; which, though contorted and twisted, are yet spun out of the same elementary nature, the same thread as we are. Considering how odd these characters are, the success of Sterne is marvellous, and his art in this respect consummate. But yet on a point most nearly allied it is very faulty. Though each individual character is shaded off into human nature, the whole is not shaded off into the world. This society of originals and oddities is left to stand by itself, as if it were a natural and ordinary society,—a society easily conceivable and needing no explanation. Such is not the manner of the great masters; in their best works a constant atmosphere of half commonplace personages surrounds and shades off, illustrates and explains every central group of singular persons.

On the whole, therefore, the judgment of criticism on *Tristram Shandy* is concise and easy. It is immortal because of certain scenes suggested by Sterne's curious experience, detected by his singular sensibility, and heightened by his delineative and discriminative imagination. It is defective because its style is fantastic, its method illogical and provoking; because its indecency is of the worst sort, as far as in such matters an artistic judgment can speak of worst and best; because its world of characters forms an incongruous group of singular persons utterly dissimilar to and irreconcilable with the world in which we live. It is a great work of art, but of barbarous art. Its mirth is boisterous. It is *provincial*. It is redolent of an inferior society; of those who think crude animal spirits in themselves delightful, who do not know that, without wit to point them or humour to convey them, they are disagreeable to others; who like disturbing transitions, blank pages, and tricks of style; who do not know that a simple and logical form of expression is the most effective, if not the easiest—the least laborious to readers, if not always the most easily attained by writers.

The oddity of *Tristram Shandy* was, however, a great aid to its immediate popularity. If an author were to stand on his head now and then in Cheapside, his eccentricity would bring him into contact with the police, but it would advertise his writings; they would sell better: people would like to see what was said by a great author who was so odd as to stand so. Sterne put his eccentricity into his writings, and therefore came into collision with the critics; but he attained the same end. His book sold capitally. As with all popular authors, he went to London; he was fêted. ' The *man* Sterne,' growled Dr. Johnson, ' has dinner engagements for three months.' The upper world—ever desirous of novelty, ever tired of itself, ever anxious to be amused—was in hopes of a new wit. It naturally hoped that the author of *Tristram Shandy* would talk well, and it sent for him to talk.

He did talk well, it appears, though not always very correctly, and never very clerically. His appearance was curious, but yet refined. Eager eyes, a wild look, a long lean frame, and what he called a cadaverous bale of goods for a body, made up an odd exterior, which attracted notice, and did not repel liking. He looked like a scarecrow with bright eyes. With a random manner, but not without a nice calculation, he discharged witticisms at London parties. His keen nerves told him which were fit witticisms; *they* took, and *he* was applauded.

He published some sermons too. That tolerant age liked, it is instructive as well as amusing to think, sermons by the author of *Tristram Shandy*. People wonder at the rise of Methodism; but ought they to wonder? If a clergyman publishes his sermons *because* he has written an indecent novel—a novel which is purely pagan—which is outside the ideas of Christianity, whose author can scarcely have been inside of them—if a man so made and so circumstanced is *as such* to publish Christian sermons, surely Christianity is a joke and a dream. Wesley was right in this at least; if Christianity be true, the upper life of the last century was based on rotten falsehood. A world which is really secular—which professes to be Christian, is the worst of worlds.

The only point in which Sterne resembles a clergyman of our own time is, that he lost his voice. That peculiar affection of the chest and throat, which is hardly known among barristers, but which inflicts such suffering upon parsons, attacked him also. Sterne too, as might be expected, went abroad for it. He ' spluttered French,' he tells us, with success in Paris; the accuracy of the grammar some phrases in his letters would lead us to doubt; but few, very few Yorkshire parsons could then talk French at all, and there was doubtless a fine tact and sensibility in what he said. A literary phenomenon wishing to enjoy society, and able to amuse society, has ever been welcome in the Parisian world. After Paris, Sterne went to the south of France, and on to Italy, lounging easily in pretty places, and living comfortably, as far as one can see, upon the profits of *Tristram Shandy*. Literary success has seldom changed more suddenly and completely the course of a man's life. For years Sterne resided in a country parsonage, and the sources of his highest excitement were a country-town full of provincial oddities, and a ' Crazy Castle ' full of the license and the whims of a country squire. On a sudden London, Paris, and Italy were opened to him. From a few familiar things he was suddenly transferred to many unfamiliar things. He was equal to them, though the change came so suddenly in middle life—though the change from a secluded English district to the great and interesting scenes was far greater, far fuller of unexpected sights and unforeseen phenomena, than it can be now—when travelling is common—when the newspaper is 'abroad'—when every one has in his head some feeble image of Europe and the world. Sterne showed the delicate docility which belongs to a sensitive and experiencing nature. He understood and enjoyed very much of this new and strange life, if not the whole.

The proof of this remains written in the *Sentimental Journey*. There is no better painting of first and easy impressions than that book. After all which has been written on the *ancien régime*, an Englishman at least will feel a fresh instruction on reading these simple observations. They are instructive *because* of their simplicity. The old world at heart was not like that; there were depths and realities, latent forces and concealed results, which were hidden from Sterne's eye, which it would have been quite out of his way to think of or observe. But the old world *seemed* like that. This was the spectacle of it as it was seen by an observing stranger; and we take it up, not to know what was the truth, but to know what we should have thought to be the truth if we had lived in those times. People say *Eöthen* is not like the real East; very likely it is not, but it is like what an imaginative young Englishman would *think* the East. Just so, the *Sentimental Journey* is not the true France of the old monarchy, but it is exactly what an observant quick-eyed Englishman might fancy that France to be. This has given it popularity; this still makes it a valuable relic of the past. It is not true to the outward nature of real life, but it is true to the reflected image of that life in an imaginative and sensitive man.

Here is the actual description of the old chivalry of France; the 'cheap defence of nations,' as Mr. Burke called it a little while afterwards—

'When states and empires have their periods of declension, and feel in their turns what distress and poverty is—I stop not to tell the causes which gradually brought the house d'E——

in Brittany into decay. The Marquis d'E—— had fought up against his condition with great firmness; wishing to preserve, and still show to the world, some little fragments of what his ancestors had been—their indiscretions had put it out of his power. There was enough left for the little exigencies of *obscurity*. But he had two boys who look'd up to him for *light* —he thought they deserved it. He had tried his sword—it could not open the way—the *mounting* was too expensive—and simple economy was not a match for it—there was no resource but commerce.

'In any other province in France, save Brittany, this was smiting the root for ever of the little tree his pride and affection wish'd to see reblossom. But in Brittany, there being a provision for this, he avail'd himself of it; and taking an occasion when the states were assembled at Rennes, the Marquis, attended with his two boys, entered the court; and having pleaded the right of an ancient law of the duchy, which, though seldom claim'd, he said, was no less in force, he took his sword from his side—Here, said he, take it; and be trusty guardians of it, till better times put me in condition to reclaim it.

'The president accepted the Marquis's sword—he stayed a few minutes to see it deposited in the archives of his house— and departed.

'The Marquis and his whole family embarked the next day for Martinico, and in about nineteen or twenty years of successful application to business, with some unlook'd-for bequests from distant branches of his house, return'd home to reclaim his nobility and to support it.

'It was an incident of good fortune which will never happen to any traveller but a sentimental one, that I should be at Rennes at the very time of this solemn requisition: I call it solemn—it was so to me—

'The Marquis enter'd the court with his whole family; he supported his lady—his eldest son supported his sister, and his youngest was at the other extreme of the line next his mother— he put his handkerchief to his face twice—

'—There was a dead silence. When the Marquis had approach'd within six paces of the tribunal, he gave the Marchioness to his youngest son, and advancing three steps before his family—he reclaim'd his sword. His sword was given him; and the moment he got it into his hand he drew it almost out of the scabbard—'twas the shining face of a friend he had once given up—he look'd attentively along it, beginning at the hilt, as if to see whether it was the same—when observing a little rust which it had contracted near the point, he brought it near his eye, and bending his head down over it—I think I saw a tear fall upon the place: I could not be deceived by what followed.

' " I shall find," said he, " some *other* way to get it off."

' When the Marquis had said this, he return'd his sword into its scabbard, made a bow to the guardians of it—and with his wife and daughter, and his two sons following him, walk'd out.

' O how I envied him his feelings ! '

It shows a touching innocence of the imagination to believe, —for probably Sterne did believe,—or to expect his readers to believe, in a *noblesse* at once so honourable and so theatrical.

In two points the *Sentimental Journey*, viewed with the critic's eye and as a mere work of art, is a great improvement upon *Tristram Shandy*. The style is simpler and better; it is far more connected; it does not jump about, or leave a topic *because* it is interesting; it does not worry the reader with fantastic transitions, with childish contrivances and rhetorical intricacies. Highly elaborate the style certainly is, and in a certain sense artificial; it is full of nice touches, which must have come only upon reflection—a careful polish and judicious enhancement, in which the critic sees many a trace of time and toil. But a style delicately adjusted and exquisitely polished belongs to such a subject. Sterne undertook to write, *not* of the coarse business of life—very strong common sort of words are best for that—*not* even of interesting outward realities, which may be best described in a nice and simple style; but of the passing moods of human nature, of the impressions which a sensitive nature receives from the world without; and it is only the nicest art and the most dexterous care which can fit an obtuse language to such fine employment. How language was first invented and made we may not know; but beyond doubt it was shaped and fashioned into its present state by common ordinary men and women using it for common and ordinary purposes. They wanted a carving-knife, not a razor or lancet. And those great artists who have to use

language for more exquisite purposes, who employ it to
describe changing sentiments and momentary fancies and the
fluctuating and indefinite inner world, must use curious nicety,
and hidden but effectual artifice, else they cannot duly punctuate their thoughts and slice the fine edges of their reflexions.
A hair's-breadth is as important to them as a yard's-breadth
to a common workman. Sterne's style has been criticised as
artificial; but it is justly and rightly artificial, because language
used in its natural and common mode was not framed to
delineate, cannot delineate, the delicate subjects with which
he occupies himself.

That contact with the world, and with the French world
especially, should teach Sterne to abandon the arbitrary and
fantastic structure of *Tristram Shandy* is most natural. French
prose may be unreasonable in its meaning, but is ever rational
in its structure; it is logic itself. It will not endure that the
reader's mind should be jarred by rough transitions, or distracted by irrelevant oddities. *Antics* in style are prohibited by
its severe code, just as eccentricities in manner are kept down
by the critical tone of a fastidious society. In a barbarous
country oddity may be attractive; in the great world it never
is, except for a moment; it is on trial to see whether it is really
oddity, to see if it does not contain elements which may be
useful to, which may be naturalised in society at large. But
inherent eccentricity, oddity *pur et simple,* is *immiscible* in the
great ocean of universal thought; it is apart from it, even when
it floats in and is contained in it; very, very soon it is cast out
from the busy waters, and left alone upon the beach. Sterne
had the sense to be taught by the sharp touch of the world; he
threw aside the ' player's garb ' which he had been tempted to
assume. He discarded too, as was equally natural, the ugly
indecency of *Tristram Shandy.* We will not undertake to defend
the morality of certain scenes in the *Sentimental Journey;*
there are several which might easily do much harm; but there
is nothing displeasing to the natural man in them. They are
nice enough; to those whose æsthetic nature has not been laid
waste by their moral nature they are attractive. They have a
dangerous prettiness, which may easily incite to practical evil;
but in itself, and separated from its censurable consequences,
such prettiness is an artistic perfection. It was natural that the
aristocratic world should easily teach Sterne that separation

between the laws of beauty and the laws of morality which has been familiar to it during many ages—which makes so much of its essence.

Mrs. Sterne did not prosper all this time. She went abroad and stayed at Montpellier with her husband; but it is not wonderful that a mere ' wife,' taken out of Yorkshire, should be unfit for the great world. The domestic appendices of men who rise much hardly ever suit the high places at which they arrive. Mrs. Sterne was no exception. She seems to have been sensible, but it was *domestic* sense. It was of the small world, small: it was fit to regulate the Yorkshire parsonage, it was suitable to a small *ménage* even at Montpellier. But there was a deficiency in general mind. She did not, we apprehend, comprehend or appreciate the new thoughts and feelings which a new and great experience had awakened in her husband's mind. His mind moved, but hers could not; she was anchored, but he was at sea.

To fastidious writers who will only use very dignified words, there is much difficulty in describing Sterne's life in his celebrity. But to humbler persons, who can only describe the things of society in the words of society, the case is simple. Sterne was ' an old flirt.' These are short and expressive words, and they tell the whole truth. There is no good reason to suspect his morals, but he dawdled about pretty women. He talked at fifty with the admiring tone of twenty; pretended to ' freshness ' of feeling; though he had become mature, did not put away immature things. That he had any real influence over women is very unlikely; he was a celebrity, and they liked to exhibit him; he was amusing, and they liked him to amuse them. But they doubtless felt that he too was himself a joke. Women much respect real virtue; they much admire strong and successful immorality; but they neither admire nor respect the timid age which affects the forms of vice without its substance; which preserves the exterior of youth, though the reality is departed; which is insidious but not dangerous, sentimental but not passionate. Of this sort was Sterne, and he had his reward. Women of the world are willing to accept any admiration, but this sort they accept with suppressed and latent sarcasm. They ridiculed his imbecility while they accepted his attentions and enjoyed his society.

Many men have lived this life with but minor penalties, and

justly; for though perhaps a feeble and contemptible, it is not a bad or immoral life. But Sterne has suffered a very severe though a delayed and posthumous penalty. He was foolish enough to write letters to some of his friends, and after his death, to get money, his family published them. This is the sort of thing:

' Eliza will receive my books with this. The sermons came all hot from the heart; I wish that I could give them any title to be offered to yours.—The others came from the head—I am more indifferent about their reception.

' I know not how it comes about, but I am half in love with you—I ought to be wholly so; for I never valued (or saw more good qualities to value) or thought more of one of your sex than of you; so adieu.

' Yours faithfully,
' if not affectionately,
' L. STERNE.'

' I cannot rest, Eliza, though I shall call on you at half-past twelve, till I know how you do.—May thy dear face smile, as thou risest, like the sun of this morning. I was much grieved to hear of your alarming indisposition yesterday; and disappointed too, at not being let in. Remember, my dear, that a friend has the same right as a physician. The etiquettes of this town (you'll say) say otherwise.—No matter! Delicacy and propriety do not always consist in observing their frigid doctrines.

' I am going out to breakfast, but shall be at my lodgings by eleven, when I hope to read a single line under thy own hand, that thou art better, and wilt be glad to see thy Bramin.'

This Eliza was a Mrs. Draper, the wife of a judge in India, ' much respected in that part of the world.' We know little of Eliza, except that there is a stone in Bristol cathedral

SACRED

TO THE MEMORY

OF

MRS. ELIZABETH DRAPER,

IN WHOM

GENIUS AND BENEVOLENCE

WERE UNITED.

SHE DIED AUGUST 3, 1778, AGED 35.

Let us hope she possessed, in addition to genius and benevolence, the good sense to laugh at Sterne's letters.

In truth, much of the gloss and delicacy of Sterne's pagan instinct had faded away by this time. He still retained his fine sensibility, his exquisite power of entering into and of delineating plain human nature. But the world had produced its inevitable effect on that soft and voluptuous disposition. It is not, as we have said, that he was guilty of grave offences or misdeeds; he made what he would have called a 'splutter of vice,' but he would seem to have committed very little. Yet, as with most minds which have exempted themselves from rigid principle, there was a diffused texture of general laxity. The fibre had become imperfect; the moral constitution was impaired; the high colour of rottenness had come at last out, and replaced the delicate bloom and softness of the early fruit. There is no need to write commonplace sermons on an ancient text. The beauty and charm of natural paganism will not endure the stress and destruction of this rough and complicated world. An instinctive purity will preserve men for a brief time, but hardly through a long and varied life of threescore and ten years.

Sterne, however, did not live so long. In 1768 he came to London for the last time, and enjoyed himself much. He dined with literary friends and supped with fast friends. He liked both. But the end was at hand. His chest had long been delicate; he got a bad cold which became a pleurisy, and died in a London lodging—a footman sent by 'some gentlemen who were dining,' and a hired nurse, being the only persons present. His family were away; and he had devoted himself to intellectual and luxurious enjoyments, which are at least as sure to make a lonely deathbed as a refined and cultivated life. 'Self-scanned, self-centred, self-secure,' a man may perhaps live, but even so *by himself* he will be sure to die. For self-absorbed men the world at large cares little; as soon as they cease to amuse, or to be useful, it flings them aside, and they die alone. Even Sterne's grave, they say, was so obscure and neglected that the corpse-stealers ventured to open it, and his body was dissected without being recognised. The life of literary men is often a kind of sermon in itself; for the pursuit of fame, when it is contrasted with the grave realities of life, seems more absurd and trifling than most pursuits, and to leave less behind it. Mere *amusers* are never respected. It would be harsh to call Sterne a mere amuser, he is much more; but so the contemporary world regarded him. They laughed at his jests, disregarded his death-bed, and neglected his grave.

What, it may be asked, is there in such a career, or such a character as this, to remind us of the great writer whom we have just lost? In externals there seems little resemblance, or rather there seems to be great contrast. On the one side a respected manhood, a long industry, an honoured memory; on the other hand a life lax, if not dissolute, little labour, and a dishonoured grave. Mr. Thackeray, too, has written a most severe criticism on Sterne's character. Can we, then, venture to compare the two? We do so venture; and we allege, and that in spite of many superficial differences, that there was one fundamental and ineradicable resemblance between the two.

Thackeray, like Sterne, looked at everything—at nature, at life, at art—from a *sensitive* aspect. His mind was, to some considerable extent, like a woman's mind. It could comprehend abstractions when they were unrolled and explained before it, but it never naturally created them; never of itself, and without external obligation, devoted itself to them. The visible scene of life—the streets, the servants, the clubs, the gossip, the West End—fastened on his brain. These were to him reality. They burnt in upon his brain; they pained his nerves; their influence reached him through many avenues, which ordinary men do not feel much, or to which they are altogether impervious. He had distinct and rather painful sensations where most men have but confused and blurred ones. Most men have felt the *instructive* headache, during which they are more acutely conscious than usual of all which goes on around them,—during which everything seems to pain them, and in which they understand it, because it pains them, and they cannot get their imagination away from it. Thackeray had a nerve-ache of this sort always. He acutely felt every possible passing fact—every trivial interlude in society. Hazlitt used to say of himself, and used to say truly, that he could not enjoy the society in a drawing-room for thinking of the opinion which the footman formed of his odd appearance as he went upstairs. Thackeray had too healthy and stable a nature to be thrown so wholly off his balance; but the footman's view of life was never out of his head. The obvious facts which suggest it to the footman poured it in upon him; he could not exempt himself from them. As most men say that the earth *may* go round the sun, but in fact, when we look at the sun, we cannot help believing it goes round the earth,—just so this most impressible, susceptible genius could not help half accepting, half believing the common ordinary sensitive view of life, although he perfectly knew in his inner mind and deeper nature that this apparent and superficial view of life was misleading, inadequate, and deceptive. He could not help seeing everything, and what he saw made so near and keen an impression upon him, that he could not again exclude it from his understanding; it stayed there, and disturbed his thoughts.

If, he often says, 'people could write about that of which they are really thinking, how interesting books would be!' More than most writers of fiction he felt the difficulty of abstracting his thoughts and imagination from near facts which *would* make themselves felt. The sick wife in the next room, the unpaid baker's bill, the lodging-house keeper who doubts your solvency; these, and such as these,—the usual accompaniments of an early literary life,—are constantly alluded to in his writings. Perhaps he could never take a grand enough view of literature, or accept the truth of 'high art,' because of his natural tendency to this stern and humble realism. He knew that he was writing a tale which would appear in a green magazine (with others) on the 1st of March, and would be paid for perhaps on the 11th, by which time, probably, 'Mr. Smith' would have to 'make up a sum,' and would again present his little account. There are many minds besides his who feel an interest in these realities, though they yawn over 'high art' and elaborate judgments.

A painfulness certainly clings like an atmosphere round Mr. Thackeray's writings, in consequence of his inseparable and ever-present realism. We hardly know where it is, yet we are all conscious of it less or more. A free and bold writer, Sir Walter Scott throws himself far away into fictitious worlds, and soars there without effort, without pain, and with unceasing enjoyment. You see as it were between the lines of Mr. Thackeray's writings, that his thoughts were never long away from the close proximate scene. His writings might be better if it had been otherwise; but they would have been less peculiar, less individual; they would have wanted their character,

their flavour, if he had been able while writing them to forget
for many moments the ever-attending, the ever-painful sense
of himself.

Hence have arisen most of the censures upon him, both as
he seemed to be in society and as he was in his writings. He
was certainly uneasy in the common and general world, and
it was natural that he should be so. The world poured in upon
him, and *inflicted* upon his delicate sensibility a number of
petty pains and impressions which others do not feel at all, or
which they feel but very indistinctly. As he sat he seemed to
read off the passing thoughts—the base, common, ordinary
impressions—of every one else. Could such a man be at ease?
Could even a quick intellect be asked to set in order with such
velocity so many data? Could any temper, however excellent,
be asked to bear the contemporaneous influx of innumerable
minute annoyances? Men of ordinary nerves who feel a little
of the pains of society, who perceive what really passes, who are
not absorbed in the petty pleasures of sociability, could well
observe how keen was Thackeray's *sensation* of common events,
could easily understand how difficult it must have been for him
to keep mind and temper undisturbed by a miscellaneous tide
at once so incessant and so forcible.

He could not emancipate himself from such impressions
even in a case where most men hardly feel them. Many people
have—it is not difficult to have—some vague sensitive perception of what is passing in the minds of the guests, of the ideas
of such as sit at meat; but who remembers that there are also
nervous apprehensions, also a latent mental life among those
who ' stand and wait '—among the floating figures which pass
and carve? But there was no impression to which Mr.
Thackeray was more constantly alive, or which he was more
apt in his writings to express. He observes:

' Between me and those fellow-creatures of mine who are
sitting in the room below, how strange and wonderful is the
partition! We meet at every hour of the daylight, and are
indebted to each other for a hundred offices of duty and comfort of life; and we live together for years, and don't know each
other. John's voice to me is quite different from John's voice
when it addresses his mates below. If I met Hannah in the
street with a bonnet on, I doubt whether I should know her.

And all these good people, with whom I may live for years and years, have cares, interests, dear friends and relatives, mayhap schemes, passions, longing hopes, tragedies of their own, from which a carpet and a few planks and beams utterly separate me. When we were at the sea-side, and poor Ellen used to look so pale, and run after the postman's bell, and seize a letter in a great scrawling hand, and read it, and cry in a corner, how should we know that the poor little thing's heart was breaking? She fetched the water, and she smoothed the ribbons, and she laid out the dresses, and brought the early cup of tea in the morning, just as if she had had no cares to keep her awake. Henry (who lived out of the house) was the servant of a friend of mine who lived in chambers. There was a dinner one day, and Henry waited all through the dinner. The champagne was properly iced, the dinner was excellently served; every guest was attended to; the dinner disappeared; the dessert was set; the claret was in perfect order, carefully decanted, and more ready. And then Henry said, " If you please, sir, may I go home?" He had received word that his house was on fire; and, having seen through his dinner, he wished to go and look after his children, and little sticks of furniture. Why, such a man's livery is a uniform of honour. The crest on his button is a badge of bravery.'

Nothing in itself could be more admirable than this in-stinctive sympathy with humble persons; not many things are rarer than this nervous apprehension of what humble persons think. Nevertheless it cannot, we think, be effectually denied that it coloured Mr. Thackeray's writings and the more super-ficial part of his character—that part which was most obvious in common and current society—with very considerable defects. The pervading idea of the ' Snob Papers ' is too frequent, too recurring, too often insisted on, even in his highest writings; there was a slight shade of similar feeling even in his occasional society, and though it was certainly unworthy of him, it was exceedingly natural that it should be so, with such a mind as his and in a society such as ours.

There are three methods in which a society may be con-stituted. There is the equal system, which, with more or less of variation, prevails in France and in the United States. The social presumption in these countries always is that every one

s on a level with every one else. In America, the porter at the
station, the shopman at the counter, the boots at the hotel,
when neither a Negro nor an Irishman, is your equal. In
France *égalité* is a political first principle. The whole of Louis
Napoleon's *régime* depends upon it: remove that feeling, and
the whole fabric of the Empire will pass away. We once heard a
great French statesman illustrate this. He was giving a dinner
to the clergy of his neighbourhood, and was observing that he
had now no longer the power to help or hurt them, when an
eager *curé* said, with simple-minded joy, ' Oui, monsieur, main-
tenant personne ne peut rien, ni le comte, ni le prolétaire.'
The democratic priest so rejoiced at the universal levelling
which had passed over his nation, that he could not help
boasting of it when silence would have been much better
manners. We are not now able—we have no room and no
inclination—to discuss the advantages of democratic society;
but we think in England we may venture to assume that it is
neither the best nor the highest form which a society can adopt,
and that it is certainly fatal to that development of individual
originality and greatness by which the past progress of the
human race has been achieved, and from which alone, it would
seem, all future progress is to be anticipated. If it be said that
people are all alike, that the world is a plain with no natural
valleys and no natural hills, the picturesqueness of existence
is destroyed, and, what is worse, the instinctive emulation by
which the dweller in the valley is stimulated to climb the hill
is annihilated and becomes impossible.

On the other hand, there is the opposite system, which prevails in the East,—the system of irremovable inequalities, of
hedged-in castes which no one can enter but by birth, and from
which no born member can issue forth. This system likewise,
in this age and country, needs no attack, for it has no defenders.
Every one is ready to admit that it cramps originality, by
defining our work irrespective of our qualities and before we
were born; that it retards progress, by restraining the wholesome competition between class and class, and the wholesome
migration from class to class, which are the best and strongest
instruments of social improvement.

And if both these systems be condemned as undesirable and
prejudicial, there is no third system except that which we have
—the system of *removable inequalities*, where many people are

inferior to and worse off than others, but in which each may *in theory* hope to be on a level with the highest below the throne, and in which each may reasonably, and without sanguine impracticability, hope to gain one step in social elevation, to be at last on a level with those who at first were just above them. But, from the mere description of such a society, it is evident that, taking man as he is, with the faults which we know he has, and the tendencies which he invariably displays, some poison of 'snobbishness' is inevitable. Let us define it as the habit of 'pretending to be higher in the social scale than you really are.' Everybody will admit that such pretension is a fault and a vice, yet every observant man of the world would also admit that, considering what other misdemeanours men commit, this offence is not inconceivably heinous, and that, if people never did anything worse, they might be let off with a far less punitive judgment than in the actual state of human conduct would be just or conceivable. How are we to hope men will pass their lives in putting their best foot foremost, and yet will never boast that their better foot is farther advanced and more perfect than in fact it is? Is boasting to be made a capital crime? Given social ambition as a propensity of human nature; given a state of society like ours, in which there are prizes which every man may seek, degradations which every one may erase, inequalities which every one may remove,—it is idle to suppose that there will not be all sorts of striving to cease to be last and to begin to be first, and it is equally idle to imagine that all such strivings will be of the highest kind. This effort will be, like all the efforts of our mixed and imperfect human nature, partly good and partly bad, with much that is excellent and beneficial in it, and much also which is debasing and pernicious. The bad striving after unpossessed distinction is snobbishness, which from the mere definition cannot be defended, but which may be excused as a natural frailty in an emulous man who is not distinguished, who hopes to be distinguished, and who perceives that a valuable means of gaining distinction is a judicious though false pretension that it has already been obtained.

Mr. Thackeray, as we think, committed two errors in this matter. He lacerates 'snobs' in his books as if they had committed an unpardonable outrage and inexpiable crime. That man, he says, is anxious 'to know lords; and he pretends to know more of lords than he really does know. What a villain!

what a disgrace to our common nature! what an irreparable reproach to human reason!' Not at all; it is a fault which satirists should laugh at, and which moralists condemn and disapprove, but which yet does not destroy the whole vital excellence of him who possesses it,—which may leave him a good citizen, a pleasant husband, a warm friend; 'a fellow,' as the undergraduate said, '*up* in his *morals*.'

In transient society it is possible, we think, that Mr. Thackeray thought too much of social inequalities. They belonged to that common, plain, perceptible world which filled his mind, and which left him at times, and at casual moments, no room for a purely intellectual and just estimate of men as they really are in themselves and apart from social perfection or defect. He could gauge a man's reality as well as any observer, and far better than most; his attainments were great, his perception of men instinctive, his knowledge of casual matters enormous; but he had a greater difficulty than other men in relying only upon his own judgment. 'What the footman—what Mr. Yellowplush Jeames would think and say,' could not but occur to his mind, and would modify, not his settled judgment, but his transient and casual opinion of the poet or philosopher. By the constitution of his mind he thought much of social distinctions, and yet he was in his writings too severe on those who, in cruder and baser ways, showed that they also were thinking much.

Those who perceive that this irritable sensibility was the basis of Thackeray's artistic character, that it gave him his materials, his implanted knowledge of things and men, and gave him also that keen and precise style which hit in description the nice edges of all objects,—those who trace these great qualities back to their real source in a somewhat painful organisation, must have been vexed or amused, according to their temperament, at the common criticism which associates him with Fielding. Fielding's essence was the very reverse; it was a bold spirit of bounding happiness. No just observer could talk to Mr. Thackeray, or look at him, without seeing that he had deeply felt many sorrows—perhaps that he was a man *likely* to feel sorrows—that he was of an anxious temperament. Fielding was a reckless enjoyer. He saw the world—wealth and glory, the best dinner and the worst dinner, the gilded *salon* and the low sponging-house—and he saw that they were good. Down every line of his characteristic writing there runs this elemental energy of keen delight. There is no trace of such a thing in Thackeray. A musing fancifulness is far more characteristic of him than a joyful energy.

Sterne had all this sensibility also, but—and this is the cardinal discrepancy—it did not make him irritable. He was not hurried away, like Fielding, by buoyant delight; he stayed and mused on painful scenes. But they did not make him angry. He was not irritated at the ' foolish fat scullion.' He did not vex himself because of the vulgar. He did not amass petty details to prove that tenth-rate people were ever striving to be ninth-rate people. He had no tendency to rub the bloom off life. He accepted pretty-looking things, even the French aristocracy, and he owes his immortality to his making them prettier than they are. Thackeray was pained by things, and exaggerated their imperfections; Sterne brooded over things with joy or sorrow, and he idealised their sentiment—their pathetic or joyful characteristics. This is why the old lady said, ' Mr. Thackeray was an uncomfortable writer,'—and an uncomfortable writer he is.

Nor had Sterne a trace of Mr. Thackeray's peculiar and characteristic scepticism. He accepted simply the pains and pleasures, the sorrows and the joys of the world; he was not perplexed by them, nor did he seek to explain them, or account for them. There is a tinge—a mitigated, but perceptible tinge— of Swift's philosophy in Thackeray. ' Why is all this? Surely this is very strange? Am I right in sympathising with such stupid feelings, such petty sensations? Why are these things? Am I not a fool to care about or think of them? The world is dark, and the great curtain hides from us all.' This is not a steady or an habitual feeling, but it is never quite absent for many pages. It was inevitable, perhaps, that, in a sceptical and inquisitive age like this, some vestiges of puzzle and perplexity should pass into the writings of our great sentimentalist. He would not have fairly represented the moods of his time if he omitted that pervading one.

We had a little more to say of these great men, but our limits are exhausted, and we must pause. Of Thackeray it is too early to speak at length. A certain distance is needful for a just criticism. The present generation have learned too much from him to be able to judge him rightly. We do not know the merit of those great pictures which have sunk into our minds, and which have coloured our thoughts, which are become habitual memories. In the books we know best, as in the people we know best, small points, sometimes minor merits, sometimes small faults, have an undue prominence. When the young critics of this year have gray hairs, their children will tell them what is the judgment of posterity upon Mr. Thackeray.

The Waverley Novels*
(1858)

IT is not commonly on the generation which was contemporary
with the production of great works of art that they exercise
their most magical influence. Nor is it on the distant people
whom we call posterity. Contemporaries bring to new books
formed minds and stiffened creeds; posterity, if it regard them
at all, looks at them as old subjects, worn-out topics, and hears
a disputation on their merits with languid impartiality, like
aged judges in a court of appeal. Even standard authors
exercise but slender influence on the susceptible minds of a
rising generation; they are become ' papa's books;' the walls
of the library are adorned with their regular volumes; but no
hand touches them. Their fame is itself half an obstacle to their
popularity; a delicate fancy shrinks from employing so great
a celebrity as the companion of an idle hour. The generation
which is really most influenced by a work of genius is commonly
that which is still young when the first controversy respecting
its merits arises; with the eagerness of youth they read and
re-read; their vanity is not unwilling to adjudicate: in the
process their imagination is formed; the creations of the author
range themselves in the memory; they become part of the
substance of the very mind. The works of Sir Walter Scott

* *Library Edition.* Illustrated by upwards of Two Hundred Engravings on Steel, after Drawings by Turner, Landseer, Wilkie,
Stanfield, Roberts, &c., including Portraits of the Historical Per-
sonages described in the Novels. 25 vols. demy 8vo.
 Abbotsford Edition. With One Hundred and Twenty Engravings
on Steel, and nearly Two Thousand on Wood. 12 vols. super-royal
8vo.
 Author's favourite Edition. 48 vols. post 8vo.
 Cabinet Edition. 25 vols. foolscap 8vo.
 Railway Edition. Now publishing, and to be completed in 25
portable volumes, large type.
 People's Edition. 5 large volumes royal 8vo.

can hardly be said to have gone through this exact process. Their immediate popularity was unbounded. No one—a few most captious critics apart—ever questioned their peculiar power. Still they are subject to a transition, which is in principle the same. At the time of their publication mature contemporaries read them with delight. Superficial the reading of grown men in some sort must be; it is only once in a lifetime that we can know the passionate reading of youth; men soon lose its eager learning power. But from peculiarities in their structure, which we shall try to indicate, the novels of Scott suffered less than almost any book of equal excellence from this inevitable superficiality of perusal. Their plain, and, so to say, cheerful merits, suit the occupied man of genial middle life. Their appreciation was to an unusual degree coincident with their popularity. The next generation, hearing the praises of their fathers in their earliest reading time, seized with avidity on the volumes; and there is much in very many of them which is admirably fitted for the delight of boyhood. A third generation has now risen into at least the commencement of literary life, which is quite removed from the unbounded enthusiasm with which the Scotch novels were originally received, and does not always share the still more eager partiality of those who, in the opening of their minds, first received the tradition of their excellence. New books have arisen to compete with these; new interests distract us from them. The time, therefore, is not perhaps unfavourable for a slight criticism of these celebrated fictions; and their continual republication, without any criticism for many years seems almost to demand it.

There are two kinds of fiction which, though in common literature they may run very much into one another, are yet in reality distinguishable and separate. One of these, which we may call the *ubiquitous*, aims at describing the whole of human life in all its spheres, in all its aspects, with all its varied interests, aims, and objects. It searches through the whole life of man; his practical pursuits, his speculative attempts, his romantic youth, and his domestic age. It gives an entire feature of all these; or if there be any lineaments which it forbears to depict, they are only such as the inevitable repression of regulated society excludes from the admitted provi[nce] literary art. Of this kind are the novels of Cervant[es]

Sage, and, to a certain extent, of Smollett or Fielding. In our
own time, Mr. Dickens is an author whom nature intended to
write to a certain extent with this aim. He should have given
us *not* disjointed novels, with a vague attempt at a romantic
plot, but sketches of diversified scenes, and the obvious life of
varied mankind. The literary fates, however, if such beings
there are, allotted otherwise. By a very terrible example of the
way in which in this world great interests are postponed to
little ones, the genius of authors is habitually sacrificed to the
tastes of readers. In this age, the great readers of fiction are
young people. The ' addiction ' of these is to romance; and
accordingly a kind of novel has become so familiar to us as
almost to engross the name, which deals solely with the
passion of love; and if it uses other parts of human life for
the occasions of its art, it does so only cursorily and occasionally, and with a view of throwing into a stronger or more
delicate light those sentimental parts of earthly affairs which
are the special objects of delineation. All prolonged delineation of other parts of human life is considered ' dry,' stupid,
and distracts the mind of the youthful generation from the
' fantasies ' which peculiarly charm it. Mr. Olmsted has a
story of some deputation of the Indians, at which the American
orator harangued the barbarian audience about the ' great
spirit,' and ' the land of their fathers,' in the style of Mr.
Cooper's novels; during a moment's pause in the great stream,
an old Indian asked the deputation, ' why does your chief
speak thus to us? We did not wish great instruction or fine
words; we desire brandy and tobacco.' No critic in a time of
competition will speak uncourteously of any reader of either
sex; but it is indisputable that the old kind of novel, full of
' great instruction ' and varied pictures, does not afford to
some young gentlemen and some young ladies either the
peculia   or the peculiar solace which they desire.

Novels were published at a time when the
mit the sphere of fiction were coming into
they had not yet become so omnipotent as
dingly these novels everywhere bear marks
. They are not devoted with anything like
ss to the sentimental part of human life.
events, singular characters, strange
of society; they dwell with a peculiar

interest—and as if for their own sake—on antiquarian details relating to a past society. Singular customs, social practices, even political institutions which existed once in Scotland, and even elsewhere, during the middle ages, are explained with a careful minuteness. At the same time the sentimental element assumes a great deal of prominence. The book is in fact, as well as in theory, a narrative of the feelings and fortunes of the hero and heroine. An attempt more or less successful has been made to insert an interesting love-story in each novel. Sir Walter was quite aware that the best delineation of the oddest characters, or the most quaint societies, or the strangest incidents, would not in general satisfy his readers. He has invariably attempted an account of youthful, sometimes of decidedly juvenile, feelings and actions. The difference between Sir Walter's novels and the specially romantic fictions of the present day is, that in the former the love-story is always, or nearly always, connected with some great event, or the fortunes of some great historical character, or the peculiar movements and incidents of some strange state of society; and that the author did not suppose or expect that his readers would be so absorbed in the sentimental aspect of human life as to be unable or unwilling to be interested in, or to attend to, any other. There is always a *locus in quo*, if the expression may be pardoned, in the Waverley Novels. The hero and heroine walk among the trees of the forest according to rule, but we are expected to take an interest in the forest as well as in them.

No novel, therefore, of Sir Walter Scott's can be considered to come exactly within the class which we have called the ubiquitous. None of them in any material degree attempts to deal with human affairs in all their spheres—to delineate as a whole the life of man. The canvas has a large background, in some cases too large either for artistic effect or the common reader's interest; but there are always real boundaries—Sir Walter had no *thesis* to maintain. Scarcely any writer will set himself to delineate the whole of human life, unless he has a doctrine concerning human life to put forth and inculcate. The effort is *doctrinaire*. Scott's imagination was strictly conservative. He could understand (with a few exceptions) any considerable movement of human life and action, and could always describe with easy freshness everything which he did understand; but he was not obliged by stress of fanaticism to maintain a dogma concerning them, or to show their peculiar relation to the general sphere of life. He described vigorously and boldly the peculiar scene and society which in every novel he had selected as the theatre of romantic action. Partly from their fidelity to nature, and partly from a consistency in the artist's mode of representation, these pictures group themselves from the several novels in the imagination, and an habitual reader comes to think of and understand what is meant by 'Scott's world;' but the writer had no such distinct object before him. No one novel was designed to be a delineation of the world as Scott viewed it. We have vivid and fragmentary histories; it is for the slow critic of after-times to piece together their teaching.

From this intermediate position of the Waverley Novels, or at any rate in exact accordance with its requirements, is the special characteristic for which they are most remarkable. We may call this in a brief phrase their *romantic sense*; and perhaps we cannot better illustrate it than by a quotation from the novel to which the series owes its most usual name. It occurs in the description of the court ball which Charles Edward is described as giving at Holyrood House the night before his march southward on his strange adventure. The striking interest of the scene before him, and the peculiar position of his own sentimental career, are described as influencing the mind of the hero. ' Under the influence of these mixed sensations, and cheered at times by a smile of intelligence and approbation from the Prince as he passed the group, Waverley exerted his powers of fancy, animation, and eloquence, and attracted the general admiration of the company. The conversation gradually assumed the line best qualified for the display of his talents and acquisitions. The gaiety of the evening was exalted in character, rather than checked, by the approaching dangers of the morrow. All nerves were strung for the future, and prepared to enjoy the present. This mood is highly favourably for the exercise of the powers of imagination, for poetry, and for that eloquence which is allied to poetry.' Neither 'eloquence' nor 'poetry' are the exact words with which it would be appropriate to describe the fresh style of the Waverley Novels; but the imagination of their author was stimulated by a fancied mixture of sentiment and fact very much as he describes Waverley's to have been by a real experience of the two at once. The second volume of Waverley is one of the most striking illustrations of this peculiarity. The character of Charles Edward, his adventurous undertaking, his ancestral rights, the mixed selfishness and enthusiasm of the Highland chiefs, the fidelity of their hereditary followers, their striking and strange array, the contrast with the Baron of Bradwardine and the Lowland gentry; the collision of the motley and half-appointed host with the formed and finished English society, its passage by the Cumberland mountains and the blue lake of Ullswater—are unceasingly and without effort present to the mind of the writer, and incite with their historical interest the susceptibility of his imagination. But at the same time the mental struggle, or rather transition, in the mind of Waverley,—for his mind was of the faint order which scarcely struggles,—is never for an instant lost sight of. In the very midst of the inroad and the conflict, the acquiescent placidity with which the hero exchanges the service of the imperious for the appreciation of the ' nice ' heroine, is kept before us, and the imagination of Scott wandered without effort from the great scene of martial affairs to the natural but rather unheroic sentiments of a young gentleman not very difficult to please. There is no trace of effort in the transition, as is so common in the inferior works of later copyists. Many historical novelists, especially those who with care and pains have ' read up ' their detail, are often evidently in a strait how to pass from their history to their sentiment. The fancy of Sir Walter could not help connecting the two. If he had given us the English side of the race to Derby, he would have described the Bank of England paying in sixpences, and also the loves of the cashier.

It is not unremarkable in connection with this the special characteristic of the ' Scotch novels,' that their author began his literary life by collecting the old ballads of his native country. Ballad poetry is, in comparison at least with many other kinds of poetry, a sensible thing. It describes not only romantic events, but historical ones, incidents in which there is a form and body and consistence—events which have a result. Such a poem as ' Chevy Chace,' we need not explain has its prosaic side. The latest historian of Greece has nowhere been more successful than in his attempt to derive from Homer, the greatest of ballad poets, a thorough and consistent account of the political working of the Homeric state of society. The early natural imagination of men seizes firmly on all which interests the minds and hearts of natural men. We find in its delineations the council as well as the marriage; the harsh conflict as well as the deep love-affair. Scott's own poetry is essentially a modernised edition of the traditional poems which his early youth was occupied in collecting. The *Lady of the Lake* is a sort of *boudoir* ballad, yet it contains its element of common sense and broad delineation. The exact position of Lowlander and Highlander would not be more aptly described in a set treatise than in the well-known lines:

> ' Saxon, from yonder mountain high
> I marked thee send delighted eye
> Far to the south and east, where lay,
> Extended in succession gay,
> Deep waving fields and pastures green,
> With gentle slopes and hills between:
> These fertile plains, that softened vale,
> Were once the birthright of the Gael.
> The stranger came with iron hand,
> And from our fathers rent the land.
> Where dwell we now! See, rudely swell
> Crag over crag, and fell o'er fell.
> Ask we this savage hill we tread,
> For fattened steer or household bread;
> Ask we for flocks those shingles dry,—
> And well the mountain might reply,
> To you, as to your sires of yore,
> Belong the target and claymore;
> I give you shelter in my breast,
> Your own good blades must win the rest.
> Pent in this fortress of the North,
> Think'st thou we will not sally forth
> To spoil the spoiler as we may,
> And from the robber rend the prey?
> Ay, by my soul! While on yon plain
> The Saxon rears one shock of grain;
> While of ten thousand herds there strays
> But one along yon river's maze;
> The Gael, of plain and river heir,
> Shall with strong hand redeem his share.'

We need not search the same poem for specimens of the
romantic element, for the whole poem is full of them. The
incident in which Ellen discovers who Fitz-James really is, is
perhaps excessively romantic. At any rate the lines,—

> ' To him each lady's look was lent;
>   On him each courtier's eye was bent;
>   Midst furs and silks and jewels sheen,
>   He stood in simple Lincoln green,
>   The centre of the glittering ring,
>   And Snowdoun's knight is Scotland's king,'—

may be cited as very sufficient example of the sort of senti
mental incident which is separable from extreme feeling. When
Scott, according to his own half-jesting but half-serious expression, was ' beaten out of poetry ' by Byron, he began to express
in more pliable prose the same combination which his verse had
been used to convey. As might have been expected, the sense
became in the novels more free, vigorous, and flowing, because
it is less cramped by the vehicle in which it is conveyed. The
range of character which can be adequately delineated in
narrative verse is much narrower than that which can be
described in the combination of narrative with dramatic prose;
and perhaps even the sentiment of the novels is manlier and
freer; a delicate unreality hovers over the *Lady of the Lake*.

The sensible element, if we may so express it, of the
Waverley Novels appears in various forms. One of the most
striking is in the delineation of great political events and influential political institutions. We are not by any means about
to contend that Scott is to be taken as an infallible or an impartial authority for the parts of history which he delineates.
On the contrary, we believe all the world now agrees that there
are many deductions to be made from, many exceptions to be
taken to, the accuracy of his delineations. Still, whatever
period or incident we take, we shall always find in the error a
great, in one or two cases perhaps an extreme, mixture of the
mental element which we term common sense. The strongest
*un*sensible feeling in Scott was perhaps his Jacobitism, which
crept out even in small incidents and recurring prejudice
throughout the whole of his active career, and was, so to say,
the emotional aspect of his habitual Toryism. Yet no one can
have given a more sensible delineation, we might say a more

statesmanlike analysis, of the various causes which led to the momentary success, and to the speedy ruin, of the enterprise of Charles Edward. Mr. Lockhart says, that notwithstanding Scott's imaginative readiness to exalt Scotland at the expense of England, no man would have been more willing to join in emphatic opposition to an anti-English party, if any such had presented itself with a practical object. Similarly his Jacobitism, though not without moments of real influence, passed away when his mind was directed to broad masses of fact and general conclusions of political reasoning. A similar observation may be made as to Scott's Toryism; although it is certain that there was an enthusiastic, and in the malicious sense, poetical element in Scott's Toryism, yet it quite as indisputably partook largely of two other elements, which are in common repute prosaic. He shared abundantly in the love of administration and organisation, common to all men of great active powers. He liked to contemplate method at work and order in action. Everybody hates to hear that the Duke of Wellington asked ' how the king's government was to be carried on.' No amount of warning wisdom will bear so fearful a repetition. Still he *did* say it, and Scott had a sympathising foresight of the oracle before it was spoken. One element of his conservatism is his sympathy with the administrative arrangement, which is confused by the objections of a Whiggish opposition, and is liable to be altogether destroyed by uprisings of the populace. His biographer, while pointing out the strong contrast between Scott and the argumentative and parliamentary statesmen of his age, avows his opinion that in other times, and with sufficient opportunities, Scott's ability in managing men would have enabled him to ' play the part of Cecil or of Gondomar.' We may see how much an insensible enthusiasm for such abilities breaks out, not only in the description of hereditary monarchs, where the sentiment might be ascribed to a different origin, but also in the delineation of upstart rulers, who could have no hereditary sanctity in the eyes of any Tory. Roland Græme, in the *Abbot*, is well described as losing in the presence of the Regent Murray the natural impertinence of his disposition. ' He might have braved with indifference the presence of an earl merely distinguished by his belt and coronet; but he felt overawed in that of the soldier and statesman, the wielder of a nation's power, and the leader of her armies.' It is easy to perceive that the author shares the feeling of his hero by the evident pleasure with which he dwells on the Regent's demeanour: ' He then turned slowly round toward Roland Græme, and the marks of gaiety, real or assumed, disappeared from his countenance as completely as the passing bubbles leave the dark mirror of a still profound lake into which the traveller has cast a stone; in the course of a minute his noble features had assumed their natural expression of melancholy gravity,' &c. In real life Scott used to say that he never remembered feeling abashed in any one's presence except the Duke of Wellington's. Like that of the hero of his novel, his imagination was very susceptible to the influence of great achievement, and prolonged success in wide-spreading affairs.

The view which Scott seems to have taken of democracy indicates exactly the same sort of application of a plain sense to the visible parts of the subject. His imagination was singularly penetrated with the strange varieties and motley composition of human life. The extraordinary multitude and striking contrast of the characters in his novels show this at once. And even more strikingly is the same habit of mind indicated by a tendency never to omit an opportunity of describing those varied crowds and assemblages, which concentrate for a moment into a unity the scattered and unlike varieties of mankind. Thus, but a page or two before the passage which we alluded to in the *Abbot*, we find the following: ' It was indeed no common sight to Roland, the vestibule of a palace, traversed by its various groups,—some radiant with gaiety—some pensive, and apparently weighed down by affairs concerning the state, or concerning themselves. Here the hoary statesmen, with his cautious yet commanding look, his furred cloak and sable pantoufles; there the soldier in buff and steel, his long sword jarring against the pavement, and his whiskered upper lip and frowning brow looking an habitual defiance of danger, which perhaps was not always made good; there again passed my lord's serving-man, high of heart and bloody of hand, humble to his master and his master's equals, insolent to all others. To these might be added the poor suitor, with his anxious look and depressed mien—the officer, full of his brief authority, elbowing his betters, and possibly his benefactors, out of the road—the proud priest, who sought a better

benefice—the proud baron, who sought a grant of church lands
—the robber chief, who came to solicit a pardon for the
injuries he had inflicted on his neighbours—the plundered
franklin, who came to seek vengeance for that which he had
himself received. Besides there was the mustering and disposition of guards and soldiers—the despatching of messengers,
and the receiving them—the trampling and neighing of horses
without the gate—the flashing of arms, and rustling of plumes,
and jingling of spurs within it. In short, it was that gay and
splendid confusion, in which the eye of youth sees all that is
brave and brilliant, and that of experience much that is doubtful, deceitful, false, and hollow—hopes that will never be
gratified—promises which will never be fulfilled—pride in the
disguise of humility—and insolence in that of frank and
generous bounty.' As in the imagination of Shakespeare, so in
that of Scott, the principal form and object were the structure—that is a hard word—the undulation and diversified
composition of human society; the picture of this stood in the
centre, and everything else was accessory and secondary to it
The old ' rows of books,' in which Scott so peculiarly delighted,
were made to contribute their element to this varied imagination of humanity. From old family histories, odd memoirs,
old law-trials, his fancy elicited new traits to add to the
motley assemblage. His objection to democracy—an objection
of which we can only appreciate the emphatic force, when we
remember that his youth was contemporary with the first
French Revolution, and the controversy as to the uniform
and stereotyped rights of man—was, that it would sweep away
this entire picture, level prince and peasant in a common
égalité,—substitute a scientific rigidity for the irregular and
picturesque growth of centuries,—replace an abounding and
genial life by a symmetrical but lifeless mechanism. All the
descriptions of society in the novels,—whether of feudal
society, of modern Scotch society, or of English society,—
are largely coloured by this feeling. It peeps out everywhere,
and liberal critics have endeavoured to show that it was a
narrow Toryism; but in reality it is a subtle compound of the
natural instinct of the artist with the plain sagacity of the
man of the world.

It would be tedious to show how clearly the same sagacity
appears in his delineation of the various great events and move-

ments in society which are described in the Scotch novels. There is scarcely one of them which does not bear it on its surface. Objections may, as we shall show, be urged to the delineation which Scott has given of the Puritan resistance and rebellions, yet scarcely any one will say there is not a worldly sense in it. On the contrary, the very objection is, that it is too worldly, and far too exclusively sensible.

The same thoroughly well-grounded sagacity and comprehensive appreciation of human life is shown in the treatment of what we may call *anomalous* characters. In general, monstrosity is no topic for art. Every one has known in real life characters which if, apart from much experience, he had found described in books, he would have thought unnatural and impossible. Scott, however, abounds in such characters. Meg Merrilies, Edie Ochiltree, Radcliffe, are more or less of that description. That of Meg Merrilies especially is as distorted and eccentric as anything can be. Her appearance is described as making Mannering ' start; ' and well it might. ' She was full six feet high, wore a man's greatcoat over the rest of her dress, had in her hand a goodly sloethorn cudgel, and in all points of equipment except the petticoats seemed rather masculine than feminine. Her dark elf-locks shot out like the snakes of the gorgon between an old-fashioned bonnet called a bongrace, heightening the singular effect of her strong and weather-beaten features, which they partly shadowed, while her eye had a wild roll that indicated something of insanity.'

Her career in the tale corresponds with the strangeness of her exterior. ' Harlot, thief, witch, and gipsy,' as she describes herself, the hero is preserved by her virtues; half-crazed as she is described to be, he owes his safety on more than one occasion to her skill in stratagem, and ability in managing those with whom she is connected, and who are most likely to be familiar with her weakness and to detect her craft. Yet on hardly any occasion is the natural reader conscious of this strangeness. Something is of course attributable to the skill of the artist; for no other power of mind could produce the effect, unless it were aided by the unconscious tact of detailed expression. But the fundamental explanation of this remarkable success is the distinctness with which Scott saw how such a character as Meg Merrilies arose and was produced out of the peculiar circumstances of gipsy life in the localities in which he has placed his scene. He has exhibited this to his readers not by lengthy or elaborate description, but by chosen incidents, short comments, and touches of which he scarcely foresaw the effect. This is the only way in which the fundamental objection to making eccentricity the subject of artistic treatment can be obviated. Monstrosity ceases to be such when we discern the laws of nature which evolve it: when a real science explains its phenomena, we find that it is in strict accordance with what we call the natural type, but that some rare adjunct or uncommon casualty has interfered and distorted a nature which is really the same, into a phenomenon which is altogether different. Just so with eccentricity in human character; it becomes a topic of literary art only when its identity with the ordinary principles of human nature is exhibited in the midst of, and as it were, by means of, the superficial unlikeness. Such a skill, however, requires an easy careless familiarity with usual human life and common human conduct. A writer must have a sympathy with health before he can show us how, and where, and to what extent, that which is unhealthy deviates from it; and it is this consistent acquaintance with regular life which makes the irregular characters of Scott so happy a contrast to the uneasy distortions of less sagacious novelists.

A good deal of the same criticism may be applied to the delineation which Scott has given us of the *poor*. In truth, poverty is an anomaly to rich people. It is very difficult to make out why people who want dinner do not ring the bell. One half of the world, according to the saying, do not know how the other half live. Accordingly, nothing is so rare in fiction as a good delineation of the poor. Though perpetually with us in reality, we rarely meet them in our reading. The requirements of the case present an unusual difficulty to artistic delineation. A good deal of the character of the poor is an unfit topic for continuous art, and yet we wish to have in our books a lifelike exhibition of the whole of that character. Mean manners and mean vices are unfit for prolonged delineation; the everyday pressure of narrow necessities is too petty a pain and too anxious a reality to be dwelt upon. We can bear the mere description of the *Parish Register*—

' But this poor farce has neither truth nor art
To please the fancy or to touch the heart.
Dark but not awful, dismal but yet mean,
With anxious bustle moves the cumbrous scene;
Presents no objects tender or profound,
But spreads its cold unmeaning gloom around; '—

but who could bear to have a long narrative of fortunes ' dismal but yet mean,' with characters ' dark but not awful,' and no objects ' tender or profound ' ? Mr. Dickens has in various parts of his writings been led by a sort of pre-Raphaelite *cultus* of reality into an error of this species. His poor people have taken to their poverty very thoroughly; they are poor talkers and poor livers, and in all ways poor people to read about. A whole array of writers have fallen into an opposite mistake. Wishing to preserve their delineations clear from the defects of meanness and vulgarity, they have attributed to the poor a fancied happiness and Arcadian simplicity. The conventional shepherd of ancient times was scarcely displeasing: that which is by everything except express avowal removed from the sphere of reality does not annoy us by its deviations from reality; but the fictitious poor of sentimental novelists are brought almost into contact with real life, half claim to be copies of what actually exists at our very doors, are introduced in close proximity to characters moving in a higher rank, over whom no such ideal charm is diffused, and who are painted with as much truth as the writer's ability enables him to give. Accordingly, the contrast is evident and displeasing: the harsh outlines of poverty will not bear the artificial rose-tint; they are seen through it, like high cheek-bones through the delicate colours of artificial youth; we turn away with some disgust from the false elegance and undeceiving art; we prefer the rough poor of nature to the petted poor of the refining describer. Scott has most felicitously avoided both these errors. His poor people are never coarse and never vulgar; their lineaments have the rude traits which a life of conflict will inevitably leave on the minds and manners of those who are to lead it; their notions have the narrowness which is inseparable from a contracted experience; their knowledge is not more extended than their restricted means of attaining it would render possible. Almost alone among novelists Scott has given a thorough, minute, lifelike description of poor persons, which is at the same time genial and pleasing. The reason seems to be, that the firm sagacity of his genius comprehended the industrial aspect of poor people's life thoroughly and comprehensively, his experience brought it before him easily and naturally, and his artist's mind and genial disposition enabled him to dwell on those features which would be most pleasing to the world in general. In fact, his own mind of itself and by its own nature dwelt on those very peculiarities. He could not remove his firm and instructed genius into the domain of Arcadian unreality, but he was equally unable to dwell principally, peculiarly, or consecutively, on those petty, vulgar, mean details in which such a writer as Crabbe lives and breathes. Hazlitt said that Crabbe described a poor man's cottage like a man who came to distrain for rent; he catalogued every trivial piece of furniture, defects and cracks and all. Scott describes it as a cheerful but most sensible landlord would describe a cottage on his property: he has a pleasure in it. No detail, or few details, in the life of the inmates escape his experienced and interested eye; but he dwells on those which do not displease him. He sympathises with their rough industry and plain joys and sorrows. He does not fatigue himself or excite their wondering smile by theoretical plans of impossible relief. He makes the best of the life which is given, and by a sanguine sympathy makes it still better. A hard life many characters in Scott seem to lead; but he appreciates, and makes his reader appreciate, the full value of natural feelings, plain thoughts, and applied sagacity.

His ideas of political economy are equally characteristic of his strong sense and genial mind. He was always sneering at Adam Smith, and telling many legends of that philosopher's absence of mind and inaptitude for the ordinary conduct of life. A contact with the Edinburgh logicians had, doubtless, not augmented his faith in the formal deductions of abstract economy; nevertheless, with the facts before him, he could give a very plain and satisfactory exposition of the genial consequences of old abuses, the distinct necessity for stern reform, and the delicate humanity requisite for introducing that reform temperately and with feeling:

' Even so the Laird of Ellangowan ruthlessly commenced his magisterial reform, at the expense of various established and superannuated pickers and stealers, who had been his neighbours for half a century. He wrought his miracles like a second Duke Humphrey; and by the influence of the beadle's rod, caused the lame to walk, the blind to see, and the palsied to labour. He detected poachers, black-fishers, orchard-breakers, and pigeon-shooters; had the applause of the bench for his reward, and the public credit of an active magistrate.

' All this good had its rateable proportion of evil. Even an admitted nuisance, of ancient standing, should not be abated without some caution. The zeal of our worthy friend now involved in great distress sundry personages whose idle and mendicant habits his own *lâchesse* had contributed to foster, until these habits had become irreclaimable, or whose real incapacity for exertion rendered them fit objects, in their own phrase, for the charity of all well-disposed Christians. "The long-remembered beggar," who for twenty years had made his regular rounds within the neighbourhood, received rather as an humble friend than as an object of charity, was sent to the neighbouring workhouse. The decrepit dame, who travelled round the parish upon a hand-barrow, circulating from house to house like a bad shilling, which every one is in haste to pass to his neighbour; she, who used to call for her bearers as loud, or louder, than a traveller demands post-horses, even she shared the same disastrous fate. The " daft Jock," who, half knave, half idiot, had been the sport of each succeeding race of village children for a good part of a century, was remitted to the county bridewell, where, secluded from free air and sunshine, the only advantages he was capable of enjoying, he pined and died in the course of six months. The old sailor, who had so long rejoiced the smoky rafters of every kitchen in the country, by singing *Captain Ward* and *Bold Admiral Benbow*, was banished from the county for no better reason, than that he was supposed to speak with a strong Irish accent. Even the annual rounds of the pedlar were abolished by the Justice, in his hasty zeal for the administration of rural police.

' These things did not pass without notice and censure. We are not made of wood or stone, and the things which connect themselves with our hearts and habits cannot, like bark or lichen, be rent away without our missing them. The farmer's dame lacked her usual share of intelligence, perhaps also the self-applause which she had felt while distributing the *awmous*

(alms), in shape of a *gowpen* (handful) of oatmeal to the mendicant who brought the news. The cottage felt inconvenience
from interruption of the petty trade carried on by the itinerant
dealers. The children lacked their supply of sugar-plums
and toys; the young women wanted pins, ribbons, combs, and
ballads; and the old could no longer barter their eggs for salt,
snuff, and tobacco. All these circumstances brought the busy
Laird of Ellangowan into discredit, which was the more general
on account of his former popularity. Even his lineage was
brought up in judgment against him. They thought " nae-
thing of what the like of Greenside, or Burnville, or Viewforth,
might do, that were strangers in the country; but Ellangowan !
that had been a name amang them since the mirk Monanday,
and lang before—*him* to be grinding the puir at that rate !—
They ca'd his grandfather the Wicked Laird; but, though he
was whiles fractious aneuch, when he got into roving company,
and had ta'en the drap drink, he would have scorned to gang
on at this gate. Na, na, the muckle chumlay in the Auld Place
reeked like a killogie in his time, and there were as mony puir
folk riving at the banes in the court and about the door, as
there were gentles in the ha'. And the leddy, on ilka Christmas
night as it came round, gae twelve siller pennies to ilka puir
body about, in honour of the twelve apostles like. They were
fond to ca' it papistrie; but I think our great folk might take
a lesson frae the papists whiles. They gie another sort o' help
to puir folk than just dinging down a saxpence in the brod on
the Sabbath, and kilting, and scourging, and drumming them
a' the sax days o' the week besides." '

Many other indications of the same healthy and natural
sense, which gives so much of their characteristic charm to the
Scotch novels, might be pointed out, if it were necessary to
weary our readers by dwelling longer on a point we have already
laboured so much; one more, however, demands notice because
of its importance, and perhaps also because, from its somewhat
less obvious character, it might escape otherwise without notice.
There has been frequent controversy as to the penal code, if we
may so call it, of fiction; that is, as to the apportionment of
reward and punishment respectively to the good and evil personages therein delineated; and the practice of authors has
been as various as the legislation of critics. One school aban-

dons all thought on the matter, and declares that in the real life we see around us good people often fail, and wicked people continually prosper; and would deduce the precept, that it is unwise in an art which should hold the ' mirror up to nature,' not to copy the uncertain and irregular distribution of its sanctions. Another school, with an exactness which savours at times of pedantry, apportions the success and the failure, the pain and the pleasure, of fictitious life to the moral qualities of those who are living in it—does not think at all, or but little, of every other quality in those characters, and does not at all care whether the penalty and reward are evolved in natural sequence from the circumstances and characters of the tale, or are owing to some monstrous accident far removed from all relation of cause or consequence to those facts and people. Both these classes of writers produce works which jar on the natural sense of common readers, and are at issue with the analytic criticism of the best critics. One school leaves an impression of an uncared-for world, in which there is no right and no wrong; the other, of a sort of Governesses' Institution of a world, where all praise and all blame, all good and all pain, are made to turn on special graces and petty offences, pesteringly spoken of and teasingly watched for. The manner of Scott is thoroughly different; you can scarcely lay down any novel of his without a strong feeling that the world in which the fiction has been laid, and in which your imagination has been moving, is one subject to *laws* of retribution which, though not apparent on a superficial glance, are yet in steady and consistent operation, and will be quite sure to work their due effect, if time is only given to them. Sagacious men know that this is in its best aspect the condition of life. Certain of the ungodly may, notwithstanding the Psalmist, flourish even through life like a green bay-tree; for providence, in external appearance (far differently from the real truth of things, as we may one day see it), works by a scheme of averages. Most people who ought to succeed, do succeed; most people who do fail, ought to fail. But there is no exact adjustment of ' mark ' to merit; the competitive examination system appears to have an origin more recent than the creation of the world;—' on the whole,' ' speaking generally,' ' looking at life as a whole,' are the words in which we must describe the providential adjustment of visible good and evil to visible goodness and badness. And when we

look more closely, we see that these general results are the consequences of certain principles which work half unseen, and
which are effectual in the main, though thwarted here and
there. It is this comprehensive though inexact distribution of
good and evil, which is suited to the novelist, and it is exactly
this which Scott instinctively adopted. Taking a firm and genial
view of the common facts of life,—seeing it is an experienced
observer and tried man of action,—he could not help giving the
representation of it which is insensibly borne in on the minds
of such persons. He delineates it as a world moving according
to laws which are always producing their effect, never *have*
produced it; sometimes fall short a little; are always nearly
successful. Good sense produces its effect, as well as good intention; ability is valuable as well as virtue. It is this peculiarity which gives to his works, more than anything else, the
life-likeness which distinguishes them; the average of the copy
is struck on the same scale as that of reality; an unexplained,
uncommented-on adjustment works in the one, just as a
hidden, imperceptible principle of apportionment operates in
the other.

The romantic susceptibility of Scott's imagination is as
obvious in his novels as his matter-of-fact sagacity. We can
find much of it in the place in which we should naturally look
first for it,—his treatment of his heroines. We are no indiscriminate admirers of these young ladies, and shall shortly try
to show how much they are inferior as imaginative creations
to similar creations of the very highest artists. But the mode
in which the writer speaks of them everywhere indicates an
imagination continually under the illusion which we term
romance. A gentle tone of manly admiration pervades the
whole delineation of their words and actions. If we look carefully at the narratives of some remarkable female novelists—
it would be invidious to give the instances by name—we shall
be struck at once with the absence of this; they do not half
like their heroines. It would be satirical to say that they were
jealous of them; but it is certain that they analyse the mode in
which their charms produce their effects, and the minutiæ of
their operation, much in the same way in which a slightly
jealous lady examines the claims of the heroines of society.
The same writers have invented the atrocious species of *plain*
heroines. Possibly none of the frauds which are now so much

the topic of common remark are so irritating as that to which
the purchaser of a novel is a victim on finding that he has only
to peruse a narrative of the conduct and sentiments of an ugly
lady. 'Two-and-sixpence to know the heart which has high
cheek-bones!' Was there ever such an imposition? Scott
would have recoiled from such a conception. Even Jeanie
Deans, though no heroine, like Flora Macivor, is described as
'comely,' and capable of looking almost pretty when required,
and she has a compensating set-off in her sister, who is beautiful as well as unwise. Speaking generally, as is the necessity
of criticism, Scott makes his heroines, at least by profession,
attractive, and dwells on their attractiveness, though not with
the wild ecstasy of insane youth, yet with the tempered and
mellow admiration common to genial men of this world. Perhaps at times we are rather displeased at his explicitness, and
disposed to hang back and carp at the admirable qualities displayed to us. But this is only a stronger evidence of the peculiarity which we speak of,—of the unconscious sentiments
inseparable from Scott's imagination.

The same romantic tinge undeniably shows itself in Scott's
pictures of the past. Many exceptions have been taken to the
detail of mediæval life as it is described to us in *Ivanhoe*; but
one merit will always remain to it, and will be enough to secure
to it immense popularity. It describes the middle ages as we
should have wished them to have been. We do not mean that
the delineation satisfies those accomplished admirers of the old
church system who fancy that they have found among the pre-
lates and barons of the fourteenth century a close approximation to the theocracy which they would recommend for our
adoption. On the contrary, the theological merits of the
middle ages are not prominent in Scott's delineation. 'Dogma'
was not in his way: a cheerful man of the world is not anxious
for a precise definition of peculiar doctrines. The charm of
Ivanhoe is addressed to a simpler sort of imagination,—to that
kind of boyish fancy which idolises mediæval society as the
'fighting time.' Every boy has heard of tournaments, and has
a firm persuasion that in an age of tournaments life was thoroughly well understood. A martial society, where men fought
hand to hand on good horses with large lances, in peace for
pleasure, and in war for business, seems the very ideal of perfection to a bold and simply fanciful boy. *Ivanhoe* spreads

before him the full landscape of such a realm, with Richard Cœur-de-Lion, a black horse, and the passage of arms at Ashby. Of course he admires it, and thinks there was never such a writer, and will never more be such a world. And a mature critic will share his admiration, at least to the extent of admitting that nowhere else have the elements of a martial romance been so gorgeously accumulated without becoming oppressive; their fanciful charm been so powerfully delineated, and yet so constantly relieved by touches of vigorous sagacity. One single fact shows how great the romantic illusion is. The pressure of painful necessity is scarcely so great in this novel as in novels of the same writer in which the scene is laid in modern times. Much may be said in favour of the mediæval system as contradistinguished from existing society; much has been said. But no one can maintain that general comfort was as much diffused as it is now. A certain ease pervades the structure of later society. Our houses may not last so long, are not so picturesque, will leave no such ruins behind them; but they are warmed with hot water, have no draughts, and contain sofas instead of rushes. A slight daily unconscious luxury is hardly ever wanting to the dwellers in civilisation; like the gentle air of a genial climate, it is a perpetual minute enjoyment. The absence of this marks a rude barbaric time. We may avail ourselves of rough pleasures, stirring amusements, exciting actions, strange rumours; but life is hard and harsh. The cold air of the keen North may brace and invigorate, but it cannot soothe us. All sensible people know that the middle ages must have been very uncomfortable; there was a difficulty about ' good food; '—almost insuperable obstacles to the cultivation of nice detail and small enjoyment. No one knew the abstract facts on which this conclusion rests better than Scott; but his delineation gives no general idea of the result. A thoughtless reader rises with the impression that the middle ages had the same elements of happiness which we have at present, and that they had fighting besides. We do not assert that this tenet is explicitly taught; on the contrary, many facts are explained, and many customs elucidated from which a discriminating and deducing reader would infer the meanness of poverty and the harshness of barbarism. But these less imposing traits escape the rapid, and still more the boyish reader. His general impression is one of romance; and though, when

roused, Scott was quite able to take a distinct view of the opposing facts, he liked his own mind to rest for the most part in
the same pleasing illusion.

The same sort of historical romance is shown likewise in
Scott's picture of remarkable historical characters. His
Richard I. is the traditional Richard, with traits heightened and
ennobled in perfect conformity to the spirit of tradition. Some
illustration of the same quality might be drawn from his
delineations of the Puritan rebellions and the Cavalier enthusiasm. We might show that he ever dwells on the traits and
incidents most attractive to a genial and spirited imagination.
But the most remarkable instance of the power which romantic
illusion exercised over him is his delineation of Mary Queen
of Scots. He refused at one time of his life to write a biography
of that princess ' because his opinion was contrary to his feeling.' He evidently considered her guilt to be clearly established, and thought, with a distinguished lawyer, that he should
' direct a jury to find her guilty; ' but his fancy, like that of
most of his countrymen, took a peculiar and special interest in
the beautiful lady who, at any rate, had suffered so much and so
fatally at the hands of a queen of England. He could not bring
himself to dwell with nice accuracy on the evidence which substantiates her criminality, or on the still clearer indications of
that unsound and over-crafty judgment, which was the fatal
inheritance of the Stuart family, and which, in spite of advantages that scarcely any other family in the world has enjoyed,
has made their name an historical by-word for misfortune.
The picture in the *Abbot*, one of the best historical pictures
which Scott has given us, is principally the picture of the queen
as the fond tradition of his countrymen exhibited her. Her
entire innocence, it is true, is never alleged: but the enthusiasm of her followers is dwelt on with approving sympathy;
their confidence is set forth at large; her influence over them
is skilfully delineated; the fascination of charms chastened by
misfortune is delicately indicated. We see a complete picture
of the beautiful queen, of the suffering and sorrowful but yet
not insensible woman. Scott could not, however, as a close
study will show us, quite conceal the unfavourable nature
of his fundamental opinion. In one remarkable passage the
struggle of the judgment is even conspicuous, and in others
the sagacity of the practised lawyer,—the ' thread of the

attorney,' as he used to call it,—in his nature, qualifies and modifies the sentiment hereditary in his countrymen, and congenial to himself.

This romantic imagination is a habit or power (as we may choose to call it) of mind which is almost essential to the highest success in the historical novel. The aim, at any rate the effect, of this class of works seems to be to deepen and confirm the received view of historical personages. A great and acute writer may from an accurate study of original documents discover that those impressions are erroneous, and by a process of elaborate argument substitute others which he deems more accurate. But this can only be effected by writing a regular history. The essence of the achievement is the proof. If Mr. Froude had put forward his view of Henry the Eighth's character in a professed novel, he would have been laughed at. It is only by a rigid adherence to attested facts and authentic documents, that a view so original could obtain even a hearing. We start back with a little anger from a representation which is avowedly imaginative, and which contradicts our impressions. We do not like to have our opinions disturbed by reasoning; but it is impertinent to attempt to disturb them by fancies. A writer of the historical novel is bound by the popular conception of his subject; and commonly it will be found that this popular impression is to some extent a romantic one. An element of exaggeration clings to the popular judgment: great vices are made greater, great virtues greater also; interesting incidents are made more interesting, softer legends more soft. The novelist who disregards this tendency will do so at the peril of his popularity. His business is to make attraction more attractive, and not to impair the pleasant pictures of ready-made romance by an attempt at grim reality.

We may therefore sum up the indications of this characteristic excellence of Scott's novels by saying, that more than any novelist he has given us fresh pictures of practical human society, with its cares and troubles, its excitements and its pleasures; that he has delineated more distinctly than any one else the framework in which this society inheres, and by the boundaries of which it is shaped and limited; that he has made more clear the way in which strange and eccentric characters grow out of that ordinary and usual system of life; that he has extended his view over several periods of society, and given an

animated description of the external appearance of each, and a
firm representation of its social institutions; that he has shown
very graphically what we may call the worldly laws of moral
government; and that over all these he has spread the glow of
sentiment natural to a manly mind, and an atmosphere of
generosity congenial to a cheerful one. It is from the collective
effect of these causes, and from the union of sense and sentiment which is the principle of them all, that Scott derives the
peculiar healthiness which distinguishes him. There are no such
books as his for the sick-room, or for freshening the painful
intervals of a morbid mind. Mere sense is dull, mere sentiment unsubstantial; a sensation of genial healthiness is only
given by what combines the solidity of the one and the bright-
ening charm of the other.

Some guide to Scott's defects, or to the limitations of his
genius, if we would employ a less ungenial and perhaps more
correct expression, is to be discovered, as usual, from the consideration of his characteristic excellence. As it is his merit
to give bold and animated pictures of this world, it is his
defect to give but insufficient representations of qualities
which this world does not exceedingly prize,—of such as
do not thrust themselves very forward in it,—of such as
are in some sense above it. We may illustrate this in several
ways.

One of the parts of human nature which are systematically
omitted in Scott, is the searching and abstract intellect. This
did not lie in his way. No man had a stronger sagacity, better
adapted for the guidance of common men, and the conduct of
common transactions. Few could hope to form a more correct
opinion on things and subjects which were brought before him
in actual life; no man had a more useful intellect. But on the
other hand, as will be generally observed to be the case, no one
was less inclined to that probing and seeking and anxious inquiry into things in general which is the necessity of some
minds, and a sort of intellectual famine in their nature. He
had no call to investigate the theory of the universe, and he
would not have been able to comprehend those who did. Such
a mind as Shelley's would have been entirely removed from his
comprehension. He had no call to mix ' awful talk and asking
looks ' with his love of the visible scene. He could not have
addressed the universe:

'I have watched
Thy shadow, and the darkness of thy steps;
And my heart ever gazes on the depth
Of thy deep mysteries.   I have made my bed
In charnels and on coffins, where black death
Keeps record of the trophies won from thee,
Hoping to still these obstinate questionings
Of thee and thine, by forcing some lone ghost,
Thy messenger, to render up the tale
Of what we are.'

Such thoughts would have been to him 'thinking without an object,' 'abstracted speculations,' 'cobwebs of the unintelligible brain.' Above all minds his had the Baconian propensity to work upon 'stuff.' At first sight, it would not seem that this was a defect likely to be very hurtful to the works of a novelist. The labours of the searching and introspective intellect, however needful, absorbing, and in some degree delicious, to the seeker himself, are not in general very delightful to those who are not seeking. Genial men in middle life are commonly intolerant of that philosophising which their prototype in old times classed side by side with the lisping of youth. The theological novel, which was a few years ago so popular, and which is likely to have a recurring influence in times when men's belief is unsettled, and persons who cannot or will not read large treatises have thoughts in their minds and inquiries in their hearts, suggests to those who are accustomed to it the absence elsewhere of what is necessarily one of its most distinctive and prominent subjects. The desire to attain a belief, which has become one of the most familiar sentiments of heroes and heroines, would have seemed utterly incongruous to the plain sagacity of Scott, and also to his old-fashioned art. Creeds are *data* in his novels; people have different creeds, but each keeps his own. Some persons will think that this is not altogether amiss; nor do we particularly wish to take up the defence of the dogmatic novel. Nevertheless, it will strike those who are accustomed to the youthful generation of a cultivated time, that the passion of intellectual inquiry is one of the strongest impulses in many of them, and one of those which give the predominant colouring to the conversation and exterior mind of many more. And a novelist will not exercise the most potent influence over those subject to that passion if he entirely omit the delineation of it. Scott's works have only one merit in this relation: they are an excellent rest to those who have felt this passion, and have had something too much of it.

The same indisposition to the abstract exercises of the intellect shows itself in the reflective portions of Scott's novels, and perhaps contributes to their popularity with that immense majority of the world who strongly share in that same indisposition: it prevents, however, their having the most powerful intellectual influence on those who have at any time of their lives voluntarily submitted themselves to this acute and refining discipline. The reflections of a practised thinker have a peculiar charm, like the last touches of the accomplished artist. The cunning exactitude of the professional hand leaves a trace in the very language. A nice discrimination of thought makes men solicitous of the most apt expressions to diffuse their thoughts. Both words and meaning gain a metallic brilliancy, like the glittering precision of the pure Attic air. Scott's is a healthy and genial world of reflection, but it wants the charm of delicate exactitude.

The same limitation of Scott's genius shows itself in a very different portion of art—in his delineation of his heroines. The same blunt sagacity of imagination, which fitted him to excel in the rough description of obvious life, rather unfitted him for delineating the less substantial essence of the female character. The nice *minutiæ* of society, by means of which female novelists have been so successful in delineating their own sex, were rather too small for his robust and powerful mind. Perhaps, too, a certain unworldliness of *imagination* is necessary to enable men to comprehend or delineate that essence: unworldliness of *life* is no doubt not requisite; rather, perhaps, worldliness is necessary to the acquisition of a sufficient experience. But an absorption in the practical world does not seem favourable to a comprehension of anything which does not precisely belong to it. Its interests are too engrossing; its excitements too keen; it modifies the fancy, and in the change unfits it for everything else. Something, too, in Scott's character and history made it more difficult for him to give a representation of women than of men. Goethe used to say, that his idea of woman was not drawn from his experience, but that it came to him before experience, and that he explained his experience by a reference to it. And though this is a German, and not very happy, form of expression, yet it appears to indicate a very important distinction. Some efforts of the imagination are made so early in life, just as it were at the dawn of the conscious faculites, that we are never able to fancy ourselves as destitute of them. They are part of the mental constitution with which, so to speak, we awoke to existence. These are always far more firm, vivid, and definite, than any other images of our fancy, and we apply them, half unconsciously, to any facts and sentiments and actions which may occur to us later in life, whether arising from within or thrust upon us from the outward world. Goethe doubtless meant that the idea of the female character was to him one of these first elements of imagination; not a thing puzzled out, or which he remembered having conceived, but a part of the primitive conceptions which, being coeval with his memory, seemed inseparable from his consciousness. The descriptions of women likely to be given by this sort of imagination will probably be the best descriptions. A mind which would arrive at this idea of the female character by this process, and so early, would be one obviously of more than usual susceptibility. The early imagination does not commonly take this direction; it thinks most of horses and lances, tournaments and knights; only a mind with an unusual and instinctive tendency to this kind of thought, would be borne thither so early or so effectually. And even independently of this probable peculiarity of the individual, the primitive imagination in general is likely to be the most accurate which men can form; not, of course, of the external manifestations and detailed manners, but of the inner sentiment and characteristic feeling of women. The early imagination conceives what it does conceive very justly; fresh from the facts, stirred by the new aspect of things, undimmed by the daily passage of constantly forgotten images, not misled by the irregular analogies of a dislocated life,—the early mind sees what it does see with a spirit and an intentness never given to it again. A mind like Goethe's, of very strong imagination, aroused at the earliest age,—not of course by passions, but by an unusual strength in that undefined longing which is the prelude to our passions,—will form the best idea of the inmost female nature which masculine nature can form. The trace is evident in the characters of women formed by Goethe's imagination or Shakespeare's, and those formed by such an imagination as that of Scott. The latter seem so external. We have traits, features, manners; we know the heroine as she appeared in the street; in some degree we know how she talked, but we never know how she felt—least of all what she was: we always feel there is a world behind, unanalysed, unrepresented, which we cannot attain to. Such a character as Margaret in *Faust* is known to us to the very soul; so is Imogen; so is Ophelia. Edith Bellenden, Flora Macivor, Miss Wardour, are young ladies who, we are told, were good-looking, and well-dressed (according to the old fashion), and sensible; but we feel we know but very little of them, and they do not haunt our imaginations. The failure of Scott in this line of art is more conspicuous, because he had not in any remarkable degree the later experience of female detail, with which some minds have endeavoured to supply the want of the early essential imagination, and which Goethe possessed in addition to it. It was rather late, according to his biographer, before Scott set up for a 'squire of dames;' he was a 'lame young man, very enthusiastic about ballad poetry;' he was deeply in love with a young lady, supposed to be imaginatively represented by Flora Macivor, but he was unsuccessful. It would be over-ingenious to argue, from his failing in a single love-affair, that he had no peculiar interest in young ladies in general; but the whole description of his youth shows that young ladies exercised over him a rather more divided influence than is usual. Other pursuits intervened, much more than is common with persons of the imaginative temperament, and he never led the life of flirtation from which Goethe believed that he derived so much instruction. Scott's heroines, therefore, are, not unnaturally, faulty, since from a want of the very peculiar instinctive imagination he could not give us the essence of women, and from the habits of his life he could not delineate to us their detailed life with the appreciative accuracy of habitual experience. Jeanie Deans is probably the best of his heroines, and she is so because she is the least of a heroine. The plain matter-of-fact element in the peasant-girl's life and circumstances suited a robust imagination. There is little in the part of her character that is very finely described which is characteristically feminine. She is not a masculine, but she is an epicene heroine. Her love-affair with Butler, a single remarkable scene excepted, is rather commonplace than otherwise.

A similar criticism might be applied to Scott's heroes. Everyone feels how commonplace they are—Waverley excepted, whose very vacillation gives him a sort of character. They have little personality. They are all of the same type;—excellent young men—rather strong—able to ride and climb and jump. They are always said to be sensible, and bear out the character by being not unwilling sometimes to talk platitudes. But we know nothing of their inner life. They are said to be in love; but we have no special account of their individual sentiments. People show their character in their love more than in anything else. These young gentlemen all love in the same way—in the vague commonplace way of this world. We have no sketch or dramatic expression of the life within. Their souls are quite unknown to us. If there is an exception, it is Edgar Ravenswood. But if we look closely, we may observe that the notion which we obtain of his character, unusually broad as it is, is not a notion of him in his capacity of hero, but in his capacity of distressed peer. His proud poverty gives a distinctness which otherwise his lineaments would not have. We think little of his love; we think much of his narrow circumstances and compressed haughtiness.

The same exterior delineation of character shows itself in his treatment of men's religious nature. A novelist is scarcely, in the notion of ordinary readers, bound to deal with this at all; if he does, it will be one of his great difficulties to indicate it graphically, yet without dwelling on it. Men who purchase a novel do not wish a stone or a sermon. All lengthened reflections must be omitted; the whole armoury of pulpit eloquence. But no delineation of human nature can be considered complete which omits to deal with man in relation to the questions which occupy him as man, with his convictions as to the theory of the universe and his own destiny; the human heart throbs on few subjects with a passion so intense, so peculiar, and so typical. From an artistic view, it is a blunder to omit an element which is so characteristic of human life, which contributes so much to its animation, and which is so picturesque. A reader of a more simple mind, little apt to indulge in such criticism, feels 'a want of depth,' as he would speak, in delineations from which so large an element of his own most passionate and deepest nature is omitted. It can hardly be said that there is an omission of the religious nature in Scott. But at the same time there is no adequate delineation of it. If we refer to the facts of his life, and the view of his character which we collect from them, we shall find that his religion was of a qualified and double sort. He was a genial man of the world, and had the easy faith in the kindly *Dieu des bons gens* which is natural to such a person; and he had also a half-poetic principle of superstition in his nature, inclining him to believe in ghosts, legends, fairies, and elfs, which did not affect his daily life, or possibly his superficial belief, but was nevertheless very constantly present to his fancy, and affected, as is the constitution of human nature, by that frequency, the indefined, half-expressed, inexpressible feelings which are at the root of that belief. Superstition was a kind of Jacobitism in his religion; as a sort of absurd reliance on the hereditary principle modified insensibly his leanings in the practical world, so a belief in the existence of unevidenced, and often absurd, supernatural beings qualified his commonest speculations on the higher world. Both these elements may be thought to enter into the highest religion; there is a principle of cheerfulness which will justify in its measure a genial enjoyment, and also a principle of fear which those who think only of that enjoyment will deem superstition, and which will really become superstition in the over-anxious and credulous acceptor of it. But in a true religion these two elements will be combined. The character of God images itself very imperfectly in any human soul; but in the highest it images itself as a whole; it leaves an abiding impression which will justify anxiety and allow of happiness. The highest aim of the religious novelist would be to show how this operates in human character; to exhibit in their curious modification our religious love, and also our religious fear. In the novels of Scott the two elements appear in a state of separation, as they did in his own mind. We have the superstition of the peasantry in the *Antiquary*, in *Guy Mannering*, everywhere almost; we have likewise a pervading tone of genial easy reflection characteristic of the man of the world who produced, and agreeable to the people of the world who read, these works. But we have no picture of the two in combination. We are scarcely led to think on the subject at all, so much do other subjects distract our interest; but if we do think, we are puzzled at the contrast. We do not know which is true, the uneasy belief of superstition, or the easy satisfaction of the world; we waver between the two, and have no suggestion even hinted to us of the possibility of a reconciliation. The character of the Puritans certainly did not in general embody such a reconciliation, but it might have been made by a sympathising artist the vehicle for a delineation of a struggle after it. The two elements of love and fear ranked side by side in their minds with an intensity which is rare even in minds that feel only one of them. The delineation of Scott is amusing, but superficial. He caught the ludicrous traits which tempt the mirthful imagination, but no other side of the character pleased him. The man of the world was displeased with their obstinate interfering zeal; their intensity of faith was an opposition force in the old Scotch polity, of which he liked to fancy the harmonious working. They were superstitious enough; but nobody likes other people's superstitions. Scott's were of a wholly different kind. He made no difficulty as to the observance of Christmas-day, and would have eaten potatoes without the faintest scruple, although their name does not occur in Scripture. Doubtless also his residence in the land of Puritanism did not incline him to give anything except a satirical representation of that belief. You must not expect from a Dissenter a faithful appreciation of the creed from which he dissents. You cannot be impartial on the religion of the place in which you live; you may believe it, or you may dislike it; it crosses your path in too many forms for you to be able to look at it with equanimity. Scott had rather a rigid form of Puritanism forced upon him in his infancy; it is asking too much to expect him to be partial to it. The aspect of religion which Scott delineates best is that which appears in griefs, especially in the grief of strong characters. His strong *natural* nature felt the power of death. He has given us many pictures of rude and simple men subdued, if only for a moment, into devotion by its presence.

On the whole, and speaking roughly, these defects in the delineation which Scott has given us of human life are but two. He omits to give us a delineation of the soul. We have mind, manners, animation, but it is the stir of this world. We miss the consecrating power; and we miss it not only in its own peculiar sphere, which, from the difficulty of introducing the deepest elements into a novel, would have been scarcely matter for a harsh criticism, but in the place in which a novelist might most be expected to delineate it. There are perhaps such things as the love affairs of immortal beings, but no one would learn it from Scott. His heroes and heroines are well dressed for this world, but not for another; there is nothing even in their love which is suitable for immortality. As has been noticed, Scott also omits any delineation of the abstract unworldly intellect. This too might not have been so severe a reproach, considering its undramatic, unanimated nature, if it had stood alone; but taken in connection with the omission which we have just spoken of, it is most important. As the union of sense and romance makes the world of Scott so characteristically agreeable,—a fascinating picture of this world in the light in which we like best to dwell on it, so the deficiency in the attenuated, striving intellect, as well as in the supernatural soul, gives to the ' world ' of Scott the cumbrousness and temporality, in short, the materialism, which is characteristic of the world.

We have dwelt so much on what we think are the characteristic features of Scott's imaginative representations, that we have left ourselves no room to criticise the two most natural points of criticism in a novelist—plot and style. This is not, however, so important in Scott's case as it would commonly be. He used to say, ' It was no use having a plot; you could not keep to it.' He modified and changed his thread of story from day to day,—sometimes even from bookselling reasons, and on the suggestion of others. An elaborate work of narrative art could not be produced in this way, every one will concede; the highest imagination, able to look far over the work, is necessary for that task. But the plots produced, so to say, by the pen of the writer as he passes over the events are likely to have a freshness and a suitableness to those events, which is not possessed by the inferior writers who make up a mechanical plot before they commence. The procedure of the highest genius doubtless is scarcely a procedure; the view of the whole story comes at once upon its imagination like the delicate end and the distinct beginning of some long vista. But all minds do not possess the highest mode of conception; and among lower modes, it is doubtless better to possess the vigorous fancy which creates each separate scene in

2   G

succession as it goes, than the pedantic intellect which design
everything long before it is wanted. There is a play in uncon
scious creation which no voluntary elaboration and precon
ceived fitting of distinct ideas can ever hope to produce. I
the whole cannot be created by one bounding effort, it is bette
that each part should be created separately and in detail.

The style of Scott would deserve the highest praise if M
Thiers could establish his theory of narrative language. H
maintains that an historian's language approaches perfection ir
proportion as it aptly communicates what is meant to be
narrated without drawing any attention to itself. Scott's style
fulfils this condition. Nobody rises from his works without a
most vivid idea of what is related, and no one is able to quote a
single phrase in which it has been narrated. We are inclined
however, to differ from the great French historian, and to
oppose to him a theory derived from a very different writer
Coleridge used to maintain that all good poetry was untrans
latable into words of the same language without injury to the
sense; the meaning was, in his view, to be so inseparably
intertwined even with the shades of the language, that the
change of a single expression would make a difference in the
accompanying feeling, if not in the bare signification: con
sequently, all good poetry must be remembered exactly,—to
change a word is to modify the essence. Rigidly this theory
can only be applied to a few kinds of poetry, or special passages
in which the imagination is exerting itself to the utmost, and
collecting from the whole range of associated language the
very expressions which it requires. The highest excitation of
feeling is necessary to this peculiar felicity of choice. In
calmer moments the mind has either a less choice, or less
acuteness of selective power. Accordingly, in prose it would
be absurd to expect any such nicety. Still, on great occasions
in imaginative fiction, there should be passages in which the
words seem to cleave to the matter. The excitement is as
great as in poetry. The words should become part of the
sense. They should attract our attention, as this is necessary
to impress them on the memory; but they should not in so
doing distract attention from the meaning conveyed. On the
contrary, it is their inseparability from their meaning which
gives them their charm and their power. In truth, Scott's
language, like his sense, was such as became a bold sagacious

man of the world. He used the first sufficient words which
came uppermost, and seems hardly to have been sensible, even
in the works of others, of that exquisite accuracy and inexplicable appropriateness of which we have been speaking.

To analyse in detail the faults and merits of even a few of
the greatest of the Waverley Novels would be impossible in
the space at our command on the present occasion. We have
only attempted a general account of a few main characteristics.
Every critic must, however, regret to have to leave topics so
tempting to remark as many of Scott's stories, and a yet
greater number of his characters.

Charles Dickens*
(1858)

IT must give Mr. Dickens much pleasure to look at the collected
series of his writings. He has told us of the beginnings of
Pickwick. 'I was,' he relates in what is now the preface to
that work, 'a young man of three-and-twenty, when the
present publishers, attracted by some pieces I was at that
time writing in the *Morning Chronicle* newspaper (of which one
series had lately been collected and published in two volumes,
illustrated by my esteemed friend Mr. George Cruikshank),
waited upon me to propose a something that should be published in shilling numbers—then only known to me, or I
believe to anybody else, by a dim recollection of certain inter-
minable novels in that form, which used, some five-and-
twenty years ago, to be carried about the country by pedlars,
and over some of which I remember to have shed innumerable
tears, before I served my apprenticeship to Life. When I
opened my door in Furnival's Inn to the managing partner
who represented the firm, I recognised in him the person from
whose hands I had bought, two or three years previously,
and whom I had never seen before or since, my first copy of
the magazine in which my first effusion—dropped stealthily
one evening at twilight, with fear and trembling, into a dark
letter-box, in a dark office, up a dark court in Fleet Street—
appeared in all the glory of print; on which occasion, by the by,
—how well I recollect it!—I walked down to Westminster
Hall, and turned into it for half-an-hour, because my eyes were
so dimmed with joy and pride, that they could not bear the
street, and were not fit to be seen there. I told my visitor
of the coincidence, which we both hailed as a good omen;
and so fell to business.'

*Cheap Edition of the Works of Mr. Charles Dickens. The Pick-
wick Papers, Nicholas Nickleby, &c.* London, 1857-8. Chapman and
Hall.

After such a beginning, there must be great enjoyment in looking at the long series of closely printed green volumes, in remembering their marvellous popularity, in knowing that they are a familiar literature wherever the English language is spoken,—that they are read with admiring appreciation by persons of the highest culture at the centre of civilisation,—that they amuse, and are fit to amuse, the roughest settler in Vancouver's Island.

The penetrating power of this remarkable genius among all classes at home is not inferior to its diffusive energy abroad. The phrase ' household book ' has, when applied to the works of Mr. Dickens, a peculiar propriety. There is no contemporary English writer, whose works are read so generally through the whole house, who can give pleasure to the servants as well as to the mistress, to the children as well as to the master. Mr. Thackeray without doubt exercises a more potent and plastic fascination within his sphere, but that sphere is limited. It is restricted to that part of the middle class which gazes inquisitively at the ' Vanity Fair ' world. The delicate touches of our great satirist have, for such readers, not only the charm of wit, but likewise the interest of valuable information; he tells them of the topics which they want to know. But below this class there is another and far larger, which is incapable of comprehending the idling world, or of appreciating the accuracy of delineations drawn from it,—which would not know the difference between a picture of Grosvenor Square by Mr. Thackeray and the picture of it in a Minerva-Press novel,—which only cares for or knows of its own multifarious, industrial, fig-selling world,—and over these also Mr. Dickens has power.

It cannot be amiss to take this opportunity of investigating, even slightly, the causes of so great a popularity. And if, in the course of our article, we may seem to be ready with over-refining criticism, or to be unduly captious with theoretical objection, we hope not to forget that so great and so diffused an influence is a *datum* for literary investigation,—that books which have been thus *tried* upon mankind and have thus succeeded, must be books of immense genius,—and that it is our duty as critics to explain, as far as we can, the nature and the limits of that genius, but never for one moment to deny or question its existence.

Men of genius may be divided into regular and irregular
Certain minds, the moment we think of them, suggest to us
the ideas of symmetry and proportion. Plato's name, for
example, calls up at once the impression of something ordered
measured, and settled: it is the exact contrary of everything
eccentric, immature, or undeveloped. The opinions of such a
mind are often erroneous, and some of them may, from change
of time, of intellectual *data*, or from chance, seem not to be quite
worthy of it; but the mode in which those opinions are
expressed, and (as far as we can make it out) the mode in which
they are framed, affect us, as we have said, with a sensation of
symmetricalness. It is not very easy to define exactly to what
peculiar internal characteristic this external effect is due: the
feeling is distinct, but the cause is obscure; it lies hid in the
peculiar constitution of great minds, and we should not wonder
that it is not very easy either to conceive or to describe. On
the whole, however, the effect seems to be produced by a
peculiar proportionateness, in each instance, of the mind to
the tasks which it undertakes, amid which we see it, and by
which we measure it. Thus we feel that the powers and
tendencies of Plato's mind and nature were more fit than those
of any other philosopher for the due consideration and
exposition of the highest problems of philosophy, of the doubts
and difficulties which concern man as man. His genius was
adapted to its element; any change would mar the delicacy
of the thought, or the polished accuracy of the expression.
The weapon was fitted to its aim. Every instance of proportionateness does not, however, lead us to attribute this
peculiar symmetry to the whole mind we are observing. The
powers must not only be suited to the task undertaken,
but the task itself must also be suited to a human being, and
employ all the marvellous faculties with which he is endowed.
The neat perfection of such a mind as Talleyrand's is the
antithesis to the symmetry of genius; the niceties neither of
diplomacy nor of conversation give scope to the entire powers
of a great nature. We may lay down as the condition of a
regular or symmetrical genius, that it should have the exact
combination of powers suited to graceful and easy success in
an exercise of mind great enough to task the whole intellectual
nature.

On the other hand, men of irregular or unsymmetrical genius

are eminent either for some one or some few peculiarities of mind, have possibly special defects on other sides of their intellectual nature, at any rate want what the scientific men of the present day would call the *definite proportion* of faculties and qualities suited to the exact work they have in hand. The foundation of many criticisms of Shakespeare is that he is deficient in this peculiar proportion. His overteeming imagination gives at times, and not unfrequently, a great feeling of irregularity: there seems to be confusion. We have the tall trees of the forest, the majestic creations of the highest genius; but we have besides, a bushy second growth, an obtrusion of secondary images and fancies, which prevent our taking an exact measure of such grandeur. We have not the sensation of intense simplicity, which must probably accompany the highest conceivable greatness. Such is also the basis of Mr. Hallam's criticism on Shakespeare's language, which Mr. Arnold has lately revived. ' His expression is often faulty,' because his illustrative imagination, somewhat predominating over his other faculties, diffuses about the main expression a supplement of minor metaphors which sometimes distract the comprehension, and almost always deprive his style of the charm that arises from undeviating directness. Doubtless this is an instance of the very highest kind of irregular genius, in which all the powers exist in the mind in a very high, and almost all of them in the very highest measure, but in which from a slight excess in a single one, the charm of proportion is lessened. The most ordinary cases of irregular genius are those in which single faculties are abnormally developed, and call off the attention from all the rest of the mind by their prominence and activity. Literature, as the ' fragment of fragments,' is so full of the fragments of such minds that it is needless to specify instances.

Possibly it may be laid down that one of two elements is essential to a symmetrical mind. It is evident that such a mind must either apply itself to that which is theoretical or that which is practical, to the world of abstraction or to the world of objects and realities. In the former case the deductive understanding, which masters first principles, and makes deductions from them, the thin ether of the intellect,—the ' mind itself by itself,'—must evidently assume a great prominence. To attempt to comprehend principles without it, is to try to swim without arms, or to fly without wings. Accordingly, in the mind of Plato, and in others like him, the abstract and deducing understanding fills a great place; the imagination seems a kind of eye to descry its data; the artistic instinct an arranging impulse, which sets in order its inferences and conclusions. On the other hand, if a symmetrical mind busy itself with the active side of human life, with the world of concrete men and real things, its principal quality will be a practical sagacity, which forms with ease a distinct view and just appreciation of all the mingled objects that the world presents,—which allots to each its own place, and its intrinsic and appropriate rank. Possibly no mind gives such an idea of this sort of symmetry as Chaucer's. Everything in it seems in its place. A healthy sagacious man of the world has gone through the world; he loves it, and knows it; he dwells on it with a fond appreciation; every object of the old life of 'merry England' seems to fall into its precise niche in his ordered and symmetrical comprehension. The *Prologue to the Canterbury Tales* is in itself a series of memorial tablets to mediæval society; each class has its tomb, and each its apt inscription. A man without such an apprehensive and broad sagacity must fail in every extensive delineation of various life; he might attempt to describe what he did not penetrate, or if by a rare discretion he avoided that mistake, his works would want the *binding element;* he would be deficient in that distinct sense of relation and combination which is necessary for the depiction of the whole of life, which gives to it unity at first, and imparts to it a mass in the memory ever afterwards. And eminence in one or other of these marking faculties,—either in the deductive abstract intellect, or the practical seeing sagacity,—seems essential to the mental constitution of a symmetrical genius, at least in man. There are, after all, but two principal all-important spheres in human life—thought and action; and we can hardly conceive of a masculine mind symmetrically developed, which did not evince its symmetry by an evident perfection in one or other of those pursuits, which did not leave the trace of its distinct reflection upon the one, or of its large insight upon the other of them. Possibly it may be thought that in the sphere of pure art there may be room for a symmetrical development different from these; but it will perhaps be found, on examination

Charles Dickens 169

of such cases, either that under peculiar and appropriate disguises one of these great qualities is present, or that the apparent symmetry is the narrow perfection of a limited nature, which may be most excellent in itself, as in the stricter form of sacred art, but which, as we explained, is quite opposed to that broad perfection of the thinking being to which we have applied the name of the symmetry of genius.

If this classification of men of genius be admitted, there can be no hesitation in assigning to Mr. Dickens his place in it. His genius is essentially irregular and unsymmetrical. Hardly any English writer perhaps is much more so. His style is an example of it. It is descriptive, racy, and flowing; it is instinct with new imagery and singular illustration; but it does not indicate that due proportion of the faculties to one another which is a beauty in itself, and which cannot help diffusing beauty over every happy word and moulded clause. We may choose an illustration at random. The following graphic description will do:

'If Lord George Gordon had appeared in the eyes of Mr. Willet, overnight, a nobleman of somewhat quaint and odd exterior, the impression was confirmed this morning, and increased an hundredfold. Sitting bolt upright upon his bony steed, with his long, straight hair, dangling about his face and fluttering in the wind; his limbs all angular and rigid, his elbows stuck out on either side ungracefully, and his whole frame jogged and shaken at every motion of his horse's feet; a more grotesque or more ungainly figure can hardly be conceived. In lieu of whip, he carried in his hand a great gold-headed cane, as large as any footman carries in these days; and his various modes of holding this unwieldy weapon—now upright before his face like the sabre of a horse-soldier, now over his shoulder like a musket, now between his finger and thumb, but always in some uncouth and awkward fashion—contributed in no small degree to the absurdity of his appearance. Stiff, lank, and solemn, dressed in an unusual manner, and ostentatiously exhibiting—whether by design or accident—all his peculiarities of carriage, gesture, and conduct: all the qualities, natural and artificial, in which he differed from other men; he might have moved the sternest looker-on to laughter, and fully provoked the smiles and

G2

whispered jests which greeted his departure from the Maypole Inn.

' Quite unconscious, however, of the effect he produced, he trotted on beside his secretary, talking to himself nearly all the way, until they came within a mile or two of London, when now and then some passenger went by who knew him by sight, and pointed him out to some one else, and perhaps stood looking after him, or cried in jest or earnest as it might be, " Hurrah, Geordie ! No Popery ! " At which he would gravely pull off his hat, and bow. When they reached the town and rode along the streets, these notices became more frequent; some laughed, some hissed, some turned their heads and smiled, some wondered who he was, some ran along the pavement by his side and cheered. When this happened in a crush of carts and chairs and coaches, he would make a dead stop, and pulling off his hat, cry, " Gentlemen, No Popery ! " to which the gentlemen would respond with lusty voices, and with three times three; and then, on he would go again with a score or so of the raggedest, following at his horse's heels, and shouting till their throats were parched.

' The old ladies too—there were a great many old ladies in the streets, and these all knew him. Some of them—not those of the highest rank, but such as sold fruit from baskets and carried burdens—clapped their shrivelled hands, and raised a weazen, piping, shrill " Hurrah, my lord." Others waved their hands or handkerchiefs, or shook their fans or parasols, or threw up windows, and called in haste to those within, to come and see. All these marks of popular esteem he received with profound gravity and respect; bowing very low, and so frequently that his hat was more off his head than on; and looking up at the houses as he passed along, with the air of one who was making a public entry, and yet was not puffed-up or proud.'

No one would think of citing such a passage as this, as exemplifying the proportioned beauty of finished writing; it is not the writing of an evenly developed or of a highly cultured mind; it abounds in jolts and odd turns; it is full of singular twists and needless complexities; but, on the other hand, no one can deny its great and peculiar merit. It is an odd style, and it is very odd how much you read it. It is the overflow of a copious mind, though not the chastened expression of an harmonious one.

The same quality characterises the matter of his works. His range is very varied. He has attempted to describe every kind of scene in English life, from quite the lowest to almost the highest. He has not endeavoured to secure success by confining himself to a single path, nor wearied the public with repetitions of the subjects by the delineation of which he originally obtained fame. In his earlier works he never writes long without saying something well; something which no other man would have said; but even in them it is the characteristic of his power that it is apt to fail him at once; from masterly strength we pass without interval to almost infantine weakness,—something like disgust succeeds in a moment to an extreme admiration. Such is the natural fate of an unequal mind employing itself on a vast and various subject. On a recent occasion we ventured to make a division of novels into the ubiquitous,—it would have been perhaps better to say the miscellaneous,—and the sentimental; the first, as its name implies, busying itself with the whole of human life, the second restricting itself within a peculiar and limited theme. Mr. Dickens's novels are all of the former class. They aim to delineate nearly all that part of our national life which can be delineated, —at least, within the limits which social morality prescribes to social art; but you cannot read his delineation of any part without being struck with its singular incompleteness. An artist once said of the best work of another artist, ' Yes, it is a pretty patch.' If we might venture on the phrase, we should say that Mr. Dickens's pictures are graphic scraps; his best books are compilations of them.

The truth is, that Mr. Dickens wholly wants the two elements which we have spoken of as one or other requisite for a symmetrical genius. He is utterly deficient in the faculty of reasoning. ' Mamma, what shall I think about ? ' said the small girl. ' My dear, don't think,' was the old-fashioned reply. We do not allege that in the strict theory of education this was a correct reply; modern writers think otherwise; but we wish some one would say it to Mr. Dickens. He is often troubled with the idea that he must reflect, and his reflections are perhaps the worst reading in the world. There is a sentimental confusion about them; we never find the consecutive precision of mature

theory, or the cold distinctness of clear thought. Vivid facts
stand out in his imagination; and a fresh illustrative style
brings them home to the imagination of his readers; but his
continuous philosophy utterly fails in the attempt to harmonise
them,—to educe a theory or elaborate a precept from them.
Of his social thinking we shall have a few words to say in
detail; his didactic humour is very unfortunate: no writer is
less fitted for an excursion to the imperative mood. At
present, we only say, what is so obvious as scarcely to need
saying, that his abstract understanding is so far inferior to his
picturesque imagination as to give even to his best works the
sense of jar and incompleteness, and to deprive them altogether
of the crystalline finish which is characteristic of the clear and
cultured understanding.

Nor has Mr. Dickens the easy and various sagacity which,
as has been said, gives a unity to all which it touches. He
has, indeed, a quality which is near allied to it in appearance.
His shrewdness in some things, especially in traits and small
things, is wonderful. His works are full of acute remarks on
petty doings, and well exemplify the telling power of minute
circumstantiality. But the minor species of perceptive sharp-
ness is so different from diffused sagacity, that the two scarcely
ever are to be found in the same mind. There is nothing less
like the great lawyer, acquainted with broad principles and
applying them with distinct deduction, than the attorney's
clerk who catches at small points like a dog biting at flies.
'Over-sharpness' in the student is the most unpromising
symptom of the logical jurist. You must not ask a horse in
blinkers for a large view of a landscape. In the same way, a
detective ingenuity in microscopic detail is of all mental
qualities most unlike the broad sagacity by which the great
painters of human affairs have unintentionally stamped the
mark of unity on their productions. They show by their
treatment of each case that they understand the whole of life;
the special delineator of fragments and points shows that he
understands them only. In one respect the defect is more
striking in Mr. Dickens than in any other novelist of the present
day. The most remarkable deficiency in modern fiction is its
omission of the business of life, of all those countless occupations, pursuits, and callings in which most men live and move,
and by which they have their being. In most novels money

grows. You have no idea of the toil, the patience, and the wearing anxiety by which men of action provide for the day, and lay up for the future, and support those that are given into their care. Mr. Dickens is not chargeable with this omission. He perpetually deals with the pecuniary part of life. Almost all his characters have determined occupations, of which he is apt to talk even at too much length. When he rises from the toiling to the luxurious classes, his genius in most cases deserts him. The delicate refinement and discriminating taste of the idling orders are not in his way; he knows the dry arches of London Bridge better than Belgravia. He excels in inventories of poor furniture, and is learned in pawnbrokers' tickets. But, although his creative power lives and works among the middle class and industrial section of English society, he has never painted the highest part of their daily intellectual life. He made, indeed, an attempt to paint specimens of the apt and able man of business in *Nicholas Nickleby*; but the Messrs. Cheeryble are among the stupidest of his characters. He forgot that breadth of platitude is rather different from breadth of sagacity. His delineations of middle-class life have in consequence a harshness and meanness which do not belong to that life in reality. He omits the relieving element. He describes the figs which are sold, but not the talent which sells figs well. And it is the same want of the diffused sagacity in his own nature which has made his pictures of life so odd and disjointed, and which has deprived them of symmetry and unity.

The *bizarrerie* of Mr. Dickens's genius is rendered more remarkable by the inordinate measure of his special excellences. The first of these is his power of observation in detail. We have heard,—we do not know whether correctly or incorrectly,—that he can go down a crowded street, and tell you all that is in it, what each shop was, what the grocer's name was, how many scraps of orange-peel there were on the pavement. His works give you exactly the same idea. The amount of detail which there is in them is something amazing,—to an ordinary writer something incredible. There are single pages containing telling minutiæ which other people would have thought enough for a volume. Nor is his sensibility to external objects, though omnivorous, insensible to the artistic effect of each. There are scarcely anywhere such pictures of London as he draws. No writer has equally comprehended the artistic material which is given by its extent, its congregation of different elements, its mouldiness, its brilliancy.

Nor does his genius, though, from some idiosyncrasy of mind or accident of external situation, it is more especially directed to city life—at all stop at the city wall. He is especially at home in the picturesque and obvious parts of country life, particularly in the comfortable and (so to say) mouldering portion of it. The following is an instance; if not the best that could be cited, still one of the best:—

' They arranged to proceed upon their journey next evening, as a stage-wagon, which travelled for some distance on the same road as they must take, would stop at the inn to change horses, and the driver for a small gratuity would give Nell a place inside. A bargain was soon struck when the wagon came; and in due time it rolled away; with the child comfortably bestowed among the softer packages, her grandfather and the schoolmaster walking on beside the driver, and the landlady and all the good folks of the inn screaming out their good wishes and farewells.

' What a soothing, luxurious, drowsy way of travelling, to lie inside that slowly-moving mountain, listening to the tinkling of the horses' bells, the occasional smacking of the carter's whip, the smooth rolling of the great broad wheels, the rattle of the harness, the cheery goodnights of passing travellers jogging past on little short-stepped horses—all made pleasantly indistinct by the thick awning, which seemed made for lazy listening under, till one fell asleep! The very going to sleep, still with an indistinct idea, as the head jogged to and fro upon the pillow, of moving onward with no trouble or fatigue, and hearing all these sounds like dreamy music, lulling to the senses—and the slow waking up, and finding one's self staring out through the breezy curtain half-opened in the front, far up into the cold bright sky with its countless stars, and downward at the driver's lantern dancing on like its namesake Jack of the swamps and marshes, and sideways at the dark grim trees, and forward at the long bare road rising up, up, up, until it stopped abruptly at a sharp high ridge as if there were no more road, and all beyond was sky—and the stopping at the inn to bait, and being helped out, and going into a room with fire and candles, and winking very much, and being agreeably reminded that the night was cold, and anxious for very comfort's sake to think it colder than it was!—What a delicious journey was that journey in the wagon!

' Then the going on again—so fresh at first, and shortly afterwards so sleepy. The waking from a sound nap as the mail came dashing past like a highway comet, with gleaming lamps and rattling hoofs, and visions of a guard behind, standing up to keep his feet warm, and of a gentleman in a fur cap opening his eyes and looking wild and stupefied—the stopping at the turnpike, where the man was gone to bed, and knocking at the door until he answered with a smothered shout from under the bed-clothes in the little room above, where the faint light was burning, and presently came down, night-capped and shivering, to throw the gate wide open, and wish all wagons off the road except by day. The cold sharp interval between night and morning—the distant streak of light widening and spreading, and turning from gray to white, and from white to yellow, and from yellow to burning red—the presence of day, with all its cheerfulness and life—men and horses at the plough—birds in the trees and hedges, and boys in solitary fields frightening them away with rattles. The coming to a town—people busy in the market; light carts and chaises round the tavern yard; tradesmen standing at their doors; men running horses up and down the streets for sale; pigs plunging and grunting in the dirty distance, getting off with long strings at their legs, running into clean chemists' shops and being dislodged with brooms by 'prentices; the night-coach changing horses—the passengers cheerless, cold, ugly, and discontented, with three months' growth of hair in one night—the coachmen fresh as from a bandbox, and exquisitely beautiful by contrast:—so much bustle, so many things in motion, such a variety of incidents—when was there a journey with so many delights as that journey in the wagon!'

Or, as a relief from a very painful series of accompanying characters, it is pleasant to read and remember the description of the fine morning on which Mr. Jonas Chuzzlewit does not reflect. Mr. Dickens has, however, no feeling analogous to the nature-worship of some other recent writers. There is nothing Wordsworthian in his bent; the interpreting inspiration (as that school speak) is not his. Nor has he the erudition in difficult names which has filled some pages in late novelists with mineralogy and botany. His descriptions of nature are fresh and superficial; they are not sermonic or scientific.

Nevertheless, it may be said that Mr. Dickens's genius is especially suited to the delineation of city life. London is like a newspaper. Everything is there, and everything is disconnected. There is every kind of person in some houses; but there is no more connection between the houses than between the neighbours in the lists of ' births, marriages, and deaths.' As we change from the broad leader to the squalid police-report, we pass a corner and we are in a changed world. This is advantageous to Mr. Dickens's genius. His memory is full of instances of old buildings and curious people, and he does not care to piece them together. On the contrary, each scene, to his mind, is a separate scene,—each street a separate street. He has, too, the peculiar alertness of observation that is observable in those who live by it. He describes London like a special correspondent for posterity.

A second most wonderful special faculty which Mr. Dickens possesses is what we may call his *vivification* of character, or rather of characteristics. His marvellous power of observation has been exercised upon men and women even more than upon town or country; and the store of human detail, so to speak, in his books is endless and enormous. The boots at the inn, the pickpocket in the street, the undertaker, the Mrs. Gamp, are all of them at his disposal; he knows each trait and incident, and he invests them with a kind of perfection in detail which in reality they do not possess. He has a very peculiar power of taking hold of some particular traits, and making a character out of them. He is especially apt to incarnate particular professions in this way. Many of his people never speak without some allusion to their occupation. You cannot separate them from it. Nor does the writer ever separate them. What would Mr. Mould be if not an undertaker? or Mrs. Gamp if not a nurse? or Charley Bates if not a pickpocket? Not only is human nature in them subdued to what it works in, but there seems to be no nature to subdue; the whole character is the idealisation of a trade, and is not in fancy or thought distinguishable from it. Accordingly, of necessity, such delineations become caricatures. We do not in general contrast them with reality; but as soon as we do, we are struck with the monstrous exaggerations which they present. You could no more fancy

Sam Weller, or Mark Tapley, or the Artful Dodger really existing, walking about among common ordinary men and women,
than you can fancy a talking duck or a writing bear. They are
utterly beyond the pale of ordinary social intercourse. We suspect, indeed, that Mr. Dickens does not conceive his characters
to himself as mixing in the society he mixes in. He sees people
in the street, doing certain things, talking in a certain way, and
his fancy petrifies them in the act. He goes on fancying hundreds of reduplications of that act and that speech; he frames
an existence in which there is nothing else but that aspect
which attracted his attention. Sam Weller is an example. He
is a man-servant, who makes a peculiar kind of jokes, and is
wonderfully felicitous in certain similes. You see him at his
first introduction:—

' " My friend," said the thin gentleman.

' " You're one o' the adwice gratis order," thought Sam,
" or you wouldn't be so werry fond o' me all at once." But he
only said—" Well, sir ? "

' " My friend," said the thin gentleman, with a conciliatory
hem—" Have you got many people stopping here, now?
Pretty busy? Eh? "

' Sam stole a look at the inquirer. He was a little high-
dried man, with a dark squeezed-up face, and small restless
black eyes, that kept winking and twinkling on each side of his
little inquisitive nose, as if they were playing a perpetual game
of peep-bo with that feature. He was dressed all in black, with
boots as shiny as his eyes, a low white neckcloth, and a clean
shirt with a frill to it. A gold watch-chain, and seals, depended from his fob. He carried his black kid gloves *in* his
hands, not *on* them; and as he spoke, thrust his wrists beneath
his coat-tails, with the air of a man who was in the habit of
propounding some regular posers.

' " Pretty busy, eh? " said the little man.

' " Oh, werry well, sir," replied Sam, " we shan't be bank-
rupts, and we shan't make our fort'ns. We eats our biled
mutton without capers, and don't care for horse-radish wen ve
can get beef ? "

' " Ah," said the little man, " you're a wag, ain't you? "

' " My eldest brother was troubled with that complaint,"
said Sam, " it may be catching—I used to sleep with him."

' " This is a curious old house of yours," said the little man, looking round him.

' " If you'd sent word you was a coming, we'd ha' had it repaired," replied the imperturbable Sam.

' The little man seemed rather baffled by these several repulses, and a short consultation took place between him and the two plump gentlemen. At its conclusion, the little man took a pinch of snuff from an oblong silver box, and was apparently on the point of renewing the conversation, when one of the plump gentlemen, who, in addition to a benevolent countenance, possessed a pair of spectacles, and a pair of black gaiters, interfered—

' " The fact of the matter is," said the benevolent gentleman, " that my friend here " (pointing to the other plump gentleman) " will give you half a guinea, if you'll answer one or two—"

' " Now, my dear sir—my dear sir," said the little man, " pray allow me—my dear sir, the very first principle to be observed in these cases, is this: if you place a matter in the hands of a professional man, you must in no way interfere in the progress of the business; you must repose implicit confidence in him. Really, Mr. (he turned to the other plump gentleman, and said)—I forget your friend's name."

' " Pickwick," said Mr. Wardle, for it was no other than that jolly personage.

' " Ah, Pickwick—really Mr. Pickwick, my dear sir, excuse me—I shall be happy to receive any private suggestions of yours, as *amicus curiæ*, but you must see the impropriety of your interfering with my conduct in this case, with such an *ad captandum* argument as the offer of half a guinea. Really, my dear sir, really," and the little man took an argumentative pinch of snuff, and looked very profound.

' " My only wish, sir," said Mr. Pickwick, " was to bring this very unpleasant matter to as speedy a close as possible."

' " Quite right—quite right," said the little man.

' " With which view," continued Mr. Pickwick, " I made use of the argument which my experience of men has taught me is the most likely to succeed in any case."

' " Ay, ay," said the little man, " very good, very good indeed; but you should have suggested it to *me*. My dear sir,

I'm quite certain you cannot be ignorant of the extent of confidence which must be placed in professional men. If any authority can be necessary on such a point, my dear sir, let me refer you to the well-known case in Barnwell and—"

' " Never mind George Barnwell," interrupted Sam, who had remained a wondering listener during this short colloquy; " everybody knows vhat sort of a case his was, tho' it's always been my opinion, mind you, that the young 'ooman deserved scragging a precious sight more than he did. Hows'ever, that's neither here nor there. You want me to except of half a guinea. Werry well, I'm agreeable: I can't say no fairer than that, can I, sir? (Mr. Pickwick smiled.) Then the next question is, what the devil do you want with me, as the man said wen he see the ghost? "

' " We want to know—" said Mr. Wardle.

' " Now, my dear sir—my dear sir," interposed the busy little man.

' Mr. Wardle shrugged his shoulders, and was silent.

' " We want to know," said the little man, solemnly; " and we ask the question of you, in order that we may not awaken apprehensions inside—we want to know who you've got in this house at present."

' " Who there is in the house! " said Sam, in whose mind the inmates were always represented by that particular article of their costume, which came under his immediate superintendence. " There's a wooden leg in number six; there's a pair of Hessians in thirteen; there's two pair of halves in the commercial; there's these here painted tops in the snuggery inside the bar; and five more tops in the coffee-room."

' " Nothing more? " said the little man.

' " Stop a bit," replied Sam, suddenly recollecting himself. " Yes; there's a pair of Wellingtons a good deal worn, and a pair o' lady's shoes, in number five."

' " What sort of shoes? " hastily inquired Wardle, who, together with Mr. Pickwick, had been lost in bewilderment at the singular catalogue of visitors.

' " Country make," replied Sam.

' " Any maker's name? "

' " Brown."

' " Where of? "

' " Muggleton,"

' " It *is* them," exclaimed Wardle. " By heavens, we've found them,"

' " Hush ! " said Sam. " The Wellingtons has gone to Doctors Commons."

' " No," said the little man.

' " Yes, for a license."

' " We're in time," exclaimed Wardle. " Show us the room; not a moment is to be lost."

' " Pray, my dear sir—pray," said the little man; " caution, caution." He draw from his pocket a red silk purse, and looked very hard at Sam as he drew out a sovereign.

' Sam grinned expressively.

' " Show us into the room at once, without announcing us," said the little man, " and it's yours." '

One can fancy Mr. Dickens hearing a dialogue of this sort, —not nearly so good, but something like it,—and immediately setting to work to make it better and put it in a book; then changing a little the situation, putting the boots one step up in the scale of service, engaging him as footman to a stout gentleman (but without for a moment losing sight of the peculiar kind of professional conversation and humour which his first dialogue presents), and astonishing all his readers by the marvellous fertility and magical humour with which he maintains that style. Sam Weller's father is even a stronger and simpler instance. He is simply nothing but an old coachman of the stout and extinct sort: you cannot separate him from the idea of that occupation. But how amusing he is ! We dare not quote a single word of his talk; because we should go on quoting so long, and every one knows it so well. Some persons may think that this is not a very high species of delineative art. The idea of personifying traits and trades may seem to them poor and meagre. Anybody, they may fancy, can do that. But how would they do it ? Whose fancy would not break down in a page,—in five lines ? Who could carry on the vivification with zest and energy and humour for volume after volume ? Endless fertility in laughter-causing detail is Mr. Dickens's most astonishing peculiarity. It requires a continuous and careful reading of his works to be aware of his enormous wealth. Writers have attained the greatest reputation for wit and humour, whose whole works do not contain so much of either as are to be found in a very few pages of his.

Mr. Dickens's humour is indeed very much a result of the two peculiarities of which we have been speaking. His power of detailed observation and his power of idealising individual traits of character—sometimes of one or other of them, sometimes of both of them together. His similes on matters of external observation are so admirable that everybody appreciates them, and it would be absurd to quote specimens of them; nor is it the sort of excellence which best bears to be paraded for the purposes of critical example. Its off-hand air and natural connection with the adjacent circumstances are inherent parts of its peculiar merit. Every reader of Mr. Dickens's works knows well what we mean. And who is not a reader of them?

But his peculiar humour is even more indebted to his habit of vivifying external traits, than to his power of external observation. He, as we have explained, expands traits into people; and it is a source of true humour to place these, when so expanded, in circumstances in which only people—that is complete human beings—can appropriately act. The humour of Mr. Pickwick's character is entirely of this kind. He is a kind of incarnation of simple-mindedness and what we may call obvious-mindedness. The conclusion which each occurrence or position in life most immediately presents to the unsophisticated mind is that which Mr. Pickwick is sure to accept. The proper accompaniments are given to him. He is a stout gentleman in easy circumstances, who is irritated into originality by no impulse from within, and by no stimulus from without. He is stated to have 'retired from business.' But no one can fancy what he was in business. Such guileless simplicity of heart and easy impressibility of disposition would soon have induced a painful failure amid the harsh struggles and the tempting speculations of pecuniary life. As he is represented in the narrative, however, nobody dreams of such antecedents. Mr. Pickwick moves easily over all the surface of English life from Goswell Street to Dingley Dell, from Dingley Dell to the Ipswich elections, from drinking milk-punch in a wheelbarrow to sleeping in the approximate pound, and no one ever thinks of applying to him the ordinary maxims which we should apply to any common person in life, or to any common personage in a fiction. Nobody thinks it is wrong in Mr. Pickwick to drink too much milk-punch in a wheelbarrow, to introduce worthless people of whom he knows nothing to the families of people for whom he really cares; nobody holds him responsible for the consequences; nobody thinks there is anything wrong in his taking Mr. Bob Sawyer and Mr. Benjamin Allen to visit Mr. Winkle senior, and thereby almost irretrievably offending him with his son's marriage. We do not reject moral remarks such as these, but they never occur to us. Indeed the indistinct consciousness that such observations are possible, and that they are hovering about our minds, enhances the humour of the narrative. We are in a conventional world, where the mere maxims of common life do not apply, and yet which has all the amusing detail, and picturesque elements, and singular eccentricities of common life. Mr. Pickwick is a personified ideal; a kind of amateur in life, whose course we watch through all the circumstances of ordinary existence, and at whose follies we are amused just as really skilled people are at the mistakes of an amateur in their art. His being in the pound is not wrong; his being the victim of Messrs. Dodson is not foolish. 'Always shout with the mob,' said Mr. Pickwick. 'But suppose there are two mobs,' said Mr. Snodgrass. 'Then shout with the loudest,' said Mr. Pickwick. This is not in him weakness or time-serving, or want of principle, as in most even of fictitious people it would be. It is his way. Mr. Pickwick was expected to say something, so he said 'Ah' in a grave voice. This is not pompous as we might fancy, or clever as it might be if intentionally devised; it is simply his way. Mr. Pickwick gets late at night over the wall behind the back-door of a young-ladies' school, is found in that sequestered place by the schoolmistress and the boarders and the cook, and there is a dialogue between them. There is nothing out of possibility in this; it is his way. The humour essentially consists in treating as a moral agent a being who really is not a moral agent. We treat a vivified accident as a man, and we are surprised at the absurd results. We are reading about an acting thing, and we wonder at its scrapes, and laugh at them as if they were those of the man. There is something of this humour in every sort of farce. Everybody knows these are not real beings acting in real life, though they talk as if they were, and want us to believe that they are. Here, as in Mr. Dickens's books, we have exaggerations pretending to comport themselves as ordinary beings, caricatures acting as if they were characters.

At the same time it is essential to remember, that however great may be and is the charm of such exaggerated personifications, the best specimens of them are immensely less excellent, belong to an altogether lower range of intellectual achievements, than the real depiction of actual living men. It is amusing to read of beings *out of* the laws of morality, but it is more profoundly interesting, as well as more instructive, to read of those whose life in its moral conditions resembles our own. We see this most distinctly when the representations are given by the genius of the same writer. Falstaff is a sort of sack-holding paunch, an exaggerated over-development which no one thinks of holding down to the commonplace rules of the ten commandments and the statute-law. We do not think of them in connection with him. They belong to a world apart. Accordingly we are vexed when the king discards him and reproves him. Such a fate was a necessary adherence on Shakespeare's part to the historical tradition; he never probably thought of departing from it, nor would his audience have perhaps endured his doing so. But to those who look at the historical plays as pure works of imaginative art, it seems certainly an artistic misconception to have developed so marvellous an *un*moral impersonation, and then to have subjected it to an ethical and punitive judgment. Still, notwithstanding this error, which was very likely inevitable, Falstaff is probably the most remarkable specimen of caricature-representation to be found in literature. And its very excellence of execution only shows how inferior is the kind of art which creates only such representations. Who could compare the genius, marvellous as must be its fertility, which was needful to create a Falstaff with that shown in the higher productions of the same mind in Hamlet, Ophelia, and Lear? We feel instantaneously the difference between the aggregating accident which rakes up from the externalities of life other accidents analogous to itself, and the central ideal of a real character which cannot show itself wholly in any accidents, but which exemplifies itself partially in many, which unfolds itself gradually in wide spheres of action, and yet, as with those we know best in life, leaves something hardly to be understood, and after years of familiarity is a problem and a difficulty to the last. In the same way the embodied characteristics and grotesque exaggerations of Mr. Dickens, notwithstanding all their humour and all their marvellous abundance, can never be for a moment compared with the great works of the real painters of essential human nature.

There is one class of Mr. Dickens's pictures which may seem to form an exception to this criticism. It is the delineation of the outlaw, we might say the anti-law, world in *Oliver Twist*. In one or two instances Mr. Dickens has been so fortunate as to hit on characteristics which, by his system of idealisation and continual repetition, might really be brought to look like a character. A man's trade or profession in regular life can only exhaust a very small portion of his nature; no approach is made to the essence of humanity by the exaggeration of the traits which typify a beadle or an undertaker. With the outlaw world it is somewhat different. The bare fact of a man belonging to that world is so important to his nature, that if it is artistically developed with coherent accessories, some approximation to a distinctly natural character will be almost inevitably made. In the characters of Bill Sykes and Nancy this is so. The former is the skulking ruffian who may be seen any day at the police-courts, and whom anyone may fancy he sees by walking through St. Giles's. You cannot attempt to figure to your imagination the existence of such a person without being thrown into the region of the passions, the will, and the conscience; the mere fact of his maintaining, as a condition of life and by settled profession, a struggle with regular society necessarily brings these deep parts of his nature into prominence; great crime usually proceeds from abnormal impulses or strange effort. Accordingly Mr. Sykes is the character most approaching to a coherent man who is to be found in Mr. Dickens's works. We do not say that even here there is not some undue heightening admixture of caricature,—but this defect is scarcely thought of amid the general coherence of the picture, the painful subject, and the wonderful command of strange accessories. Miss Nancy is a still more delicate artistic effort. She is an idealisation of the girl who may also be seen at the police-courts and St. Giles's; as bad, according to occupation and common character, as a woman can be, yet retaining a tinge of womanhood, and a certain compassion for interesting suffering, which under favouring circumstances might be the germ of a regenerating influence. We need not stay to prove how much the imaginative development of such a personage must concern itself with our deeper humanity; how strongly, if excellent, it must be contrasted with everything conventional or casual or superficial. Mr. Dickens's delineation is in the highest degree excellent. It possesses not only the more obvious merits belonging to the subject, but also that of a singular delicacy of expression and idea. Nobody fancies for a moment that they are reading about anything beyond the pale of ordinary propriety. We read the account of the life which Miss Nancy leads with Bill Sykes without such an idea occurring to us: yet when we reflect upon it, few things in literary painting are more wonderful than the depiction of a professional life of sin and sorrow, so as not even to startle those to whom the deeper forms of either are but names and shadows. Other writers would have given as vivid a picture: Defoe would have poured out even a more copious measure of telling circumstantiality, but he would have narrated his story with an inhuman distinctness, which if not impure is *un*pure; French writers, whom we need not name, would have enhanced the interest of their narrative by trading on the excitement of stimulating scenes. It would be injustice to Mr. Dickens to say that he has surmounted these temptations; the unconscious evidence of innumerable details proves that, from a certain delicacy of imagination and purity of spirit, he has not even experienced them. Criticism is the more bound to dwell at length on the merits of these delineations, because no artistic merit can make *Oliver Twist* a pleasing work. The squalid detail of crime and misery oppresses us too much. If it is to be read at all, it should be read in the first hardness of the youthful imagination, which no touch can move too deeply, and which is never stirred with tremulous suffering at the ' still sad music of humanity.' The coldest critic in later life may never hope to have again the apathy of his boyhood.

It perhaps follows from what has been said of the characteristics of Mr. Dickens's genius, that he would be little skilled in planning plots for his novels. He certainly is not so skilled. He says in his preface to the *Pickwick Papers* ' that they were designed for the introduction of diverting characters and incidents; that no ingenuity of plot was attempted, or even at that time considered feasible by the author in connection with the desultory plan of publication adopted;' and he adds an expression of regret that 'these chapters had not been strung together on a thread of more general interest.' It is extremely fortunate that no such attempt was made. In the cases in which Mr. Dickens has attempted to make a long connected story, or to develop into scenes or incidents a plan in any degree elaborate, the result has been a complete failure. A certain consistency of genius seems necessary for the construction of a consecutive plot. An irregular mind naturally shows itself in incoherency of incident and aberration of character. The method in which Mr. Dickens's mind works, if we are correct in our criticism upon it, tends naturally to these blemishes. Caricatures are necessarily isolated; they are produced by the exaggeration of certain conspicuous traits and features; each being is enlarged on its greatest side; and we laugh at the grotesque grouping and the startling contrast. But the connection between human beings on which a plot depends is rather severed than elucidated by the enhancement of their diversities. Interesting stories are founded on the intimate relations of men and women. These intimate relations are based not on their superficial traits, or common occupations, or most visible externalities, but on the inner life of heart and feeling. You simply divert attention from that secret life by enhancing the perceptible diversities of common human nature, and the strange anomalies into which it may be distorted. The original germ of *Pickwick* was a ' Club of Oddities.' The idea was professedly abandoned; but traces of it are to be found in all Mr. Dickens's books. It illustrates the professed grotesqueness of the characters as well as their slender connection.

The defect of plot is heightened by Mr. Dickens's great, we might say complete, inability to make a love-story. A pair of lovers is by custom a necessity of narrative fiction, and writers who possess a great general range of mundane knowledge, and but little knowledge of the special sentimental subject, are often in amusing difficulties. The watchful reader observes the transition from the hearty description of well-known scenes, of prosaic streets, or journeys by wood and river, to the pale colours of ill-attempted poetry, to such sights as the novelist wishes he need not try to see. But few writers exhibit the difficulty in so aggravated a form as Mr. Dickens. Most men

by taking thought can make a lay figure to look not so very
unlike a young gentleman, and can compose a telling schedule
of ladylike charms. Mr. Dickens has no power of doing either.
The heroic character—we do not mean the form of character
so called in life and action, but that which is hereditary in the
heroes of novels—is not suited to his style of art. Hazlitt wrote
an essay to inquire ' Why the heroes of romances are insipid; '
and without going that length it may safely be said that the character of the agreeable young gentleman who loves and is loved
should not be of the most marked sort. Flirtation ought not to
be an exaggerated pursuit. Young ladies and their admirers
should not express themselves in the heightened and imaginative
phraseology suited to Charley Bates and the Dodger. Humour
is of no use, for no one makes love in jokes: a tinge of insidious
satire may perhaps be permitted as a rare and occasional relief,
but it will not be thought ' a pretty book,' if so malicious an
element be at all habitually perceptible. The broad farce in
which Mr. Dickens indulges is thoroughly out of place. If
you caricature a pair of lovers ever so little, by the necessity of
their calling you make them ridiculous. One of Sheridan's best
comedies is remarkable for having no scene in which the hero
and heroine are on the stage together; and Mr. Moore suggests
that the shrewd wit distrusted his skill in the light dropping
love-talk which would have been necessary. Mr. Dickens would
have done well to imitate so astute a policy; but he has none of
the managing shrewdness which those who look at Sheridan's
career attentively will probably think not the least remarkable
feature in his singular character. Mr. Dickens, on the contrary, pours out painful sentiments as if he wished the abundance should make up for the inferior quality. The excruciating
writing which is expended on Miss Ruth Pinch passes belief.
Mr. Dickens is not only unable to make lovers to talk, but to
describe heroines in mere narrative. As has been said, most
men can make a tumble of blue eyes and fair hair and pearly
teeth, that does very well for a young lady, at least for a good
while; but Mr. Dickens will not, probably cannot, attain even
to this humble measure of descriptive art. He vitiates the
repose by broad humour, or disenchants the delicacy by an
unctuous admiration.

    This deficiency is probably nearly connected with one of
Mr. Dickens's most remarkable excellences. No one can read

Mr. Thackeray's writings without feeling that he is perpetually treading as close as he dare to the border-line that separates the world which may be described in books from the world which it is prohibited so to describe. No one knows better than this accomplished artist where that line is, and how curious are its windings and turns. The charge against him is that he knows it but too well; that with an anxious care and a wistful eye he is ever approximating to its edge, and hinting with subtle art how thoroughly he is familiar with, and how interesting he could make the interdicted region on the other side. He never violates a single conventional rule; but at the same time the shadow of the immorality that is not seen is scarcely ever wanting to his delineation of the society that is seen. Every one may perceive what is passing in his fancy. Mr. Dickens is chargeable with no such defect: he does not seem to feel the temptation. By what we may fairly call an instinctive purity of genius, he not only observes the conventional rules, but makes excursions into topics which no other novelist could safely handle, and, by a felicitous instinct, deprives them of all impropriety. No other writer could have managed the humour of Mrs. Gamp without becoming unendurable. At the same time it is difficult not to believe that this singular insensibility to the temptations to which many of the greatest novelists have succumbed is in some measure connected with his utter inaptitude for delineating the portion of life to which their art is specially inclined. He delineates neither the love-affairs which ought to be nor those which ought not to be.

Mr. Dickens's indisposition to ' make capital ' out of the most commonly tempting part of human sentiment is the more remarkable because he certainly does not show the same indisposition in other cases. He has naturally great powers of pathos; his imagination is familiar with the common sorts of human suffering; and his marvellous conversancy with the detail of existence enables him to describe sick-beds and death-beds with an excellence very rarely seen in literature. A nature far more sympathetic than that of most authors has familiarised him with such subjects. In general, a certain apathy is characteristic of book-writers, and dulls the efficacy of their pathos. Mr. Dickens is quite exempt from this defect; but, on the other hand, is exceedingly prone to a very ostentatious exhibition of the opposite excellence. He dwells on dismal scenes with a kind of fawning fondness; and he seems unwilling to leave them, long after his readers have had more than enough of them. He describes Mr. Dennis the hangman as having a professional fondness for his occupation: he has the same sort of fondness apparently for the profession of death-painter. The painful details he accumulates are a very serious drawback from the agreeableness of his writings. Dismal 'light literature' is the dismallest of reading. The reality of the police-reports is sufficiently bad, but a fictitious police-report would be the most disagreeable of conceivable compositions. Some portions of Mr. Dickens's books are liable to a good many of the same objections. They are squalid from noisome trivialities, and horrid with terrifying crime. In his earlier books this is commonly relieved at frequent intervals by a graphic and original mirth. As we will not say age, but maturity, has passed over his powers, this counteractive element has been lessened; the humour is not so happy as it was, but the wonderful fertility in painful minutiæ still remains.

Mr. Dickens's political opinions have subjected him to a good deal of criticism, and to some ridicule. He has shown, on many occasions, the desire—which we see so frequent among able and influential men—to start as a political reformer. Mr. Spurgeon said, with an application to himself, ' If you've got the ear of the public, *of course* you must begin to tell it its faults.' Mr. Dickens has been quite disposed to make this use of his popular influence. Even in *Pickwick* there are many traces of this tendency; and the way in which it shows itself in that book and in others is very characteristic of the time at which they appeared. The most instructive political characteristic of the years from 1825 to 1845 is the growth and influence of the scheme of opinion which we call Radicalism. There are several species of creeds which are comprehended under this generic name, but they all evince a marked reaction against the worship of the English constitution and the affection for the English *status quo*, which were then the established creed and sentiment. All Radicals are anti-Eldonites. This is equally true of the Benthamite or philosophical radicalism of the early period, and the Manchester, or ' definite-grievance radicalism,' among the last vestiges of which we are now living. Mr. Dickens represents a species different from either. His is what we may call the ' sentimental radicalism; ' and if we recur to the history of the time, we shall find that there would not originally have been any opprobrium attaching to such a name. The whole course of the legislation, and still more of the administration, of the first twenty years of the nineteenth century was marked by a harsh unfeelingness which is of all faults the most contrary to any with which we are chargeable now. The world of the ' Six Acts,' of the frequent executions for death, of the Draconic criminal law, is so far removed from us that we cannot comprehend its having ever existed. It is more easy to understand the recoil which has followed. All the social speculation, and much of the social action of the few years succeeding the Reform Bill bear the most marked traces of the reaction. The spirit which animates Mr. Dickens's political reasonings and observations expresses it exactly. The vice of the then existing social authorities and of the then existing public had been the forgetfulness of the pain which their own acts evidently produced,—an unrealising habit which adhered to official rules and established maxims, and which would not be shocked by the evident consequences, by proximate human suffering. The sure result of this habit was the excitement of the habit precisely opposed to it. Mr. Carlyle, in his *Chartism*, we think, observes of the poor-law reform: ' It was then, above all things, necessary that outdoor relief should cease. But how? What means did great Nature take for accomplishing that most desirable end? She created a race of men who believed the cessation of outdoor relief to be the one thing needful.' In the same way, and by the same propensity to exaggerated opposition which is inherent in human nature, the unfeeling obtuseness of the early part of this century was to be corrected by an extreme, perhaps an excessive, sensibility to human suffering in the years which have followed. There was most adequate reason for the sentiment in its origin, and it had a great task to perform in ameliorating harsh customs and repealing dreadful penalties; but it has continued to repine at such evils long after they ceased to exist, and when the only facts that at all resemble them are the necessary painfulness of due punishment and the necessary rigidity of established law. Mr. Dickens is an example both of the proper use and of the abuse of the sentiment. His earlier works have many excellent descriptions of the abuses which had descended to the present generation from others whose sympathy with pain was less tender. Nothing can be better than the description of the poor debtors' gaols in *Pickwick*, or of the old parochial authorities in *Oliver Twist*. No doubt these descriptions are caricatures, all his delineations are so; but the beneficial use of such art can hardly be better exemplified. Human nature endures the aggravation of vices and foibles in written description better than that of excellencies. We cannot bear to hear even the hero of a book for ever called ' just;' we detest the recurring praise even of beauty, much more of virtue. The moment you begin to exaggerate a character of true excellence, you spoil it; the traits are too delicate not to be injured by heightening or marred by over-emphasis. But a beadle is made for caricature. The slight measure of pomposity that humanises his unfeelingness introduces the requisite comic element; even the turnkeys of a debtors' prison may by skilful hands be similarly used. The contrast between the destitute condition of Job Trotter and Mr. Jingle and their former swindling triumph, is made comic by a rarer touch of unconscious art. Mr. Pickwick's warm heart takes so eager an interest in the misery of his old enemies, that our colder nature is tempted to smile. We endure the over-intensity, at any rate the unnecessary aggravation, of the surrounding misery; and we endure it willingly, because it brings out better than anything else could have done the half-comic intensity of a sympathetic nature.

It is painful to pass from these happy instances of well-used power to the glaring abuses of the same faculty in Mr. Dickens's later books. He began by describing really removable evils in a style which would induce all persons, however insensible, to remove them if they could; he has ended by describing the natural evils and inevitable pains of the present state of being in such a manner as must tend to excite discontent and repining. The result is aggravated, because Mr. Dickens never ceases to hint that these evils are removable, though he does not say by what means. Nothing is easier than to show the evils of anything. Mr. Dickens has not unfrequently spoken, and what is worse, he has taught a great number of parrot-like imitators to speak, in what really is, if they knew it, a tone of objection to the necessary constitution of human society. If you will only write a description of it, any form of government will seem ridiculous. What is more absurd than a despotism, even at its best? A king of ability or an able minister sits in an orderly room filled with memorials, and returns, and documents, and memoranda. These are his world; among these he of necessity lives and moves. Yet how little of the real life of the nation he governs can be represented in an official form! How much of real suffering is there that statistics can never tell! how much of obvious good is there that no memorandum to a minister will ever mention! how much deception is there in what such documents contain! how monstrous must be the ignorance of the closet statesman, after all his life of labour, of much that a ploughman could tell him of! A free government is almost worse, as it must read in a written delineation. Instead of the real attention of a laborious and anxious statesman, we have now the shifting caprices of a popular assembly—elected for one object, deciding on another; changing with the turn of debate; shifting in its very composition; one set of men coming down to vote to-day, to-morrow another and often unlike set, most of them eager for the dinner-hour, actuated by unseen influences—by a respect for their constituents, by the dread of an attorney in a far-off borough. What people are these to control a nation's destinies, and wield the power of an empire, and regulate the happiness of millions! Either way we are at fault. Free government seems an absurdity, and despotism is so too. Again, every form of law has a distinct expression, a rigid procedure, customary rules and forms. It is administered by human beings liable to mistake, confusion, and forgetfulness, and in the long run, and on the average, is sure to be tainted with vice and fraud. Nothing can be easier than to make a case, as we may say, against any particular system, by pointing out with emphatic caricature its inevitable miscarriages and by pointing out nothing else. Those who so address us may assume a tone of philanthropy, and for ever exult that they are not so unfeeling as other men are; but the real tendency of their exhortations is to make men dissatisfied with their inevitable condition, and what is worse, to make them fancy that its irremediable evils can be remedied, and indulge in a succession of vague strivings and restless changes. Such, however,—though in a style of expression somewhat different,—is very much the tone with which Mr. Dickens and his followers have in later years made us familiar. To the second-hand repeaters of a cry so feeble, we can have nothing to say; if silly people cry because they think the world is silly, let them cry; but the founder of the school cannot, we are persuaded, peruse without mirth the lachrymose eloquence which his disciples have perpetrated. The soft moisture of irrelevant sentiment cannot have entirely entered into his soul. A truthful genius must have forbidden it. Let us hope that his pernicious example may incite some one of equal genius to preach with equal efficiency a sterner and a wiser gospel; but there is no need just now for us to preach it without genius.

There has been much controversy about Mr. Dickens's taste. A great many cultivated people will scarcely concede that he has any taste at all; a still larger number of fervent admirers point, on the other hand, to a hundred felicitous descriptions and delineations which abound in apt expressions and skilful turns and happy images,—in which it would be impossible to alter a single word without altering for the worse; and naturally inquire whether such excellences in what is written do not indicate good taste in the writer. The truth is, that Mr. Dickens has what we may call creative taste; that is to say, the habit or faculty, whichever we may choose to call it, which at the critical instant of artistic production offers to the mind the right word, and the right word only. If he is engaged on a good subject for caricature, there will be no defect of taste to preclude the caricature from being excellent. But it is only in moments of imaginative production that he has any taste at all. His works nowhere indicate that he possesses in any degree the passive taste which decides what is good in the writings of other people and what is not, and which performs the same critical duty upon a writer's own efforts when the confusing mists of productive imagination have passed away. Nor has Mr. Dickens the gentlemanly instinct which in many minds supplies the place of purely critical discernment, and which, by constant association with those who know what is best, acquires a second-hand perception of that which is best. He has no tendency to conventionalism for good or for evil; his merits are far removed from the ordinary path of writers, and it was not probably so much effort to him as to other men to step so far out of that path: he scarcely knew how far it was. For the same reason he cannot tell how faulty his writing will often be thought, for he cannot tell what people will think.

A few pedantic critics have regretted that Mr. Dickens had

not received what they call a regular education. And if we understand their meaning, we believe they mean to regret that he had not received a course of discipline which would probably have impaired his powers. A regular education should mean that ordinary system of regulation and instruction which experience has shown to fit men best for the ordinary pursuits of life. It applies the requisite discipline to each faculty in the exact proportion in which that faculty is wanted in the pursuits of life; it develops understanding and memory, and imagination, each in accordance with the scale prescribed. To men of ordinary faculties this is nearly essential; it is the only mode in which they can be fitted for the inevitable competition of existence. To men of regular and symmetrical genius also, such a training will often be beneficial. The world knows pretty well what are the great tasks of the human mind, and has learnt in the course of ages with some accuracy what is the kind of culture likely to promote their exact performance. A man of abilities extraordinary in degree but harmonious in proportion, will be the better for having submitted to the kind of discipline which has been ascertained to fit a man for the work to which powers in that proportion are best fitted; he will do what he has to do better and more gracefully; culture will add a touch to the finish of nature. But the case is very different with men of irregular and anomalous genius, whose excellences consist in the *aggravation* of some special faculty, or at the most of one or two. The discipline which will fit him for the production of great literary works is that which will most develop the peculiar powers in which he excels; the rest of the mind will be far less important, it will not be likely that the culture which is adapted to promote this special development will also be that which is most fitted for expanding the powers of common men in common directions. The precise problem is to develop the powers of a strange man in a strange direction. In the case of Mr. Dickens, it would have been absurd to have shut up his observant youth within the walls of a college. They would have taught him nothing about Mrs. Gamp there; Sam Weller took no degree. The kind of early life fitted to develop the power of apprehensive observation is a brooding life in stirring scenes; the idler in the streets of life knows the streets; the bystander knows the picturesque effect of life better than the player, and the meditative idler amid the hum of existence is much more likely to know its sound and to take in and comprehend its depths and meanings than the scholastic student intent on books, which, if they represent any world, represent one which has long passed away,—which commonly try rather to develop the reasoning understanding than the seeing observation,—which are written in languages that have long been dead. You will not train by such discipline a caricaturist of obvious manners.

Perhaps, too, a regular instruction and daily experience of the searching ridicule of critical associates would have detracted from the *pluck* which Mr. Dickens shows in all his writings. It requires a great deal of courage to be a humorous writer; you are always afraid that people will laugh at you instead of with you: undoubtedly there is a certain eccentricity about it. You take up the esteemed writers, Thucydides and the *Saturday Review*; after all, they do not make you laugh. It is not the function of really artistic productions to contribute to the mirth of human beings. All sensible men are afraid of it, and it is only with an extreme effort that a printed joke attains to the perusal of the public; the chances are many to one that the anxious producer loses heart in the correction of the press, and that the world never laughs at all. Mr. Dickens is quite exempt from this weakness. He has what a Frenchman might call the courage of his faculty. The real daring which is shown in *Pickwick Papers*, in the whole character of Mr. Weller senior, as well as in that of his son, is immense, far surpassing any which has been shown by any other contemporary writer. The brooding irregular mind is in its first stage prone to this sort of courage. It perhaps knows that its ideas are ' out of the way;' but with the infantine simplicity of youth, it supposes that originality is an advantage. Persons more familiar with the ridicule of their equals in station (and this is to most men the great instructress of the college time) well know that of all qualities this one most requires to be clipped and pared and measured. Posterity we doubt not will be entirely perfect in every conceivable element of judgment; but the existing generation like what they have heard before—it is much easier. It required great courage in Mr. Dickens to write what his genius has compelled them to appreciate.

We have throughout spoken of Mr. Dickens as he was, rather than as he is; or, to use a less discourteous phrase, and we hope a truer, of his early works rather than of those which are more recent. We could not do otherwise consistently with the true code of criticism. A man of great genius, who has written great and enduring works, must be judged mainly by them; and not by the inferior productions which, from the necessities of personal position, a fatal facility of composition, or other cause, he may pour forth at moments less favourable to his powers. Those who are called on to review these inferior productions themselves, must speak of them in the terms they may deserve; but those who have the more pleasant task of estimating as a whole the genius of the writer, may confine their attention almost wholly to those happier efforts which illustrate that genius. We should not like to have to speak in detail of Mr. Dickens's later works, and we have not done so. There are, indeed, peculiar reasons why a genius constituted as his is (at least if we are correct in the view which we have taken of it) would not endure without injury during a long life the applause of the many, the temptations of composition, and the general excitement of existence. Even in his earlier works it was impossible not to fancy that there was a weakness of fibre unfavourable to the longevity of excellence. This was the effect of his deficiency in those masculine faculties of which we have said so much,—the reasoning understanding and firm far-seeing sagacity. It is these two component elements which stiffen the mind, and give a consistency to the creed and a coherence to its effects,—which enable it to protect itself from the rush of circumstances. If to a deficiency in these we add an extreme sensibility to circumstances,—a mobility, as Lord Byron used to call it, of emotion, which is easily impressed, and still more easily carried away by impression,—we have the idea of a character peculiarly unfitted to bear the flux of time and chance. A man of very great determination could hardly bear up against them with such slight aids from within and with such peculiar sensibility to temptation. A man of merely ordinary determination would succumb to it; and Mr. Dickens has succumbed. His position was certainly unfavourable. He has told us that the works of his later years, inferior as all good critics have deemed them, have yet been more read than those of his earlier and healthier years. The most characteristic part of his audience, the lower middle-class, were ready to receive with delight the least favourable productions of his genius. Human

nature cannot endure this; it is too much to have to endure
a coincident temptation both from within and from without.
Mr. Dickens was too much inclined by natural disposition to
lachrymose eloquence and exaggerated caricature. Such was
the kind of writing which he wrote most easily. He found
likewise that such was the kind of writing that was read most
readily; and of course he wrote that kind. Who would have
done otherwise? No critic is entitled to speak very harshly of
such degeneracy, if he is not sure that he could have coped
with difficulties so peculiar. If that rule is to be observed, who
is there that will not be silent? No other Englishman has
attained such a hold on the vast populace; it is little, therefore,
to say that no other has surmounted its attendant temptations.

Mr. Macaulay*
(1856)

THIS is a marvellous book. Everybody has read it, and every one has read it with pleasure. It has little advantage of subject. When the volumes came out, an honest man said, 'I suppose something happened between the years 1689 and 1697; but what happened I do not know.' Every one knows now. No period with so little obvious interest will henceforth be so familiarly known. Only a most felicitous and rather curious genius could and would shed such a light on such an age. If in the following pages we seem to cavil and find fault, let it be remembered, that the business of a critic is criticism; that is it *not* his business to be thankful; that he must attempt an estimate rather than a eulogy.

Mr. Macaulay seems to have in a high degree the temperament most likely to be that of a historian. This may be summarily defined as the temperament which inclines men to take an interest in actions as contrasted with objects, and in past actions in preference to present actions. We should expand our meaning. Some people are unfortunately born scientific. They take much interest in the objects of nature. They feel a curiosity about shells, snails, horses, butterflies. They are delighted at an ichthyosaurus, and excited at a polyp; they are learned in minerals, vegetables, animals; they have skill in fishes, and attain renown in pebbles; in the highest cases they know the great causes of grand phenomena, can indicate the courses of the stars or the current of the waves; but in every case their minds are directed not to the actions of man, but to the scenery amidst which he lives; not to the inhabitants of this world, but to the world itself; not to what most resembles themselves, but to that which is most unlike. What compels

*The History of England from the Accession of James the Second. By Thomas Babington Macaulay. Longmans.

men to take an interest in what they do take an interest is commonly a difficult question—for the most part, indeed, it is an insoluble one; but in this case it would seem to have a negative cause—to result from the absence of an intense and vivid nature. The inclination of mind which abstracts the attention from that in which it can feel sympathy to that in which they cannot, seems to arise from a want of sympathy. A tendency to devote the mind to trees and stones as much as, or in preference to, men and women, appears to imply that the intellectual qualities, the abstract reason, and the inductive scrutiny which can be applied equally to trees and to men, to stones and to women, predominate over the more special qualities solely applicable to our own race,—the keen love, the eager admiration, the lasting hatred, the lust of rule which fastens men's interests on people and to people. As a confirmation of this, we see, that, even in the greatest cases, scientific men have been calm men. Their actions are unexceptionable; scarcely a spot stains their excellence: if a doubt is to be thrown on their character, it would be rather that they were insensible to the temptations than that they were involved in the offences of ordinary men. An aloofness and abstractedness cleave to their greatness. There is a coldness in their fame. We think of Euclid as of fine ice; we admire Newton as we admire the Peak of Teneriffe. Even the intensest labours, the most remote triumphs of the abstract intellect, seem to carry us into a region different from our own—to be in a *terra incognita* of pure reasoning, to cast a chill on human glory.

We know that the taste of most persons is quite opposite. The tendency of man is to take an interest in man, and almost in man only. The world has a vested interest in itself. Analyse the minds of the crowd of men, and what will you find? Something of the outer earth, no doubt,—odd geography, odd astronomy, doubts whether Scutari is in the Crimea, investigations whether the moon is less or greater than Jupiter; some idea of herbs, more of horses; ideas, too, more or less vague, of the remote and supernatural,—notions which the tongue cannot speak, which it would seem the world would hardly bear if thoroughly spoken. Yet, setting aside these which fill the remote corners and lesser outworks of the brain, the whole stress and vigour of the ordinary faculties is expended on their possessor and his associates, on the man and on his fellows.

In almost all men, indeed, this is not simply an intellectual contemplation; we not only look on, but act. The impulse to busy ourselves with the affairs of men goes further than the simple attempt to know and comprehend them: it warms us with a further life; it incites us to stir and influence those affairs; its animated energy will not rest till it has hurried us into toil and conflict. At this stage the mind of the historian, as we abstractedly fancy it, naturally breaks off; it has more interest in human affairs than the naturalist; it instinctively selects the actions of man for occupation and scrutiny, in preference to the habits of fishes or the structure of stones; but it has not so much vivid interest in them as the warm and active man. To know is sufficient for it; it can bear not to take a part. A want of impulse seems born with the disposition. To be constantly occupied about the actions of others; to have constantly presented to your contemplation and attention events and occurrences memorable only as evincing certain qualities of mind and will, which very qualities in a measure you feel within yourself, and yet be without an impulse to exhibit them in the real world, ' which is the world of all of us; ' to contemplate, yet never act; 'to have the House before you,' and yet to be content with the reporters' gallery,—shows a chill impassiveness of temperament, a sluggish insensibility to ardent impulse, a heavy immobility under ordinary emotion. The image of the stout Gibbon placidly contemplating the animated conflicts, the stirring pleadings of Fox and Burke, watching a revolution and heavily taking no part in it, gives an idea of the historian as he is likely to be. ' Why,' it is often asked, ' is history dull? It is a narrative of life, and life is of all things the most interesting.' The answer is, that it is written by men too dull to take the common interest in life, in whom languor predominates over zeal, and sluggishness over passion.

Macaulay is not dull, and it may seem hard to attempt to bring him within the scope of a theory which is so successful in explaining dulness. Yet, in a modified and peculiar form, we can perhaps find in his remarkable character unusually distinct traces of the insensibility which we ascribe to the historian. The means of scrutiny are ample; Mr. Macaulay has not spent his life in a corner; if posterity should refuse—of course they will not refuse—to read a line of his writings, they would yet be sought out by studious inquirers, as those of a man of high political position, great notoriety, and greater oratorical power. We are not therefore obliged, as in so many cases even among contemporaries, to search for the author's character in his books alone; we are able from other sources to find out his character, and then apply it to explain the peculiarities of his works. Macaulay has exhibited many high attainments, many dazzling talents, much singular and well-trained power; but the quality which would most strike the observers of the interior man is what may be called his *in*experiencing nature. Men of genius are in general distinguished by their extreme susceptibility to external experience. Finer and softer than other men, every exertion of their will, every incident of their lives, influences them more deeply than it would others. Their essence is at once finer and more impressible; it receives a distincter mark, and receives it more easily than the souls of the herd. From a peculiar sensibility, the man of genius bears the stamp of life commonly more clearly than his fellows; even casual associations make a deep impression on him; examine his mind, and you may discern his fortunes. Mr. Macaulay has nothing of this. You could not tell what he has been. His mind shows no trace of change. What he is, he was; and what he was, he is. He early attained a high development, but he has not increased it since; years have come, but they have whispered little; as was said of the second Pitt, 'He never grew, he was cast.' The volume of 'speeches' which he has published places the proof of this in every man's hand. His first speeches are as good as his last; his last scarcely richer than his first. He came into public life at an exciting season; he shared of course in that excitement, and the same excitement still quivers in his mind. He delivered marvellous rhetorical exercises on the Reform Bill when it passed; he speaks of it with rhetorical interest even now. He is still the man of '32. From that era he looks on the past. He sees 'Old Sarum' in the seventeenth century, and Gatton in the civil wars. You may fancy an undertone. The Norman barons commenced the series of reforms which ' *we* consummated;' Hampden was ' preparing for the occasion in which I had a part;' William ' for the debate in which I took occasion to observe.' With a view to that era everything begins; up to that moment everything ascends. That was the ' fifth act ' of the human race;

the remainder of history is only an afterpiece. All this was very
natural at the moment; nothing could be more probable than
that a young man of the greatest talents, entering at once into
important life at a conspicuous opportunity, should exaggerate
its importance; he would fancy it was the ' crowning achievement,' the greatest ' in the tide of time.' But the singularity is,
that he should retain the idea now; that years have brought no
influence, experience no change. The events of twenty years
have been full of rich instruction on the events of twenty years
ago; but they have not instructed him. His creed is a fixture.
It is the same on his peculiar topic—on India. Before he went
there he made a speech on the subject; Lord Canterbury, who
must have heard a million speeches, said it was the best he had
ever heard. It is difficult to fancy that so much vivid knowledge could be gained from books—from horrible Indian
treatises; that such imaginative mastery should be possible
without actual experience. Not forgetting, or excepting, the
orations of Burke, it was perhaps as remarkable a speech as was
ever made on India by an Englishman who had not been in
India. Now he has been there he speaks no better—rather
worse; he spoke excellently without experience, he speaks no
better with it,—if anything, it rather puts him out. His speech
on the Indian charter a year or two ago was not finer than that
on the charter of 1833. Before he went to India he recommended
that writers should be examined in the classics; after being in
India he recommended that they should be examined in the
same way. He did not say he had seen the place in the meantime, he did not think that had anything to do with it. You
could never tell from any difference in his style what he had
seen, or what he had not seen. He is so insensible to passing
objects, that they leave no distinctive mark, no intimate peculiar trace.

Such a man would naturally think literature more instructive than life. Hazlitt said of Mackintosh, ' He might like to
read an *account* of India; but India itself, with its burning,
shining face, was a mere blank, an endless waste to him. Persons of this class have no more to say to a plain matter of fact
staring them in the face than they have to a *hippopotamus*.'
This was a keen criticism on Sir James, savouring of the
splenetic mind from which it came. As a complete estimate, it
would be a most unjust one of Macaulay; but we know that

there are a whole class of minds which prefers the literary delineation of objects to the actual eyesight of them. To some life is difficult. An insensible nature, like a rough hide, resists the breath of passing things; an unobserving retina in vain depicts whatever a quicker eye does not explain. But any one can understand a book; the work is done, the facts observed, the formulæ suggested, the subjects classified. Of course, it needs labour, and a following fancy, to peruse the long lucubrations and descriptions of others; but a fine detective sensibility is unnecessary; type is plain, an earnest attention will follow it and know it. To this class Mr. Macaulay belongs: and he has characteristically maintained that dead authors are more fascinating than living people.

'Those friendships,' he tells us, 'are exposed to no danger from the occurrences by which other attachments are weakened or dissolved. Time glides by; fortune is inconstant; tempers are soured; bonds which seemed indissoluble are daily sundered by interest, by emulation, or by caprice. But no such cause can affect the silent converse which we hold with the highest of human intellects. That placid intercourse is disturbed by no jealousies or resentments. These are the old friends who are never seen with new faces; who are the same in wealth and in poverty, in glory and in obscurity. With the dead there is no rivalry. In the dead there is no change. Plato is never sullen. Cervantes is never petulant. Demosthenes never comes unseasonably. Dante never stays too long. No difference of political opinion can alienate Cicero. No heresy can excite the horror of Bossuet.'

But Bossuet is dead; and Cicero was a Roman; and Plato wrote in Greek. Years and manners separate us from the great. After dinner, Demosthenes *may* come unseasonably; Dante *might* stay too long. *We* are alienated from the politician, and have a horror of the theologian. Dreadful idea, having Demosthenes for an intimate friend! He had pebbles in his mouth; he was always urging action; he spoke such good Greek; we cannot dwell on it,—it is too much. Only a mind impassive to our daily life, unalive to bores and evils, to joys and sorrows, incapable of the deepest sympathies, a prey to print, could imagine it. The mass of men have stronger ties and warmer hopes. The exclusive devotion to books tires. We require to love and hate, to act and live.

It is not unnatural that a person of this temperament should preserve a certain aloofness even in the busiest life. Mr. Macaulay has ever done so. He has been in the thick of political warfare, in the van of party conflict. Whatever a keen excitability would select for food and opportunity, has been his; but he has not been excited. He has never thrown himself upon action, he has never followed trivial details with an anxious passion. He has ever been a man for a great occasion. He was by nature a *deus ex machinâ*. Somebody has had to fetch him. His heart was in Queen Anne's time. When he came, he spoke as Lord Halifax might have spoken. Of course, it may be contended that this is the *eximia ars*; that this solitary removed excellence is particularly and essentially sublime. But, simply and really, greater men have been more deeply ' immersed in matter.' The highest eloquence quivers with excitement; there is life-blood in the deepest action; a man like Strafford seems flung upon the world. An orator should never talk like an observatory; no coldness should strike upon the hearer.

It is characteristic also that he should be continually thinking of posterity. In general, that expected authority is most ungrateful; those who think of it most, it thinks of least. The way to secure its favour is, to give vivid essential pictures of the life before you; to leave a fresh glowing delineation of the scene to which you were born, of the society to which you have peculiar access. This is gained, not by thinking of your posterity, but by living in society; not by poring on what is to be, but by enjoying what is. That spirit of thorough enjoyment which pervades the great delineators of human life and human manners, was not caused by ' being made after supper, out of a cheese-paring; ' it drew its sustenance from a relishing, enjoying, sensitive life, and the flavour of the description is the reality of the enjoyment. Of course, this is not so in science. You may leave a name by an abstract discovery, without having led a vigorous existence; yet what a name is this ! Taylor's theorem will go down to posterity,—possibly its discoverer was for ever dreaming and expecting that it would; but what does posterity know of the deceased Taylor ? *Nominis umbra* is rather a compliment; for it is not substantial enough to have a shadow. But in other walks,—say in political oratory, which is the part of Mr. Macaulay's composition in which his value for posterity's opinion is most apparent—the way to interest posterity is to think but little of it. What gives to the speeches of Demosthenes the interest they have? The intense, vivid, glowing interest of the speaker in all that he is speaking about. Philip is not a person whom 'posterity will censure,' but the man 'whom I hate:' the matter in hand not one whose interest depends on the memory of men, but in which an eager intense nature would have been absorbed if there had been no posterity at all, on which he wished to deliver his own soul. A *casual* character, so to speak, is natural to the most intense words; externally, even, they will interest the 'after world' more for having interested the present world; they must have a life of *some* place and *some* time before they can have one of all space and all time. Mr. Macaulay's oratory is the very opposite of this. School-boyish it is not, for it is the oratory of a very sensible man; but the theme of a school-boy is not more devoid of the salt of circumstance. The speeches on the Reform Bill have been headed, 'Now, a man came up from college and spoke thus;' and, like a college man, he spoke rather to the abstract world than to the present. He knew no more of the people who actually did live in London than of people who would live in London, and there was therefore no reason for speaking to one more than to the other. After years of politics, he speaks so still. He looks on a question (he says) as posterity will look on it; he appeals from this to future generations; he regards existing men as painful prerequisites of great-grandchildren. This seems to proceed, as has been said, from a distant and unimpressible nature. But it is impossible to deny that it has one great advantage: it has made him take pains. A man who speaks to people a thousand years off will naturally speak carefully: he tries to be heard over the clang of ages, over the rumours of myriads. Writing for posterity is like writing on foreign post paper: you cannot say to a man at Calcutta what you would say to a man at Hackney; you think 'the yellow man is a very long way off; this is fine paper, it will go by a ship;' so you try to say something worthy of the ship, something noble, which will keep and travel. Writers like Macaulay, who think of future people, have a respect for future people. Each syllable is

solemn, each word distinct. No author trained to periodical
writing has so little of its slovenliness and its imperfection.

This singularly constant contemplation of posterity has
coloured his estimate of social characters. He has no toleration
for those great men in whom a lively sensibility to momentary
honours has prevailed over a consistent reference to the posthumous tribunal. He is justly severe on Lord Bacon:

'In his library all his rare powers were under the guidance
of an honest ambition, of an enlarged philanthropy, of a sincere love of truth. There no temptation drew him away from
the right course. Thomas Aquinas could pay no fees, Duns
Scotus could confer no peerages. The "Master of the Sentences" had no rich reversions in his gift. Far different was
the situation of the great philosopher when he came forth from
his study and his laboratory to mingle with the crowd which
filled the galleries of Whitehall. In all that crowd there was
no man equally qualified to render great and lasting services
to mankind. But in all that crowd there was not a heart more
set on things which no man ought to suffer to be necessary
to his happiness,—on things which can often be obtained only
by the sacrifice of integrity and honour. To be the leader of the
human race in the career of improvement, to found on the ruins
of ancient intellectual dynasties a more prosperous and more
enduring empire, to be revered to the latest generations as the
most illustrious among the benefactors of mankind,—all this
was within his reach. But all this availed him nothing, while
some quibbling special pleader was promoted before him to
the Bench,—while some heavy country gentleman took pre-
cedence of him by virtue of a purchased coronet,—while
some pander, happy in a fair wife, could obtain a more cordial
salute from Buckingham,—while some buffoon, versed in all
the latest scandal of the Court, could draw a louder laugh from
James.'

Yet a less experience, or a less opportunity of experience,
would have warned a mind more observant that the bare desire
for long posthumous renown is but a feeble principle in common
human nature. Bacon had as much of it as most men. The
keen excitability to this world's temptations must be opposed
by more exciting impulses, by more retarding discouragements,
by conscience, by religion, by fear. If you would vanquish

earth, you must 'invent heaven.' It is the fiction of a cold abstractedness that the possible respect of unseen people can commonly be more desired than the certain homage of existing people.

In a more conspicuous manner the chill nature of the most brilliant among English historians is shown in his defective dealing with the passionate eras of our history. He has never been attracted or not proportionately attracted, by the singular mixture of heroism and slavishness, of high passion and base passion, which mark the Tudor period. The defect is apparent in his treatment of a period on which he has written powerfully—the time of the civil wars. He has never in the highest manner appreciated either of the two great characters—the Puritan and the Cavalier—which are the form and life of those years. What historian, indeed, has ever estimated the Cavalier character? There is Clarendon—the grave, rhetorical, decorous lawyer—piling words, congealing arguments,—very stately, a little grim. There is Hume—the Scotch metaphysician—who has made out the best case for such people as never were, for a Charles who never died, for a Strafford who would never have been attainted,—a saving, calculating north-countryman,—fat, impassive, who lived on eightpence a day. What have these people to do with an enjoying English gentleman? It is easy for a *doctrinaire* to bear a *post-mortem* examination,—it is much the same whether he be alive or dead; but not so with those who live during their life, whose essence is existence, whose being is in animation. There seem to be some characters who are not made for history, as there are some who are not made for old age. A Cavalier is always young. The buoyant life arises before us rich in hope, strong in vigour, irregular in action; men young and ardent, framed in the 'prodigality of nature;' open to every enjoyment, alive to every passion; eager, impulsive; brave without discipline; noble without principle; prizing luxury, despising danger, capable of high sentiment, but in each of whom the

> 'Addiction was to courses vain;
> His companies unlettered, rude, and shallow,
> His hours filled up with riots, banquets, sports,
> And never noted in him any study,
> Any retirement, any sequestration
> From open haunts and popularity.'

We see these men setting forth or assembling to defend their king and church; and we see it without surprise; a rich daring loves danger; a deep excitability likes excitement. If we look around us, we may see what is analogous. Some say that the battle of the Alma was won by the 'uneducated gentry;' the 'uneducated gentry' would be Cavaliers now. The political sentiment is part of the character. The essence of Toryism is enjoyment. Talk of the ways of spreading a wholesome Conservatism throughout this country: give painful lectures, distribute weary tracts (and perhaps this is as well— you may be able to give an argumentative answer to a few objections, you may diffuse a distinct notion of the dignified dullness of politics); but as far as communicating and establishing your creed are concerned—try a little pleasure. The way to keep up old customs is, to enjoy old customs; the way to be satisfied with the present state of things is, to enjoy that state of things. Over the 'Cavalier' mind this world passes with a thrill of delight; there is an exultation in a daily event, zest in the 'regular thing,' joy at an old feast. Sir Walter Scott is an example of this. Every habit and practice of old Scotland was inseparably in his mind associated with genial enjoyment. To propose to touch one of her institutions, to abolish one of those practices, was to touch a personal pleasure —a point on which his mind reposed, a thing of memory and hope. So long as this world is this world, will a buoyant life be the proper source of an animated Conservatism. The 'church-and-king' enthusiasm has even a deeper connection with the Cavaliers. Carlyle has said, in his vivid way, 'Two or three young gentlemen have said, "Go to, I will *make* a religion."' This is the exact opposite of what the irregular enjoying man can think or conceive. What! is he, with his untrained mind and his changeful heart and his ruleless practice, to create a creed? Is the gushing life to be asked to construct a cistern? Is the varying heart to be its own master, the evil practice its own guide? Sooner will a ship invent its own rudder, devise its own pilot, than the eager being will find out the doctrine which is to restrain him. The very intellect is a type of the confusion of the soul. It has little arguments on a thousand subjects, hearsay sayings, original flashes, small and bright, struck from the heedless mind by the strong impact of the world. And it has nothing else. It has no systematic knowledge; it has a hatred of regular attention. What can an understanding of this sort do with refined questioning or subtle investigation? It is obliged in a sense by its very nature to take what comes; it is overshadowed in a manner by the religion to which it is born; its conscience tells it that it owes obedience to something; it craves to worship something; that something, in both cases, it takes from the past. ' Thou hast not chosen me, but I have chosen thee,' might his faith say to a believer of this kind. A certain bigotry is altogether natural to him. His creed seems to him a primitive fact, as certain and evident as the stars. The political faith (for it is a faith) of these persons is of a kind analogous. The virtue of loyalty assumes in them a passionate aspect, and overflows, as it were, all the intellect which belongs to the topic. This virtue, this need of our nature, arises, as political philosophers tell us, from the conscious necessity which man is under of obeying an external moral rule. We feel that we are by nature and by the constitution of all things under an obligation to conform to a certain standard, and we seek to find or to establish in the sphere without an authority which shall enforce it, shall aid us in compelling others and also in mastering ourselves. When a man impressed with this principle comes in contact with the institution of civil government as it now exists and as it has always existed, he finds what he wants—he discovers an authority; and he feels bound to submit to it. We do not, of course, mean that all this takes place distinctly and consciously in the mind of the person; on the contrary, the class of minds most subject to its influence are precisely those which have in general the least defined and accurate consciousness of their own operations, or of what befalls them. In matter of fact, they find themselves under the control of laws and of a polity from the earliest moment that they can remember, and they obey it from habit and custom years before they know why. Only in later life, when distinct thought is from an outward occurrence forced upon them, do they feel the necessity of some such power; and in proportion to their passionate and impulsive disposition they feel it the more. The law has in a less degree on them the same effect which military discipline has in a greater. It braces them to defined duties, and subjects them to a known authority. Quieter minds find this authority in an internal conscience; but in riotous natures its still small voice is lost if it be not echoed in loud harsh tones from the firm and outer world:

> ' Their breath is agitation, and their life
> A storm whereon they ride.'

From without they crave a bridle and a curb. The doctrine of non-resistance is no *accident* of the Cavalier character, though it seems at first sight singular in an eager tumultuous disposition. So inconsistent is human nature, that it proceeds from the very extremity of that tumult. They know that they cannot allow themselves to question the authority which is upon them; they feel its necessity too acutely, their intellect is untrained in subtle disquisitions, their conscience fluctuating, their passions rising. They are sure that if they once depart from that authority, their whole soul will be in anarchy. As a riotous state tends to fall under a martial tyranny, a passionate mind tends to subject itself to an extrinsic law—to enslave itself to an outward discipline. ' That is what the king says, boy, and that was ever enough for Sir Henry Lee.' An hereditary monarch is, indeed, the very embodiment of this principle. The authority is so defined, so clearly vested, so evidently intelligible; it descends so distinctly from the past, it is imposed so conspicuously from without. Anything free refers to the people; anything elected seems self-chosen. ' The divinity that doth hedge a king ' consists in his evidently representing an unmade, unchosen, hereditary duty.

The greatness of this character is not in Mr. Macaulay's way, and its faults are. Its license affronts him; its riot alienates him. He is for ever contrasting the dissoluteness of Prince Rupert's horse with the restraint of Cromwell's pikemen. A deep enjoying nature finds no sympathy. The brilliant style passes forward: we dwell on its brilliancy, but it is cold. He has no tears for that warm life, no tenderness for that extinct joy. The ignorance of the Cavalier, too, moves his wrath: ' They were ignorant of what every schoolgirl knows.'' Their loyalty to their sovereign is the devotion of the Egyptians to the god Apis, who selected ' a calf to adore.' Their non-resistance offends the philosopher: their license is commented on with the tone of a precisian. Their indecorum does not suit the dignity of the narrator. Their rich free nature is unappreciated; the tingling intensity of their joy is unnoticed. In a word, there is something of the schoolboy about the Cavalier —there is somewhat of a schoolmaster about the historian.

It might be thought, at first sight, that the insensibility and coldness which are unfavourable to the appreciation of the Cavalier would be particularly favourable to that of the Puritan. Some may say that a natural aloofness from things earthly would dispose a man to the doctrines of a sect which enjoins above all other commandments abstinence and aloofness *from* those things. In Mr. Macaulay's case it certainly has had no such consequence. He was bred up in the circle which more than any other has resembled that of the greatest and best Puritans—in the circle which has presented the evangelical doctrine in its most influential and celebrated, and not its least genial form. Yet he has revolted against it. The bray of 'Exeter Hall' is a phrase which has become celebrated: it is an odd one for his father's son. The who lecourse of his personal fortunes, the entire scope of his historical narrative, show an utter want of sympathy with the Puritan disposition. It would be idle to quote passages; it will be enough to recollect the contrast between the estimate—say of Cromwell—by Carlyle and that by Macaulay, to be aware of the enormous discrepancy. The one's manner evinces an instinctive sympathy, the other's an instinctive aversion.

We believe that this is but a consequence of the same impassibility of nature which we have said so much of. M. Montalembert, in a striking *éloge* on a French historian—a man of the Southey type—after speaking of his life in Paris during youth (a youth cast in the early and exciting years of the first revolution, and of the prelude to it), and graphically portraying a man subject to scepticism, but not given to vice; staid in habits, but unbelieving in opinion; without faith and without irregularity,—winds up the whole by the sentence, that '*he was hardened at once against good and evil.*' In his view, the insensibility which was a guard against exterior temptation was also a hindrance to inward belief: and there is a philosophy in this. The nature of man is not two things, but one thing. We have not one set of affections, hopes, sensibilities, to be affected by the present world, and another and a different to be affected by the invisible world: we are moved by grandeur, or we are not; we are stirred by sublimity, or we are not; we hunger after righteousness, or we do not; we hate vice, or we do not; we are passionate, or not passionate; loving, or not loving; cold, or not cold; our heart is dull, or it is wakeful; our soul is alive, or it is dead. Deep under the surface of the intellect lies the *stratum* of the passions, of the intense, peculiar, simple impulses which constitute the heart of man; there is the eager essence, the primitive desiring being. What stirs this latent being we know. In general it is stirred by everything. Sluggish natures are stirred little, wild natures are stirred much; but all are stirred somewhat. It is not important whether the object be in the visible or invisible world: whoso loves what he has seen, will love what he has not seen; whoso hates what he has seen, will hate what he has not seen. Creation is, as it were, but the garment of the Creator: whoever is blind to the beauty on its surface, will be insensible to the beauty beneath; whoso is dead to the sublimity before his senses, will be dull to that which he imagines; whoso is untouched by the visible man, will be unmoved by the invisible God. These are no new ideas; and the conspicuous evidence of history confirms them. Everywhere the deep religious organisation has been deeply sensitive to this world. If we compare what are called sacred and profane literatures, the depth of human affection is deepest in the sacred. A warmth as of life is on the Hebrew, a chill as of marble is on the Greek. In Jewish history the most tenderly religious character is the most sensitive to earth. Along every lyric of the great Psalmist thrills a deep spirit of human enjoyment; he was alive as a child to the simple aspects of the world; the very errors of his mingled career are but those to which the open, enjoying character is most prone; its principle, so to speak, was a tremulous passion for that which he had seen, as well as that which he had not seen. There is no paradox, therefore, in saying that the same character which least appreciates the impulsive and ardent Cavalier is also the most likely not to appreciate the warm zeal of an overpowering devotion.

Some years ago it would have been necessary to show at length that the Puritans had such a devotion. The notion had been that they were fanatics, who simulated zeal, and hypocrites, who misquoted the Old Testament. A new era has arrived; one of the great discoveries which the competition of authors has introduced into historical researches has attained a singular popularity. Times are changed. We are rather now, in general, in danger of holding too high an estimate of the puritanical character than a too low or contemptuous one. Among the disciples of Carlyle it is considered that having been a Puritan is the next best thing to having been in Germany. But though we cannot sympathise with everything that the expounders of the new theory allege, and though we should not select for praise the exact peculiarities most agreeable to the slightly grim ' gospel of earnestness,' we acknowledge the great service which they have rendered to English history. No one will now ever overlook, that in the greater, in the original Puritans—in Cromwell, for example—the whole basis of the character was a passionate, deep, rich, religious organisation.

This is not in Mr. Macaulay's way. It is not that he is sceptical; far from it. ' Divines of all persuasions,' he tells us, ' are agreed that there is a religion; ' and he acquiesces in their teaching. But he has no passionate self-questionings, no indomitable fears, no asking perplexities. He is probably pleased at the exemption. He has praised Lord Bacon for a similar want of interest. ' Nor did he ever meddle with those enigmas which have puzzled hundreds of generations, and will puzzle hundreds more. He said nothing about the grounds of moral obligation, or the freedom of the human will. He had no inclination to employ himself in labours resembling those of the damned in the Grecian Tartarus—to spin for ever on the same wheel round the same pivot. He lived in an age in which disputes on the most subtle points of divinity excited an intense interest throughout Europe; and nowhere more than in England. He was placed in the very thick of the conflict. He was in power at the time of the Synod of Dort, and must for months have been daily deafened with talk about election, reprobation, and final perseverance. Yet we do not remember a line in his works from which it can be inferred that he was either a Calvinist or an Arminian. While the world was resounding with the noise of a disputatious philosophy and a disputatious theology, the Baconian school, like Alworthy seated between Square and Thwackum, preserved a calm neutrality,—half-scornful, half-benevolent,—and, content with adding to the sum of practical good, left the war of words to those who liked it.' This may be the writing of good sense, but it is not the expression of an anxious or passionate religious nature.

Such is the explanation of his not prizing so highly as he

should prize the essential excellences of the Puritan character.
He is defective in the one point in which they were very great;
he is eminent in the very point in which they were most
defective. A spirit of easy cheerfulness pervades his writings,
a pleasant geniality overflows in history: the rigid asceticism,
the pain for pain's sake of the Puritan is altogether alien to
him. Retribution he would deny; sin is hardly a part of his
creed. His religion is one of thanksgiving. His notion of
philosophy—it would be a better notion of his own writing—
is *illustrans commoda vitæ*.

The English Revolution is the very topic for a person of this
character. It is eminently an unimpassioned movement. It
requires no appreciation of the Cavalier or of the zealot; no
sympathy with the romance of this world; no inclination to
pass beyond, and absorb the mind's energies in another. It had
neither the rough enthusiasm of barbarism nor the delicate
grace of high civilisation; the man who conducted it had neither
the deep spirit of Cromwell's Puritans nor the chivalric loyalty
of the enjoying English gentleman. They were hard-headed
sensible men, who knew that politics were a kind of business,
that the essence of business is compromise, of practicality
concession. They drove no theory to excess; for they had no
theory. Their passions did not hurry them away; for their
temperament was still, their reason calculating and calm.
Locke is the type of the best character of his era. There is
nothing in him which a historian such as we have described
could fail to comprehend, or could not sympathise with when
he did comprehend. He was the very reverse of a Cavalier; he
came of a Puritan stock; he retained through life a kind of
chilled Puritanism: he had nothing of its excessive, overpowering, interior zeal, but he retained the formal decorum which it
had given to the manners, the solid earnestness of its intellect,
the heavy respectability of its character. In all the nations
across which Puritanism has passed you may notice something
of its indifference to this world's lighter enjoyments; no one of
them has been quite able to retain its singular interest in what
is beyond the veil of time and sense. The generation to which
we owe our revolution was in the first stage of the descent.
Locke thought a zealot a dangerous person, and a poet little
better than a rascal. It has been said, with perhaps an allusion
to Macaulay, that our historians have held that ' all the people

who lived before 1688 were either knaves or fools.' This is, of course, an exaggeration; but those who have considered what sort of person a historian is likely to be, will not be surprised at his preference for the people of that era. They had the equable sense which he appreciates; they had not the deep animated passions to which his nature is insensible.

Yet, though Mr. Macaulay shares in the common temperament of historians, and in the sympathy with, and appreciation of, the characters most congenial to that temperament, he is singularly contrasted with them in one respect—he has a vivid fancy, they have a dull one. History is generally written on the principle that human life is a transaction; that people come to it with defined intentions and a calm self-possessed air, as stockjobbers would buy 'omnium,' as timber-merchants buy 'best middling;' people are alike, and things are alike; everything is a little dull, every one a little slow; manners are not depicted, traits are not noticed; the narrative is confined to those great transactions which can be understood without any imaginative delineation of their accompaniments. There are two kinds of things—those which you need only to *understand*, and those which you need also to *imagine*. That a man bought nine hundredweight of hops is an intelligible idea—you do not want the hops delineated or the man described; that he went into society suggests an inquiry—you want to know what the society was like, and how far he was fitted to be there. The great business transactions of the political world are of the intelligible description. Macaulay has himself said:

' A history, in which every particular incident may be true, may on the whole be false. The circumstances which have most influence on the happiness of mankind, the changes of manners and morals, the transition of communities from poverty to wealth, from knowledge to ignorance, from ferocity to humanity,—these are, for the most part, noiseless revolutions. Their progress is rarely indicated by what historians are pleased to call important events. They are not achieved by armies, or enacted by senates. They are sanctioned by no treaties, and recorded in no archives. They are carried on in every school, in every church, behind ten thousand counters, at ten thousand firesides. The upper current of society presents no certain criterion by which we can judge of the direction in which the under current flows. We read of defeats and victories; but we know that nations may be miserable amidst victories, and prosperous amidst defeats. We read of the fall of wise ministers, and of the rise of profligate favourites; but we must remember how small a proportion the good or evil effected by a single statesman can bear to the good or evil of a great social system.'

But of this sluggishness of imagination he has certainly no trace himself. He is willing to be ' behind ten thousand counters,' to be a guest ' at ten thousand firesides.' He is willing to see ' ordinary men as they appear in their ordinary business and in their ordinary pleasures.' He has no objection to 'mingle in the crowds of the Exchange and the coffee-house.' He would ' obtain admittance to the convivial table and the domestic hearth.' So far as his dignity will permit, ' he will bear with vulgar expressions.' And a singular efficacy of fancy gives him the power to do so. Some portion of the essence of human nature is concealed from him; but all its accessories are at his command. He delineates any trait; he can paint, and justly paint, any manners he chooses.

' A perfect historian,' he tells us, ' is he in whose work the character and spirit of an age is exhibited in miniature. He relates no fact, he attributes no expression to his characters, which is not authenticated by sufficient testimony; but, by judicious selection, rejection, and arrangement, he gives to truth those attractions which have been usurped by fiction. In his narrative a due subordination is observed—some transactions are prominent, others retire; but the scale on which he represents them is increased or diminished, not according to the dignity of the persons concerned in them, but according to the degree in which they elucidate the condition of society and the nature of man. He shows us the court, the camp, and the senate; but he shows us also the nation. He considers no anecdote, no peculiarity of manner, no familiar saying, as too insignificant for his notice, which is not too insignificant to illustrate the operation of laws, of religion, and of education, and to mark the progress of the human mind. Men will not merely be described, but will be made intimately known to us. The changes of manners will be indicated, not merely by a few general phrases, or a few extracts from statistical documents, but by appropriate images presented in every line. If a man, such as we are supposing, should write the history of England, he would assuredly not omit the battles, the sieges, the negotiations, the seditions, the ministerial changes; but with these he would intersperse the details which are the charm of historical romances. At Lincoln Cathedral there is a beautiful painted window, which was made by an apprentice out of the pieces of glass which had been rejected by his master. It is so far superior to every other in the church, that, according to the tradition, the vanquished artist killed himself from mortification. Sir Walter Scott, in the same manner, has used those fragments of truth which historians have scornfully thrown behind them in a manner which may well excite their envy. He has constructed out of their gleanings works which, even considered as histories, are scarcely less valuable than theirs. But a truly great historian would reclaim those materials which the novelist has appropriated. The history of the government, and the history of the people, would be exhibited in that mode in which alone they can be exhibited justly, in inseparable conjunction and intermixture. We should not then have to look for the wars and votes of the Puritans in Clarendon, and for their phraseology in *Old Mortality*; for one half of King James in Hume, and for the other half in the *Fortunes of Nigel*.'

So far as the graphic description of exterior life goes, he has completely realised his idea.

This union of a flowing fancy with an insensible organisation is very rare. In general a delicate fancy is joined with a poetic organisation. Exactly why, it would be difficult to explain. It is for metaphysicians in large volumes to explain the genesis of the human faculties; but, as a fact, it seems to be clear that, for the most part, imaginative men are the most sensitive to the poetic side of human life and natural scenery. They are drawn by a strong instinct to what is sublime, grand, and beautiful. They do not care for the coarse business of life. They dislike to be cursed with its ordinary cares. Their nature is vivid; it is interested by all which naturally interests; it dwells on the great, the graceful, and the grand. On this account it naturally runs away from history. The very name of it is too oppressive. Are not all such works written in the *Index Expurgatorius* of the genial satirist as works which it was impossible to read? The coarse and cumbrous matter revolts the soul of the fine and fanciful voluptuary. Take it as you will, human life is like the earth on which man dwells. There are exquisite beauties, grand imposing objects, scattered here and there; but the spaces between these are wide; the mass of common clay is huge; the dead level of vacant life, of commonplace geography, is immense. The poetic nature cannot bear the preponderance; it seeks relief in selected scenes, in special topics, in favourite beauties. History, which is the record of human existence, is a faithful representative of it, at least in this: the poetic mind cannot bear the weight of its narrations and the commonplaceness of its events.

This peculiarity of character gives to Macaulay's writing one of its most curious characteristics. He throws over matters which are in their nature dry and dull,—transactions—budgets —bills,—the charm of fancy which a poetical mind employs to enhance and set forth the charm of what is beautiful. An attractive style is generally devoted to what is in itself specially attractive; here it is devoted to subjects which are often unattractive, are sometimes even repelling, at the best are commonly neutral, not inviting attention, if they do not excite dislike. In these new volumes there is a currency reform, pages on Scotch Presbyterianism, a heap of Parliamentary debates. Who could be expected to make anything interesting of such topics? It is not cheerful to read in the morning papers the debates of yesterday, though they happened last night; one cannot like a Calvinistic divine when we see him in the pulpit; it is awful to read on the currency, even when it concerns the bank-notes which we use. How, then, can we care for a narrative when the divine is dead, the shillings extinct, the whole topic of the debate forgotten and past away? Yet such is the power of style, so great is the charm of very skilful words, of narration which is always passing forward, of illustration which always hits the mark, that such subjects as these not only become interesting, but very interesting. The proof is evident. No book is so sought after. The Chancellor of the Exchequer said, ' all members of Parliament had read it.' What other books could ever be fancied to have been read by them? A county member—a real county member—hardly reads two volumes *per* existence. Years ago Macaulay said a History of England might become more in demand at the

circulating libraries than the last novel. He has actually made
his words true. It is no longer a phrase of rhetoric, it is a
simple fact.

The explanation of this remarkable notoriety is, the contrast of the topic and the treatment. Those who read for the
sake of entertainment are attracted by the one; those who
read for the sake of instruction are attracted by the other.
Macaulay has something that suits the readers of Mr. Hallam;
he has something which will please the readers of Mr.
Thackeray. The first wonder to find themselves reading such
a style; the last are astonished at reading on such topics—at
finding themselves studying by casualty. This marks the
author. Only a buoyant fancy and an impassive temperament
could produce a book so combining weight with levity.

Something similar may be remarked of the writings of a
still greater man—of Edmund Burke. The contrast of the
manner of his characteristic writings to their matter is very
remarkable. He, too, threw over the detail of business and of
politics those graces and attractions of manner which seem in
some sort inconsistent with them; which are adapted for topics
more intrinsically sublime and beautiful. It was for this reason
that Hazlitt asserted that ' no woman ever cared for Burke's
writings.' The matter, he said, was ' hard and dry,' and no
superficial glitter or eloquence could make it agreeable to
those who liked what is, in its very nature, fine and delicate.
The charm of exquisite narration has, in a great degree, in
Mr. Macaulay's case, supplied the deficiency; but it may be
perhaps remarked, that some trace of the same phenomenon
has again occurred, from similar causes, and that his popularity,
though great among both sexes, is in some sense more masculine than feminine. The absence of this charm of narration,
to which accomplished women are, it would seem, peculiarly
sensitive, is very characteristic of Burke. His mind was the
reverse of historical. Although he had rather a coarse, incon-
dite temperament, not finely susceptible to the best influences,
to the most exquisite beauties of the world in which he lived,
yet lived in that world thoroughly and completely. He did not
take an interest, as a poet does, in the sublime because it is
sublime, in the beautiful because it is beautiful; but he had
the passions of more ordinary men in a degree, and of an
intensity, which ordinary men may be most thankful that they

have not. In no one has the intense faculty of intellectual hatred—the hatred which the absolute dogmatist has for those in whom he incarnates and personifies the opposing dogma— been fiercer or stronger; in no one has the intense ambition to rule and govern,—in scarcely any one has the daily ambition of the daily politician, been fiercer and stronger: he, if any man, cast himself upon his time. After one of his speeches peruse one of Macaulay's: you seem transported to another sphere. The fierce living interest of the one contrasts with the cold rhetorical interest of the other; you are in a different part of the animal kingdom; you have left the viviparous intellect; you have left products warm and struggling with hasty life; you have reached the oviparous, and products smooth and polished, cold and stately.

In addition to this impassive nature, inclining him to write on past transactions—to this fancy, enabling him to adorn and describe them—Mr. Macaulay has a marvellous memory to recall them; and what we may call the Scotch intellect, enabling him to conceive them. The memory is his most obvious power. An enormous reading seems always present to him. No effort seems wanted—no mental excogitation. According to his own description of a like faculty, ' it would have been strange indeed, if you had asked for anything that was not to be found in that immense storehouse. The article you required was not only there, it was ready. It was in its own compartment. In a moment it was brought down, unpacked, and explained.' He has a literary illustration for everything; and his fancy enables him to make a skilful use of his wealth. He always selects the exact likeness of the idea which he wishes to explain. And though it be less obvious, yet his writing would have been deficient in one of its most essential characteristics if it had not been for what we have called his Scotch intellect, which is a curious matter to explain. It may be thought that Adam Smith had little in common with Sir Walter Scott. Sir Walter was always making fun of him; telling odd tales of his abstraction and singularity; not obscurely hinting, that a man who could hardly put on his own coat, and certainly could not buy his own dinner, was scarcely fit to decide on the proper course of industry and the mercantile dealings of nations. Yet, when Sir Walter's own works come to be closely examined, they will be found to contain a good deal of political economy of a certain sort,—and not a very bad sort. Any one who will study his description of the Highland clans in *Waverley;* his observations on the industrial side (if so it is to be called) of the Border-life; his plans for dealing with the poor of his own time,—will be struck not only with a plain sagacity, which we could equal in England, but with the digested accuracy and theoretical completeness which they show. You might cut paragraphs, even from his lighter writings, which would be thought acute in the *Wealth of Nations.* There appears to be in the genius of the Scotch people—fostered, no doubt, by the abstract metaphysical education of their Universities, but also, by way of natural taste, supporting that education, and rendering it possible and popular—a power of reducing human actions to formulæ or principles. An instance is now in a high place. People who are not lawyers,—rural people, who have sense of their own, but have no access to the general repute and opinion which expresses the collective sense of the great world,—never can be brought to believe that Lord Campbell is a great man. They read his speeches in the House of Lords—his occasional flights of eloquence on the bench—his attempts at pathos—his stupendous *gaucheries*—and they cannot be persuaded that a person so guilty of such things can have really first-rate talent. If you ask them how he came to be Chief Justice of England, they mutter something angry, and 'Well, Scotchmen *do* get on somehow.' This is really the true explanation. In spite of a hundred defects, Lord Campbell has the Scotch faculties in perfection. He reduces legal matters to a sound broad principle better than any man who is now a judge. He has a steady, comprehensive, abstract, distinct consistency, which elaborates a formula and adheres to a formula; and it is this which has raised him from a plain—a very plain—Scotch adventurer to be Lord Chief Justice of England. Mr. Macaulay has this too. Among his more brilliant qualities, it has escaped the attention of critics; the more so, because his powers of exposition and expression make it impossible to conceive for a moment that the amusing matter we are reading is really Scotch economy.

'During the interval,' he tells us, 'between the Restoration and the Revolution, the riches of the nation had been rapidly

increasing. Thousands of busy men found every Christmas
that, after the expenses of the year's housekeeping had been
defrayed out of the year's income, a surplus remained; and
how that surplus was to be employed was a question of some
difficulty. In our time, to invest such a surplus, at something
more than three per cent., on the best security that has ever
been known in the world, is the work of a few minutes. But in
the seventeenth century, a lawyer, a physician, a retired
merchant, who had saved some thousands, and who wished to
place them safely and profitably, was often greatly embarrassed.
Three generations earlier, a man who had accumulated wealth
in a profession generally purchased real property, or lent his
savings on mortgage. But the number of acres in the kingdom
had remained the same; and the value of those acres, though
it had greatly increased, had by no means increased so fast as the
quantity of capital which was seeking for employment. Many,
too, wished to put their money where they could find it at an
hour's notice, and looked about for some species of property
which could be more readily transferred than a house or a
field. A capitalist might lend on bottomry or on personal
security; but, if he did so, he ran a great risk of losing interest
and principal. There were a few joint-stock companies, among
which the East India Company held the foremost place; but
the demand for the stock of such companies was far greater
than the supply. Indeed, the cry for a new East India Company was chiefly raised by persons who had found difficulty
in placing their savings at interest on good security. So great
was that difficulty, that the practice of hoarding was common. We are told that the father of Pope the poet, who retired
from business in the City about the time of the Revolution,
carried to a retreat in the country a strong box containing
near twenty thousand pounds, and took out from time to time
what was required for household expenses; and it is highly
probable that this was not a solitary case. At present the
quantity of coin which is hoarded by private persons is so
small, that it would, if brought forth, make no perceptible
addition to the circulation. But, in the earlier part of the
reign of William the Third, all the greatest writers on currency
were of opinion that a very considerable mass of gold and
silver was hidden in secret drawers and behind wainscots.

' The natural effect of this state of things was, that a crowd of projectors, ingenious and absurd, honest and knavish, employed themselves in devising new schemes for the employment of redundant capital. It was about the year 1688 that the word stockjobber was first heard in London. In the short space of four years a crowd of companies, every one of which confidently held out to subscribers the hope of immense gains, sprang into existence: the Insurance Company, the Paper Company, the Lutestring Company, the Pearl-Fishery Company, the Glass-Bottle Company, the Alum Company, the Blythe Coal Company, the Swordblade Company. There was a Tapestry Company, which would soon furnish pretty hangings for all the parlours of the middle class and for all the bedchambers of the higher. There was a Copper Company, which proposed to explore the mines of England, and held out a hope that they would prove not less valuable than those of Potosi. There was a Diving Company, which undertook to bring up precious effects from shipwrecked vessels, and which announced that it had laid in a stock of wonderful machines, resembling complete suits of armour. In front of the helmet was a huge glass eye, like that of a Cyclop; and out of the crest went a pipe, through which the air was to be admitted. The whole process was exhibited on the Thames. Fine gentlemen and fine ladies were invited to the show, were hospitably regaled, and were delighted by seeing the divers in their panoply descend into the river, and return laden with old iron and ship's tackle. There was a Greenland Fishing Company, which could not fail to drive the Dutch whalers and herring-busses out of the Northern Ocean. There was a Tanning Company, which promised to furnish leather superior to the best that was brought from Turkey or Russia. There was a society which undertook the office of giving gentlemen a liberal education on low terms, and which assumed the sounding name of the Royal Academies Company. In a pompous advertisement it was announced that the directors of the Royal Academies Company had engaged the best masters in every branch of knowledge, and were about to issue twenty thousand tickets at twenty shillings each. There was to be a lottery: two thousand prizes were to be drawn; and the fortunate holders of the prizes were to be taught, at the charge of the company, Latin, Greek, Hebrew, French, Spanish, conic sections, trigonometry, heraldry, japanning, fortification, book-keeping, and the art of playing the theorbo. Some of these companies took large mansions, and printed their advertisements in gilded letters. Others, less ostentatious, were content with ink, and met at coffee-houses in the neighbourhood of the Royal Exchange. Jonathan's and Garraway's were in a constant ferment with brokers, buyers, sellers, meetings of directors, meetings of proprietors. Time-bargains soon came into fashion. Extensive combinations were formed, and monstrous fables were circulated, for the purpose of raising or depressing the price of shares. Our country witnessed for the first time those phenomena with which a long experience has made us familiar. A mania, of which the symptoms were essentially the same with those of the mania of 1720, of the mania of 1825, of the mania of 1845, seized the public mind. An impatience to be rich, a contempt for those slow but sure gains which are the proper reward of industry, patience, and thrift, spread through society. The spirit of the cogging dicers of Whitefriars took possession of the grave senators of the city, wardens of trades, deputies, aldermen. It was much easier and much more lucrative to put forth a lying prospectus announcing a new stock, to persuade ignorant people that the dividends could not fall short of twenty per cent., and to part with five thousand pounds of this imaginary wealth for ten thousand solid guineas, than to load a ship with a well-chosen cargo for Virginia or the Levant. Every day some new bubble was puffed into existence, rose buoyant, shone bright, burst, and was forgotten.'

You will not find the cause of panics so accurately explained in the dryest of political economists—in the Scotch M'Culloch.

These peculiarities of character and mind may be very conspicuously traced through the *History of England*, and in the *Essays*. Their first and most striking quality is the *intellectual entertainment* which they afford. This, as practical readers know, is a kind of sensation which is not very common, and which is very productive of great and healthy enjoyment. It is quite distinct from the amusement which is derived from common light works. The latter is very great; but it is passive. The mind of the reader is not awakened to any independent action: you see the farce, but you see it without effort; not simply without painful effort, but without any perceptible mental activity whatever. Again, entertainment of intellect is contrasted with the high enjoyment of consciously following pure and difficult reasoning; such a sensation is a sort of sublimated pain. The highest and most intense action of the intellectual powers is like the most intense action of the bodily on a high mountain. We climb and climb; we have a thrill of pleasure, but we have also a sense of effort and anguish. Nor is the sensation to be confounded with that which we experience from the best and purest works of art. The pleasure of high tragedy is also painful: the whole soul is stretched; the spirit pants; the passions scarcely breathe: it is a rapt and eager moment, too intense for continuance— so overpowering, that we scarcely know whether it be joy or pain. The sensation of intellectual entertainment is altogether distinguished from these by not being accompanied by any pain, and yet being consequent on, or being contemporaneous with, a high and constant exercise of mind. While we read works which so delight us, we are conscious that we are delighted, and are conscious that we are not idle. The opposite pleasures of indolence and exertion seem for a moment combined. A sort of elasticity pervades us; thoughts come easily and quickly; we seem capable of many ideas; we follow cleverness till we fancy that we are clever. This feeling is only given by writers who stimulate the mind just to the degree which is pleasant, and who do not stimulate it more; who exact a moderate exercise of mind, and who seduce us to it insensibly. This can only be, of course, by a charm of style; by the inexplicable *je ne sais quoi* which attracts our attention; by constantly raising and constantly satisfying our curiosity. And there seems to be a further condition. A writer who wishes to produce this constant effect must not appeal to any single separate faculty of mind, but to the whole mind at once. The fancy tires, if you appeal only to the fancy; the understanding is aware of its dullness, if you appeal only to the understanding; the curiosity is soon satiated unless you pique it with variety. This is the very opportunity for Macaulay. He has fancy, sense, abundance; he appeals to both fancy and understanding. There is no sense of effort. His books read like an elastic dream. There is a continual sense of instruction; for who had an idea of the transactions before? The emotions, too, which he appeals to are the easy admiration, the cool disapprobation, the gentle worldly curiosity, which quietly excite us, never fatigue us,—which we could bear for ever. To read Macaulay for a day, would be to pass a day of easy thought, of pleasant placid emotion.

Nor is this a small matter. In a state of high civilisation it is no simple matter to give multitudes a large and healthy enjoyment. The old bodily enjoyments are dying out; there is no room for them any more; the complex apparatus of civilisation cumbers the ground. We are thrown back upon the mind, and the mind is a barren thing. It can spin little from itself: few that describe what they see are in the way to discern much. Exaggerated emotions, violent incidents, monstrous characters, crowd our canvas; they are the resource of a weakness which would obtain the fame of strength. Reading is about to become a series of collisions against aggravated breakers, of beatings with imaginary surf. In such times a book of sensible attraction is a public benefit; it diffuses a sensation of vigour through the multitude. Perhaps there is a danger that the extreme popularity of the manner may make many persons fancy they understand the matter more perfectly than they do; some readers may become conceited; several boys believe that they too are Macaulays. Yet, duly allowing for this defect, it is a great good that so many people should learn so much on such topics so agreeably; that they should feel that they *can* understand them; that their minds should be stimulated by a consciousness of health and power.

The same peculiarities influence the style of the narrative. The art of narration is the art of writing in hooks-and-eyes. The principle consists in making the appropriate thought follow the appropriate thought, the proper fact the proper fact; in first preparing the mind for what is to come, and then letting it come. This can only be achieved by keeping continually and insensibly before the mind of the reader some one object, character, or image, whose variations are the events of the story, whose unity is the unity of it. Scott, for example, keeps before you the mind of some one person,—that of Morton in *Old Mortality*, of Rebecca in *Ivanhoe*, of Lovel in *The Antiquary*,—whose fortunes and mental changes are the central incidents, whose personality the string of unity. It is the defect of the great Scotch novels that their central figure is frequently not their most interesting topic,—that their interest is often rather in the accessories than in the essential principle—rather in that which surrounds the centre of narration than in the centre itself. Scott tries to meet this objection by varying the mind which he selects for his unit; in one of his chapters it is one character, in the next a different; he shifts the scene from the hero to the heroine, from the ' Protector of the settlement ' of the story to the evil being who mars it perpetually : but when narrowly examined, the principle of his narration will be found nearly always the same,—the changes in the position—external or mental—of some one human being. The most curiously opposite sort of narration is that of Hume. He seems to carry a *view*, as the moderns call it, through everything. He forms to himself a metaphysical—that perhaps is a harsh word—an intellectual conception of the time and character before him; and the gradual working out or development of that view is the principle of his narration. He tells the story of the conception. You rise from his pages without much remembrance of or regard for the mere people, but with a clear notion of an elaborated view, skilfully abstracted and perpetually impressed upon you. A critic of detail should scarcely require a better task than to show how insensibly and artfully the subtle historian infuses his doctrine among the facts, indicates somehow—you can scarcely say how—their relation to it; strings them, as it were, upon it, concealing it in seeming beneath them, while in fact it altogether determines their form, their grouping, and their consistency. The style of Macaulay is very different from either of these. It is a diorama of political pictures. You seem to begin with a brilliant picture,—its colours are distinct, its lines are firm; on a sudden it changes, at first gradually, you can scarcely tell how or in what, but truly and unmistakably,— a slightly different picture is before you; then the second vision seems to change,—it too is another and yet the same; then the third shines forth and fades; and so without end. The unity of this delineation is the identity—the apparent identity—of the picture; in no two moments does it seem quite different, in no two is it identically the same. It grows and alters as our bodies would appear to alter and grow, if you could fancy any one watching them, and being conscious of their daily little changes. The events are picturesque variations; the unity is a unity of political painting, of represented external form. It is evident how suitable this is to a writer whose understanding is solid, whose sense is political, whose fancy is fine and delineative.

To this merit of Macaulay is to be added another. No one describes so well what we may call the *spectacle* of a character. The art of delineating character by protracted description is one which grows in spite of the critics. In vain is it alleged that the character should be shown dramatically; that it should be illustrated by events; that it should be exhibited in its actions. The truth is, that these homilies are excellent, but incomplete; true, but out of season. There is a utility in verbal portrait, as Lord Stanhope says there is in painted. Goethe used to observe, that in society—in a *tête-à-tête*, rather —you often thought of your companion as if he was his portrait: you were silent; you did not care what he said; but you considered him as a picture, as a whole, especially as regards yourself and your relations towards him. You require something of the same kind in literature; *some* description of a man is clearly necessary as an introduction to the story of his life and actions. But more than this is wanted; you require to have the object placed before you as a whole, to have the characteristic traits mentioned, the delicate qualities drawn out, the firm features gently depicted. As the practice which Goethe hints at is, of all others, the most favourable to a just and calm judgment of character, so the literary substitute is essential as a steadying element, as a summary, to bring together and give a unity to our views. We must see the man's face. Without it, we seem to have heard a great deal about the person, but not to have known him; to be aware that he had done a good deal, but to have no settled, ineradicable notion what manner of man he was. This is the reason why critics like Macaulay, who sneer at the practice when estimating the works of others, yet make use of it at great length, and, in his case, with great skill, when they come to be historians themselves. The kind of characters whom Macaulay can describe is limited—at least we think so—by the bounds which we indicated just now. There are some men whom he is too impassive to comprehend; but he can always tell us of such as he does comprehend, what they looked like, and what they were.

Mr. Macaulay

A great deal of this vividness Macaulay of course owes to his style. Of its effectiveness there can be no doubt; its agreeability no one who has just been reading it is likely to deny. Yet it has a defect. It is not, as Bishop Butler would have expressed it, such a style as ' is suitable to such a being as man, in such a world as the present one.' It is too omniscient. Everything is too plain. All is clear; nothing is doubtful. Instead of probability being, as the great thinker expressed it, ' the very guide of life,' it has become a rare exception—an uncommon phenomenon. You rarely come across anything which is not decided; and when you do come across it, you seem to wonder that the positiveness, which has accomplished so much, should have been unwilling to decide anything. This is hardly the style for history. The data of historical narratives, especially of modern histories, are a heap of confusion. No one can tell where they lie, or where they do not lie; what is in them, or what is not in them. Literature is called the ' fragment of fragments;' little has been written, and but little of that little has been preserved. So history is a vestige of vestiges; few facts leave any trace of themselves, any witness of their occurrence; of fewer still is that witness preserved; a slight track is all anything leaves, and the confusion of life, the tumult of change sweep even that away in a moment. It is not possible that these data can be very fertile in certainties. Few people would make anything of them: a memoir here, a MS. there—two letters in a magazine—an assertion by a person whose veracity is denied,— these are the sort of evidence out of which a flowing narrative is to be educed—and of course it ought not to be too flowing. ' If you please, sir, to tell me what you do *not* know,' was the inquiry of a humble pupil addressed to a great man of science. It would have been a relief to the readers of Macaulay if he had shown a little the outside of uncertainties, which there must be—the gradations of doubt, which there ought to be—the singular accumulation of difficulties, which must beset the extraction of a very easy narrative from very confused materials.

This defect in style is, indeed, indicative of a defect in understanding. Mr. Macaulay's mind is eminently gifted, but there is a want of graduation in it. He has a fine eye for probabilities, a clear perception of evidence, a shrewd guess at missing links of fact; but each probability seems to him a certainty, each piece of evidence conclusive, each analogy exact. The heavy Scotch intellect is a little prone to this: one figures it as a heap of formulæ, and if fact *b* is reducible to formula B, that is all which it regards; the mathematical mill grinds with equal energy at flour perfect and imperfect—at matter which is quite certain, and at matter which is only a little probable. But the great cause of this error is, an abstinence from practical action. Life is a school of probability. In the writings of every man of patient practicality, in the midst of whatever other defects, you will find a careful appreciation of the degrees of likelihood; a steady balancing of them one against another; a disinclination to make things too clear, to overlook the debit side of the account in mere contemplation of the enormousness of the credit. The reason is obvious: action is a business of risk; the real question is the magnitude of that risk. Failure is ever impending; success is ever uncertain; there is always, in the very best of affairs, a slight probability of the former, a contingent possibility of the non-occurrence of the latter. For practical men, the problem ever is to test the amount of these inevitable probabilities; to make sure that no one increases too far; that by a well-varied choice the number of risks may in itself be a protection—be an insurance to you, as it were, against the capricious result of any one. A man like Macaulay, who stands aloof from life, is not so instructed; he sits secure; nothing happens in his study: he does not care to test probabilities; he loses the detective sensation.

Mr. Macaulay's so-called inaccuracy is likewise a phase of this defect. Considering the enormous advantages which a picturesque style gives to ill-disposed critics; the number of points of investigation which it suggests; the number of assertions it makes, sentence by sentence; the number of ill-disposed critics that there are in the world; remembering Mr. Macaulay's position,—set on a hill to be spied at by them,—he can scarcely be thought an inaccurate historian. Considering all things, they have found few certain blunders, hardly any direct mistakes. Every sentence of his style requires minute knowledge; the vivid picture has a hundred details; each of those details must have an evidence, an authority, a proof. An historian like Hume passes easily over a period; his chart is large; if he gets the conspicuous headlands, the large harbours, duly marked, he does not care. Macaulay puts in the depth of each wave, every remarkable rock, every tree on the shore. Nothing gives a critic so great an advantage. It is difficult to do this for a volume; simple for a page. It is easy to sele t a particular event, and learn all which any one can know about it; examine Macaulay's descriptions, say he is wrong, that X is not buried where he asserts, that a little boy was one year older than he states. But how would the critic manage, if he had to work out all this for a million facts, for a whole period? Few men, we suspect, would be able to make so few errors of simple and provable fact. On the other hand, few men would arouse a sleepy critic by such startling assertion. If Macaulay finds a new theory, he states it as a fact. Very likely it really is the most probable theory; at any rate, we know of no case in which his theory is not one among the most plausible. If it had only been so stated, it would have been well received. His view of Marlborough's character, for instance, is a specious one; it has a good deal of evidence, a large amount of real probability, but it has scarcely more. Marlborough *may* have been as bad as is said, but we can hardly be *sure* of it at this time.

Macaulay's 'party-spirit' is another consequence of his positiveness. When he inclines to a side, he inclines to it too much. His opinions are a shade too strong; his predilections some degrees at least too warm. William is too perfect, James too imperfect. The Whigs are a trifle like angels; the Tories like, let us say, 'our inferiors.' Yet this is evidently an honest party-spirit. It does not lurk in the corners of sentences, it is not insinuated without being alleged; it does not, like the unfairness of Hume, secrete itself so subtly in the turns of the words, that when you look to prove it, it is gone. On the contrary, it rushes into broad day. William is loaded with panegyric; James is always spoken evil of. Hume's is the artful pleading of a hired advocate; Macaulay's the bold eulogy of a sincere friend. As far as effect goes, this is an error. The very earnestness of the affection leads to a reaction; we are tired of having William called the 'just;' we cannot believe so many pages; 'all that' can scarcely be correct. As we said, if the historian's preference for persons and parties had been duly tempered and mitigated, if the probably good were only said to be probably good, if the rather bad were only alleged to be rather bad, the reader would have been convinced, and the historian would have escaped the savage censure of envious critics.

The one thing which detracts from the pleasure of reading these volumes, is the doubt whether they should have been written. Should not these great powers be reserved for great periods? Is this abounding, picturesque style, suited for continuous history? Are small men to be so largely described? Should not admirable delineation be kept for admirable people? We think so. You do not want Raphael to paint sign-posts, or Palladio to build dirt-pies. Much of history is necessarily of little value,—the superficies of circumstance, the scum of events. It is very well to have it described, indeed you must have it described; the chain must be kept complete; the narrative of a country's fortunes will not allow of breaks or gaps. Yet all things need not be done equally well. The life of a great painter is short. Even the industry of Macaulay will not complete this history. It is a pity to spend such powers on such events. It would have been better to have some new volumes of essays solely on great men and great things. The diffuseness of the style would have been then in place; we could have borne to hear the smallest minutiæ of magnificent epochs. If an inferior hand had executed the connecting-links, our notions would have acquired an insensible perspective; the works of the great artist, the best themes, would have stood out from the canvas. They are now confused by the equal brilliancy of the adjacent inferiorities.

Much more might be said on this narrative. As it will be read for very many years, it will employ the critics for very many years. It would be unkind to make all the best observations. Something, as Mr. Disraeli said in a budget-speech, something should be left for 'future statements of this nature.' There will be an opportunity. Whatever those who come after may say against this book, it will be, and remain, the 'Pictorial History of England.'

Beranger*
(1857)

THE invention of books has at least one great advantage. It has half-abolished one of the worst consequences of the diversity of languages. Literature enables nations to understand one another. Oral intercourse hardly does this. In English a distinguished foreigner says not what he thinks, but what he can. There is a certain intimate essence of national meaning which is as untranslatable as good poetry. Dry thoughts are cosmopolitan; but the delicate associations of language which express character, the traits of speech which mark the man, differ in every tongue, have not even cumbrous circumlocutions that are equivalent in another. National character is a deep thing—a shy thing; you cannot exhibit much of it to people who have a difficulty in understanding your language; you are in strange society, and you feel you will not be understood. 'Let an English gentleman,' writes Mr. Thackeray, 'who has dwelt two, four, or ten years in Paris, say at the end of any given period how much he knows of French society, how many French houses he has entered, and how many French friends he has made. Intimacy there is none; we see but the outsides of the people. Year by year we live in France, and grow grey and see no more. We play *écarté* with Monsieur de Trêfle every night; but what do we know of the heart of the man—of the inward ways, thoughts, and customs of Trêfle? We dance with Countess Flicflac Tuesdays and Thursdays ever since the peace; and how far are we advanced in her acquaintance since we first twirled her round a room? We know her velvet

* *Œuvres complètes de* C.-J. de Béranger. *Nouvelle édition revue par l'Auteur, contenant les Dix Chansons nouvelles, le facsimile d'une Lettre de Béranger; illustrée de cinquante-deux gravures sur acier, d'après Charlet, D'Aubigny, Johannot Grenier, De Lemud, Pauquet, Penguilly, Raffet, Sandoz, exécutées par les artistes les plus distingués, et d'un beau portrait d'après nature par* Sandoz. 2 vols. 8vo. 1855.

gown and her diamonds; we know her smiles and her simpers and her rouge, but the real, rougeless, *intime* Flicflac we know not.'* Even if our words did not stutter, as they do stutter on our tongue, she would not tell us what she is. Literature has half mended this. Books are exportable; the essence of national character lies flat on a printed page. Men of genius with the impulses of solitude produce works of art, whose words can be read and re-read and partially taken in by foreigners to whom they could never be uttered, the very thought of whose unsympathising faces would freeze them on the surface of the mind. Alexander Smith has accused poetical reviewers of beginning as far as possible from their subject. It may seem to some, though it is not so really, that we are exemplifying this saying in commencing as we have commenced an article on Béranger.

There are two kinds of poetry, which one may call poems of this world, and poems not of this world. We see a certain society on the earth held together by certain relations, performing certain acts, exhibiting certain phenomena, calling forth certain emotions. The millions of human beings who compose it have their various thoughts, feelings, and desires. They hate, act, and live. The social bond presses them closely together; and from their proximity new sentiments arise which are half superficial and do not touch the inmost soul, but which nevertheless are unspeakably important in the actual constitution of human nature, and work out their effects for good and for evil on the characters of those who are subjected to their influence. These sentiments of the world, as one may speak, differ from the more primitive impulses and emotions of our inner nature as the superficial phenomena of the material universe from what we fancy is its real essence. Passing hues, transient changes have their course before our eyes; a multiplex diorama is for ever displayed; underneath it all we fancy—such is the inevitable constitution of our thinking faculty—a primitive immovable essence, which is modified into all the ever-changing phenomena we see, which is the grey granite whereon they lie, the primary substance whose *débris* they all are. Just so from the original and primitive emotions of man, society—the evolving capacity of combined action—brings out desires which seem new, in a sense are new, which have no existence out of

* We have been obliged to abridge the above extract, and in so doing have left out the humour of it.

the society itself, are coloured by its customs at the moment,
change with the fashions of the age. Such a principle is what
we may call social gaiety: the love of combined amusement
which all men feel and variously express, and which is to the
higher faculties of the soul what a gay running stream is to the
everlasting mountain, a light, altering element which beautifies
while it modifies. Poetry does not shrink from expressing such
feelings; on the contrary, their renovating cheerfulness blends
appropriately with her inspiriting delight. Each age and each
form of the stimulating imagination has a fashion of its own.
Sir Walter sings in his modernised chivalry,

> ' Waken, lords and ladies gay,
>   On the mountain dawns the day;
>   All the jolly chase is here,
>   With hawk and horse and hunting-spear.
>   Hounds are in their couples yelling,
>   Hawks are whistling, horns are knelling,
>   Merrily, merrily, mingle they;
>   Waken, lords and ladies gay.
>
> ' Louder, louder chant the lay,
>   Waken, lords and ladies gay;
>   Tell them youth and mirth and glee
>   Run a course as well as we.
>   Time, stern huntsman, who can balk?
>   Stanch as hound and fleet as hawk;
>   Think of this, and rise with day,
>   Gentle lords and ladies gay.'

The poet of the people, ' *vilain et très vilain*,' sings with the
pauper Bohemian,

> ' Voir c'est avoir. Allons courir!
>   Vie errante
>   Est chose enivrante.
>   Voir c'est avoir. Allons courir!
>   Car tout voir c'est tout conquérir.
>
> ' Nous n'avons donc exempts d'orgueil,
>   De lois vaines,
>   De lourdes chaines;
>   Nous n'avons donc exempts d'orgueil,
>   Ni berceau, ni toit, ni cercueil;

Mais croyez-en notre gaîté,
  Noble ou prêtre,
  Valet ou maître;
Mais, croyez-en notre gaîté,
Le bonheur est la liberté.

' Oui, croyez-en notre gaîté,
  Noble ou prêtre,
  Valet ou maître;
Oui, croyez-en notre gaîté,
Le bonheur est la liberté.'

The forms of these poems of social amusement are, in truth, as various as the social amusement itself. The variety of the world, singularly various as it everywhere is, is nowhere so various as in that. Men have more ways of amusing themselves than of doing anything else they do. But the essence—the characteristic—of these poems everywhere is, that they express more or less well the lighter desires of human nature;—those that have least of unspeakable depth, partake most of what is perishable and earthly, and least of the immortal soul. The objects of these desires are social accidents; excellent, perhaps, essential, possibly—so is human nature made—in one form and variety or another, to the well-being of the soul, yet in themselves transitory, fleeting, and in other moods contemptible. The old saying was, that to endure solitude a man must either be a beast or a god. It is in the lighter play of social action, in that which is neither animal nor divine, which in its half-way character is so natural to man, that these poems of society, which we have called poems of amusement, have their place.

This species does not, however, exhaust the whole class. Society gives rise to another sort of poems, differing from this one as contemplation differs from desire. Society may be thought of as an object. The varied scene of men,—their hopes, fears, anxieties, maxims, actions,—presents a sight more interesting to man than any other which has ever existed, or which can exist; and it may be viewed in all moods of mind, and with the change of inward emotion as the external object seems to change: not that it really does so, but that some sentiments are more favourable to clear-sightedness than others are; and some bring before us one aspect of the subject, and fix our

attention upon it, others a different one, and bind our minds
to that likewise. Among the most remarkable of these varied
views is the world's view of itself. The world, such as it is,
has made up its mind what it is. Childishly deceivable by
charlatans on every other subject,—imposed on by pedantry,
by new and unfounded science, by ancient and unfounded reputation, a prey to pomposity, overrun with recondite fools,
ignorant of all else,—society knows itself. The world knows
a man of the world. A certain tradition pervades it; a *dis-
ciplina* of the market-place teaches what the collective society
of men has ever been, and what, so long as the nature of man
is the same, it cannot and will not cease to be. Literature, the
written expression of human nature in every variety, takes
up this variety likewise. Ancient literature exhibits it from
obvious causes in a more simple manner than modern literature
can. Those who are brought up in times like the present,
necessarily hear a different set of opinions, fall in with other
words, are under the shadow of a higher creed. In consequence,
they cannot have the simple *naïveté* of the old world; they
cannot speak with easy equanimity of the fugitiveness of life,
the necessity of death, of goodness as a mean, of sin as an
extreme. The theory of the universe has ceased to be an open
question. Still the spirit of Horace is alive, and as potent as
that of any man. His tone is that of prime ministers; his easy
philosophy is that of courts and parliaments; you may hear his
words where no other foreign words are ever heard. He is but
the extreme and perfect type of a whole class of writers, some
of whom exist in every literary age, and who give an expression
to what we may call the poetry of equanimity, that is, the
world's view of itself; its self-satisfaction, its conviction that
you must bear what comes, not hope for much, think *some* evil,
never be excited, admire little, and then you will be at peace.
This creed does not sound attractive in description. Nothing,
it has been said, is so easy as to be ' religious on paper: ' on the
other hand, it is rather difficult to be worldly in speculation;
the mind of man, when its daily maxims are put before it,
revolts from anything so stupid, so mean, so poor. It requires
a consummate art to reconcile men in print to that moderate
and insidious philosophy which creeps into all hearts, colours
all speech, influences all action. We may not stiffen common
sense into a creed; our very ambition forbids:—

' It hears a voice within us tell
  Calm's not life's crown, though calm is well:
  'Tis all perhaps which man acquires;
  But 'tis not what our youth desires.'

Still a great artist may succeed in making ' calm ' interesting.
Equanimity has its place in literature; the poetry of equipoise
is possible. Poems of society have, thus, two divisions: that
which we mentioned first, the expression of the feelings which
are called out by the accidents of society; next, the harmonised
expression of that philosophy of indifference with which the
world regards the fortunes of individuals and its own.

We have said that no modern nation can produce literature
embodying this kind of cool reflection and delineation as it was
once produced. By way of compensation, however, it may be,
it no doubt is, easier now to produce the lyrical kind of poems of
society—the light expression of its light emotions—than it was
in ancient times. Society itself is better. There is something
hard in Paganism, which is always felt even in the softest traits
of the most delicate society in antiquity. The social influence of
women in modern times gives an interest, a little pervading
excitement, to social events. Civilisation, besides, has made
comfort possible; it has, at least in part, created a scene in
which society can be conducted. Its petty conveniences may or
may not be great benefits according to a recondite philosophy;
but there can be no doubt that for actual men and women in
actual conversation it is of the greatest importance that their
feet should not be cold; that their eyes and mouth should not
be troubled with smoke; that sofas should be good, and attractive chairs many. Modern times have the advantage of the
ancient in the scenery of flirtation. The little boy complained
that you could not find ' drawing-room ' in the dictionary. Perhaps even because our reflections are deeper, our inner life less
purely pagan, our apparent life is softer and easier. Some have
said, that one reason why physical science made so little progress in ancient times was, that people were in doubt about
more interesting things; men must have, it has been alleged, a
settled creed as to human life and human hopes, before they
will attend to shells and snails and pressures. And whether
this be so or not, perhaps a pleasant society is only possible to
persons at ease as to what is beyond society. Those only can lie

on the grass who fear no volcano underneath, and can bear to
look at the blue vault above.

Among modern nations it is not difficult to say where we
should look for success in the art of social poetry. 'Wherever,'
said Mr. Lewes the other day, 'the French go, they take what
they call their civilisation—that is, a *café* and a theatre.' And
though this be a trifle severe, yet in its essence its meaning is
correct. The French have in some manner or other put their
mark on all the externals of European life. The essence of
every country remains little affected by their teaching; but
in all the superficial embellishments of society they have enjoined the fashion; and the very language in which those
embellishments are spoken of, shows at once whence they were
derived. Something of this is doubtless due to the accidents of
a central position, and an early and prolonged political influence; but more to a certain neatness of nature, a certain finish
of the senses, which enables them more easily than others to
touch lightly the light things of society, to see the *comme-il-
faut*. 'I like,' said a good judge, 'to hear a Frenchman talk;
he strikes a light.' On a hundred topics he gives the bright,
sharp edge, where others have only a blunt approximation.

Nor is this anticipation disappointed. Reviewers do not
advance such theories unless they correspond with known
results. For many years the French have not been more celebrated for memoirs which professedly describe a real society
than they have been for the light social song which embodies
its sentiments and pours forth its spirit. The principle on which
such writings are composed is the taking some incident—not
voluntarily (for the incident doubtless of itself takes a hold on
the poet's mind)—and out of that incident developing all which
there is in it. A grave form is of course inconsistent with such
art. The spirit of such things is half-mirthful; a very profound
meaning is rarely to be expected; but little incidents are not
destitute of meaning, and a delicate touch will delineate it in
words. A profound excitement likewise such poems cannot
produce; they do not address the passions or the intuitions, the
heart or the soul, but a gentle pleasure, half sympathy, half
amusement, is that at which they aim. They do not please us
equally in all moods of mind: sometimes they seem nothing
and nonsense, like society itself. We must not be too active or
too inactive, to like them; the tension of mind must not be too

great; in our highest moods the littlenesses of life are petty;
the mind must not be obtusely passive; light touches will not
stimulate a sluggish inaction. This dependence on the mood of
mind of the reader makes it dangerous to elucidate this sort of
art by quotation; Béranger has, however, the following:—

'*Laideur et Beauté.*

'Sa trop grande beauté m'obsède;
C'est un masque aisément trompeur.
Oui, je voudrais qu'elle fût laide,
Mais laide, laide à faire peur.
Belle ainsi faut-il que je l'aime!
Dieu, reprends ce don éclatant;
Je le demande à l'enfer même:
Qu'elle soit laide et que je l'aime autant.

'A ces mots m'apparaît le diable;
C'est le père de la laideur.
"Rendons-la," dit-il, "effroyable,
De tes rivaux trompons l'ardeur.
J'aime assez ces métamorphoses.
Ta belle ici vient en chantant;
Perles, tombez; fanez-vous, roses:
La voilà laide et tu l'aimes autant."

'—Laide! moi! dit-elle étonnée;
Elle s'approche d'un miroir,
Doute d'abord, puis, consternée,
Tombe en un morne désespoir.
"Pour moi seul tu jurais de vivre,"
Lui dis-je, à ses pieds me jetant;
"A mon seul amour il te livre.
Plus laide encore, je t'aimerais autant."

'Ses yeux éteints fondent en larmes,
Alors sa douleur m'attendrit.
"Ah! rendez, rendez-lui ses charmes."
"—Soit!" répond Satan qui sourit.
Ainsi que naît la fraîche aurore,
Sa beauté renaît à l'instant.
Elle est, je crois, plus belle encore:
Elle est plus belle, et moi je l'aime autant.

'Vite au miroir elle s'assure
Qu'on lui rend bien tous ses appas;
Des pleurs restent sur sa figure
Qu'elle essuie en grondant tout bas.
Satan s'envole, et la cruelle
Fuit et s'écrie en me quittant:
"Jamais fille que Dieu fit belle
Ne doit aimer qui peut l'aimer autant."'

And this is even a more characteristic specimen:

La Mouche.

'Au bruit de notre gaîté folle,
Au bruit des verres, des chansons,
Quelle mouche murmure et vole,
Et revient quand nous la chassons? (bis.)
C'est quelque dieu, je le soupçonne,
Qu'un peu de bonheur rend jaloux.
Ne souffrons point qu'elle bourdonne, } (bis.)
Qu'elle bourdonne autour de nous.

'Transformée en mouche hideuse,
Amis, oui, c'est, j'en suis certain,
La Raison, déité grondeuse,
Qu'irrite un si joyeux festin,
L'orage approche, le ciel tonne;
Voilà ce que dit son courroux.
Ne souffrons point qu'elle bourdonne,
Qu'elle bourdonne autour de nous.

'C'est la Raison qui vient me dire:
"A ton âge on vit en reclus.
Ne bois plus tant, cesse de rire,
Cesse d'aimer, ne chante plus."
Ainsi son beffroi toujours sonne
Aux lueurs des feux les plus doux.
Ne souffrons point qu'elle bourdonne,
Qu'elle bourdonne autour de nous.

'C'est la Raison; gare à Lisette!
Son dard la menace toujours.
Dieux! il perce la collerette:
Le sang coule! accourez, Amours!

Amours, poursuivez la félonne ;
Qu'elle expire enfin sous vos coups.
Ne souffrons point qu'elle bourdonne,
Qu'elle bourdonne autour de nous.

'Victoire ! amis, elle se noie
Dans l'aï que Lise a versé.
Victoire ! et qu'aux mains de la Joie
Le sceptre enfin soit replacé. (*bis*.)
Un souffle ébranle sa couronne ;
Une mouche nous troublait tous.
Ne craignons plus qu'elle bourdonne, ⎫
Qu'elle bourdonne autour de nous.' ⎭ (*bis*.)

To make poetry out of a fly is a difficult operation. It used to be said of the Lake school of criticism, in Mr. Wordsworth's early and more rigid days, that there was no such term as ' elegant ' in its nomenclature. The reason is that, dealing, or attempting to deal, only with the essential aboriginal principles of human nature, that school had no room and no occasion for those minor contrivances of thought and language which are necessary to express the complex accumulation of little feelings, the secondary growth of human emotion. The underwood of nature is ' elegant '; the bare ascending forest-tree despises what is so trivial,—it is grave and solemn. Of such verses, on the other hand, as have been quoted, ' elegance ' is essential; the delicate finish of fleeting forms is the only excellence they can have.

The characteristic deficiencies of French literature have no room to show themselves in this class of art. ' Though France herself denies,' says a recent writer, ' yet all other nations with one voice proclaim her inferiority to her rivals in poetry and romance, and in all the other elevated fields of fiction. A French Dante, or Michael Angelo, or Cervantes, or Murillo, or Goethe, or Shakespeare, or Milton, we at once perceive to be a mere anomaly; a supposition which may, indeed, be proposed in terms, but which in reality is inconceivable and impossible.' In metaphysics, the reason seems to be that the French character is incapable of being mastered by an unseen idea, without being so tyrannised over by it as to be incapable of artistic development. Such a character as Robespierre's may explain what we mean. His entire nature was taken up, and absorbed

in certain ideas; he had almost a vanity in them; he was of
them, and they were of him. But they appear in his mind,
in his speeches, in his life, in their driest and barest form;
they have no motion, life, or roundness. We are obliged to
use many metaphors remotely and with difficulty to indicate
the procedure of the imagination. In one of these metaphors
we figure an idea of imagination as a living thing, a kind of
growing plant, with a peculiar form, and ever preserving its
identity, but absorbing from the earth and air all kindred,
suitable, and, so to say, annexable materials. In a mind such
as Robespierre's, in the type of the fanatic mind, there is no
such thing. The ideas seem a kind of dry hard capsules, never
growing, never enlarging, never uniting. Development is denied
them; they cannot expand, or ripen, or mellow. Dogma is a
dry hard husk; poetry has the soft down of the real fruit.
Ideas seize on the fanatic mind just as they do on the poetical;
they have the same imperious ruling power. The difference
is, that in the one the impelling force is immutable, iron,
tyrannical; in the other the rule is expansive, growing, free,
taking up from all around it moment by moment whatever is
fit, as in the political world a great constitution arises through
centuries, with a shape that does not vary, but with movement
for its essence and the fluctuation of elements for its vitality.
A thin poor mind like Robespierre's seems pressed and ham-
pered by the bony fingers of a skeleton hand; a poet's is expanded and warmed at the same time that it is impelled by a
pure life-blood of imagination. The French, as we have said,
are hardly capable of this. When great remote ideas seize upon
them at all, they become fanatics. The wild, chimerical revolutionary, mad Frenchman has the stiffest of human minds.
He is under the law of his creed; he has not attained to the
higher freedom of the impelling imagination. The prosing
rhetoric of the French tragedy shows the same defect in another
form. The ideas which should have become living realities,
remain as lean abstractions. The characters are speaking
officials, jets of attenuated oratory. But exactly on this very
account the French mind has a genius for the poetry of society.
Unable to remove itself into the higher region of imagined
forms, it has the quickest detective insight into the exact
relation of surrounding superficial phenomena. There are two
ways of putting it: either, being fascinated by the present,

they cannot rise to what is not present; or, being by defect of nature unable to rise to what is not present, they are concentrated and absorbed in that which is so. Of course there ought not to be, but there *is*, a world of *bonbons*, of *salons*, of *esprit*. Living in the present they have the poetry of the present. The English genius is just the opposite. Our cumbrous intellect has no call to light artificialities. We do not excel in punctuated detail or nicely-squared elaboration. It puts us out of patience that others should. A respectable Englishman murmured in the *Café de Paris*, ' I wish I had a hunch of mutton.' He could not bear the secondary niceties with which he was surrounded. Our art has the same principle. We excel in strong noble imagination, in solid stuff. Shakespeare is tough work; he has the play of the rising energy, the buoyant freedom of the unbounded mind; but no writer is so destitute of the simplifying dexterities of the manipulating intellect.

It is dangerous for a foreigner to give an opinion on minutiæ of style, especially on points affecting the characteristic excellencies of national style. The French language is always neat ; all French styles somehow seem good. But Béranger appears to have a peculiar neatness. He tells us that all his songs are the production of a painful effort. If so, the reader should be most grateful; *he* suffers no pain. The delicate elaboration of the writer has given a singular currency to the words. Difficult writing is rarely easy reading. It can never be so when the labour is spent in piecing together elements not joined by an insensible touch of imagination. The highest praise is due to a writer whose ideas are more delicately connected by unconscious genius than other men's are, and yet who spends labour and toil in giving the production a yet cunninger finish, a still smoother connection. The characteristic aloofness of the Gothic mind, its tendency to devote itself to what is not present, is represented in composition by a want of care in the pettinesses of style. A certain clumsiness pervades all tongues of German origin. Instead of the language having been sharpened and improved by the constant keenness of attentive minds, it has been habitually used obtusely and crudely. Light loquacious Gaul has for ages been the contrast. If you take up a pen just used by a good writer, for a moment you seem to write rather well. A language long employed by a delicate and critical society is a treasure of dextrous felicities. It is not, according to the fine expression of Mr. Emerson, ' fossil poetry;' it is crystallised *esprit*.

A French critic has praised Béranger for having retained the *refrain*, or burden, ' *la rime de l'air*,' as he calls it. Perhaps music is more necessary as an accompaniment to the poetry of society than it is to any other poetry. Without a sensuous reminder, we might forget that it was poetry; especially in a sparkling, glittering, attenuated language, we might be absorbed as in the defined elegances of prose. In half trivial compositions we easily forget the little central fancy. The music prevents this: it gives oneness to the parts, pieces together the shavings of the intellect, makes audible the flow of imagination.

The poetry of society tends to the poetry of love. All poetry tends that way. By some very subtle links, which no metaphysician has skilfully tracked, the imagination, even in effects and employments which seem remote, is singularly so connected. One smiles to see the feeling recur. Half the poets can scarcely keep away from it: in the high and dry epic you may see the poet return to it. And perhaps this is not unaccountable. The more delicate and stealing the sensuous element, the more the mind is disposed to brood upon it; the more we dwell on it in stillness, the more it influences the wandering hovering which we term imagination. The first constructive effort of imagination is beyond the limit of consciousness; the faculty works unseen. But we know that it works in a certain soft leisure only: and this in ordinary minds is almost confined to, in the highest is most commonly accompanied by, the subtlest emotion of reverie. So insinuating is that feeling, that no poet is alive to all its influences; so potent is it, that the words of a great poet, in our complex modern time, are rarely ever free from its traces. The phrase ' stealing calm,' which most naturally and graphically describes the state of soul in which the imagination works, quite equally expresses, it is said, the coming in and continuance of the not uncommon emotion. Passing, however, from such metaphysics, there is no difficulty in believing that the poetry of society will tend to the most romantic part of society,—away from aunts and uncles, antiquaries and wigs, to younger and pleasanter elements. The talk of society does so, probably its literature will do so likewise. There are, never-theless, some limiting considerations, which make this tendency less all-powerful than we might expect it to be. In the first place, the poetry of society cannot deal with passion. Its light touch is not competent to express eager intense emotion. Rather, we should say, the essential nature of the poetry of amusement is inconsistent with those rugged, firm, aboriginal elements which passion brings to the surface. The volcano is inconsistent with careless talk; you cannot comfortably associate with lava. Such songs as those of Burns are the very antithesis to the levity of society. A certain explicit-ness pervades them:

> ' Come, let me take thee to my breast,
>   And pledge we ne'er shall sunder;
> And I shall spurn as vilest dust
>   The warld's wealth and grandeur.'

There is a story of his having addressed a lady in society, some time after he came to Edinburgh, in this direct style, and being offended that she took notice of it. The verses were in English, and were not intended to mean anything particular, only to be an elegant attention; but you might as well ask a young lady to take brandy with you as compliment her in this intense manner. The eager peasant-poet was at fault in the polished refinements of the half-feeling drawing-room. Again, the poetry of society can scarcely deal with affection. No poetry, except in hints, and for moments, perhaps ever can. You might as well tell secrets to the town-crier. The essence of poetry somehow is publicity. It is very odd when one reads many of the sentiments which are expressed there,—the brooding thought, the delicate feeling, the high conception. What is the use of telling these to the mass of men? Will the grocer feel them?—will the greasy butcher in the blue coat feel them? Are there not some emphatic remarks by Lord Byron on Mr. Sanders (' the d—d saltfish-seller ' of Venice), who could not appreciate *Don Juan*? Nevertheless, for some subtle reason or other, poets do crave, almost more than other men, the public approbation. To have a work of art in your imagination, and that no one else should know of it, is a great pain. But even this craving has its limits. Art can only deal with the universal. Characters, sentiments, actions, must be described in what in the old language might be called their conceptual shape. There must always be an idea in them. If one compares a great character in fiction, say that of Hamlet, with a well-known character in life, we are struck almost at once by the typical and representative nature of the former. We seem to have a more *summary* conception of it, if the phrase may be allowed, than we have of the people we know best in reality. Indeed, our notion of the fictitious character rather resembles a notion of actual persons of whom we know a little, and but a little,—of a public man, suppose, of whom from his speeches and writings we know something, but with whom we never exchanged a word. We generalise a few traits; we do what the historian will have to do hereafter; we *make* a man, so to speak, resembling the real one, but more defined, more simple and comprehensible. The objects on which affection turns are exactly the opposite. In their essence they are individual, peculiar. Perhaps they become known under a kind of confidence; but even if not, nature has hallowed the details of near life by an inevitable secrecy. You cannot expect other persons to feel them; you cannot tell your own intellect what they are. An individuality lurks in our nature. Each soul (as the divines speak) clings to each soul. Poetry is impossible on such points as these: they seem too sacred, too essential. The most that it can do is, by hints and little marks in the interstices of a universalised delineation, to suggest that there is something more than what is stated, and more inward and potent than what is stated. Affection as a settled subject is incompatible with art. And thus the poetry of society is limited on its romantic side in two ways: first, by the infinite intense nature of passion, which forces the voice of art beyond the social tone; and by the confidential, incomprehensible nature of affection, which will not bear to be developed for the public by the fancy in any way.

Being so bounded within the ordinary sphere of their art, poets of this world have contrived or found a substitute. In every country there is a society which is no society. The French, which is the most worldly of literatures, has devoted itself to the delineation of this outside world. There is no form, comic or serious, dramatic or lyrical, in which the subject has not been treated: the burden is—

> 'Lisette, ma Lisette,
> Tu m'as trompé toujours;
> Mais vive la grisette!
> Je veux, Lisette,
> Boire à nos amours.'

There is obviously no need of affection in *this* society. The whole plot of the notorious novel, *La Dame aux Camélias*,—and a very remarkable one it is,—is founded on the incongruity of real feeling with this world, and the singular and inappropriate consequences which result if by any rare chance it does appear there. Passion is almost *à fortiori* out of the question. The depths of human nature have nothing to do with this life. On this account, perhaps, it is that it harmonises so little with the English literature and character. An Englishman can scarcely live on the surface; his passions are too strong, his power of *finesse* too little. Accordingly, since Defoe, who treated the subject with a coarse matter-of-factness, there has been nothing in our literature of this kind—nothing at least professedly devoted to it. How far this is due to real excellence, how far to the *bourgeois* and not very outspoken temper of our recent writers, we need not in this place discuss. There is no occasion to quote in this country the early poetry of Béranger, at least not the sentimental part of it. We may take, in preference, one of his poems written in old, or rather in middle, age:

> *'Cinquante Ans.*
>
> 'Pourquoi ces fleurs? est-ce ma fête?
> Non; ce bouquet vient m'annoncer
> Qu'un demi-siècle sur ma tête
> Achève aujourd'hui de passer.
> Oh! combien nos jours sont rapides!
> Oh! combien j'ai perdu d'instants!
> Oh! combien je me sens de rides!
> Hélas! hélas! j'ai cinquante ans.
>
> 'A cet âge, tout nous échappe;
> Le fruit meurt sur l'arbre jauni.
> Mais à ma porte quelqu'un frappe;
> N'ouvrons point: mon rôle est fini.
> C'est, je gage, un docteur qui jette

Sa carte où s'est logé le temps.
Jadis, j'aurais dit: C'est Lisette.
Hélas! hélas! j'ai cinquante ans.

' En maux cuisants vieillesse abonde:
C'est la goutte qui nous meurtrit;
La cécité, prison profonde;
La surdité dont chacun rit.
Puis la raison, lampe qui baisse,
N'a plus que des feux tremblotants.
Enfants, honorez la vieillesse!
Hélas! hélas! j'ai cinquante ans!

' Ciel! j'entends la Mort qui, joyeuse,
Arrive en se frottant les mains.
A ma porte la fossoyeuse
Frappe; adieu, messieurs les humains!
En bas, guerre, famine et peste;
En haut, plus d'astres éclatants.
Ouvrons, tandis que Dieu me reste.
Hélas! hélas! j'ai cinquante ans.

' Mais non! c'est vous! vous, jeune amie!
Sœur de charité des amours!
Vous tirez mon âme endormie
Du cauchemar des mauvais jours.
Semant les roses de votre âge.
Partout, comme fait le printemps,
Parfumez les rêves d'un sage.
Hélas! hélas! j'ai cinquante ans.'

This is the last scene of the *grisette*, of whom we read in so many songs sparkling with youth and gaiety.

A certain intellectuality, however, pervades Béranger's love-songs. You seem to feel, to see, not merely the emotion, but the mind, in the background viewing that emotion. You are conscious of a considerateness qualifying and contrasting with the effervescing champagne of the feelings described. Desire is rarefied; sense half becomes an idea. You may trace a similar metamorphosis in the poetry of passion itself. If we contrast such a poem as Shelley's *Epipsychidion* with the natural language of common passion, we see how curiously the intellect can take its share in the dizziness of sense. In the same way, in the lightest poems of Béranger we feel that it may be infused, may interpenetrate the most buoyant effervescence.

Nothing is more odd than to contrast the luxurious and voluptuous nature of much of Béranger's poetry with the circumstances of his life. He never in all his productive time had more than 80l. a year; the smallest party of pleasure made him live, he tells us himself, most ascetically for a week; so far from leading the life of a Sybarite, his youth was one of anxiety and privation. A more worldly poet has probably never written, but no poet has shown in life so philosophic an estimate of this world's goods. His origin is very unaristocratic. He was born in August, 1780, at the house of his grandfather, a poor old tailor. Of his mother we hear nothing. His father was a speculative sanguine man, who never succeeded. His principal education was given him by an aunt, who taught him to read and to write, and perhaps generally incited his mind. His school-teaching tells of the philosophy of the revolutionary time. By way of primary school for the town of Péronne, a patriotic member of the National Assembly had founded an *institut d'enfants*. ' It offered,' we are told, ' at once the image of a club and that of a camp; the boys wore a military uniform; at every public event they named deputations, delivered orations, voted addresses: letters were written to the citizen Robespierre and the citizen Tallien.' Naturally amid so great affairs there was no time for mere grammar; they did not teach *Latin*. Nor did Béranger ever acquire any knowledge of that language; and he may be said to be destitute of what is in the usual sense called culture. Accordingly it has in these days been made a matter of wonder by critics, whom we may think pedantic, that one so destitute should be able to produce such works. But a far keener judge has pronounced the contrary. Goethe, who certainly did not undervalue the most elaborate and artful cultivation, at once pronounced Béranger to have ' a nature most happily endowed, firmly grounded in himself, purely developed from himself, and quite in harmony with himself.' In fact, as these words mean, Béranger, by happiness of nature or self-attention, has that *centrality* of mind which is the really valuable result of colleges and teaching. He puts things together; he refers things to a principle; rather, they group themselves in his intelligence insensibly round a principle. There is nothing *distrait* in his genius; the man has attained to be himself; a cool oneness, a poised personality, pervades him. 'The unlearned,' it has been said, 'judge at random.' Béranger is not unlearned in this sense. There is no one who judges more simply, smoothly, and uniformly. His ideas refer to an exact measure. He has mastered what comes before him. And though doubtless unacquainted with foreign and incongruous literatures, he has mastered his own literature, which was shaped by kindred persons, and has been the expression of analogous natures; and this has helped him in expressing himself.

In the same way, his poor youth and boyhood have given a reality to his productions. He seems to have had this in mind in praising the 'practical education which I have received.' He was bred a printer; and the highest post he attained was a clerkship at the university, worth, as has been said, 8*ol.* per annum. Accordingly he has everywhere a sympathy with the common people, an unsought familiarity with them and their life. Sybarite poetry commonly wants this. The aristocratic nature is superficial; it relates to a life protected from simple wants, depending on luxurious artifices. 'Mamma,' said the simple-minded nobleman, 'when poor people have no bread, why do not they eat buns? they are much better.' An over-perfumed softness pervades the poetry of society. You see this in the songs of Moore, the best of the sort we have; all is beautiful, soft, half-sincere. There is a little falsetto in the tone, everything reminds you of the drawing-room and the *piano-forte*; and not only so—for all poetry of society must in a measure do this—but it seems fit for no other scene. Natural-ness is the last word of praise that would be suitable. In the scented air we forget that there is a *pavé* and a multitude. Perhaps France is of all countries which have ever existed the one in which we might seek an exception from this luxurious limitation. A certain *égalité* may pervade its art as its society. There is no such difference as with us between the shoeblack and the gentleman. A certain refinement is very common; an extreme refinement possibly rare. Béranger was able to write his poems in poverty: they are popular with the poor.

A success even greater than what we have described as having been achieved by Béranger in the first class of the poems of society—that of amusement—has been attained by

him in the second class, expressive of epicurean speculation.
Perhaps it is one of his characteristics that the two are for ever
running one into another. There is animation in his thinking,
there is meaning in his gaiety. It requires no elaborate explanation to make evident the connection between scepticism
and luxuriousness. Every one thinks of the Sadducee as in cool
halls and soft robes; no one supposes that the Sybarite believes.
Pain not only purifies the mind, but deepens the nature. A
simple happy life is animal; it is pleasant, and it perishes. All
writers who have devoted themselves to the explanation of this
world's view of itself are necessarily in a certain measure
Sadducees. The world is a Sadducee itself; it cannot be anything else without recognising a higher creed, a more binding
law, a more solemn reality—without ceasing to be the world.
Equanimity is incredulous; impartiality does not care; an
indifferent politeness is sceptical. Though not a single speculative opinion is expressed, we may feel this in *Roger Bontemps*:—

' *Roger Bontemps.*

' Aux gens atrabilaires
  Pour exemple donné,
  En un temps de misères
  Roger Bontemps est né,
  Vivre obscur à sa guise,
  Narguer les mécontents;
  Eh gai ! c'est la devise
  Du gros Roger Bontemps.

' Du chapeau de son père
  Coiffé dans les grands jours,
  De roses ou de lierre
  Le rajeunir toujours;
  Mettre un manteau du bure,
  Vieil ami de vingt ans;
  Eh gai ! c'est la parure
  Du gros Roger Bontemps.

' Posséder dans sa hutte
  Une table, un vieux lit,
  Des cartes, une flûte,
  Un broc que Dieu remplit,

Un portrait de maîtresse,
Un coffre et rien dedans;
Eh gai! c'est la richesse
Du gros Roger Bontemps.

'Aux enfans de la ville
Montrer de petits jeux;
Etre un faiser habile
De contes graveleux;
Ne parler que de danse
Et d'almanachs chantants;
Eh gai! c'est la science
Du gros Roger Bontemps.

'Faute de vin d'élite,
Sabler ceux du canton;
Préférer Marguerite
Aux dames du grand ton;
De joie et de tendresse
Remplir tous ses instants;
Eh gai! c'est la sagesse
Du gros Roger Bontemps.

'Dire au ciel: Je me fie,
Mon père, à ta bonté;
De ma philosophie
Pardonne la gaîté;
Que ma saison dernière
Soit encore un printemps;
Eh gai! c'est la prière
Du gros Roger Bontemps.

'Vous, pauvres pleins d'envie,
Vous, riches désireux,
Vous, dont le char dévie
Après un cours heureux;
Vous, qui perdrez peut-être
Des titres éclatants,
Eh gai! prenez pour maître
Le gros Roger Bontemps.'

At the same time, in Béranger the scepticism is not extreme.
The skeleton is not paraded. That the world is a passing show,
a painted scene, is admitted; you seem to know that it is all
acting and rouge and illusion; still the pleasantness of the acting is dwelt on, the rouge is never rubbed off, the dream runs
lightly and easily. No nightmare haunts you, you have no
uneasy sense that you are about to awaken. Persons who require
a sense of reality may complain; pain is perhaps necessary to
sharpen their nerves, a tough effort to harden their consciousness: but if you pass by this objection of the threshold, if you
admit the possibility of a superficial and fleeting world, you will
not find a better one than Béranger's world. Suppose all the
world were a *restaurant*, his is a good *restaurant*; admit that
life is an effervescing champagne, his is the best for the moment.

In several respects Béranger contrasts with Horace, the poet
whom in general he most resembles. The song of *Roger Bontemps* suggests one of the most obvious differences. It is
essentially democratic. As we have said before, Béranger is the
poet of the people; he himself says, *Le peuple c'est ma muse*.
Throughout Horace's writings, however much he may speak,
and speak justly, of the simplicity of his tastes, you are always
conscious that his position is exceptional. Everybody cannot
be the friend of Mæcenas; every cheerful man of the world
cannot see the springs of the great world. The intellect of
most self-indulgent men must satisfy itself with small indul-
gences. Without a hard ascent you can rarely see a great
view. Horace had the almost unequalled felicity of watching
the characters and thoughts and tendencies of the governors
of the world; the nicest manipulation of the most ingenious
statesmen; the inner tastes and predilections which are the
origin of the most important transactions; and yet had the ease
and pleasantness of common and effortless life. So rare a
fortune cannot be a general model; the gospel of Epicureanism
must not ask a close imitation of one who had such very special
advantages. Béranger gives the acceptors of that creed a
commoner type. Out of nothing but the most ordinary advantages—the garret, the almost empty purse, the not over-attired
grisette—he has given them a model of the sparkling and
quick existence for which their fancy is longing. You cannot
imagine commoner materials. In another respect Horace and
Béranger are remarkably contrasted. Béranger, sceptical and

indifferent as he is, has a faith in, and zeal for, liberty. It seems odd that he should care for that sort of thing; but he does care for it. Horace probably had a little personal shame attaching to such ideas. No regimental officer of our own time can have 'joined' in a state of more crass ignorance than did the stout little student from Athens in all probability the army of Brutus; the legionaries must have taken the measure of him, as the sergeants of our living friends. Anyhow he was not partial to such reflections; zeal for political institutions is quite as foreign to him as any other zeal. A certain hope in the future is characteristic of Béranger—

> ' Qui découvrit un nouveau monde?
> Un fou qu'on raillait en tout lieu.'

Modern faith colours even bystanding scepticism. Though probably with no very accurate ideas of the nature of liberty, Béranger believes that it is a great good, and that France will have it.

The point in which Béranger most resembles Horace is that which is the most essential in the characters of them both— their geniality. This is the very essence of the poems of society; it springs in the verses of amusement, it harmonises with acquiescing sympathy the poems of indifference. And yet few qualities in writing are so rare. A certain malevolence enters into literary ink; the point of the pen pricks. Pope is the very best example of this. With every desire to imitate Horace, he cannot touch any of his subjects, or any kindred subjects, without infusing a bitter ingredient. It is not given to the children of men to be philosophers without envy. Lookers-on can hardly bear the spectacle of the great world. If you watch the carriages rolling down to the House of Lords, you will try to depreciate the House of Lords. Idleness is cynical. Both Béranger and Horace are exceptions to this. Both enjoy the roll of the wheels; both love the glitter of the carriages; neither is angry at the sun. Each knows that he is as happy as he can be—that he is all that he can be in his contemplative philosophy. In his means of expression, for the purpose in hand, the French-man has the advantage. The Latin language is clumsy. Light pleasure was an exotic in the Roman world; the terms in which you strive to describe it, suit rather the shrill camp and the droning law-court. In English, as we hinted just now, we have this too. Business is in our words; a too heavy sense clogs our literature: even in a writer so apt as Pope at the *finesse* of words, you feel the solid Gothic roots impede him. It is difficult not to be cumbrous. The horse may be fleet and light, but the wheels are ponderous and the road goes heavily. Béranger certainly has not this difficulty; nobody ever denied that a Frenchman could be light, that the French language was adapted for levity.

When we ascribed an absence of bitterness and malevolence to Béranger, we were far from meaning that he is not a satirist. Every light writer in a measure must be so. Mirth is the imagery of society; and mirth must make fun of somebody. The nineteenth century has not had many shrewder critics than its easy natured poet. Its intense dullness particularly strikes him. He dreads the dreariness of the Academy; pomposity bores him; formalism tires him; he thinks, and may well think, it dreary to have

> ' Pour grands hommes des journalistes,
>   Pour amusement l'Opéra.'

But skilful as is the mirth, its spirit is genial and good-natured. ' You have been making fun of me, Sydney, for twenty years,' said a friend to the late Canon of St. Paul's, ' and I do not think you have said a single thing I should have wished you not to say.' So far as its essential features are concerned, the nineteenth century may say the same of its musical satirist. Perhaps, however, the Bourbons might a little object. Clever people have always a *little* malice against the stupid.

There is no more striking example of the degree in which the gospel of good works has penetrated our modern society, than that Béranger has talked of 'utilising his talent.' The epicurean poet considers that he has been a political missionary. Well may others be condemned to the penal servitude of industry, if the lightest and idlest of skilful men boasts of being subjected to it. If Béranger thinks it necessary to think he has been useful, others may well think so too; let us accept the heavy doctrine of hard labour; there is no other way to heave the rubbish of this world. The mode in which Béranger is anxious to prove that he made his genius of use is by diffusing a taste for liberty, and expressing an enthusiasm for it; and also, as we suppose, in quizzing those rulers of

France who have not shared either the taste or the enthusiasm. Although, however, such may be the idea of the poet himself, posterity will scarcely confirm it. Political satire is the most ephemeral kind of literature. The circumstances to which it applies are local and temporary; the persons to whom it applies die. A very few months will make unintelligible what was at first strikingly plain. Béranger has illustrated this by an admission. There was a delay in publishing the last volume of his poems, many of which relate to the years or months immediately preceding the Revolution of 1830; the delay was not long, as the volume appeared in the first month of 1833, yet he says that many of the songs relate to the passing occurrences of a period ' *déjà loin de nous.*' On so shifting a scene as that of French political life, the jests of each act are forgotten with the act itself; the eager interest of each moment withdraws the mind from thinking of or dwelling on anything past. And in all countries administration is ephemeral; what relates to it is transitory. Satires on its detail are like the jests of a public office; the clerks change, oblivion covers their peculiarities; the point of the joke is forgotten. There are some considerable exceptions to the saying that foreign literary opinion is a ' contemporary posterity'; but in relation to satires on transitory transactions it is exactly expressive. No Englishman will now care for many of Béranger's songs which were once in the mouths of all his countrymen, which coloured the manners of revolutions, perhaps influenced their course. The fame of a poet may have a reference to politics; but it will be only to the wider species, to those social questions which never die, the elements of that active human nature which is the same age after age. Béranger can hardly hope for this. Even the songs which relate to liberty can hardly hope for this immortality. They have the vagueness which has made French aspirations for freedom futile. So far as they express distinct feeling, their tendency is rather anti-aristocratic than in favour of simple real liberty. And an objection to mere rank, though a potent, is neither a very agreeable nor a very poetical sentiment. Moreover, when the love of liberty is to be imaginatively expressed, it requires to an Englishman's ear a sound bigger and more trumpet-tongued than the voice of Béranger.

On a deeper view, however, an attentive student will dis-

cover a great deal that is most instructive in the political
career of the not very business-like poet. His life has been
contemporaneous with the course of a great change; and
throughout it the view which he has taken of the current events
is that which sensible men took at the time, and which a sensible posterity (and these events will from their size attract
attention enough to insure their being viewed sensibly) is
likely to take. Béranger was present at the taking of the
Bastille, but he was then only nine years old; the accuracy of
opinion which we are claiming for him did not commence so
early. His mature judgment begins with the career of Napoleon; and no one of the thousands who have written on that
subject has viewed it perhaps more justly. He had no love for
the despotism of the Empire, was alive to the harshness of its
administration, did not care too much for its glory, must have
felt more than once the social exhaustion. At the same time,
no man was penetrated more profoundly, no literary man half
so profoundly, with the popular admiration for the genius of the
Empire. His own verse has given the truest and most lasting
expression of it:

> ' *Les Souvenirs du Peuple.*
> On parlera de sa gloire
> Sous le chaume bien longtemps.
> L'humble toit, dans cinquante ans,
> Ne connaîtra plus d'autre histoire.
> Là viendront les villageois
> Dire alors à quelque vieille:
> " Par des récits d'autrefois,
> Mère, abrégez notre veille.
> Bien, dit-on, qu'il nous ait nui,
> Le peuple encor le révère,
>   Oui, le révère.
> Parlez-nous de lui, grand'mère;
>   Parlez-nous de lui." (*bis.*)
>
> " Mes enfants, dans ce village,
> Suivi de rois, il passa.
> Voilà bien longtemps de ça:
> Je venais d'entrer en ménage.
> A pied grimpant le coteau,
> Où pour voir je m'étais mise,

Il avait petit chapeau
Avec redingote grise.
Près de lui je me troublai;
Il me dit: ' Bonjour, ma chère,
Bonjour, ma chère.' "
—" Il vous a parlé, grand'mère!
Il vous a parlé!"

" L'an d'après, moi, pauvre femme,
A Paris étant un jour,
Je le vis avec sa cour:
Il se rendait à Notre-Dame.
Tous les cœurs étaient contents;
On admirait son cortége.
Chacun disait: ' Quel beau temps!
Le ciel toujours le protége.'
Son sourire était bien doux;
D'un fils Dieu le rendait père,
Le rendait père."
—" Quel beau jour pour vous, grand'mère!
Quel beau jour pour vous!"

" Mais, quand la pauvre Champagne
Fut en proie aux étrangers,
Lui, bravant tous les dangers,
Semblait seul tenir la campagne.
Un soir, tout comme aujourd'hui,
J'entends frapper à la porte;
J'ouvre. Bon Dieu! c'était lui,
Suivi d'une faible escorte.
Il s'asseoit où me voilà,
S'écriant: 'Oh! quelle guerre!
Oh! quelle guerre!' "
—" Il s'est assis là, grand'mère!
Il s'est assis là!"

" ' J'ai faim,' dit-il; et bien vite
Je sers piquette et pain bis;
Puis il sèche ses habits;
Même à dormir le feu l'invite.
Au réveil, voyant mes pleurs,
Il me dit: ' Bonne espérance!

Je cours de tous ses malheurs,
Sous Paris, venger la France.'
Il part; et comme un trésor
J'ai depuis gardé son verre,
    Gardé son verre."
" Vous l'avez encor, grand'mère!
    Vous l'avez encor!"

" Le voici. Mais à sa perte
Le héros fut entraîné.
Lui, qu'un pape a couronné,
Est mort dans une île déserte.
Longtemps aucun ne l'a cru;
On disait: ' Il va paraître;
Par mer il est accouru;
L'étranger va voir son maître.'
Quand d'erreur on nous tira,
Ma douleur fut bien amère!
    Fut bien amère!"
—" Dieu vous bénira, grand'mère;
    Dieu vous bénira."'

This is a great exception to the transitoriness of political
poetry. Such a character as that of Napoleon displayed on so
large a stage, so great a genius amid such scenery of action,
insures an immortality. ' The page of universal history ' which
he was always coveting, he has attained; and it is a page which,
from its singularity and its errors, its shame and its glory, will
distract the attention from other pages. No one who has ever
had in his mind the idea of Napoleon's character can forget it.
Nothing too can be more natural than that the French should
remember it. It has the primary imagination, the elementary
conceiving power, in which they are deficient. So far from
being restricted to the poetry of society, he would not have
even appreciated it. A certain bareness marks his mind;
his style is curt; the imaginative product is left rude; there
is the distinct abstraction of the military diagram. The
tact of light and passing talk; the detective imagination which
is akin to that tact, and discovers the quick essence of social
things,—he never had. In speaking of his power over popular
fancies, Béranger has called him ' the greatest poet of modern
times.' No genius can be more unlike his own, and therefore

perhaps it is that he admires it so much. During the Hundred Days, Béranger says he was never under the illusion, then not rare, that the Emperor could become a constitutional monarch. The lion, he felt, would not change his skin. After the return of the Bourbons, he says, doubtless with truth, that his ' *instinct du peuple* ' told him they could never ally themselves with liberal principles, or unite with that new order of society which, though dating from the Revolution, had acquired in five-and-twenty years a half-prescriptive right. They and their followers came in to *take* possession, and it was impossible they could unite with what *was* in possession. During the whole reign of the hereditary Bourbon dynasty, Béranger was in opposition; representing the natural sentiments of the new Frenchman, he could not bear the natural tendency of the ruling power to the half-forgotten practices of old France. The legitimate Bourbons were by their position the chieftains of the party advocating their right by birth; they could not be the kings of a people; and the poet of the people was against them. After the genius of Napoleon, all other governing minds would seem tame and contracted; and Charles X. was not a man to diminish the inevitable feeling. Béranger despised him. As the poet warred with the weapons of poetry, the Government retorted with the penalties of State. He was turned out of his petty clerkship, he was twice imprisoned; but these things only increased his popularity; and a firm and genial mind, so far from being moved, sang songs at La Force itself. The Revolution of 1830 was willing to make his fortune.

' Je l'ai traitée,' he says, ' comme une puissance qui peut avoir des caprices auxquels il faut être en mesure de résister. Tous ou presque tous mes amis ont passé au ministère: j'en ai même encore un ou deux qui restent suspendus à ce mât de cocagne. Je me plais à croire qu'ils y sont accrochés par la basque, malgré les efforts qu'ils font pour descendre. J'aurais donc pu avoir part à la distribution des emplois. Malheureusement je n'ai pas l'amour des sinécures, et tout travail obligé m'est devenu insupportable, hors peut-être encore celui d'expéditionnaire. Des médisants ont prétendu que je faisais de la vertu. Fi donc! je faisais de la paresse. Ce défaut m'a tenu lieu de bien des qualités; aussi je le recommande à beaucoup de nos honnêtes gens. Il expose pourtant à de singuliers reproches. C'est à cette paresse si douce, que des censeurs rigides ont attribué l'éloignement où je me suis tenu de ceux de mes honorables amis qui ont eu le malheur d'arriver au pouvoir. Faisant trop d'honneur à ce qu'ils veulent bien appeler ma bonne tête, et oubliant trop combien il y a loin du simple bon sens à la science des grandes affaires, ces censeurs prétendent que mes conseils eussent éclairé plus d'un ministre. A les en croire, tapi derrière le fauteuil de velours de nos hommes d'état, j'aurais conjuré les vents, dissipé les orages, et fait nager la France dans un océan de délices. Nous aurions tous de la liberté à revendre ou plutôt à donner, car nous n'en savons pas bien encore le prix. Eh! messieurs mes deux ou trois amis, qui prenez un chansonnier pour un magicien, on ne vous a donc pas dit que le pouvoir est une cloche qui empêche ceux qui la mettent en branle d'entendre aucun autre son?   Sans doute des ministres consultent quelquefois ceux qu'ils ont sous la main: consulter est un moyen de parler de soi qu'on néglige rarement. Mais il ne suffirait pas de consulter de bonne foi des gens qui conseilleraient de même. Il faudrait encore exécuter: ceci est la part du caractère. Les intentions les plus pures, le patriotisme le plus éclairé ne le donnent pas toujours. Qui n'a vu de hauts personnages quitter un donneur d'avis avec une pensée courageuse, et, l'instant d'après, revenir vers lui, de je ne sais quel lieu de fascination, avec l'embarras d'un démenti donné aux résolutions les plus sages? "Oh!" disent-ils, "nous n'y serons plus repris! quelle galère!" Le plus honteux ajoute: "Je voudrais bien vous voir à ma place!" Quand un ministre dit cela, soyez sûr qu'il n'a plus la tête à lui. Cependant il en est un, mais un seul, qui, sans avoir perdu la tête, a répété souvent ce mot de la meilleure foi du monde; aussi ne l'adressait-il jamais à un ami.'

The statesman alluded to in the last paragraph is Manuel, his intimate friend, from whom he declares he could never have been separated, but whose death prevented his obtaining political honours. Nobody can read the above passage without feeling its tone of political sense. An enthusiasm for, yet half distrust of, the Revolution of July seems as sound a sentiment as could be looked for even in the most sensible contemporary. What he has thought of the present dynasty we do not know.

He probably has as little concurred in the silly encomiums of its mere partisans as in the wild execrations of its disapponted enemies. His opinion could not have been either that of the English who *fêted* Louis Napoleon in 1855, or of those who despised him in 1851. The political fortunes of France during the last ten years must have been a painful scene of observation to one who remembered the taking of the Bastille. If there be such a thing as failure in the world, this looks like it.

Although we are very far from thinking that Béranger's claims on posterity are founded on his having utilised his talent in favour of liberty, it is very natural that he should think or half-think himself that it is so. His power over the multitude must have given him great pleasure; it is something to be able to write mottoes for a revolution; to write words for people to use, and hear people use those words. The same sort of pleasure which Horace derived from his nearness to the centre of great action, Béranger has derived from the power which his thorough sympathy with his countrymen has given him over them. A political satire may be ephemeral from the rapid oblivion of its circumstances; but it is not unnatural that the author, inevitably proud of its effect, may consider it of higher worth than mere verses of society.

This shrewd sense gives a solidity to the verses of Béranger which the social and amusing sort of poetry commonly wants; but nothing can redeem it from the reproach of wanting *back* thought. This is inevitable in such literature; as it professes to delineate for us the light essence of a fugitive world, it cannot be expected to dwell on those deep and eternal principles on which that world is based. It ignores them as light talk ignores them. The most opposite thing to the poetry of society is the poetry of inspiration. There exists, of course, a kind of imagination which detects the secrets of the universe—which fills us sometimes with dread, sometimes with hope—which awakens the soul, which makes pure the feelings, which explains nature, reveals what is above nature, chastens ' the deep heart of man.' Our senses teach us what the world is; our intuitions where it is. We see the blue and gold of the world, its lively amusements, its gorgeous if superficial splendour, its currents of men; we feel its light spirits, we enjoy its happiness; we enjoy it, and we are puzzled. What is the object of all this? Why do we do all this? What is the universe *for*? Such a book as Béranger suggests this difficulty in its strongest form. It embodies the essence of all that pleasure-loving, pleasure-giving, unaccountable world in which men spend their lives,— which they are compelled to live in, but which the moment you get out of it seems so odd that you can hardly believe it is real. On this account, as we were saying before, there is no book the impression of which varies so much in different moods of mind. Sometimes no reading is so pleasant; at others you half-despise the idea of it and half-hate; it seems to sum up and make clear the littleness of your own nature. Few can bear the theory of their amusements; it is essential to the pride of man to believe that he is industrious. We are irritated at literary laughter, and wroth at printed mirth. We turn angrily away to that higher poetry which gives the outline within which all these light colours are painted. From the capital of levity, and its self-amusing crowds; from the elastic *vaudeville* and the grinning actors; from *chansons* and *cafés* we turn away to the solemn nature, to the blue over-arching sky: the one remains, the many pass; no number of seasons impairs the bloom of those hues, they are as soft to-morrow as to-day. The immeasurable depth folds us in. 'Eternity,' as the orig nal thinker said, 'is everlasting.' We breathe a deep breath. And perhaps we have higher moments. We comprehend the 'unintelligible world;' we see into 'the life of things;' we fancy we know whence we come and whither we go; words we have repeated for years have a meaning for the first time; texts of old Scripture seem to apply to *us*. . . . . And—and—Mr. Thackeray would say, You come back into the town, and order dinner at a *restaurant*, and read Béranger once more .

And though this is true—though the author of *Le Dieu des Bonnes Gens* has certainly no claim to be called a profound divine—though we do not find in him any proper expression, scarcely any momentary recognition, of those intuitions which explain in a measure the scheme and idea of things, and form the back-thought and inner structure of such minds as ours,— his sense and sympathy with the people enable him, perhaps compel him, to delineate those essential conditions which constitute the structure of exterior life, and determine with inevitable certainty the common life of common persons. He has no call to deal with heaven or the universe, but he knows the earth; he is restricted to the boundaries of time, but he under-

stands time. He has extended his delineations beyond what in
this country would be considered correct; *Les Cinq Étages* can
scarcely be quoted here; but a perhaps higher example of the
same kind of art may be so:

' *Le Vieux Vagabond.*

' Dans ce fossé cessons de vivre;
  Je finis vieux, infirme et las;
  Les passants vont dire: " Il est ivre."
  Tant mieux ! ils ne me plaindront pas.
  J'en vois qui détournent la tête;
  D'autres me jettent quelques sous.
  Courez vite, allez à la fête.
Vieux vagabond, je puis mourir sans vous.

' Oui, je meurs ici de vieillesse,
  Parce qu'on ne meurt pas de faim.
  J'espérais voir de ma détresse
  L'hôpital adoucir la fin.
  Mais tout est plein dans chaque hospice,
  Tant le peuple est infortuné.
  La rue, hélas ! fut ma nourrice.
Vieux vagabond, mourons où je suis né.

' Aux artisans, dans mon jeune âge,
  J'ai dit: " Qu'on m'enseigne un métier."
  " Va, nous n'avons pas trop d'ouvrage,"
  Répondaient-ils, " va mendier."
  Riches, qui me disiez: " Travaille,"
  J'eus bien des os de vos repas;
  J'ai bien dormi sur votre paille.
Vieux vagabond, je ne vous maudis pas.

' J'aurais pu voler, moi, pauvre homme;
  Mais non: mieux vaut tendre la main.
  Au plus, j'ai dérobé la pomme
  Qui mûrit au bord du chemin.
  Vingt fois pourtant on me verrouille
  Dans les cachots, de par le roi.
  De mon seul bien on me dépouille.
Vieux vagabond, le soleil est à moi.

'Le pauvre a-t-il une patrie?
Que me font vos vins et vos blés,
Votre gloire et votre industrie,
Et vos orateurs assemblés?
Dans vos murs ouverts à ses armes
Lorsque l'étranger s'engraissait,
Comme un sot j'ai versé des larmes.
  Vieux vagabond, sa main me nourrissait.

'Comme un insecte fait pour nuire,
Hommes, que ne m'écrasiez-vous?
Ah! plutôt vous deviez m'instruire
A travailler au bien de tous.
Mis à l'abri du vent contraire,
Le ver fût devenu fourmi;
Je vous aurais chéris en frère.
  Vieux vagabond, je meurs votre ennemi.'

Pathos in such a song as this enters into poetry. We sympathise with the essential lot of man. Poems of this kind are doubtless rare in Béranger. His commoner style is lighter and more cheerful; but no poet who has painted so well the light effervescence of light society can, when he likes, paint so well the solid stubborn forms with which it is encompassed. The genial firm sense of a large mind sees and comprehends all of human life which lies within the sphere of sense. He is an epicurean, as all merely sensible men by inevitable consequence are; and as an epicurean, he prefers to deal with the superficial and gay forms of life; but he can deal with others when he chooses to be serious. Indeed, there is no melancholy like the melancholy of the epicurean. He is alive to the fixed conditions of earth, but not to that which is above earth. He muses on the temporary, as such; he admits the skeleton, but not the soul. It is wonderful that Béranger is so cheerful as he is.

We may conclude as we began. In all his works, in lyrics of levity, of politics, of worldly reflection,—Béranger, if he had not a single object, has attained a uniform result. He has given us an idea of the essential French character, such as we fancy it must be, but can never for ourselves hope to see that it is. We understand the nice tact, the quick intelligence, the gay precision; the essence of the drama we know—the spirit of what we have seen. We know his feeling:

> ' J'aime qu'un Russe soit Russe,
> Et qu'un Anglais soit Anglais ;
> Si l'on est Prussien en Prusse,
> En France soyons Français.'

He has acted accordingly: he has delineated to us the essentia
Frenchman.

Mr. Clough's Poems*
(1862)

No one can be more rigid than we are in our rules as to the publication of remains and memoirs. It is very natural that the friends of a cultivated man who seemed about to do something, but who died before he did it, should desire to publish to the world the grounds of their faith, and the little symptoms of his immature excellence. But though they act very naturally, they act very unwisely. In the present state of the world there are too many half-excellent people: there is a superfluity of persons who have all the knowledge, all the culture, all the requisite taste,—all the tools, in short, of achievement, but who are deficient in the latent impulse and secret vigour which alone can turn such instruments to account. They have all the outward and visible signs of future success; they want the invisible spirit, which can only be demonstrated by trial and victory. Nothing, therefore, is more tedious or more worthless than the posthumous delineation of the possible successes of one who did not succeed. The dreadful remains of nice young persons which abound among us prove almost nothing as to the future fate of those persons if they had survived. We can only tell that any one is a man of genius by his having produced some work of genius. Young men must practise themselves in youthful essays; and to some of their friends these may seem works not only of fair promise, but of achieved excellence. The cold world of critics and readers will not, however, think so; that world well understands the distinction between promise and performance, and sees that these laudable *juvenilia* differ from good books as much as legitimate bills of exchange differ from actual cash.

If we did not believe that Mr. Clough's poems, or at least

* *Poems.* By Arthur Hugh Clough, sometime Fellow of Oriel College, Oxford. With a Memoir. Macmillan.

several of them, had real merit, not as promissory germs, but as completed performances, it would not seem to us to be within our province to notice them. Nor if Mr. Clough were now living among us, would he wish us to do so. The marked peculiarity, and, so to say, the *flavour* of his mind, was a sort of truthful scepticism, which made him anxious never to overstate his own assurance of anything; disinclined him to over-rate the doings of his friends; and absolutely compelled him to underrate his own past writings, as well as his capability for future literary success. He could not have borne to have his poems reviewed with ' nice remarks ' and sentimental epithets of insincere praise. He was equal to his precept:

' Where are the great, whom thou wouldst wish to praise thee ?
　Where are the pure, whom thou wouldst choose to love thee ?
　Where are the brave, to stand supreme above thee,
　Whose high commands would cheer, whose chiding raise
　　thee ?
　　Seek, seeker, in thyself; submit to find
　　In the stones bread, and life in the blank mind.'

To offer petty praise and posthumous compliments to a stoic of this temper is like buying sugar-plums for St. Simon Stylites. We venture to write an article on Mr. Clough, because we believe that his poems depict an intellect in a state which is always natural ' to such a being as man in such a world as the present,' which is peculiarly natural to us just now; and because we believe that many of these poems are very remark-able for true vigour and artistic excellence, although they certainly have several defects and shortcomings, which would have been lessened, if not removed, if their author had lived longer and had written more.

In a certain sense there are two great opinions about every-thing. There are so about the universe itself. The world as we know it is this. There is a vast, visible, indisputable sphere, of which we never lose the consciousness, of which no one seriously denies the existence, about the most important part of which most people agree tolerably and fairly. On the other hand, there is the invisible world, about which men are not agreed at all, which all but the faintest minority admit to exist somehow and somewhere, but as to the nature or locality of which there is no efficient popular demonstration; there is no such compulsory argument as will *force* the unwilling conviction of any one disposed to denial. As our minds rise, as our knowledge enlarges, as our wisdom grows, as our instincts deepen, our conviction of this invisible world is daily strengthened, and our estimate of its nature is continually improved. But— and this is the most striking peculiarity of the whole subject— the more we improve, the higher we rise, the nobler we conceive the unseen world which is in us and about us, in which we live and move, the more unlike that world becomes to the world which we *do* see. The divinities of Olympus were in a very plain and intelligible sense part and parcel of this earth; they were better specimens than could be found below, but they belonged to extant species; they were better editions of visible existences; they were like the heroines whom young men imagine after the young ladies of their vicinity—they were better and handsomer, but they were of the same sort; they had never been seen, but they might have been seen any day. So too of the God with whom the Patriarch wrestled: he might have been wrestled with even if he was not; he was that sort of person. If we contrast with these the God of whom Christ speaks—the God who has not been seen at any time, whom no man hath seen or can see, who is infinite in nature, whose ways are past finding out, the transition is palpable. We have passed from gods—from an invisible world which is similar to, which is a *natural appendix* to, the world in which we live,—and we have come to believe in an invisible world, which is altogether unlike that which we see, which is certainly not opposed to our experience, but is altogether beyond and unlike our experience; which belongs to another set of things altogether; which is, as we speak, transcendental. The 'possible' of early barbarism is like the reality of early barbarism; the 'may be,' the 'great perhaps,' of late civilisation, is most unlike the earth, whether barbaric or civilised.

Two opinions as to the universe naturally result from this fundamental contrast. There are plenty of minds like that of Voltaire, who have simply no sense or perception of the invisible world whatever, who have no ear for religion, who are in the technical sense unconverted, whom no conceivable process could convert without altering what to bystanders and ordinary observers is their identity. They are, as a rule, acute, sensible, discerning, and humane; but the first observation which the most ordinary person would make as to them is, that they are 'limited;' they understand palpable existence; they elaborate it, and beautify and improve it; but an admiring bystander who can do none of these things, who can beautify nothing, who, if he tried, would only make what is ugly uglier, is conscious of a latent superiority which he can hardly help connecting with his apparent inferiority. We cannot write Voltaire's sentences; we cannot make things as clear as he made them; but we do not much care for our deficiency. Perhaps we think 'things ought not to be so plain as all that.' There is a hidden, secret, unknown side to this universe, which these picturesque painters of the visible, these many-handed manipulators of the palpable, are not aware of, which would spoil their dexterity if it were displayed to them. Sleep-walkers can tread safely on the very edge of any precipice; but those who see, cannot. On the other hand, there are those whose minds have not only been converted, but in some sense *inverted*. They are so occupied with the invisible world as to be absorbed in it entirely; they have no true conception of that which stands plainly before them; they never look coolly at it, and are cross with those who do; they are wrapt up in their own faith as to an unseen existence; they rush upon mankind with, 'Ah, there it is! there it is!—don't you see it?' and so incur the ridicule of an age.

The best of us try to avoid both fates. We strive, more or less, to 'make the best of both worlds.' We know that the invisible world cannot be duly discerned, or perfectly appreciated. We know that we see as in a glass darkly; but still we look on the glass. We frame to ourselves some image which we know to be incomplete, which probably is in part untrue, which we try to improve day by day, of which we do not deny the defects,—but which nevertheless is our 'all;' which we hope, when the accounts are taken, may be found not utterly *unlike* the unknown reality. This is, as it seems, the best religion for finite beings, living, if we may say so, on the very edge of two dissimilar worlds, on the very line on which the infinite, unfathomable sea surges up, and just where the queer little bay of this world ends. We count the pebbles on the shore, and image to ourselves as best we may the secrets of the great deep.

There are, however, some minds (and of these Mr. Clough's

was one) which will not accept what appears to be an intellectual destiny. They struggle against the limitations of mortality, and will not condescend to use the natural and needful aids of human thought. They will not *make their image.* They struggle after an 'actual abstract.' They feel, and they rightly feel, that every image, every translation, every mode of conception by which the human mind tries to place before itself the Divine mind, is imperfect, halting, changing. They feel, from their own experience, that there is no one such mode of representation which will suit their own minds at all times, and they smile with bitterness at the notion that they could contrive an image which will suit all other minds. They could not become fanatics or missionaries, or even common preachers, without forfeiting their natural dignity, and foregoing their very essence. To cry in the streets, to uplift their voice in Israel, to be 'pained with hot thoughts,' to be 'preachers of a dream,' would reverse their whole cast of mind. It would metamorphose them into something which omits every striking trait for which they were remarked, and which contains every trait for which they were not remarked. On the other hand, it would be quite as opposite to their whole nature to become followers of Voltaire. No one knows more certainly and feels more surely that there is an invisible world, than those very persons who decline to make an image or representation of it, who shrink with a nervous horror from every such attempt when it is made by any others. All this inevitably leads to what common practical people term a 'curious' sort of mind. You do not know how to describe these 'universal negatives,' as they seem to be. They will not fall into place in the ordinary intellectual world any how. If you offer them any known religion, they 'won't have that;' if you offer them no religion, they will not have that either; if you ask them to accept a new and as yet unrecognised religion, they altogether refuse to do so. They seem not only to believe in an 'unknown God,' but in a God whom no man can ever know. Mr. Clough has expressed, in a sort of lyric, what may be called their essential religion.

> 'O Thou whose image in the shrine
>   Of human spirits dwells divine !
>   Which from that precinct once conveyed,
>   To be to outer day displayed,

Doth vanish, part, and leave behind
Mere blank and void of empty mind,
Which wilful fancy seeks in vain
With casual shapes to fill again!

'O Thou, that in our bosom's shrine
Dost dwell, unknown because divine!
I thought to speak, I thought to say,
" The light is here," " behold the way,"
" The voice was thus " and " thus the word,"
And " thus I saw," and " that I heard,"—
But from the lips that half essayed
The imperfect utterance fell unmade.

'O Thou, in that mysterious shrine
Enthroned, as I must say, divine!
I will not frame one thought of what
Thou mayest either be or not.
I will not prate of " thus " and " so,"
And be profane with " yes " and " no."
Enough that in our soul and heart
Thou, whatso'er Thou mayst be, art.'

It was exceedingly natural that Mr. Clough should incline
to some such creed as this, with his character and in his circumstances. He had by nature, probably, an exceedingly real
mind, in the good sense of that expression and the bad sense.
The actual visible world as it was, and he saw it, exercised
over him a compulsory influence. The hills among which he
had wandered, the cities he had visited, the friends whom he
knew,—these were his world. Many minds of the poetic sort
easily melt down these palpable facts into some impalpable
ether of their own. To such a mind as Shelley's the 'solid
earth ' is an immaterial fact; it is not even a cumbersome
difficulty—it is a preposterous imposture. Whatever may exist,
all that *clay* does not exist; it would be too absurd to think so.
Common persons can make nothing of this dreaminess; and
Mr. Clough, though superficial observers set him down as a
dreamer, could not make much either. To him, as to the mass of
men, the vulgar outward world was a primitive fact. ' Taxes
is true,' as the miser said. Reconcile what you have to say
with green peas, for green peas are certain; such was Mr.

Clough's idea. He could not dissolve the world into credible
ideas and then believe those ideas, as many poets have done.
He could not catch up a creed, as ordinary men do. He had a
straining, inquisitive, critical mind; he scrutinised every idea
before he took it in; he did not allow the moral forces of life
to act as they should; he was not content to gain a belief
' by going on living.' He said,

> ' *Action will furnish belief;* but will that belief be the true
> one ?
> This is the point, you know.'

He felt the coarse facts of the plain world so thoroughly, that
he could not readily take in anything which did not seem in
accordance with them and like them. And what common idea
of the invisible world seems in the least in accordance with
them or like them ?

 A journal-writer, in one of his poems, has expressed this:

> ' Comfort has come to me here in the dreary streets of the city,
> Comfort—how do you think ?—with a barrel-organ to bring it.
> Moping along the streets, and cursing my day as I wandered,
> All of a sudden my ear met the sound of an English psalm-
>   tune.
> Comfort me it did, till indeed I was very near crying.
> Ah, there is some great truth, partial very likely, but needful,
> Lodged, I am strangely sure, in the tones of the English psalm-
>   tune:
> Comfort it was at least; and I must take without question
> Comfort, however it come, in the dreary streets of the city.

> ' What with trusting myself, and seeking support from within
>   me,
> Almost I could believe I had gained a religious assurance,
> Formed in my own poor soul a great moral basis to rest on.
> Ah, but indeed I see, I feel it factitious entirely;
> I refuse, reject, and put it utterly from me;
> I will look straight out, see things, not try to evade them;
> Fact shall be fact for me, and the Truth the Truth as ever,
> Flexible, changeable, vague, and multiform, and doubtful.—
> Off, and depart to the void, thou subtle, fanatical tempter ! '

Mr. Clough's fate in life had been such as to exaggerate this naturally peculiar temper. He was a pupil of Arnold's; one of his best, most susceptible, and favourite pupils. Some years since there was much doubt and interest as to the effect of Arnold's teaching. His sudden death, so to say, cut his life in the middle, and opened a tempting discussion as to the effect of his teaching when those taught by him should have become men and not boys. The interest which his own character then awakened, and must always awaken, stimulated the discussion, and there was much doubt about it. But now we need doubt no longer. The Rugby ' men ' are *real* men, and the world can pronounce its judgment. Perhaps that part of the world which cares for such things has pronounced it. Dr. Arnold was almost indisputably an admirable master for a common English boy,—the small, apple-eating animal whom we know. He worked, he pounded, if the phrase may be used, into the boy a belief, or at any rate a floating, confused conception, that there are great subjects, that there are strange problems, that knowledge has an indefinite value, that life is a serious and solemn thing. The influence of Arnold's teaching upon the majority of his pupils was probably very vague, but very good. To impress on the ordinary Englishman a general notion of the importance of what is intellectual and the reality of what is supernatural, is the greatest benefit which can be conferred upon him. The common English mind is too coarse, sluggish, and worldly to take such lessons too much to heart. It is improved by them in many ways, and is not harmed by them at all. But there are a few minds which are very likely to think too much of such things. A susceptible, serious, intellectual boy may be injured by the incessant inculcation of the awfulness of life and the magnitude of great problems. It is not desirable to take this world too much *au sérieux*; most persons will not; and the one in a thousand who will, should not. Mr. Clough was one of those who will. He was one of Arnold's favourite pupils, because he gave heed so much to Arnold's teaching; and exactly because he gave heed to it was it bad for him. He required quite another sort of teaching: to be told to take things easily; not to try to be wise overmuch; to be ' something beside critical; ' to go on living quietly and obviously, and see what truth would come to him. Mr. Clough had to his latest years what may be noticed in others of

Arnold's disciples,—a fatigued way of looking at great subjects. It seemed as if he had been put into them before his time, had seen through them, heard all which could be said about them, had been bored by them, and had come to want something else.

A still worse consequence was, that the faith, the doctrinal teaching which Arnold impressed on the youths about him was one personal to Arnold himself, which arose out of the peculiarities of his own character, which can only be explained by them. As soon as an inquisitive mind was thrown into a new intellectual atmosphere, and was obliged to naturalise itself in it, to consider the creed it had learned with reference to the facts which it encountered and met, much of that creed must fade away. There were inevitable difficulties in it, which only the personal peculiarities of Arnold prevented his perceiving, and which everyone else must soon perceive. The new intellectual atmosphere into which Mr. Clough was thrown was peculiarly likely to have this disenchanting effect. It was the Oxford of Father Newman; an Oxford utterly different from Oxford as it is, or from the same place as it had been twenty years before. A complete estimate of that remarkable thinker cannot be given here; it would be no easy task even now, many years after his influence has declined, nor is it necessary for the present purpose. Two points are quite certain of Father Newman, and they are the only two which are at present material. He was undeniably a consummate master of the difficulties in the creeds of other men. With a profoundly religious organisation which was hard to satisfy, with an imagination which could not help setting before itself simply and exactly what different creeds would come to and mean in life, with an analysing and most subtle intellect which was sure to detect the weak point in an argument if a weak point there was, with a manner at once grave and fascinating,—he was a nearly perfect religious disputant, whatever may be his deficiencies as a religious teacher. The most accomplished theologian of another faith would have looked anxiously to the joints of his harness before entering the lists with an adversary so prompt and keen. To suppose that a youth fresh from Arnold's teaching, with a hasty faith in a scheme of thought radically inconsistent, should be able to endure such an encounter was absurd. Arnold flattered himself that he was a principal opponent of Mr. Newman; but he was rather a principal fellow-labourer. There was but one quality in a common English boy which would have enabled him to resist such a reasoner as Mr. Newman. We have a heavy apathy on exciting topics, which enables us to leave dilemmas unsolved, to forget difficulties, to go about our pleasure or our business, and to leave the reasoner to pursue his logic: ' any how he is very *long* '—*that* we comprehend. But it was exactly this happy apathy, this commonplace indifference, that Arnold prided himself on removing. He objected strenuously to Mr. Newman's creed, but he prepared anxiously the very soil in which that creed was sure to grow. A multitude of such minds as Mr. Clough's, from being Arnoldites, became Newmanites. A second quality in Mr. Newman is at least equally clear. He was much better skilled in finding out the difficulties of other men's creeds than in discovering and stating a distinct basis for his own. In most of his characteristic works he does not even attempt it. His argument is essentially an argument *ad hominem*; an argument addressed to the present creed of the person with whom he is reasoning. He says: ' Give up what you hold already, or accept what I now say; for that which you already hold involves it.' Even in books where he is especially called on to deal with matters of first principle, the result is unsatisfactory. We have heard it said that he has in later life accounted for the argumentative vehemence of his book *against* the Church of Rome by saying: ' I did it as a duty; I *put* myself into a state of mind to write that book.' And this is just the impression which his arguments give. His elementary principles seem *made*, not born. Very likely he would admit the fact, and yet defend his practice. He would say: ' Such a being as man is, in such a world as this is, *must* do so; he must make a venture for his religion; he may see a greater probability that the doctrine of the Church is true than that it is false; he may see before he believes in her that she has greater evidence than any other creed; but he must do the rest for himself. *By means of his will* he must put himself into a new state of mind; he must cast in his lot with the Church here and hereafter; *then* his belief will gradually strengthen; he will in time become sure of what she says.' He undoubtedly in the time of his power persuaded many young men to try some such process as this. The weaker, the more credulous and the more fervent, were able to persevere; those who had not distinct perceptions of real truth, who were dreamy and fanciful by nature, persevered without difficulty. But Mr. Clough could not do so; he felt it was ' something factitious.' He began to speak of the ' ruinous force of the will,' and ' our terrible notions of duty.' He ceased to be a Newmanite.

Thus Mr. Clough's career and life were exactly those most likely to develop and foster a morbid peculiarity of his intellect. He had, as we have explained, by nature an unusual difficulty in forming a creed as to the unseen world; he could not get the visible world out of his head; his strong grasp of plain facts and obvious matters was a difficulty to him. Too easily one great teacher inculcated a remarkable creed; then another great teacher took it away; then this second teacher made him believe for a time some of his own artificial faith; then it would not do. He fell back on that vague, impalpable, unembodied religion which we have attempted to describe.

He has himself given in a poem, now first published, a very remarkable description of this curious state of mind. He has prefixed to it the characteristic motto, ' *Il doutait de tout, même de l'amour.*' It is the delineation of a certain love-passage in the life of a hesitating young gentleman, who was in Rome at the time of the revolution of 1848; who could not make up his mind about the revolution, who could not make up his mind whether he liked Rome, who could not make up his mind whether he liked the young lady, who let her go away without him, who went in pursuit of her, and could not make out which way to look for her, who, in fine, has some sort of religion, but cannot himself tell what it is. The poem was not published in the author's lifetime, and there are some lines which we are persuaded he would have further polished, and some parts which he would have improved, if he had seen them in print. It is written in conversational hexameters, in a tone of semi-satire and half-belief. Part of the commencement is a good example of them:

' Rome disappoints me much; I hardly as yet understand, but
Rubbishy seems the word that most exactly would suit it.
All the foolish destructions, and all the sillier savings,
All the incongruous things of past incompatible ages,
Seem to be treasured up here to make fools of present and
  future.
Would to heaven the old Goths had made a cleaner sweep of it !

Would to heaven some new ones would come and destroy
    these churches!
However, one can live in Rome as also in London.
Rome is better than London, because it is other than London.
It is a blessing, no doubt, to be rid, at least for a time, of
All one's friends and relations,—yourself (forgive me!)
    included,—
All the *assujettissement* of having been what one has been,
What one thinks one is, or thinks that others suppose one;
Yet, in despite of all, we turn like fools to the English.
Vernon has been my fate; who is here the same that you knew
    him,—
Making the tour, it seems, with friends of the name of
    Trevellyn.

' Rome disappoints me still; but I shrink and adapt myself
    to it.
Somehow a tyrannous sense of a superincumbent oppression
Still, wherever I go, accompanies ever, and makes me
Feel like a tree (shall I say?) buried under a ruin of brickwork.
Rome, believe me, my friend, is like its own Monte Testaceo,
Merely a marvellous mass of broken and castaway wine-pots.
Ye Gods! what do I want with this rubbish of ages departed,
Things that Nature abhors, the experiments that she has
    failed in?
What do I find in the Forum? An archway and two or three
    pillars.
Well, but St. Peter's? Alas, Bernini has filled it with
    sculpture!
No one can cavil, I grant, at the size of the great Coliseum.
Doubtless the notion of grand and capacious and massive
    amusement,
This the old Romans had; but tell me, is this an idea?
Yet of solidity much, but of splendour little is extant:
" Brickwork I found thee, and marble I left thee!" their
    Emperor vaunted;
" Marble I thought thee, and brickwork I find thee!" the
    Tourist may answer.'

As he goes on, he likes Rome rather better, but hazards the
following imprecation on the Jesuits:

' Luther, they say, was unwise; he didn't see how things were
      going;
Luther was foolish,—but, O great God! what call you
      Ignatius!
O my tolerant soul, be still! but you talk of barbarians,
Alaric, Attila, Genseric;—why, they came, they killed, they
Ravaged, and went on their way; but these vile, tyrannous
      Spaniards,
These are here still,—how long, O ye heavens, in the country
      of Dante?
These, that fanaticised Europe, which now can forget them,
      release not
This, their choicest of prey, this Italy; here you see them,—
Here, with emasculate pupils and gimcrack churches of Gesù,
Pseudo-learning and lies, confessional-boxes and postures,—
Here, with metallic beliefs and regimental devotions,—
Here, overcrusting with slime, perverting, defacing, debasing,
Michael Angelo's dome, that had hung the Pantheon in heaven,
Raphael's Joys and Graces, and thy clear stars, Galileo!'

The plot of the poem is very simple, and certainly is not
very exciting. The moving force, as in most novels of verse or
prose, is the love of the hero for the heroine; but this love
assuredly is not of a very impetuous and overpowering
character. The interest of this story is precisely that it is not
overpowering. The over-intellectual hero, over-anxious to be
composed, will not submit himself to his love; over-fearful
of what is voluntary and factitious, he will not make an effort
and cast in his lot with it. He states his view of the subject
better than we can state it:

' I am in love, meantime, you think; no doubt you would think
      so.
I am in love, you say, with those letters, of course, you would
      say so.
I am in love, you declare. I think not so; yet I grant you
It is a pleasure indeed to converse with this girl. Oh, rare gift,
Rare felicity, this! she can talk in a rational way, can
Speak upon subjects that really are matters of mind and of
      thinking.
Yet in perfection retain her simplicity; never, one moment,

Never, however you urge it, however you tempt her, consents
    to
Step from ideas and fancies and loving sensations to those
    vain
Conscious understandings that vex the minds of mankind.
No, though she talk, it is music; her fingers desert not the
    keys; 'tis
Song, though you hear in the song the articulate vocables
    sounded,
Syllables singly and sweetly the words of melodious meaning.
    I am in love, you say; I do not think so, exactly.
There are two different kinds, I believe, of human attraction:
One which simply disturbs, unsettles, and makes you uneasy,
And another that poises, retains, and fixes and holds you.
I have no doubt, for myself, in giving my voice for the latter.
I do not wish to be moved, but growing where I was growing,
There more truly to grow, to live where as yet I had languished.
I do not like being moved: for the will is excited; and action
Is a most dangerous thing; I tremble for something factitious,
Some malpractice of heart and illegitimate process;
We are so prone to these things, with our terrible notions of
    duty.
Ah, let me look, let me watch, let me wait, unhurried, un-
    prompted!
Bid me not venture on aught that could alter or end what is
    present!
Say not, Time flies, and Occasion, that never returns, is
    departing!
Drive me not out, ye ill angels with fiery swords, from my
    Eden,
Waiting, and watching, and looking! Let love be its own
    inspiration!
Shall not a voice, if a voice there must be, from the airs that
    environ,
Yea, from the conscious heavens, without our knowledge or
    effort,
Break into audible words? And love be its own inspiration?'

It appears, however, that even this hesitating hero would
have come to the point at last. In a book, at least, the hero
has nothing else to do. The inevitable restrictions of a pretty

story hem him in; to wind up the plot, he must either propose
or die, and usually he prefers proposing. Mr. Claude, for such
is the name of Mr. Clough's hero, is evidently on his road
towards the inevitable alternative, when his fate intercepts him
by the help of a person who meant nothing less. There is a
sister of the heroine, who is herself engaged to a rather quick
person, and who cannot make out anyone's conducting himself
differently from her George Vernon. She writes:

' Mr. Claude, you must know, is behaving a little bit better;
  He and Papa are great friends; but he really is too *shilly-
      shally*,—
  So unlike George! Yet I hope that the matter is going on
      fairly.
  I shall, however, get George, before he goes, to say something.
  Dearest Louise, how delightful to bring young people
      together!'

As the heroine says, ' dear Georgina ' wishes for nothing so
much as to show her adroitness. George Vernon does interfere,
and Mr. Claude may describe for himself the change it makes
in his fate:

' Tibur is beautiful too, and the orchard slopes, and the Anio
  Falling, falling yet, to the ancient lyrical cadence;
  Tibur and Anio's tide; and cool from Lucretilis ever,
  With the Digentian stream, and with the Bandusian fountain,
  Folded in Sabine recesses, the valley and villa of Horace:—
  So not seeing I sung; so seeing and listening say I,
  Here as I sit by the stream, as I gaze at the cell of the Sibyl,
  Here with Albunea's home and the grove of Tiburnus beside
      me;*
  Tivoli beautiful is, and musical, O Teverone,
  Dashing from mountain to plain, thy parted impetuous
      waters!
  Tivoli's waters and rocks; and fair under Monte Gennaro,
  (Haunt even yet, I must think, as I wander and gaze, of the
      shadows,

        *   '——domus Albuneæ resonantis,
            Et præceps Anio, et Tiburni lucus, et uda
            Mobilibus pomaria rivis.'

Faded and pale, yet immortal, of Faunus, the Nymphs, and
    the Graces,)
Fair in itself, and yet fairer with human completing creations,
Folded in Sabine recesses the valley and villa of Horace:—
So not seeing I sung; so now—Nor seeing, nor hearing,
Neither by waterfall lulled, nor folded in sylvan embraces,
Neither by cell of the Sibyl, nor stepping the Monte Gennaro,
Seated on Anio's bank, nor sipping Bandusian waters,
But on Montorio's height, looking down on the tile-clad
    streets, the
Cupolas, crosses, and domes, the bushes and kitchen-gardens,
Which, by the grace of the Tibur, proclaim themselves Rome
    of the Roman,—
But on Montorio's height, looking forth to the vapoury
    mountains,
Cheating the prisoner Hope with illusions of vision and
    fancy,—
But on Montorio's height, with these weary soldiers by me,
Waiting till Oudinot enter, to reinstate Pope and Tourist.

Yes, on Montorio's height for a last farewell of the city,—
So it appears; though then I was quite uncertain about it.
So, however, it was. And now to explain the proceeding.
  I was to go, as I told you, I think, with the people to
    Florence.
Only the day before, the foolish family Vernon
Made some uneasy remarks, as we walked to our lodging
    together,
As to intentions, forsooth, and so forth. I was astounded,
Horrified quite; and obtaining just then, as it happened, an
    offer
(No common favour) of seeing the great Ludovisi collection,
Why, I made this a pretence, and wrote that they must excuse me
How could I go? Great Heavens! to conduct a permitted
    flirtation
Under those vulgar eyes, the observed of such observers!
Well, but I now, by a series of fine diplomatic inquiries,
Find from a sort of relation, a good and sensible woman,
Who is remaining at Rome with a brother too ill for removal,
That it was wholly unsanctioned, unknown,—not, I think,
    by Georgina:

She, however, ere this,—and that is the best of the story—
She and the Vernon, thank Heaven, are wedded and gone—
    honeymooning.
So—on Montorio's height for a last farewell of the city.
Tibur I have not seen, nor the lakes that of old I had dreamt
    of;
Tibur I shall not see, nor Anio's waters, nor deep en-
Folded in Sabine recesses the valley and villa of Horace;
Tibur I shall not see;—but something better I shall see.
Twice I have tried before, and failed in getting the horses;
Twice I have tried and failed: this time it shall not be a
    failure.'

But, of course, he does not reach Florence till the heroine
and her family are gone; and he hunts after them through
North Italy, not very skilfully, and then he returns to Rome;
and he reflects, certainly not in a very dignified or heroic
manner:

' I cannot stay at Florence, not even to wait for a letter.
Galleries only oppress me. Remembrance of hope I had
    cherished
(Almost more than as hope, when I passed through Florence
    the first time)
Lies like a sword in my soul. I am more a coward than ever,
Chicken-hearted, past thought. The *cafés* and waiters distress
    me.
All is unkind, and, alas! I am ready for any one's kindness.
Oh, I knew it of old, and knew it, I thought, to perfection,
If there is any one thing in the world to preclude all kind-
    ness,
It is the need of it,—it is this sad, self-defeating dependence.
Why is this, Eustace? Myself, were I stronger, I think I could
    tell you.
But it is odd when it comes. So plumb I the deeps of
    depression,
Daily in deeper, and find no support, no will, no purpose.
All my old strengths are gone. And yet I shall have to do
    something.
Ah, the key of our life, that passes all wards, opens all locks,
Is not *I will*, but *I must*. I must,—I must,—and I do it.

After all, do I know that I really cared so about her?
Do whatever I will, I cannot call up her image;
For when I close my eyes, I see, very likely, St. Peter's,
Or the Pantheon façade, or Michael Angelo's figures,
Or, at a wish, when I please, the Alban hills and the Forum,—
But that face, those eyes,—ah no, never anything like them;
Only, try as I will, a sort of featureless outline,
And a pale blank orb, which no recollection will add to.
After all, perhaps there was something factitious about it;
I have had pain, it is true: I have wept, and so have the
  actors.

'At the last moment I have your letter, for which I was
  waiting;
I have taken my place, and see no good in inquiries.
Do nothing more, good Eustace, I pray you. It only will vex
  me.
Take no measures. Indeed, should we meet, I could not be
  certain;
All might be changed, you know. Or perhaps there was
  nothing to be changed.
It is a curious history, this; and yet I foresaw it;
I could have told it before. The Fates, it is clear, are against
  us;
For it is certain enough I met with the people you mention;
They were at Florence the day I returned there, and spoke
  to me even;
Stayed a week, saw me often; departed, and whither I know
  not.
Great is Fate, and is best. I believe in Providence partly.
What is ordained is right, and all that happens is ordered.
Ah, no, that isn't it. But yet I retain my conclusion.
I will go where I am led, and will not dictate to the chances.
Do nothing more, I beg. If you love me, forbear interfering.'

And the heroine, like a sensible, quiet girl, sums up:

'You have heard nothing; of course, I know you can have
  heard nothing.
Ah, well, more than once I have broken my purpose, and
  sometimes,

Only too often, have looked for the little lake-steamer to bring
    him.
But it is only fancy,—I do not really expect it.
Oh, and you see I know so exactly how he would take it:
Finding the chances prevail against meeting again, he would
    banish
Forthwith every thought of the poor little possible hope,
    which
I myself could not help, perhaps, thinking only too much of;
He would resign himself, and go. I see it exactly.
So I also submit, although in a different manner.
Can you not really come? We go very shortly to England.'

And there let us hope she found a more satisfactory lover and
husband.

The same defect which prevented Mr. Claude from obtaining his bride will prevent this poem from obtaining universal
popularity. The public like stories which come to something;
Mr. Arnold teaches that a great poem must be founded on a
great action, and this one is founded on a long inaction. But
Art has many mansions. Many poets, whose cast of thought
unfits them for very diffused popularity, have yet a concentrated
popularity which suits them, and which lasts. Henry Taylor has
wisely said ' that a poet does not deserve the name who would
not rather be read a thousand times by one man, than a single
time by a thousand.' This repeated perusal, this testing by
continual repetition and close contact, is the very test of
intellectual poetry; unless such poetry can identify itself with
our nature, and dissolve itself into our constant thought, it is
nothing, or less than nothing; it is an ineffectual attempt to
confer a rare pleasure; it teazes by reminding us of that
pleasure, and tires by the effort which it demands from us. But
if a poem really possess this capacity of intellectual absorption
—if it really is in matter of fact accepted, apprehended,
delighted in, and retained by a large number of cultivated and
thoughtful minds,—its non-recognition by what is called the
public is no more against it than its non-recognition by the coal-
heavers. The half-educated and busy crowd, whom we call the
public, have no more right to impose their limitations on highly
educated and meditative thinkers, than the uneducated and yet
more numerous crowd have to impose their still narrower

mitations on the half-educated. The coal-heaver will not read
any books whatever; the mass of men will not read an intellectual poem: it can hardly ever be otherwise. But timid
thinkers must not dread to have a secret and rare faith. Little
deep poetry is very popular, and *no* severe art. Such poetry as
Mr. Clough's, especially, can never be so; its subjects would
forbid it, even if its treatment were perfect: but it may have
a better fate; it may have a tenacious hold on the solitary,
the meditative, and the calm. It is this which Mr. Clough
would have wished; he did not desire to be liked by ' inferior
people '—at least he would have distrusted any poem of his
own which they did like.

The artistic skill of these poems, especially of the poem
from which we have extracted so much, and of a long-vacation
pastoral published in the Highlands, is often excellent, and
occasionally fails when you least expect it. There was an odd
peculiarity in Mr. Clough's mind; you never could tell whether
it was that he would not show himself to the best advantage, or
whether he *could* not; it is certain that he very often did not,
whether in life or in books. His intellect moved with a great
difficulty, and it had a larger inertia than any other which we
have ever known. Probably there was an awkwardness born
with him, and his shyness and pride prevented him from curing
that awkwardness as most men would have done. He felt he
might fail, and he knew that he hated to fail. He neglected,
therefore, many of the thousand petty trials which fashion and
form the accomplished man of the world. Accordingly, when
at last he wanted to do something, or was obliged to attempt
something, he had occasionally a singular difficulty. He could
not get his matter out of him.

In poetry he had a further difficulty, arising from perhaps
an over-cultivated taste. He was so good a disciple of Wordsworth, he hated so thoroughly the common sing-song metres of
Moore and Byron, that he was apt to try to write what will
seem to many persons to have scarcely a metre at all. It is
quite true that the metre of intellectual poetry should not be
so pretty as that of songs, or so plain and impressive as that of
vigorous passion. The rhythm should pervade it and animate
it, but should not protrude itself upon the surface, or intrude
itself upon the attention. It should be a latent charm, though
a real one. Yet though this doctrine is true, it is nevertheless

a dangerous doctrine. Most writers need the strict fetters of
familiar metre; as soon as they are emancipated from this,
they fancy that *any* words of theirs are metrical. If a man will
read any expressive and favourite words of his own often enough,
he will come to believe that they are rhythmical; probably they
have a rhythm as he reads them; but no notation of pauses
and accents could tell the reader how to read them in that
manner; and when read in any other mode they may be prose
itself. Some of Mr. Clough's early poems, which are placed at
the beginning of this volume, are perhaps examples of more or
less of this natural self-delusion. Their writer could read them
as verse, but that was scarcely his business; and the common
reader fails.

Of one metre, however, the hexameter, we believe the most
accomplished judges, and also common readers, agree that Mr.
Clough possessed a very peculiar mastery. Perhaps he first
showed in English its *flexibility*. Whether any consummate
poem of great length and sustained dignity can be written in
this metre, and in our language, we do not know. Until a
great poet has written his poem, there are commonly no lack of
plausible arguments that seem to prove he cannot write it; but
Mr. Clough has certainly shown that in the hands of a skilful
and animated artist it is capable of adapting itself to varied
descriptions of life and manners, to noble sentiments, and to
changing thoughts. It is perhaps the most flexible of English
metres. Better than any others it changes from grave to gay
without desecrating what should be solemn, or disenchanting
that which should be graceful. And Mr. Clough was the first
to prove this, by writing a noble poem, in which it was
done.

In one principal respect Mr. Clough's two poems in hexameters, and especially the Roman one, from which we made
so many extracts, are very excellent. Somehow or other he
makes you understand what the people of whom he is writing
precisely were. You may object to the means, but you cannot
deny the result. By fate he was thrown into a vortex of
theological and metaphysical speculation, but his genius was
better suited to be the spectator of a more active and moving
scene. The play of mind upon mind; the contrasted view
which contrasted minds take of great subjects; the odd irony
of life which so often thrusts into conspicuous places exactly

what no one would expect to find in those places,—these were his subjects. Under happy circumstances he might have produced on such themes something which the mass of readers would have greatly liked; as it is, he has produced a little which meditative readers will much value, and which they will long remember.

Of Mr. Clough's character it would be out of place to say anything, except in so far as it elucidates his poems. The sort of conversation for which he was most remarkable rises again in the *Amours de Voyage*, and gives them to those who knew him in life a very peculiar charm. It would not be exact to call its best lines a pleasant cynicism; for cynicism has a bad name, and the ill-nature and other offensive qualities which have given it that name were utterly out of Mr. Clough's way. Though without much fame, he had no envy. But he had a strong realism. He saw what it is considered cynical to see—the absurdities of many persons, the pomposities of many creeds, the splendid zeal with which missionaries rush on to teach what they do not know, the wonderful earnestness with which most incomplete solutions of the universe are thrust upon us as complete and satisfying. ' *Le fond de la Providence*,' says the French novelist, ' *c'est l'ironie*.' Mr. Clough would not have said that; but he knew what it meant, and what was the portion of truth contained in it. Undeniably this *is* an *odd* world, whether it should have been so or no; and all our speculations upon it should begin with some admission of its strangeness and singularity. The habit of dwelling on such thoughts as these will not of itself make a man happy, and may make unhappy one who is inclined to be so. Mr. Clough in his time felt more than most men the weight of the unintelligible world; but such thoughts make an instructive man. Several survivors may think they owe much to Mr. Clough's quiet question, ' Ah, then you think——? ' Many pretending creeds, and many wonderful demonstrations, passed away before that calm inquiry. He had a habit of putting your own doctrine concisely before you, so that you might see what it came to, and that you did not like it. Even now that he is gone, some may feel the recollection of his society a check on unreal theories and half-mastered thoughts. Let us part from him in his own words:

' Some future day when what is now is not,
  When all old faults and follies are forgot,
  And thoughts of difference passed like dreams away,
  We'll meet again, upon some future day.

' When all that hindered, all that vexed our love,
  As tall rank weeds will climb the blade above,
  When all but it has yielded to decay,
  We'll meet again, upon some future day.

' When we have proved, each on his course alone,
  The wider world, and learnt what's now unknown,
  Have made life clear, and worked out each a way,
  We'll meet again,—we shall have much to say.

' With happier mood, and feelings born anew,
  Our boyhood's bygone fancies we'll review,
  Talk o'er old talks, play as we used to play,
  And meet again, on many a future day.

· Some day, which oft our hearts shall yearn to see,
  In some far year, though distant yet to be,
  Shall we indeed,—ye winds and waters, say!—
  Meet yet again, upon some future day ? '

Henry Crabb Robinson[*]
(1869)

PERHAPS I should be ashamed to confess it, but I own I opened the three large volumes of Mr. Robinson's memoirs with much anxiety. Their bulk, in the first place, appalled me; but that was by no means my greatest apprehension. I knew I had a hundred times heard Mr. Robinson say that he hoped something he would leave behind would ' be published and be worth publishing.' I was aware too—for it was no deep secret —that for half a century or more he had kept a diary, and that he had been preserving correspondence besides; and I was dubious what sort of things these would be, and what—to use Carlyle's words—any human editor could make of them. Even when Mr. Robinson used to talk so I used to shudder; for the men who have tried to be memoir-writers and failed, are as numerous, or nearly so, as those who have tried to be poets and failed. A specific talent is as necessary for the one as for the other. But as soon as I had read a little of the volumes, all these doubts passed away. I saw at once that Mr. Robinson had an excellent power of narrative-writing, and that the editor of his remains had made a judicious use of excellent materials.

Perhaps more than anything it was the modesty of my old friend (I think I may call Mr. Robinson my old friend, for though he *thought* me a modern youth, I *did* know him twenty years)—perhaps, I say, it was his modesty which made me nervous about his memoirs more than anything else. I have so often heard him say (and say it with a vigour of emphasis which is rarer in our generation even than in his),—' Sir, I have no literary talent. I cannot write. I never *could* write anything,

* *Diary, Reminiscences, and Correspondence of Henry Crabb Robinson, Barrister-at-Law, F.S.A.* Selected and Edited by Thomas Sadler, Ph.D. In Three Volumes. London, 1869.

and I never *would* write anything,'—that being so taught, and so vehemently, I came to believe. And there was this to justify my creed. The notes Mr. Robinson used to scatter about him —and he was fond of writing rather elaborate ones—were not always very good. At least they were too long for the busy race of the present generation, and introduced Schiller and Goethe where they need not have come. But in these memoirs (especially in the Reminiscences and the Diary—for the moment he gets to a letter the style is worse) the words flow with such an effectual simplicity, that even Southey, the great master of such prose, could hardly have written better. Possibly it was his real interest in his old stories which preserved Mr. Robinson; in his letters he was not so interested and he fell into words and amplifications; but in those ancient anecdotes, which for years were his life and being, the style, as it seems to me, could scarcely be mended even in a word. And though, undoubtedly, the book is much too long in the latter half, I do not blame Dr. Sadler, the editor and biographer, for it, or indeed blame anyone. Mr. Robinson has led a very long and very varied life, and some of his old friends had an interest in one part of his reminiscences and some in another. An unhappy editor entrusted with ' a deceased's papers,' cannot really and in practice omit much that any surviving friends much want to have put in. One man calls with a letter ' in which my dear and honoured friend gave me advice that was of such inestimable value, I hope, I cannot but think you will find room for it.' And another calls with memoranda of a dinner —a most ' superior occasion,' as they say in the north—at which, he says, ' there was conversation to which I never, or scarcely ever, heard anything equal. There were A. B. and C. D. and E. F., all masters, as you remember, of the purest conversational eloquence; surely I need not hesitate to believe that you will say something of that dinner.' And so an oppressed biographer has to serve up the crumbs of ancient feasts, though well knowing in his heart that they are crumbs, and though he feels, too, that the critics will attack him, and cruelly say it is his fault. But remembering this, and considering that Mr. Robinson wrote a diary beginning in 1811, going down to 1867, and occupying thirty-five closely written volumes, and that there were ' Reminiscences ' and vast unsorted papers, I think Dr. Sadler has managed admirably well. His book is brief

Henry Crabb Robinson 293

to what it might have been, and all his own part is written
with delicacy, feeling, and knowledge. He quotes, too, from
Wordsworth by way of motto—

> ' A man he seems of cheerful yesterdays
> And confident to-morrows; with a face
> Not worldly minded, for it bears too much
> A nation's impress,—gaiety and health,
> Freedom and hope;—but keen withal and shrewd:
> His gestures note,—and, hark, his tones of voice
> Are all vivacious as his mien and looks.'

It was a happy feeling of Mr. Robinson's character that selected
these lines to stand at the beginning of his memoirs.

And yet in one material respect—in this case perhaps the
most material respect—Dr. Sadler has failed, and not in the
least from any fault of his. Sydney Smith used to complain
that ' no one had ever made him his trustee or executor; ' being
really a very sound and sensible man of business, he felt that it
was a kind of imputation on him, and that he was not appreciated. But some one more justly replied, ' But how could *you*,
Sydney Smith, expect to be made an executor? Is there any
one who wants their " remains " to be made fun of? ' Now
every trustee of biographical papers is exactly in this difficulty,
that he cannot make fun. The melancholy friends who left the
papers would not at all like it. And, besides, there grows upon
every such biographer an ' official ' feeling—a confused sense of
vague responsibilities—a wish not to impair the gravity of the
occasion, or to offend anyone by levity. But there are some
men who cannot be justly described quite gravely; and Crabb
Robinson is one of them. A certain grotesqueness was a part
of him, and unless you liked it you lost the very best of him.
He is called, and properly called, in these memoirs Mr. Robinson; but no well-judging person ever called him so in life. He
was always called ' old Crabb,' and that is the only name which
will ever bring up his curious image to me. He was, in the
true old English sense of the word, a ' character; ' one whom
a very peculiar life, certainly, and perhaps also a rather peculiar
nature to begin with, had formed and moulded into something
so exceptional and singular that it did not seem to belong to
ordinary life, and almost moved a smile when you saw it
moving there. ' Aberrant forms,' I believe, the naturalists call

seals and such things in natural history; odd shapes that can only be explained by a long past, and which swim with a certain incongruity in their present *milieu*. Now 'old Crabb' was (to me at least) just like that. You watched with interest and pleasure his singular gestures, and his odd way of saying things, and muttered, as if to keep up the recollection, 'And *this* is the man who was the friend of Goethe, and is the friend of Wordsworth!' There was a certain animal oddity about 'old Crabb' which made it a kind of mental joke to couple him with such great names, and yet he was to his heart's core thoroughly coupled with them. If you leave out all his strange ways (I do not say Dr. Sadler has quite left them out), but to some extent he has been obliged, by place and decorum, to omit them, you lose the life of the man. You cut from the negro his skin, and from the leopard his spots. I well remember poor Clough, who was then fresh from Oxford, and was much puzzled by the corner of London to which he had drifted, looking at 'old Crabb' in a kind of terror for a whole breakfast time, and muttering in mute wonder, and almost to himself, as he came away, 'Not at all the regular patriarch.' And certainly no one could accuse Mr. Robinson of an insipid regularity either in face or nature.

Mr. Robinson was one of the original founders of University College, and was for many years both on its senate and council; and as he lived near the college he was fond of collecting at breakfast all the elder students—especially those who had any sort of interest in literature. Probably he never appeared to so much advantage, or showed all the best of his nature, so well as in those parties. Like most very cheerful old people, he at heart preferred the company of the very young; and a set of young students, even after he was seventy, suited him better as society than a set of grave old men. Sometimes, indeed, he would have—I do not say some of his contemporaries, few of them even in 1847 were up to breakfast parties, but persons of fifty and sixty—those whom young students call old gentlemen. And it was amusing to watch the consternation of some of them at the surprising youth and levity of their host. They shuddered at the freedom with which we treated him. Middle-aged men, of feeble heads and half-made reputations, have a nice dislike to the sharp arguments and the unsparing jests of 'boys at college;' they cannot bear the rough society of those who, never having tried their own strength, have not yet acquired a fellow-feeling for weakness. Many such persons, I am sure, were half hurt with Mr. Robinson for not keeping those ' impertinent boys ' more at a just distance; but Mr. Robinson liked fun and movement, and disliked the sort of dignity which shelters stupidity. There was little to gratify the unintellectual part of man at these breakfasts, and what there was was not easy to be got at. Your host, just as you were sitting down to breakfast, found he had forgotten to make the tea, then he could not find his keys, then he rang the bell to have them searched for; but long before the servant came he had gone off into ' Schiller-Goethe,' and could not the least remember what he had wanted. The more astute of his guests used to breakfast before they came, and then there was much interest in seeing a steady literary man, who did not understand the region, in agonies at having to hear three stories before he got his tea, one again between his milk and his sugar, another between his butter and his toast, and additional zest in making a stealthy inquiry that was sure to intercept the coming delicacies by bringing on Schiller and Goethe.

It is said in these memoirs that Mr. Robinson's parents were very good-looking, and that when married they were called the handsome couple. But in his old age very little regular beauty adhered to him, if he ever had any. His face was pleasing from its animation, its kindness, and its shrewdness, but the nose was one of the most slovenly which nature had ever turned out, and the chin of excessive length, with portentous power of extension. But, perhaps, for the purpose of a social narrator (and in later years this was Mr. Robinson's position), this oddity of feature was a gift. It was said, and justly said, that Lord Brougham used to punctuate his sentences with his nose; just at the end of a long parenthesis he *could*, and did, turn up his nose, which served to note the change of subject as well, or better, than a printed mark. Mr. Robinson was not so skilful as this, but he had a very able use of the chin at a conversational crisis, and just at the point of a story pushed it out, and then very slowly drew it in again, so that you always knew when to laugh, and the oddity of the gesture helped you in laughing.

Mr. Robinson had known nearly every literary man worth knowing in England and Germany for fifty years or more. He had studied at Jena in the ' great time,' when Goethe, and

Schiller, and Wieland were all at their zenith; he had lived with Charles Lamb and his set, and Rogers and his set, besides an infinite lot of little London people; he had taught Madame de Staël German philosophy in Germany, and helped her in business afterwards in England; he was the real friend of Wordsworth, and had known Coleridge and Southey almost from their ' coming out ' to their death. And he was not a mere literary man. He had been a *Times* correspondent in the days of Napoleon's early German battles, now more than ' seventy years since;' he had been off Corunna in Sir John Moore's time; and last, but almost first it should have been, he was an English barrister, who had for years a considerable business, and who was full of picturesque stories about old judges. Such a varied life and experience belong to very few men, and his social nature—at once accessible and assailant—was just the one to take advantage of it. He seemed to be lucky all through: in childhood he remembered when John Gilpin came out; then he had seen—he could not hear—John Wesley preach; then he had heard Erskine, and criticised him intelligently, in some of the finest of the well-known ' State trials; ' and so on during all his vigorous period.

I do not know that it would be possible to give a better idea of Mr. Robinson's best conversations than by quoting almost at random from the earlier part of these memoirs:—

' At the Spring assizes of 1791, when I had nearly attained my sixteenth year, I had the delight of hearing Erskine. It was a high enjoyment, and I was able to profit by it. The subject of the trial was the validity of a will—Braham *v.* Rivett. Erskine came down specially retained for the plaintiff, and Mingay for the defendant. The trial lasted two days. The title of the heir being admitted, the proof of the will was gone into at once. I have a recollection of many of the circumstances after more than fifty-four years; but of nothing do I retain so perfect a recollection as of the figure and voice of Erskine. There was a charm in his voice, a fascination in his eye, and so completely had he won my affection, that I am sure had the verdict been given against him I should have burst out crying. Of the facts and of the evidence I do not pretend to recollect anything beyond my impressions and sensations. My pocket-book records that Erskine was engaged

two and a half hours in opening the case, and Mingay two
hours and twenty minutes in his speech for the defence. E.'s
reply occupied three hours. The testatrix was an old
lady in a state of imbecility. The evil spirit of the case was
an attorney. Mingay was loud and violent, and gave Erskine
an opportunity of turning into ridicule his imagery and illustrations. For instance, M. having compared R. to the Devil
going into the Garden of Eden, E. drew a closer parallel than
M. intended. Satan's first sight of Eve was related in Milton's
words—

' " Grace was in all her steps, heaven in her eye,
    In every gesture dignity and love; "

and then a picture of idiotcy from Swift was contrasted. But
the sentence that weighed on my spirits was a pathetic exclama-
tion—" If, gentlemen, you should by your verdict annihilate
an instrument so solemnly framed, *I should retire a troubled
man from this court*." And as he uttered the word *court*, he
beat his breast and I had a difficulty in not crying out. When
in bed the following night I awoke several times in a state of
excitement approaching fever—the words " *troubled man from
this court* " rang in my ears.

' A new trial was granted, and ultimately the will was set
aside. I have said I profited by Erskine. I remarked his
great artifice, if I may call it so; and in a small way I afterwards
practised it. It lay in his frequent repetitions. He had one
or two leading arguments and main facts on which he was
constantly dwelling. But then he had marvellous skill in
varying his phraseology, so that no one was sensible of tauto-
logy in the expressions. Like the doubling of a hare, he was
perpetually coming to his old place. Other great advocates I
have remarked were ambitious of a great variety of arguments.

' About the same time that I thus first heard the most perfect of forensic orators I was also present at an exhibition
equally admirable, and which had a powerful effect upon my
mind. It was, I believe, in October, 1790, and not long before
his death, that I heard John Wesley in the great round Meet-
ing-House at Colchester. He stood in a wide pulpit, and on
each side of him stood a minister, and the two held him up,
having their hands under his armpits. His feeble voice was

barely audible. But his reverend countenance, especially his long white locks, formed a picture never to be forgotten. There was a vast crowd of lovers and admirers. It was for the most part pantomime, but the pantomime went to the heart. Of the kind I never saw anything comparable to it in after life.'

And again :—

'It was at the Summer Circuit that Rolfe made his first appearance. He had been at the preceding Sessions. I have a pleasure in recollecting that I at once foresaw that he would become a distinguished man. In my Diary I wrote, "Our new junior, Mr. Rolfe, made his appearance. His manners are genteel; his conversation easy and sensible. He is a very acceptable companion, but I fear a dangerous rival." And my brother asking me who the new man was, I said, "I will venture to predict that you will live to see that young man attain a higher rank than any one you ever saw upon the cir- cuit." It is true he is not higher than Leblanc, who was also a puisne judge, but Leblanc was never Solicitor-General; nor, probably, is Rolfe yet at the end of his career. One day, when some one remarked, "Christianity is part and parcel of the law of the land," Rolfe said to me, "Were you ever employed to draw an indictment against a man for not loving his neighbour as himself ? "

'Rolfe is, by universal repute, if not the very best, at least one of the best judges on the Bench. He is one of the few with whom I have kept up an acquaintance.'*

Of course, these stories came over and over again. It is the excellence of a reminiscent to have a few good stories, and his misfortune that people will remember what he says. In

* 'Since writing the above, Baron Rolfe has verified my prediction more strikingly by being created a peer, by the title of Lord Cran- worth, and appointed a Vice-Chancellor. Soon after his appoint- ment, he called on me, and I dined with him. I related to Lady Cranworth the anecdote given above, of my conversation with my brother, with which she was evidently pleased. Lady Cranworth was the daughter of Mr. Carr, Solicitor to the Excise, whom I for- merly used to visit, and ought soon to find some mention of in my journals. Lord Cranworth continues to enjoy universal respect.— H. C. R. 1851.'

Mr. Robinson's case an unskilled person could often see the anecdote somewhere impending, and there was often much interest in trying whether you could ward it off or not. There was one great misfortune which had happened to his guests, though he used to tell it as one of the best things that had ever happened to himself. He had picked up a certain bust of Wieland by Schadow, which it appears had been lost, and in the finding of which Goethe, even Goethe, rejoiced. After a very long interval I still shudder to think how often I have heard that story; it was one which no skill or care could long avert, for the thing stood opposite our host's chair, and the sight of it was sure to recall him. Among the ungrateful students to whom he was so kind, the first question always asked of anyone who had breakfasted at his house was, ' Did you undergo the *bust* ? '

A reader of these memoirs would naturally and justly think that the great interest of Mr. Robinson's conversation was the strength of his past memory; but quite as amusing or more was the present weakness. He never could remember names, and was very ingenious in his devices to elude the defect. There is a story in these Memoirs:—

' I was engaged to dine with Mr. Wansey at Walthamstow. When I arrived there I was in the greatest distress, through having forgotten his name. And it was not till after half an hour's worry that I recollected he was a Unitarian, which would answer as well; for I instantly proceeded to Mr. Cogan's. Having been shown into a room, young Mr. Cogan came— " Your commands, sir ? "—" Mr. Cogan, I have taken the liberty to call on you in order to know where I am to dine to-day." He smiled. I went on: " The truth is, I have accepted an invitation to dine with a gentleman, a recent acquaintance, whose name I have forgotten; but I am sure you can tell me, for he is a Unitarian, and the Unitarians are very few here." '

And at his breakfasts it was always the same; he was always in difficulty as to some person's name or other, and he had regular descriptions which recurred, like Homeric epithets, and which he expected you to apply to the individual. Thus poor Clough always appeared—' That admirable and accomplished man. You know whom I mean. The one who never says anything.'

And of another living poet he used to say: ' Probably the most able, and certainly the most consequential, of all the young persons I know. You know which it is. The one with whom I could never *presume* to be intimate. The one whose father I knew so many years.' And another particular friend of my own always occurred as—' That great friend of yours that has been in Germany—that most accomplished and interesting person—that most able and excellent young man. Sometimes I like him, and sometimes I *hate* him. You,' turning to me, ' know whom I mean, you villain ! ' And certainly I did know; for I had heard the same adjectives, and been referred to in the same manner, very many times.

Of course a main part of Mr. Robinson's conversation was on literary subjects; but of this, except when it related to persons whom he had known, or sonnets to ' the conception of which he was privy,' I do not think it would be just to speak very highly. He spoke sensibly and clearly—he could not on any subject speak otherwise; but the critical faculty is as special and as peculiar almost as the poetical; and Mr. Robinson in serious moments was quite aware of it, and he used to deny that he had one faculty more than the other. He used to read much of Wordsworth to me; but I doubt—though many of his friends will think I am a great heretic—I doubt if he read the best poems; and even those he did read (and he read very well) rather suffered from coming in the middle of a meal, and at a time when you wanted to laugh, and not to meditate. Wordsworth was a solitary man, and it is only in solitude that his best poems, or indeed any of his characteristic poems, can be truly felt or really apprehended. There are some at which I never look, even now, without thinking of the wonderful and dreary faces which Clough used to make while Mr. Robinson was reading them. To Clough certain of Wordsworth's poems were part of his inner being, and he suffered at hearing them obtruded at meal times, just as a High Churchman would suffer at hearing the collects of the Church. Indeed, these poems were among the collects of Clough's Church.

Still less do I believe that there is any special value in the expositions of German philosophy in these volumes, or that there was any in those which Mr. Robinson used to give on such matters in conversation. They are clear, no doubt, and accurate, but they are not the expositions of a born metaphysician. He speaks in these Memoirs of his having a difficulty in concentrating his 'attention on works of speculation.' And such books as Kant can only be really mastered, can perhaps only be usefully studied, by those who have an unusual facility in concentrating their mind on impalpable abstractions, and an uncommon inclination to do so. Mr. Robinson had neither; and I think the critical philosophy had really very little effect on him, and had, during the busy years which had elapsed since he studied it, very nearly run off him. There was something very curious in the sudden way that anything mystical would stop in him. At the end of a Sunday breakfast, after inflicting on you much which was transcendental in Wordsworth or Goethe, he would say, as we left him, with an air of relish, ' Now I am going to run down to Exeter Street to hear Madge. I shall not be in time for the prayers; but I do not so much care about that; what I do like is the sermon; it is so clear.' Mr. Madge was a Unitarian of the old school, with as little mystical and transcendental in his nature as any one who ever lived. There was a living piquancy in the friend of Goethe—the man who *would* explain to you his writings—being also the admirer of ' Madge;' it was like a proser, lengthily eulogising Kant to you, and then saying, 'Ah! but I do love Condillac; he is so clear.'

But, on the other hand, I used to hold—I was reading law at the time, and so had some interest in the matter—that Mr. Robinson much underrated his legal knowledge, and his practical power as a lawyer. What he used to say was, ' I never knew any law, sir, but I knew the practice. . . . I left the bar, sir, because I feared my incompetence might be discovered. I was a tolerable junior, but I was rising to be a leader, which I was unfit to be, and so I retired, not to disgrace myself by some fearful mistake.' In these Memoirs he says that he retired when he had made the sum of money which he thought enough for a bachelor with few wants and not a single expensive taste. The simplicity of his tastes is certain; very few Englishmen indeed could live with so little show or pretence. But the idea of the gross incompetence is absurd. No one who was so ever said so. There are, I am confident, plenty of substantial and well-satisfied men at the English bar who do not know nearly as much law as Mr. Robinson knew, and who have not a tithe of his natural sagacity, but who believe in themselves and in whom their clients believe. On the other hand, Mr. Robinson had many great qualifications for success at the bar. He was a really good speaker: when over seventy I have heard him make a speech that good speakers in their full vigour would be glad to make. He had a good deal of the actor in his nature, which is thought, and I fancy justly thought, to be necessary to the success of all great advocates, and perhaps of all great orators. He was well acquainted with the petty technicalities which intellectual men in middle life in general cannot learn, for he had passed some years in an attorney's office. Above all, he was a very thinking man, and had an ' idea of business '—that inscrutable something which at once and altogether distinguishes the man who is safe in the affairs of life from those who are unsafe. I do not suppose he knew much black-letter law; but there are plenty of judges on the bench who, unless they are much belied, also know very little—perhaps none. And a man who can intelligently read Kant, like Mr. Robinson, need not fear the book-work of English law. A very little serious study would have taught him law enough to lead the Norfolk circuit. He really had a sound, moderate, money-making business, and only a little pains was wanted to give him more.

The real reason why he did not take the trouble I fancy was that, being a bachelor, he was a kind of amateur in life, and did not really care. He could not spend what he had on himself, and used to give away largely, though in private. And even more, as with most men who have not thoroughly worked when young, daily, regular industry was exceedingly trying to him. No man could be less idle; far from it, he was always doing something; but then he was doing what he chose. Sir Walter Scott, one of the best workers of his time, used always to say that ' he had no temptation to be idle, but the greatest temptation, when one thing was wanted of him, to go and do something else.' Perhaps the only persons who, not being forced by mere necessity, really conquer this temptation, are those who were early broken to the yoke, and are fixed to the furrow by habit. Mr. Robinson loitered in Germany, so he was not one of these.

I am not regretting this. It would be a base idolatry of

practical life to require every man to succeed in it as far as he could, and to devote to it all his mind. The world certainly does not need it; it pays well, and it will never lack good servants. There will always be enough of sound, strong men to be working barristers and judges, let who will object to become so. But I own I think a man ought to be able to be a ' Philistine ' if he chose; there is a sickly incompleteness about people too fine for the world, and too nice to work their way in it. And when a man like Mr. Robinson had a real sagacity for affairs, it is for those who respect his memory to see that his reputation does not suffer from his modesty, and that his habitual self-depreciations—which, indeed, extended not only to his powers of writing as well as to those of acting—are not taken to be exactly true.

In fact, Mr. Robinson was usefully occupied in University College business and University Hall business, and other such things. But there is no special need to write on them in connection with his name, and it would need a good deal of writing to make them intelligible to those who do not know them now. And the greater part of his life was spent in society where his influence was always manly and vigorous. I do not mean that he was universally popular, it would be defacing his likeness to say so. ' I am a man,' he once told me, ' to whom a great number of persons entertain the very strongest objection.' Indeed he had some subjects on which he could hardly bear opposition. Twice he nearly quarrelled with me: once for writing in favour of Louis Napoleon, which, as he had caught in Germany a thorough antipathy to the first Napoleon, seemed to him quite wicked; and next for my urging that Hazlitt was a much greater writer than Charles Lamb—a harmless opinion which I still hold, but which Mr. Robinson met with this outburst: ' You, sir, you prefer the works of that scoundrel, that odious, that malignant writer, to the exquisite essays of that angelic creature!' I protested that there was no evidence that angels could write particularly well, but it was in vain, and it was some time before he forgave me. Some persons who casually encountered peculiarities like these, did not always understand them. In his last years, too, augmenting infirmities almost disqualified Mr. Robinson for general society, and quite disabled him from showing his old abilities in it. Indeed, I think that these Memoirs will give almost a new idea of his power to many young men who had only seen him casually, and at times of feebleness. After ninety it is not easy to make new friends. And, in any case, this book will always have a great charm for those who knew Mr. Robinson well when they were themselves young, because it will keep alive to them the image of his buoyant sagacity, and his wise and careless kindness.

Wordsworth, Tennyson, and Browning; or, Pure, Ornate, and Grotesque Art in English Poetry* (1864)

WE couple these two books together, not because of their likeness, for they are as dissimilar as books can be, nor on account of the eminence of their authors, for in general two great authors are too much for one essay, but because they are the best possible illustration of something we have to say upon poetical art—because they may give to it life and freshness. The accident of contemporaneous publication has here brought together two books, very characteristic of modern art, and we want to show how they are characteristic.

Neither English poetry nor English criticism have ever recovered the *eruption* which they both made at the beginning of this century into the fashionable world. The poems of Lord Byron were received with an avidity that resembles our present avidity for sensation novels, and were read by a class which at present reads little but such novels. Old men who remember those days may be heard to say, 'We hear nothing of poetry now-a-days; it seems quite down.' And 'down' it certainly is, if for poetry it be a descent to be no longer the favourite excitement of the more frivolous part of the 'upper' world. That stimulating poetry is now little read. A stray schoolboy may still be detected in a wild admiration for the *Giaour* or the *Corsair* (and it is suitable to his age, and he should not be reproached for it), but the *real* posterity—the quiet students of a past literature—never read them or think of them. A line

---

* *Enoch Arden, &c.* By Alfred Tennyson, D.C.L., Poet Laureate. *Dramatis Personæ.* By Robert Browning.

or two linger in the memory; a few telling strokes of occasional and felicitous energy are quoted, but this is all. As wholes, these exaggerated stories were worthless; they taught nothing, and, therefore, they are forgotten. If now-a-days a dismal poet were, like Byron, to lament the fact of his birth, and to hint that he was too good for the world, the *Saturday Review* would say that 'they doubted if he *was* too good; that a sulky poet was a questionable addition to a tolerable world; that he need not have been born, as far as they were concerned.' Doubtless, there is much in Byron besides his dismal exaggeration, but it was that exaggeration which made 'the sensation,' which gave him a wild moment of dangerous name. As so often happens, the cause of his momentary fashion is the cause also of his lasting oblivion. Moore's former reputation was less excessive, yet it has not been more permanent. The prettiness of a few songs preserves the memory of his name, but as a poet to *read* he is forgotten. There is nothing to read in him; no exquisite thought, no sublime feeling, no consummate description of true character. Almost the sole result of the poetry of that time is the harm which it has done. It degraded for a time the whole character of the art. It said by practice, by a most efficient and successful practice, that it was the aim, the *duty* of poets, to catch the attention of the passing, the fashionable, the busy world. If a poem 'fell dead,' it was nothing; it was composed to please the 'London' of the year, and if that London did not like it, why it had failed. It fixed upon the minds of a whole generation, it engraved in popular memory and tradition, a vague conviction that poetry is but one of the many *amusements* for the light classes, for the lighter hours of all classes. The mere notion, the bare idea, that poetry is a deep thing, a teaching thing, the most surely and wisely elevating of human things, is even now to the coarse public mind nearly unknown.

As was the fate of poetry, so inevitably was that of criticism. The science that expounds which poetry is good and which is bad is dependent for its popular reputation on the popular estimate of poetry itself. The critics of that day had *a* day, which is more than can be said for some since; they professed to tell the fashionable world in what books it would find new pleasure, and therefore they were read by the fashionable world. Byron counted the critic and poet equal. The *Edinburgh*

Review penetrated among the young, and into places of female resort where it does not go now. As people ask, ' Have you read *Henry Dunbar*? and what do you think of it?' so they then asked, ' Have you read the *Giaour*? and what do you think of it?' Lord Jeffrey, a shrewd judge of the world, employed himself in telling it what to think; not so much what it ought to think, as what at bottom it did think, and so by dexterous sympathy with current society he gained contemporary fame and power. Such fame no critic must hope for now. His articles will not penetrate where the poems themselves do not penetrate. When poetry was noisy, criticism was loud; now poetry is a still small voice, and criticism must be smaller and stiller. As the function of such criticism was limited so was its subject. For the great and (as time now proves) the *permanent* part of the poetry of his time—for Shelley and for Wordsworth—Lord Jeffrey had but one word. He said* ' It won't do.' And it will not do to amuse a drawing-room.

The doctrine that poetry is a light amusement for idle hours, a metrical species of sensational novel, has not indeed been without gainsayers wildly popular. Thirty years ago, Mr. Carlyle most rudely contradicted it. But perhaps this is about all that he has done. He has denied, but he has not disproved. He has contradicted the floating paganism, but he has not founded the deep religion. All about and around us a *faith* in poetry struggles to be extricated, but it is not extricated. Some day, at the touch of the true word, the whole confusion will by magic cease; the broken and shapeless notions cohere and crystallise into a bright and true theory. But this cannot be yet.

But though no complete theory of the poetic art as yet be possible for us, though perhaps only our children's children will be able to speak on this subject with the assured confidence which belongs to accepted truth, yet something of some certainty may be stated on the easier elements, and something that will throw light on these two new books. But it will be necessary to assign reasons, and the assigning of reasons is a dry task. Years ago, when criticism only tried to show how poetry could be made a good amusement, it was not impossible that criticism itself should be amusing. But now it must at

---

* The first words in Lord Jeffrey's celebrated review of the *Excursion* were, ' This will never do.'

least be serious, for we believe that poetry is a serious and a deep thing.

There should be a word in the language of literary art to express what the word ' picturesque ' expresses for the fine arts. *Picturesque* means fit to be put into a picture; we want a word *literatesque*, ' fit to be put into a book.' An artist goes through a hundred different country scenes, rich with beauties, charms and merits, but he does not paint any of them. He leaves them alone; he idles on till he finds the hundred-and-first—a scene which many observers would not think much of, but which *he* knows by virtue of his art will look well on canvas, and this he paints and preserves. Susceptible observers, though not artists, feel this quality too; they say of a scene, ' How picturesque ! ' meaning by this a quality distinct from that of beauty, or sublimity, or grandeur—meaning to speak not only of the scene as it is in itself, but also of its fitness for imitation by art; meaning not only that it is good, but that its goodness is such as ought to be transferred to paper; meaning not simply that it fascinates, but also that its fascination is such as ought to be copied by man. A fine and insensible instinct has put language to this subtle use; it expresses an idea without which fine art criticism could not go on, and it is very natural that the language of pictorial should be better supplied with words than that of literary criticism, for the eye was used before the mind, and language embodies primitive sensuous ideas, long ere it expresses, or need express, abstract and literary ones.

The reason why a landscape is ' picturesque ' is often said to be that such landscape represents an ' idea.' But this explanation, though in the minds of some who use it it is near akin to the truth, fails to explain that truth to those who did not know it before; the word ' idea,' is so often used in these subjects when people do not know anything else to say; it represents so often a kind of intellectual insolvency, when philosophers are at their wits' end, that shrewd people will never readily on any occasion give it credit for meaning anything. A wise explainer must, therefore, look out for other words to convey what he has to say. *Landscapes*, like everything else in nature, divide themselves as we look at them into a sort of rude classification. We go down a river, for example, and we see a hundred landscapes on both sides of it, resembling one another in much, yet differing in something; with trees here, and a farmhouse there, and shadows on one side, and a deep pool far on; a collection of circumstances most familiar in themselves, but making a perpetual novelty by the magic of their various combinations. We travel so for miles and hours, and then we come to a scene which also has these various circumstances and adjuncts, but which combines them best, which makes the best whole of them, which shows them in their best proportion at a single glance before the eye. Then we say, ' This is the place to paint the river; this is the picturesque point !' Or, if not artists or critics of art, we feel without analysis or examination that somehow this bend or sweep of the river shall in future *be the river to us*: that it is the image of it which we will retain in our mind's eye, by which we will remember it, which we will call up when we want to describe or think of it. Some fine countries, some beautiful rivers, have not this picturesque quality; they give us elements of beauty, but they do not combine them together; we go on for a time delighted, but *after* a time somehow we get wearied; we feel that we are taking in nothing and learning nothing; we get no collected image before our mind; we see the accidents and circumstances of that sort of scenery, but the summary scene we do not see; we find *disjecta membra,* but no form; various and many and faulty approximations are displayed in succession; but the absolute perfection in that country's or river's scenery—its *type*—is withheld. We go away from such places in part delighted, but in part baffled; we have been puzzled by pretty things; we have beheld a hundred different inconsistent specimens of the same sort of beauty; but the rememberable idea, the full development, the characteristic individuality of it, we have not seen.

We find the same sort of quality in all parts of painting. We see a portrait of a person we know, and we say, ' It is like —yes, like, of course, but it is not *the man*;' we feel it could not be anyone else, but still, somehow it fails to bring home to us the individual as we know him to be. *He* is not there. An accumulation of features like his are painted, but his essence is not painted; an approximation more or less excellent is given, but the characteristic expression, the *typical* form, of the man is withheld.

Literature—the painting of words—has the same quality

but wants the analogous word. The word '*literatesque*' would mean, if we possessed it, that perfect combination in the *subject-matter* of literature, which suits the *art* of literature. We often meet people, and say to them, sometimes meaning well and sometimes ill, 'How well so-and-so would do in a book!' Such people are by no means the best people; but they are the most effective people—the most rememberable people. Frequently when we first know them, we like them because they explain to us so much of our experience; we have known many people 'like that,' in one way or another, but we did not seem to understand them; they were nothing to us, for their traits were indistinct; we forgot them, for they *hitched* on to nothing, and we could not classify them; but when we see the *type* of the genus, at once we seem to comprehend its character; the inferior specimens are explained by the perfect embodiment; the approximations are definable when we know the ideal to which they draw near. There are the infinite number of classes of human beings, but in each of these classes there is a distinctive type which, if we could expand it out in words, would define the class. We cannot expand it in formal terms any more than a landscape or a species of landscape; but we have an art, an art of words, which can draw it. Travellers and others often bring home, in addition to their long journals —which though so living to them, are so dead, so inanimate, so undescriptive to all else—a pen-and-ink sketch, rudely done very likely, but which, perhaps, even the more for the blots and strokes, gives a distinct notion, an emphatic image, to all who see it. They say at once, *now* we know the sort of thing. The sketch has *hit* the mind. True literature does the same. It describes sorts, varieties, and permutations, by delineating the type of each sort, the ideal of each variety, the central, the marking trait of each permutation.

On this account, the greatest artists of the world have ever shown an enthusiasm for reality. To care for notions, and abstractions; to philosophise; to reason out conclusions; to care for schemes of thought, are signs in the artistic mind of secondary excellence. A Schiller, an Euripides, a Ben Jonson, cares for *ideas*—for the parings of the intellect, and the distillation of the mind; a Shakespeare, a Homer, a Goethe, finds his mental occupation, the true home of his natural thoughts, in the real world—' which is the world of all of us '—where the face of nature, the moving masses of men and women, are ever changing, ever multiplying, ever mixing one with the other. The reason is plain—the business of the poet, of the artist, is with *types*; and those types are mirrored in reality. As a painter must not only have a hand to execute, but an eye to distinguish—as he must go here and there through the real world to catch the picturesque man, the picturesque scene, which is to live on his canvas—so the poet must find in that reality, the *literatesque* man, the *literatesque* scene which nature intends for him, and which will live in his page. Even in reality he will not find this type complete, or the characteristics perfect; but there, at least, he will find *something*, some hint, some intimation, some suggestion; whereas, in the stagnant home of his own thoughts he will find nothing pure, nothing *as it is*, nothing which does not bear his own mark, which is not somehow altered by a mixture with himself.

The first conversation of Goethe and Schiller illustrates this conception of the poet's art. Goethe was at that time prejudiced against Schiller, we must remember, partly from what he considered the *outrages* of the *Robbers*, partly because of the philosophy of Kant. Schiller's 'Essay on *Grace and Dignity*,' he tells us, 'Was yet less of a kind to reconcile me. The philosophy of Kant, which exalts the dignity of mind so highly, while appearing to restrict it, Schiller had joyfully embraced: it unfolded the extraordinary qualities which Nature had implanted in him; and in the lively feeling of freedom and self-direction, he showed himself unthankful to the Great Mother, who surely had not acted like a step-dame towards him. Instead of viewing her as self-subsisting, as producing with a living force, and according to appointed laws, alike the highest and the lowest of her works, he took her up under the aspect of some empirical native qualities of the human mind. Certain harsh passages I could even directly apply to myself: they exhibited my confession of faith in a false light; and I felt that if written without particular attention to me, they were still worse; for in that case, the vast chasm which lay between us, gaped but so much the more distinctly.' After a casual meeting at a Society for Natural History, they walked home, and Goethe proceeds.

' We reached his house; the talk induced me to go in. I

then expounded to him, with as much vivacity as possible, the *Metamorphosis of Plants*,* drawing out on paper, with many characteristic strokes, a symbolic plant for him, as I proceeded. He heard and saw all this, with much interest and distinct comprehension; but when I had done, he shook his head and said: " This is no experiment, this is an idea." I stopped with some degree of irritation; for the point which separated us was most luminously marked by this expression. The opinions in *Dignity and Grace* again occurred to me; the old grudge was just awakening; but I smothered it, and merely said: " I was happy to find that I had got ideas without knowing it, nay that I saw them before my eyes."

' Schiller had much more prudence and dexterity of management than I; he was also thinking of his periodical the *Horen*, about this time, and of course rather wished to attract than repel me. Accordingly he answered me like an accomplished Kantite; and as my stiff-necked Realism gave occasion to many contradictions, much battling took place between us, and at last a truce, in which neither party would consent to yield the victory, but each held himself invincible. Positions like the following grieved me to the very soul: *How can there ever be an experiment, that shall correspond with an idea? The specific quality of an idea is, that no experiment can reach it or agree with it.* Yet if he held as an idea, the same thing which I looked upon as an experiment, there must certainly, I thought, be some community between us, some ground whereon both of us might meet! '

With Goethe's natural history, or with Kant's philosophy, we have here no concern, but we can combine the expressions of the two great poets into a nearly complete description of poetry. The ' symbolic plant ' is the *type* of which we speak, the ideal at which inferior specimens aim, the class-characteristic in which they all share, but which none shows forth fully. Goethe was right in searching for this in reality and nature; Schiller was right in saying that it was an ' idea,' a transcending notion to which approximations could be found in experience, but only approximations—which could not be found

---

* ' A curious physiologico-botanical theory by Goethe, which appears to be entirely unknown in this country: though several eminent continental botanists have noticed it with commendation. It is explained at considerable length, in this same *Morphologie*.'

there itself. Goethe, as a poet, rightly felt the primary necessity of outward suggestion and experience; Schiller as a philosopher, rightly felt its imperfection.

But in these delicate matters, it is easy to misapprehend. There is, undoubtedly, a sort of poetry which is produced as it were out of the author's mind. The description of the poet's own moods and feelings is a common sort of poetry—perhaps the commonest sort. But the peculiarity of such cases is, that the poet does not describe himself *as* himself: autobiography is not his object; he takes himself as a specimen of human nature; he describes, not himself, but a distillation of himself: he takes such of his moods as are most characteristic, as most typify certain moods of certain men, or certain moods of all men; he chooses preponderant feelings of special sorts of men, or occasional feelings of men of all sorts; but with whatever other difference and diversity, the essence is that such self-describing poets describe what is *in* them, but not *peculiar* to them,—what is generic, not what is special and individual. Gray's *Elegy* describes a mood which Gray felt more than other men, but which most others, perhaps all others, feel too. It is more popular, perhaps, than any English poem, because that sort of feeling is the most diffused of high feelings, and because Gray added to a singular nicety of fancy an habitual proneness to a *contemplative*—a discerning but unbiassed— meditation on death and on life. Other poets cannot hope for such success: a subject so popular, so grave, so wise, and yet so suitable to the writer's nature is hardly to be found. But the same ideal, the same unautobiographical character is to be found in the writings of meaner men. Take sonnets of Hartley Coleridge, for example:—

I.

TO A FRIEND.

' When we were idlers with the loitering rills,
  The need of human love we little noted:
  Our love was nature; and the peace that floated
  On the white mist, and dwelt upon the hills,
  To sweet accord subdued our wayward wills:
  One soul was ours, one mind, one heart devoted,
  That, wisely doating, ask'd not why it doated,
  And ours the unknown joy, which knowing kills.

But now I find, how dear thou wert to me;
That man is more than half of nature's treasure,
Of that fair Beauty which no eye can see,
Of that sweet music which no ear can measure;
And now the streams may sing for others' pleasure,
The hills sleep on in their eternity.'

II.

TO THE SAME.

' In the great city we are met again,
Where many souls there are, that breathe and die,
Scarce knowing more of nature's potency,
Than what they learn from heat, or cold, or rain,
The sad vicissitude of weary pain;—
For busy man is lord of ear and eye,
And what hath nature, but the vast, void sky,
And the thronged river toiling to the main?
Oh! say not so, for she shall have her part
In every smile, in every tear that falls,
And she shall hide her in the secret heart,
Where love persuades, and sterner duty calls:
But worse it were than death, or sorrow's smart,
To live without a friend within these walls.'

III.

TO THE SAME.

' We parted on the mountains, as two streams
From one clear spring pursue their several ways;
And thy fleet course hath been through many a maze
In foreign lands, where silvery Padus gleams
To that delicious sky, whose glowing beams
Brightened the tresses that old Poets praise;
Where Petrarch's patient love, and artful lays,
And Ariosto's song of many themes,
Moved the soft air. But I, a lazy brook,
As close pent up within my native dell,
Have crept along from nook to shady nook,
Where flowrets blow, and whispering Naiads dwell
Yet now we meet, that parted were so wide,
O'er rough and smooth to travel side by side.'

The contrast of instructive and enviable locomotion with refining but instructive meditation is not special and peculiar to these two, but general and universal. It was set down by Hartley Coleridge because he was the most meditative and refining of men.

What sort of literatesque types are fit to be described in the sort of literature called poetry, is a matter on which much might be written. Mr. Arnold, some years since, put forth a theory that the art of poetry could only delineate *great actions*. But though, rightly interpreted and understood—using the word action so as to include high and sound activity in contemplation—this definition may suit the highest poetry, it certainly cannot be stretched to include many inferior sorts and even many good sorts. Nobody in their senses would describe Gray's *Elegy* as the delineation of a ' great action; ' some kinds of mental contemplation may be energetic enough to deserve this name, but Gray would have been frightened at the very word. He loved scholarlike calm and quiet inaction; his very greatness depended on his *not* acting, on his ' wise passiveness,' on his indulging the grave idleness which so well appreciates so much of human life. But the best answer—the *reductio ad absurdum*—of Mr. Arnold's doctrine, is the mutilation which it has caused him to make of his own writings. It has forbidden him, he tells us, to reprint *Empedocles*—a poem undoubtedly containing defects and even excesses, but containing also these lines:—

> ' And yet what days were those, Parmenides!
> When we were young, when we could number friends
> In all the Italian cities like ourselves,
> When with elated hearts we join'd your train,
> Ye Sun-born virgins! on the road of Truth.
> Then we could still enjoy, then neither thought
> Nor outward things were clos'd and dead to us,
> But we receiv'd the shock of mighty thoughts
> On simple minds with a pure natural joy;
> And if the sacred load oppress'd our brain,
> We had the power to feel the pressure eas'd,
> The brow unbound, the thoughts flow free again,
> In the delightful commerce of the world.
> We had not lost our balance then, nor grown

Thought's slaves, and dead to every natural joy.
The smallest thing could give us pleasure then—
The sports of the country people;
A flute note from the woods;
Sunset over the sea:
Seed-time and harvest;
The reapers in the corn;
The vinedresser in his vineyard;
The village-girl at her wheel.

Fullness of life and power of feeling, ye
Are for the happy, for the souls at ease,
Who dwell on a firm basis of content.
But he who has outliv'd his prosperous days,
But he, whose youth fell on a different world
From that on which his exil'd age is thrown;
Whose mind was fed on other food, was train'd
By other rules than are in vogue to-day;
Whose habit of thought is fix'd, who will not change,
But in a world he loves not must subsist
In ceaseless opposition, be the guard
Of his own breast, fetter'd to what he guards,
That the world win no mastery over him;
Who has no friend, no fellow left, not one;
Who has no minute's breathing space allow'd
To nurse his dwindling faculty of joy:—
Joy and the outward world must die to him
As they are dead to me.'

What freak of criticism can induce a man who has written such poetry as this, to discard it, and say it is not poetry? Mr. Arnold is privileged to speak of his own poems, but no other critic could speak so and not be laughed at.

We are disposed to believe that no very sharp definition can be given—at least in the present state of the critical art—of the boundary line between poetry and other sorts of imaginative delineation. Between the undoubted dominions of the two kinds there is a debatable land; everybody is agreed that the 'Œdipus at Colonus' *is* poetry: everyone is agreed that the wonderful appearance of Mrs. Veal is *not* poetry. But the exact line which separates grave novels in verse like *Aylmer's Field* or *Enoch Arden,* from grave novels not in verse like *Silas Marner*

Adam Bede, we own we cannot draw with any confidence. Nor, perhaps, is it very important; whether a narrative is thrown into verse or not certainly depends in part on the taste of the age, and in part on its mechanical helps. Verse is the only mechanical help to the memory in rude times, and there is little writing till a cheap something is found to write upon, and a cheap something to write with. Poetry—verse at least—is the literature of *all work* in early ages; it is only later ages which write in what *they* think a natural and simple prose. There are other casual influences in the matter too; but they are not material now. We need only say here that poetry, because it has a more marked rhythm than prose, must be more intense in meaning and more concise in style than prose. People expect a ' marked rhythm ' to imply something worth marking; if it fails to do so they are disappointed. They are displeased at the visible waste of a powerful instrument; they call it ' doggerel,' and rightly call it, for the metrical expression of full thought and eager feeling—the burst of metre—incident to high imagination, should not be wasted on petty matters which prose does as well,—which it does better—which it suits by its very limpness and weakness, whose small changes it follows more easily, and to whose lowest details it can fully and without effort degrade itself. Verse, too, should be *more concise*, for long continued rhythm tends to jade the mind, just as brief rhythm tends to attract the attention. Poetry should be memorable and emphatic, intense, and *soon over*.

The great divisions of poetry, and of all other literary art, arise from the different modes in which these *types*—these characteristic men, these characteristic feelings—may be variously described. There are three principal modes which we shall attempt to describe—the *pure,* which is sometimes, but not very wisely, called the classical; the *ornate,* which is also unwisely called romantic; and the *grotesque,* which might be called the mediæval. We will describe the nature of these a little. Criticism we know must be brief—not, like poetry, because its charm is too intense to be sustained—but on the contrary, because its interest is too weak to be prolonged; but elementary criticism, if an evil, is a necessary evil; a little while spent among the simple principles of art is the first condition, the absolute pre-requisite, for surely apprehending and wisely judging the complete embodiments and miscellaneous forms of actual literature.

The definition of *pure* literature is that it describes the type in its simplicity, we mean, with the exact amount of accessory circumstance which is necessary to bring it before the mind in finished perfection, and *no more* than that amount. The *type* needs some accessories from its nature—a picturesque landscape does not consist wholly of picturesque features. There is a setting of surroundings—as the Americans would say, of *fixings*—without which the reality is not itself. By a traditional mode of speech, as soon as we see a picture in which a complete effect is produced by detail so rare and so harmonised as to escape us, we say how ' classical.' The whole which is to be seen appears at once and through the detail, but the detail itself is not seen: we do not think of that which gives us the idea; we are absorbed in the idea itself. Just so in literature the pure art is that which works with the fewest strokes; the fewest, that is, for its purpose, for its aim is to call up and bring home to men an idea, a form, a character, and if that idea be twisted, that form be involved, that character perplexed, many strokes of literary art will be needful. Pure art does not mutilate its object; it represents it as fully as is possible with the slightest effort which is possible; it shrinks from no needful circumstances, as little as it inserts any which are needless. The precise peculiarity is not merely that no incidental circumstance is inserted which does not tell on the main design: no art is fit to be called *art* which permits a stroke to be put in without an object; but that only the minimum of such circumstance is inserted at all. The form is sometimes said to be bare, the accessories are sometimes said to be invisible, because the appendages are so choice that the shape only is perceived.

The English literature undoubtedly contains much impure literature; impure in its style if not in its meaning; but it also contains one great, one nearly perfect, model of the pure style in the literary expression of typical *sentiment*; and one not perfect, but gigantic and close approximation to perfection in the pure delineation of objective character. Wordsworth, perhaps, comes as near to choice purity of style in sentiment as is possible; Milton, with exceptions and conditions to be explained, approaches perfection by the strenuous purity with which he depicts character.

A wit once said, that '*pretty* women had more features than *beautiful* women,' and though the expression may be criticised, the meaning is correct. Pretty women seem to have a great number of attractive points, each of which attracts your attention, and each one of which you remember afterwards; yet these points have not *grown together*, their features have not linked themselves into a single inseparable whole. But a beautiful woman is a whole as she is; you no more take her to pieces than a Greek statue; she is not an aggregate of divisible charms, she is a charm in herself. Such ever is the dividing test of pure art; if you catch yourself admiring its details, it is defective; you ought to think of it as a single whole which you must remember, which you must admire, which somehow subdues you while you admire it, which is a 'possession' to you 'for ever.'

Of course no individual poem embodies this ideal perfectly; of course every human word and phrase has its imperfections, and if we choose an instance to illustrate that ideal, the instance has scarcely a fair chance. By contrasting it with the ideal we suggest its imperfections; by protruding it as an example, we turn on its defectiveness the microscope of criticism. Yet these two sonnets of Wordsworth may be fitly read in this place, not because they are quite without faults, or because they are the very best examples of their kind of style; but because they are *luminous* examples; the compactness of the sonnet and the gravity of the sentiment, hedging in the thoughts, restraining the fancy, and helping to maintain a singleness of expression.

' THE TROSACHS.

' There's not a nook within this solemn Pass,
But were an apt Confessional for one
Taught by his summer spent, his autumn gone,
That Life is but a tale of morning grass
Withered at eve. From scenes of art which chase
That thought away, turn, and with watchful eyes
Feed it 'mid Nature's old felicities,
Rocks, rivers, and smooth lakes more clear than glass
Untouched, unbreathed upon. Thrice happy guest,
If from a golden perch of aspen spray
(October's workmanship to rival May)

> The pensive warbler of the ruddy breast
> That moral sweeten by a heaven-taught lay,
> Lulling the year, with all its cares, to rest!'

'COMPOSED UPON WESTMINSTER BRIDGE, SEPT. 3, 1802.

> 'Earth has not anything to show more fair:
> Dull would he be of soul who could pass by
> A sight so touching in its majesty:
> This city now doth, like a garment, wear
> The beauty of the morning; silent, bare,
> Ships, towers, domes, theatres, and temples lie
> Open unto the fields and to the sky;
> All bright and glittering in the smokeless air.
> Never did sun more beautifully steep
> In his first splendour, valley, rock, or hill;
> Ne'er saw I, never felt, a calm so deep!
> The river glideth at his own sweet will:
> Dear God! The very houses seem asleep;
> And all that mighty heart is lying still!'

Instances of barer style than this may easily be found, instances of colder style—few better instances of purer style. Not a single expression (the invocation in the concluding couplet of the second sonnet perhaps excepted) can be spared, yet not a single expression rivets the attention. If, indeed, we take out the phrase—

> 'The city now doth, like a garment, wear
> The beauty of the morning,'

and the description of the brilliant yellow of autumn—

> 'October's workmanship to rival May,'

they have independent value, but they are not noticed in the sonnet when we read it through; they fall into place there, and being in their place, are not seen. The great subjects of the two sonnets, the religious aspect of beautiful but grave nature—the religious aspect of a city about to awaken and be alive, are the only ideas left in our mind. To Wordsworth has been vouchsafed the last grace of the self-denying artist; you think neither of him nor his style, but you cannot help thinking of—you *must* recall—the exact phrase, the *very* sentiment he wished.

Milton's purity is more eager. In the most exciting parts of Wordsworth—and these sonnets are not very exciting—you always feel, you never forget, that what you have before you is the excitement of a recluse. There is nothing of the stir of life; nothing of the *brawl* of the world. But Milton though always a scholar by trade, though solitary in old age, was through life intent on great affairs, lived close to great scenes, watched a revolution, and if not an actor in it, was at least secretary to the actors. He was familiar—by daily experience and habitual sympathy—with the earnest debate of arduous questions, on which the life and death of the speakers certainly depended, on which the weal or woe of the country perhaps depended. He knew how profoundly the individual character of the speakers—their inner and real nature—modifies their opinion on such questions; he knew how surely that nature will appear in the expression of them. This great experience, fashioned by a fine imagination, gives to the debate of Satanic Council in Pandæmonium its reality and its life. It is a debate in the Long Parliament, and though the *theme* of *Paradise Lost* obliged Milton to side with the monarchical element in the universe, his old habits are often too much for him; and his real sympathy—the impetus and energy of his nature—side with the rebellious element. For the purposes of art this is much better—of a court, a poet can make but little; of a heaven he can make very little, but of a courtly heaven, such as Milton conceived, he can make nothing at all. The idea of a court and the idea of a heaven are so radically different, that a distinct combination of them is always grotesque and often ludicrous. *Paradise Lost*, as a whole, is radically tainted by a vicious principle. It professes to justify the ways of God to man, to account for sin and death, and it tells you that the whole originated in a political event; in a court squabble as to a particular act of patronage and the due or undue promotion of an eldest son. Satan may have been wrong, but on Milton's theory he had an *arguable* case at least. There was something arbitrary in the promotion; there were little symptoms of a job; in *Paradise Lost* it is always clear that the devils are the weaker, but it is never clear that the angels are the better. Milton's sympathy and his imagination slip back to the Puritan rebels whom he loved, and desert the courtly angels whom he could not love although he praised. There is no wonder that Milton's hell is better than his heaven, for he hated officials and he loved rebels, for he employs his genius below, and accumulates his pedantry above. On the great debate in Pandæmonium all his genius is concentrated. The question is very practical; it is, ' What are we devils to do, now we have lost heaven ? ' Satan who presides over and manipulates the assembly—Moloch

> ' The fiercest spirit
> That fought in Heaven, now fiercer by despair.'

who wants to fight again; Belial, ' the man of the world,' who does not want to fight any more; Mammon, who is for commencing an industrial career; Beelzebub, the official statesman,

> ' Deep on his front engraven,
> Deliberation sat and Public care,'

who, at Satan's instance, proposes the invasion of earth—are as distinct as so many statues. Even Belial, ' the man of the world,' the sort of man with whom Milton had least sympathy, is perfectly painted. An inferior artist would have made the actor who ' counselled ignoble ease and peaceful sloth,' a degraded and ugly creature; but Milton knew better. He knew that low notions require a better garb than high notions. Human nature is not a high thing, but at least it has a high idea of itself; it will not accept mean maxims, unless they are gilded and made beautiful. A prophet in goatskin may cry, ' Repent, repent,' but it takes ' purple and fine linen ' to be able to say ' Continue in your sins.' The world vanquishes with its speciousness and its show, and the orator who is to persuade men to worldliness must have a share in them. Milton well knew this; after the warlike speech of the fierce Moloch he introduces a brighter and a more graceful spirit.

> ' He ended frowning, and his look denounced
> Desp'rate revenge, and battle dangerous
> To less than Gods. On th' other side up rose
> Belial, in act more graceful and humane;
> A fairer person lost not Heaven; he seem'd
> For dignity composed and high exploit:
> But all was false and hollow, though his tongue
> Dropt manna, and could make the worse appear

> The better reason, to perplex and dash
> Maturest counsels; for his thoughts were low;
> To vice industrious; but to nobler deeds
> Tim'rous and slothful; yet he pleased the ear,
> And with persuasive accent thus began:'

He does not begin like a man with a strong case, but like a man with a weak case; he knows that the pride of human nature is irritated by mean advice, and though he may probably persuade men to *take* it, he must carefully apologise for *giving* it. Here, as elsewhere, though the formal address is to devils, the real address is to men: to the human nature which we know, not to the fictitious demonic nature we do not know.

> ' I should be much for open war, O Peers!
> As not behind in hate, if what was urged
> Main reason to persuade immediate war,
> Did not dissuade me most, and seem to cast
> Ominous conjecture on the whole success:
> When he who most excels in fact of arms,
> In what he counsels and in what excels
> Mistrustful, grounds his courage on despair,
> And utter dissolution, as the scope
> Of all his aim, after some dire revenge.
> First, what revenge? The tow'rs of Heav'n are fill'd
> With armed watch, that render all access
> Impregnable; oft on the bord'ring deep
> Encamp their legions, or with obscure wing
> Scout far and wide into the realm of night,
> Scorning surprise. Or could we break our way
> By force, and at our heels all hell should rise
> With blackest insurrection, to confound
> Heav'n's purest light, yet our Great Enemy,
> All incorruptible, would on his throne
> Sit unpolluted, and th' ethereal mould
> Incapable of stain would soon expel
> Her mischief, and purge off the baser fire
> Victorious. Thus repulsed, our final hope
> Is flat despair. We must exasperate
> Th' Almighty Victor to spend all his rage,
> And that must end us: that must be our cure,
> To be no more? Sad cure; for who would lose,

Though full of pain, this intellectual being,
Those thoughts that wander through eternity,
To perish rather, swallow'd up and lost
In the wide womb of uncreated night,
Devoid of sense and motion? And who knows,
Let this be good, whether our angry Foe
Can give it, or will ever? How he can
Is doubtful; that he never will is sure.
Will he, so wise, let loose at once his ire
Belike through impotence, or unaware,
To give his enemies their wish, and end
Them in his anger, whom his anger saves
To punish endless? Wherefore cease we then?
Say they who counsel war, we are decreed,
Reserved, and destined, to eternal woe;
Whatever doing, what can we suffer more,
What can we suffer worse? Is this then worst,
Thus sitting, thus consulting, thus in arms?'

*　　*　　*　　*　　*　　*

And so on.

Mr. Pitt knew this speech by heart, and Lord Macaulay has
called it incomparable; and these judges of the oratorical art
have well decided. A mean foreign policy cannot be better
defended. Its sensibleness is effectually explained, and its
tameness as much as possible disguised.

But we have not here to do with the excellence of Belial's
policy, but with the excellence of his speech; and with that
speech in a peculiar manner. This speech, taken with the few
lines of description with which Milton introduces them, embody, in as short a space as possible, with as much perfection as
possible, the delineation of the type of character common at
all times, dangerous in many times; sure to come to the surface in moments of difficulty, and never more dangerous than
then. As Milton describes it, it is one among several *typical*
characters which will ever have their place in great councils,
which will ever be heard at important decisions, which are part
of the characteristic and inalienable whole of this statesmanlike world. The debate in Pandæmonium is a debate among
these typical characters at the greatest conceivable crisis, and
with adjuncts of solemnity which no other situation could rival.

It is the greatest *classical* triumph, the highest achievement of the pure *style* in English literature; it is the greatest description of the highest and most typical characters with the most choice circumstances and in the fewest words.

It is not unremarkable that we should find in Milton and in *Paradise Lost* the best specimen of pure style. He was schoolmaster in a pedantic age, and there is nothing so un-classical—nothing so impure in style—as pedantry. The out-of-door conversational life of Athens was as opposed to bookish scholasticism as a life can be. The most perfect books have been written not by those who thought much of books, but by those who thought little, by those who were under the restraint of a sensitive talking world, to which books had contributed something, and a various eager life the rest. Milton is gene-rally unclassical in spirit where he is learned, and naturally, because the purest poets do not overlay their conceptions with book knowledge, and the classical poets, having in comparison no books, were under little temptation to impair the purity of their style by the accumulation of their research. Over and above this, there is in Milton, and a little in Wordsworth also, one defect which is in the highest degree faulty and unclassical, which mars the effect and impairs the perfection of the pure style. There is a want of *spontaneity*, and a sense of effort. It has been happily said that Plato's words must have *grown* into their places. No one would say so of Milton or even of Words-worth. About both of them there is a taint of duty; a vicious sense of the good man's task. Things seem right where they are, but they seem to be put where they are. *Flexibility* is essential to the consummate perfection of the pure style be-cause the sensation of the poet's efforts carries away our thoughts from his achievements. We are admiring his labours when we should be enjoying his words. But this is a defect in those two writers, not a defect in pure art. Of course it *is* more difficult to write in few words than to write in many; to take the best adjuncts, and those only, for what you have to say, instead of using all which comes to hand; it *is* an addi-tional labour if you write verses in a morning, to spend the rest of the day in *choosing*, or making those verses fewer. But a perfect artist in the pure style is as effortless and as natural as in any style, perhaps is more so. Take the well-known lines:—

' There was a little lawny islet
  By anemone and violet,
     Like mosaic, paven:
And its roof was flowers and leaves
Which the summer's breath enweaves,
Where nor sun, nor showers, nor breeze,
Pierce the pines and tallest trees,
     Each a gem engraven:
Girt by many an azure wave
With which the clouds and mountains pave
     A lake's blue chasm.'

Shelley had many merits and many defects. This is not the place for a complete or indeed for *any* estimate of him. But one excellence is most evident. His words are as flexible as any words; the rhythm of some modulating air seems to move them into their place without a struggle by the poet and almost without his knowledge. This is the perfection of pure art, to embody typical conceptions in the choicest, the fewest accidents, to embody them so that each of these accidents may produce its full effect, and so to embody them without effort.

The extreme opposite to this pure art is what may be called ornate art. This species of art aims also at giving a delineation of the typical idea in its perfection and its fulness, but it aims at so doing in a manner most different. It wishes to surround the type with the greatest number of circumstances which it will *bear*. It works not by choice and selection, but by accumulation and aggregation. The idea is not, as in the pure style, presented with the least clothing which it will endure, but with the richest and most involved clothing that it will admit.

We are fortunate in not having to hunt out of past literature an illustrative specimen of the ornate style. Mr. Tennyson has just given one admirable in itself, and most characteristic of the defects and the merits of this style. The story of *Enoch Arden*, as he has enhanced and presented it, is a rich and splendid composite of imagery and illustration. Yet how simple that story is in itself. A sailor who sells fish, breaks his leg, gets dismal, gives up selling fish, goes to sea, is wrecked on a desert island, stays there some years, on his return finds his wife married to a miller, speaks to a landlady on the subject, and dies. Told in the pure and simple, the unadorned and classical style, this story would not have taken three pages, but Mr. Tennyson has been able to make it the principal—the largest tale in his new volume. He has done so only by giving to every event and incident in the volume an accompanying commentary. He tells a great deal about the torrid zone which a rough sailor like Enoch Arden certainly would not have perceived; and he gives to the fishing village, to which all the characters belong, a softness and a fascination which such villages scarcely possess in reality.

The description of the tropical island on which the sailor is thrown, is an absolute model of adorned art:—

> ' The mountain wooded to the peak, the lawns
> And winding glades high up like ways to Heaven,
> The slender coco's drooping crown of plumes,
> The lightning flash of insect and of bird,
> The lustre of the long convolvuluses
> That coil'd around the stately stems, and ran
> Ev'n to the limit of the land, the glows
> And glories of the broad belt of the world,
> All these he saw; but what he fain had seen
> He could not see, the kindly human face,
> Nor ever hear a kindly voice, but heard
> The myriad shriek of wheeling ocean-fowl,
> The league-long roller thundering on the reef,
> The moving whisper of huge trees that branch'd
> And blossom'd in the zenith, or the sweep
> Of some precipitous rivulet to the wave,
> As down the shore he ranged, or all day long
> Sat often in the seaward-gazing gorge,
> A shipwreck'd sailor, waiting for a sail:
> No sail from day to day, but every day
> The sunrise broken into scarlet shafts
> Among the palms and ferns and precipices;
> The blaze upon the waters to the east;
> The blaze upon his island overhead;
> The blaze upon the waters to the west;
> Then the great stars that globed themselves in Heaven,
> The hollow-bellowing ocean, and again
> The scarlet shafts of sunrise—but no sail.'

No expressive circumstance can be added to this description, no enhancing detail suggested. A much less happy instance is the description of Enoch's life before he sailed:—

> ' While Enoch was abroad on wrathful seas,
>   Or often journeying landward; for in truth
>   Enoch's white horse, and Enoch's ocean spoil
>   In ocean-smelling osier, and his face,
>   Rough-redden'd with a thousand winter gales,
>   Not only to the market-cross were known,
>   But in the leafy lanes behind the down,
>   Far as the portal-warding lion-whelp,
>   And peacock yew-tree of the lonely Hall,
>   Whose Friday fare was Enoch's ministering.'

So much has not often been made of selling fish.

The essence of ornate art is in this manner to accumulate round the typical object, everything which can be said about it, every associated thought that can be connected with it without impairing the essence of the delineation.

The first defect which strikes a student of ornate art—the first which arrests the mere reader of it—is what is called a want of simplicity. Nothing is described as it is, everything has about it an atmosphere of *something else*. The combined and associated thoughts, though they set off and heighten particular ideas and aspects of the central and typical conception, yet complicate it: a simple thing—' a daisy by the river's brim'—is never left by itself, something else is put with it; something not more connected with it than ' lion-whelp ' and the ' peacock yew-tree ' are with the ' fresh fish for sale ' that Enoch carries past them. Even in the highest cases ornate art leaves upon a cultured and delicate taste, the conviction that it is not the highest art, that it is somehow excessive and over-rich, that it is not chaste in itself or chastening to the mind that sees it—that it is in an explained manner unsatisfactory, ' a thing in which we feel there is some hidden want!'

That want is a want of ' definition.' We must all know landscapes, river landscapes especially, which are in the highest sense beautiful, which when we first see them give us a delicate pleasure; which in some—and these the best cases—give even a gentle sense of surprise that such things should be so beautiful, and yet when we come to live in them, to spend even a few hours in them, we seem stifled and oppressed. On the other hand there are people to whom the sea-shore is a companion, an exhilaration; and not so much for the brawl of the shore as for the *limited* vastness, the finite infinite of the ocean as they see it. Such people often come home braced and nerved, and if they spoke out the truth, would have only to say, ' We have seen the horizon line; ' if they were let alone indeed, they would gaze on it hour after hour, so great to them is the fascination, so full the sustaining calm, which they gain from that union of form and greatness. To a very inferior extent, but still, perhaps, to an extent which most people understand better, a common arch will have the same effect. A bridge completes a river landscape; if of the old and many-arched sort it regulates by a long series of defined forms the vague outline of wood and river which before had nothing to measure it; if of the new scientific sort it introduces still more strictly a geometrical element; it stiffens the scenery which was before too soft, too delicate, too vegetable. Just such is the effect of pure style in literary art. It calms by conciseness; while the ornate style leaves on the mind a mist of beauty, an excess of fascination, a complication of charm, the pure style leaves behind it the simple, defined, measured idea, as it is, and by itself. That which is chaste chastens; there is a poised energy—a state half thrill, and half tranquillity—which pure art gives, which no other can give; a pleasure justified as well as felt; an ennobled satisfaction at what ought to satisfy us, and must ennoble us.

Ornate art is to pure art what a painted statue is to an unpainted. It is impossible to deny that a touch of colour *does* bring out certain parts, does convey certain expressions, does heighten certain features, but it leaves on the work as a whole, a want, as we say, ' of something; ' a want of that inseparable chasteness which clings to simple sculpture, an impairing predominance of alluring details which impairs our satisfaction with our own satisfaction; which makes us doubt whether a higher being than ourselves will be satisfied even though we are so. In the very same manner, though the *rouge* of ornate literature excites our eye, it also impairs our confidence.

Mr. Arnold has justly observed that this self-justifying, self-*proving* purity of style, is commoner in ancient literature than in modern literature, and also that Shakespeare is not a great or an unmixed example of it. No one can say that he is. His works are full of undergrowth, are full of complexity, are not models of style; except by a miracle nothing in the Elizabethan age could be a model of style; the restraining taste of that age was feebler and more mistaken than that of any other equally great age. Shakespeare's mind so teemed with creation that he required the most just, most forcible, most constant restraint from without. He most needed to be guided of poets, and he was the least and worst guided. As a whole no one can call his works finished models of the pure style, or of any style. But he has many passages of the most pure style, passages which could be easily cited if space served. And we must remember that the task which Shakespeare undertook was the most difficult which any poet has ever attempted, and that it is a task in which after a million efforts every other poet has failed. The Elizabethan drama—as Shakespeare has immortalised it—undertakes to delineate in five acts, under stage restrictions, and in mere dialogue, a whole list of *dramatis personæ*, a set of characters enough for a modern novel, and with the distinctness of a modern novel. Shakespeare is not content to give two or three great characters in solitude and in dignity, like the classical dramatists; he wishes to give a whole *party* of characters in the play of life, and according to the nature of each. He would ' hold the mirror up to nature,' not to catch a monarch in a tragic posture, but a whole group of characters engaged in many actions, intent on many purposes, thinking many thoughts. There is life enough, there is action enough, in single plays of Shakespeare to set up an ancient dramatist for a long career. And Shakespeare succeeded. His characters, taken *en masse*, and as a whole, are as well known as any novelist's characters; cultivated men know all about them, as young ladies know all about Mr. Trollope's novels. But no other dramatist has succeeded in such an aim. No one else's characters are staple people in English literature, hereditary people whom everyone knows all about in every generation. The contemporary dramatists, Beaumont and Fletcher, Ben Jonson, Marlowe, &c., had many merits, some of them were great men. But a critic must say of them the worst thing he has to say: ' they were men who failed in their characteristic aim; ' they attempted to describe numerous sets of complicated characters, and they failed. No one of such characters, or hardly one, lives in common memory; the Faustus of Marlowe, a really great idea, is not remembered. They undertook to write what they could not write, five acts full of real characters, and in consequence, the fine individual things they conceived are forgotten by the mixed multitude, and known only to a few of the few. Of the Spanish theatre we cannot speak; but there are no such characters in any French tragedy: the whole aim of that tragedy forbad it. Goethe has added to literature a few great characters; he may be said almost to have added to literature the idea of 'intellectual creation,'—the idea of describing the great characters through the intellect; but he has not added to the common stock what Shakespeare added, a new *multitude* of men and women; and these not in simple attitudes, but amid the most complex parts of life, with all their various natures roused, mixed, and strained. The severest art must have allowed many details, much overflowing circumstance to a poet who undertook to describe what almost defies description. Pure art would have *commanded* him to use details lavishly, for only by a multiplicity of such could the required effect have been at all produced. Shakespeare could accomplish it, for his mind was a *spring*, an inexhaustible fountain of human nature, and it is no wonder that being compelled by the task of his time to let the fulness of his nature overflow, he sometimes let it overflow too much, and covered with erroneous conceits and superfluous images characters and conceptions which would have been far more justly, far more effectually, delineated with conciseness and simplicity. But there is an infinity of pure art *in* Shakespeare, although there is a great deal else also.

It will be said, if ornate art be as you say, an inferior species of art, why should it ever be used? If pure art be the best sort of art, why should it not always be used?

The reason is this: literary art, as we just now explained, is concerned with literatesque characters in literatesque situations; and the *best* art is concerned with the *most* literatesque characters in the *most* literatesque situations. Such are the subjects of pure art; it embodies with the fewest touches, and under the most select and choice circumstances, the highest conceptions; but it does not follow that only the best subjects are to be treated by art, and then only in the very best way. Human nature could not endure such a critical commandment

as that, and it would be an erroneous criticism which gave it.
Any literatesque character may be described in literature
under *any* circumstances which exhibit its literatesqueness.

The essence of pure art consists in its describing what is
as it is, and this is very well for what can bear it, but there
are many inferior things which will not bear it, and which
nevertheless ought to be described in books. A certain kind
of literature deals with illusions, and this kind of literature
has given a colouring to the name romantic. A man of rare
genius, and even of poetical genius, has gone so far as to make
these illusions the true subject of poetry—almost the sole subject. 'Without,' says Father Newman, of one of his characters, 'being himself a poet, he was in the season of poetry,
in the sweet springtime, when the year is most beautiful because
it is new. Novelty was beauty to a heart so open and cheerful
as his; not only because it was novelty, and had its proper
charm as such, but because when we first see things, we see
them in a gay confusion, which is a principal element of the
poetical. As time goes on, and we number and sort and measure things,—as we gain views,—we advance towards philosophy and truth, but we recede from poetry.

' When we ourselves were young, we once on a time walked
on a hot summer day from Oxford to Newington,—a dull road,
as anyone who has gone it knows; yet it was new to us; and
we protest to you, reader, believe it or not, laugh or not, as you
will, to us it seemed on that occasion quite touchingly beautiful; and a soft melancholy came over us, of which the shadows
fall even now, when we look back upon that dusty, weary
journey? And why? because every object which met us was
unknown and full of mystery. A tree or two in the distance
seemed the beginning of a great wood, or park, stretching end-
lessly; a hill implied a vale beyond, with that vale's history;
the bye-lanes, with their green hedges, wound on and vanished,
yet were not lost to the imagination. Such was our first journey; but when we had gone it several times, the mind refused
to act, the scene ceased to enchant, stern reality alone remained; and we thought it one of the most tiresome, odious
roads we ever had occasion to traverse.' That is to say, that
the function of the poet is to introduce a 'gay confusion,' a
rich medley which does not exist in the actual world—which
perhaps could not exist in any world—but which would seem

pretty if it did exist. Everyone who reads *Enoch Arden* will perceive that this notion of all poetry is exactly applicable to this one poem. Whatever be made of Enoch's ' Ocean-spoil in ocean-smelling osier,' of the ' portal-warding lion-whelp, and the peacock yew-tree,' everyone knows that in himself Enoch could not have been charming. People who sell fish about the country (and that is what he did, though Mr. Tennyson won't speak out, and wraps it up) never are beautiful. As Enoch was and must be coarse, in itself the poem must depend for a charm on a ' gay confusion '—on a splendid accumulation of impossible accessories.

Mr. Tennyson knows this better than many of us—he knows the country world; he has proved it that no one living knows it better; he has painted with pure art—with art which describes what is a race perhaps more refined, more delicate, more conscientious, than the sailor—the ' Northern Farmer,' and we all know what a splendid, what a living thing, he has made of it. He could, if he only would, have given us the ideal sailor in like manner—the ideal of the natural sailor we mean—the characteristic present man as he lives and is. But this he has not chosen. He has endeavoured to describe an exceptional sailor, at an exceptionally refined port, performing a graceful act, an act of relinquishment. And with this task before him, his profound taste taught him that ornate art was a necessary medium—was the sole effectual instrument—for his purpose. It was necessary for him if possible to abstract the mind from reality, to induce us *not* to conceive or think of sailors as they are while we are reading of his sailors, but to think of what a person who did not know might fancy sailors to be. A casual traveller on the seashore, with the sensitive mood and the romantic imagination Mr. Newman has described, might fancy, would fancy, a seafaring village to be like that. Accordingly, Mr. Tennyson has made it his aim to call off the stress of fancy from real life, to occupy it otherwise, to bury it with pretty accessories; to engage it on the ' peacock yew-tree,' and the ' portal-warding lion-whelp.' Nothing, too, can be more splendid than the description of the tropics as Mr. Tennyson delineates them, but a sailor would not have felt the tropics in that manner. The beauties of nature would not have so much occupied him. He would have known little of the scarlet shafts of sunrise and nothing of the long convolvuluses. As in

Robinson Crusoe, his own petty contrivances and his small ailments would have been the principal subject to him. 'For three years,' he might have said, 'my back was bad, and then I put two pegs into a piece of drift wood and so made a chair, and after that it pleased God to send me a chill.' In real life his piety would scarcely have gone beyond that.

It will indeed be said, that though the sailor had no words for, and even no explicit consciousness of the splendid details of the torrid zone, yet that he had, notwithstanding, a dim latent inexpressible conception of them: though he could not speak of them or describe them, yet they were much to him. And doubtless such is the case. Rude people are impressed by what is beautiful—deeply impressed—though they could not describe what they see, or what they feel. But what is absurd in Mr. Tennyson's description—absurd when we abstract it from the gorgeous additions and ornaments with which Mr. Tennyson distracts us—is, that his hero feels nothing else but these great splendours. We hear nothing of the physical ailments, the rough devices, the low superstitions, which really would have been the *first* things, the favourite and principal occupations of his mind. Just so when he gets home he *may* have had such fine sentiments, though it is odd, and he *may* have spoken of them to his landlady, though that is odder still, —but it is incredible that his whole mind should be made up of fine sentiments. Beside those sweet feelings, if he had them, there must have been many more obvious, more prosaic, and some perhaps more healthy. Mr. Tennyson has shown a profound judgment in distracting us as he does. He has given us a classic delineation of the 'Northern Farmer' with no ornament at all—as bare a thing as can be—because he then wanted to describe a true type of real men: he has given us a sailor crowded all over with ornament and illustration, because he then wanted to describe an unreal type of fancied men,—not sailors as they are, but sailors as they might be wished.

Another prominent element in 'Enoch Arden' is yet more suitable to, yet more requires the aid of, ornate art. Mr. Tennyson undertook to deal with *half belief*. The presentiments which Annie feels are exactly of that sort which everybody has felt, and which everyone has half believed—which hardly anyone has more than half believed. Almost everyone, it has been said, would be angry if anyone else reported that he believed in ghosts; yet hardly anyone, when thinking by himself, wholly disbelieves them. Just so such presentiments as Mr. Tennyson depicts, impress the inner mind so much that the outer mind—the rational understanding—hardly likes to consider them nicely or to discuss them sceptically. For these dubious themes an ornate or complex style is needful. Classical art speaks out what it has to say plainly and simply. Pure style cannot hesitate; it describes in concisest outline what is, as it is. If a poet really believes in presentiments he can speak out in pure style. One who could have been a poet—one of the few in any age of whom one can say certainly that they could have been, and have not been—has spoken thus:—

> ' When Heaven sends sorrow,
>   Warnings go first,
>   Lest it should burst
>   With stunning might
>   On souls too bright
>   To fear the morrow.

> ' Can science bear us
>   To the hid springs
>   Of human things?
>   Why may not dream,
>   Or thought's day-gleam,
>   Startle, yet cheer us?

> ' Are such thoughts fetters,
>   While faith disowns
>   Dread of earth's tones,
>   Recks but Heaven's call,
>   And on the wall,
>   Reads but Heaven's letters?'

But if a poet is not sure whether presentiments are true or not true; if he wishes to leave his readers in doubt; if he wishes an atmosphere of indistinct illusion and of moving shadow, he must use the romantic style, the style of miscellaneous adjunct, the style ' which shirks, not meets ' your intellect, the style which as you are scrutinising disappears.

Nor is this all, or even the principal lesson, which ' Enoch Arden ' may suggest to us, of the use of ornate art. That art is the appropriate art for an *unpleasing type*. Many of the characters of real life, if brought distinctly, prominently, and plainly before the mind, as they really are, if shown in their inner nature, their actual essence, are doubtless very unpleasant. They would be horrid to meet and horrid to think of. We fear it must be owned that ' Enoch Arden ' is this kind of person. A dirty sailor who did *not* go home to his wife is not an agreeable being: a varnish must be put on him to make him shine. It is true that he acts rightly; that he is very good. But such is human nature that it finds a little tameness in mere morality. Mere virtue belongs to a charity school-girl, and has a taint of the catechism. All of us feel this, though most of us are too timid, too scrupulous, too anxious about the virtue of others, to speak out. We are ashamed of our nature in this respect, but it is not the less our nature. And if we look deeper into the matter there are many reasons why we should not be ashamed of it. The soul of man, and as we necessarily believe of beings greater than man, has many parts beside its moral part. It has an intellectual part, an artistic part, even a religious part, in which mere morals have no share. In Shakespeare or Goethe, even in Newton or Archimedes, there is much which will not be cut down to the shape of the commandments. They have thoughts, feelings, hopes—immortal thoughts and hopes—which have influenced the life of men, and the souls of men, ever since their age, but which the ' whole duty of man,' the ethical compendium, does not recognise. Nothing is more unpleasant than a virtuous person with a mean mind. A highly developed moral nature joined to an undeveloped intellectual nature, an undeveloped artistic nature, and a very limited religious nature, is of necessity repulsive. It represents a bit of human nature—a good bit, of course—but a bit only, in disproportionate, unnatural, and revolting prominence; and therefore, unless an artist use delicate care, we are offended. The dismal act of a squalid man needed many condiments to make it pleasant, and therefore Mr. Tennyson was right to mix them subtly and to use them freely.

A mere act of self-denial can indeed scarcely be pleasant upon paper. An heroic struggle with an external adversary, even though it end in a defeat, may easily be made attractive. Human nature likes to see itself look grand, and it looks grand when it is making a brave struggle with foreign foes. But it does not look grand when it is divided against itself. An excellent person striving with temptation is a very admirable being in reality, but he is not a pleasant being in description. We hope he will win and overcome his temptation, but we feel that he would be a more interesting being, a higher being, if he had not felt that temptation so much. The poet must make the struggle great in order to make the self-denial virtuous, and if the struggle be too great, we are apt to feel some mixture of contempt. The internal metaphysics of a divided nature are but an inferior subject for art, and if they are to be made attractive, much else must be combined with them. If the excellence of Hamlet had depended on the ethical qualities of Hamlet, it would not have been the masterpiece of our literature. He acts virtuously of course, and kills the people he ought to kill, but Shakespeare knew that such goodness would not much interest the pit. He made him a handsome prince, and a puzzling meditative character; these secular qualities relieve his moral excellence, and so he becomes 'nice.' In proportion as an artist has to deal with types essentially imperfect, he must disguise their imperfections; he must accumulate around them as many first-rate accessories as may make his readers forget that they are themselves second-rate. The sudden *millionaires* of the present day hope to disguise their social defects by buying old places, and hiding among aristocratic furniture; just so a great artist who has to deal with characters artistically imperfect will use an ornate style, will fit them into a scene where there is much else to look at.

For these reasons ornate art is within the limits as legitimate as pure art. It does what pure art could not do. The very excellence of pure art confines its employment. Precisely because it gives the best things by themselves and exactly as they are it fails when it is necessary to describe inferior things among other things, with a list of enhancements and a crowd of accompaniments that in reality do not belong to it. Illusion, half belief, unpleasant types, imperfect types, are as much the proper sphere of ornate art, as an inferior landscape is the proper sphere for the true efficacy of moonlight. A really great landscape needs sunlight and bears sunlight; but moonlight is an equaliser of beauties; it gives a romantic unreality to what will not stand the bare truth. And just so does romantic art.

There is, however, a third kind of art which differs from these on the point in which they most resemble one another. Ornate art and pure art have this in common, that they paint the types of literature in as good perfection as they can. Ornate art, indeed, uses undue disguises and unreal enhancements; it does not confine itself to the best types; on the contrary it is its office to make the best of imperfect types and lame approximations; but ornate art, as much as pure art, catches its subject in the best light it can, takes the most developed aspect of it which it can find, and throws upon it the most congruous colours it can use. But grotesque art does just the contrary. It takes the type, so to say, *in difficulties*. It gives a representation of it in its minimum development, amid the circumstances least favourable to it, just while it is struggling with obstacles, just where it is encumbered with incongruities. It deals, to use the language of science, not with normal types but with abnormal specimens; to use the language of old philosophy, not with what nature is striving to be, but with what by some lapse she has happened to become.

This art works by contrast. It enables you to see, it makes you see, the perfect type by painting the opposite deviation. It shows you what ought to be by what ought not to be, when complete it reminds you of the perfect image, by showing you the distorted and imperfect image. Of this art we possess in the present generation one prolific master. Mr. Browning is an artist working by incongruity. Possibly hardly one of his most considerable efforts can be found which is not great because of its odd mixture. He puts together things which no one else would have put together, and produces on our minds a result which no one else would have produced, or tried to produce. His admirers may not like all we may have to say of him. But in our way we too are among his admirers. No one ever read him without seeing not only his great ability but his great *mind*. He not only possesses superficial useable talents, but the strong something, the inner secret something which uses them and controls them; he is great, not in mere accomplishments, but in himself. He has applied a hard strong intellect to real life; he has applied the same intellect to the problems of his age. He has striven to know what *is*: he has endeavoured not to be cheated by counterfeits, not to be infatuated with illusions. His heart is in what he says. He has battered his brain against his creed till he believes it. He has accomplishments too, the more effective because they are mixed. He is at once a student of mysticism, and a citizen of the world. He brings to the club sofa distinct visions of old creeds, intense images of strange thoughts: he takes to the bookish student tidings of wild Bohemia, and little traces of the *demi-monde*. He puts down what is good for the naughty and what is naughty for the good. Over women his easier writings exercise that imperious power which belongs to the writings of a great man of the world upon such matters. He knows women, and therefore they wish to know him. If we blame many of Browning's efforts, it is in the interest of art, and not from a wish to hurt or degrade him.

If we wanted to illustrate the nature of grotesque art by an exaggerated instance we should have selected a poem which the chance of late publication brings us in this new volume. Mr. Browning has undertaken to describe what may be called *mind in difficulties*—mind set to make out the universe under the worst and hardest circumstances. He takes 'Caliban,' not perhaps exactly Shakespeare's Caliban, but an analogous and worse creature; a strong thinking power, but a nasty creature —a gross animal, uncontrolled and unelevated by any feeling of religion or duty. The delineation of him will show that Mr. Browning does not wish to take undue advantage of his readers by a choice of nice subjects.

> '[Will sprawl, now that the heat of day is best,
> Flat on his belly in the pit's much mire,
> With elbows wide, fists clenched to prop his chin;
> And, while he kicks both feet in the cool slush,
> And feels about his spine small eft-things course,
> Run in and out each arm, and make him laugh;
> And while above his head a pompion-plant,
> Coating the cave-top as a brow its eye,
> Creeps down to touch and tickle hair and beard,
> And now a flower drops with a bee inside,
> And now a fruit to snap at, catch and crunch:'

This pleasant creature proceeds to give his idea of the origin of the Universe, and it is as follows. Caliban speaks in the third person, and is of opinion that the maker of the Universe took to making it on account of his personal discomfort:—

'Setebos, Setebos, and Setebos!
'Thinketh, He dwelleth i' the cold o' the moon.

''Thinketh He made it, with the sun to match,
But not the stars: the stars came otherwise;
Only made clouds, winds, meteors, such as that:
Also this isle, what lives and grows thereon,
And snaky sea which rounds and ends the same.

''Thinketh, it came of being ill at ease:
He hated that He cannot change His cold,
Nor cure its ache. 'Hath spied an icy fish
That longed to 'scape the rock-stream where she lived,
And thaw herself within the lukewarm brine
O' the lazy sea her stream thrusts far amid,
A crystal spike 'twixt two warm walls of wave;
Only she ever sickened, found repulse
At the other kind of water, not her life,
(Green-dense and dim-delicious, bred o' the sun)
Flounced back from bliss she was not born to breathe,
And in her old bounds buried her despair,
Hating and loving warmth alike: so He.

''Thinketh, He made thereat the sun, this isle,
Trees and the fowls here, beast and creeping thing.
Yon otter, sleek-wet, black, lithe as a leech;
Yon auk, one fire-eye, in a ball of foam,
That floats and feeds; a certain badger brown
He hath watched hunt with that slant white-wedge eye
By moonlight; and the pie with the long tongue
That pricks deep into oakwarts for a worm,
And says a plain word when she finds her prize,
But will not eat the ants; the ants themselves
That build a wall of seeds and settled stalks
About their hole—He made all these and more,
Made all we see, and us, in spite: how else?'

It may seem perhaps to most readers that these lines are
very difficult, and that they are unpleasant. And so they are.
We quote them to illustrate, not the *success* of grotesque art,
but the *nature* of grotesque art. It shows the end at which
this species of art aims, and if it fails it is from over-boldness
in the choice of a subject by the artist, or from the defects of

its execution. A thinking faculty more in difficulties—a great type,—an inquisitive, searching intellect under more disagreeable conditions, with worse helps, more likely to find falsehood, less likely to find truth, can scarcely be imagined. Nor is the mere description of the thought at all bad: on the contrary, if we closely examine it, it is very clever. Hardly anyone could have amassed so many ideas at once nasty and suitable. But scarcely any readers—any casual readers—who are not of the sect of Mr. Browning's admirers will be able to examine it enough to appreciate it. From a defect, partly of subject, and partly of style, many of Mr. Browning's works make a demand upon the reader's zeal and sense of duty to which the nature of most readers is unequal. They have on the turf the convenient expression 'staying power': some horses can hold on and others cannot. But hardly any reader not of especial and peculiar nature can hold on through such composition. There is not enough of 'staying power' in human nature. One of his greatest admirers once owned to us that he seldom or never began a new poem without looking on in advance, and foreseeing with caution what length of intellectual adventure he was about to commence. Whoever will work hard at such poems will find much mind in them: they are a sort of quarry of ideas, but who ever goes there will find these ideas in such a jagged, ugly, useless shape that he can hardly bear them.

We are not judging Mr. Browning simply from a hasty recent production. All poets are liable to misconceptions, and if such a piece as ' Caliban upon Setebos ' were an isolated error, a venial and particular exception we should have given it no prominence. We have put it forward because it just elucidates both our subject and the characteristics of Mr. Browning. But many other of his best known pieces do so almost equally; what several of his devotees think his best piece is quite enough illustrative for anything we want. It appears that on Holy Cross day at Rome the Jews were obliged to listen to a Christian sermon in the hope of their conversion, though this is, according to Mr. Browning, what they really said when they came away:—

' Fee, faw, fum! bubble and squeak!
Blessedest Thursday's the fat of the week.
Rumble and tumble, sleek and rough,

Stinking and savoury, smug and gruff,
Take the church-road, for the bell's due chime
Gives us the summons—'t is sermon-time.

' Boh, here's Barnabas ! Job, that's you ?
Up stumps Solomon—bustling too ?
Shame, man ! greedy beyond your years
To handsel the bishop's shaving-shears ?
Fair play's a jewel ! leave friends in the lurch ?
Stand on a line ere you start for the church.

' Higgledy, piggledy, packed we lie,
Rats in a hamper, swine in a stye,
Wasps in a bottle, frogs in a sieve,
Worms in a carcase, fleas in a sleeve.
Hist ! square shoulders, settle your thumbs
And buzz for the bishop—here he comes.'

And after similar nice remarks for a church, the edified congregation concludes :—

' But now, while the scapegoats leave our flock,
And the rest sit silent and count the clock,
Since forced to muse the appointed time
On these precious facts and truths sublime,—
Let us fitly employ it, under our breath,
In saying Ben Ezra's Song of Death.

' For Rabbi Ben Ezra, the night he died,
Called sons and son's sons to his side,
And spoke, " This world has been harsh and strange;
Something is wrong: there needeth a change.
But what, or where ? at the last, or first ?
In one point only we sinned, at worst.

' " The Lord will have mercy on Jacob yet,
And again in his border see Israel set.
When Judah beholds Jerusalem,
The stranger-seed shall be joined to them:
To Jacob's House shall the Gentiles cleave.
So the Prophet saith and his sons believe.

' " Ay, the children of the chosen race
Shall carry and bring them to their place:
In the land of the Lord shall lead the same,

Bondsmen and handmaids. Who shall blame,
When the slave enslave, the oppressed ones o'er
The oppressor triumph for evermore?

' " God spoke, and gave us the word to keep:
Bade never fold the hands nor sleep
'Mid a faithless world,—at watch and ward,
Till Christ at the end relieve our guard.
By His servant Moses the watch was set:
Though near upon cock-crow, we keep it yet.

' " Thou! if Thou wast He, who at mid watch came,
By the starlight, naming a dubious Name!
And if, too heavy with sleep—too rash
With fear—O Thou, if that martyr-gash
Fell on Thee coming to take Thine own,
And we gave the Cross, when we owed the Throne—

' " Thou art the Judge. We are bruised thus.
But, the judgment over, join sides with us!
Thine too is the cause! and not more Thine
Than ours, is the work of these dogs and swine,
Whose life laughs through and spits at their creed,
Who maintain Thee in word, and defy Thee in deed!

' " We withstood Christ then? be mindful how
At least we withstand Barabbas now!
Was our outrage sore? But the worst we spared,
To have called these—Christians, had we dared!
Let defiance to them pay mistrust of Thee,
And Rome make amends for Calvary!

' " By the torture, prolonged from age to age,
By the infamy, Israel's heritage,
By the Ghetto's plague, by the garb's disgrace,
By the badge of shame, by the felon's place,
By the branding-too, the bloody whip,
And the summons to Christian fellowship,—

' " We boast our proof that at least the Jew
Would wrest Christ's name from the Devil's crew.
Thy face took never so deep a shade
But we fought them in it, God our aid!
A trophy to bear, as we march, Thy band
South, East, and on to the Pleasant Land! " '

It is very natural that a poet whose wishes incline, or whose genius conducts him to a grotesque art, should be attracted towards mediæval subjects. There is no age whose legends are so full of grotesque subjects, and no age where real life was so fit to suggest them. Then, more than at any other time, good principles have been under great hardships. The vestiges of ancient civilisation, the germs of modern civilisation, the little remains of what had been, the small beginnings of what is, were buried under a cumbrous mass of barbarism and cruelty. Good elements hidden in horrid accompaniments are the special theme of grotesque art, and these mediæval life and legends afford more copiously than could have been furnished before Christianity gave its new elements of good, or since modern civilisation has removed some few at least of the old elements of destruction. A *buried* life like the spiritual mediæval was Mr. Browning's natural element, and he was right to be attracted by it. His mistake has been, that he has not made it pleasant; that he has forced his art to topics on which no one could charm, or on which he, at any rate, could not; that on these occasions and in these poems he has failed in fascinating men and women of sane taste.

We say 'sane' because there is a most formidable and estimable *insane* taste. The will has great though indirect power over the taste, just as it has over the belief. There are some horrid beliefs from which human nature revolts, from which at first it shrinks, to which, at first, no effort can force it. But if we fix the mind upon them they have a power over us just because of their natural offensiveness. They are like the sight of human blood: experienced soldiers tell us that at first men are sickened by the smell and newness of blood almost to death and fainting, but that as soon as they harden their hearts and stiffen their minds, as soon as they *will* bear it, then comes an appetite for slaughter, a tendency to gloat on carnage, to love blood, at least for the moment, with a deep eager love. It is a principle that if we put down a healthy instinctive aversion, nature avenges herself by creating an unhealthy insane attraction. For this reason the most earnest truth-seeking men fall into the worst delusions; they will not let their mind alone; they force it towards some ugly thing, which a crotchet of argument, a conceit of intellect recommends, and nature punishes their disregard of her warning by subjection to the holy one, by belief in it. Just so the most industrious critics get the most admiration. They think it unjust to rest in their instinctive natural horror: they overcome it, and angry nature gives them over to ugly poems and marries them to detestable stanzas.

Mr. Browning possibly, and some of the worst of Mr. Browning's admirers certainly, will say that these grotesque objects exist in real life, and therefore they ought to be, at least may be, described in art. But though pleasure is not the end of poetry, pleasing is a condition of poetry. An exceptional monstrosity of horrid ugliness cannot be made pleasing, except it be made to suggest—to recall—the perfection, the beauty, from which it is a deviation. Perhaps in extreme cases no art is equal to this; but then such self-imposed problems should not be worked by the artist; these out-of-the-way and detestable subjects should be let alone by him. It is rather characteristic of Mr. Browning to neglect this rule. He is the most of a realist, and the least of an idealist of any poet we know. He evidently sympathises with some part at least of Bishop Blougram's apology. Anyhow this world exists. ' There *is* good wine—there *are* pretty women—there *are* comfortable benefices—there *is* money, and it is pleasant to spend it. Accept the creed of your age and you get these, reject that creed and you lose them. And for what do you lose them? For a fancy creed of your own, which no one else will accept, which hardly anyone will call a " creed," which most people will consider a sort of unbelief.' Again, Mr. Browning evidently loves what we may call the realism, the grotesque realism, of orthodox christianity. Many parts of it in which great divines have felt keen difficulties are quite pleasant to him. He must *see* his religion, he must have an ' object-lesson ' in believing. He must have a creed that will *take*, which wins and holds the miscellaneous world, which stout men will heed, which nice women will adore. The spare moments of solitary religion— the ' obdurate questionings,' the high ' instincts,' the ' first affections,' the ' shadowy recollections,'

> ' Which, do they what they may,
> Are yet the fountain-light of all our day—
> Are yet a master-light of all our seeing; '

the great but vague faith—the unutterable tenets—seem to him worthless, visionary; they are not enough immersed in matter; they move about 'in worlds not realised.' We wish he could be tried like the prophet once; he would have found God in the earthquake and the storm; he could have deciphered from them a bracing and a rough religion; he would have known that crude men and ignorant women felt them too, and he would accordingly have trusted them; but he would have distrusted and disregarded the 'still small voice;' he would have said it was 'fancy'—a thing you thought you heard to-day, but were not sure you had heard to-morrow: he would call it a nice illusion, an immaterial prettiness; he would ask triumphantly 'How are you to get the mass of men to heed this little thing?' he would have persevered and insisted ' *My wife* does not hear it.'

But although a suspicion of beauty, and a taste for ugly reality, have led Mr. Browning to exaggerate the functions, and to caricature the nature of grotesque art, we own or rather we maintain that he has given many excellent specimens of that art within its proper boundaries and limits. Take an example, his picture of what we may call the *bourgeois* nature in *difficulties;* in the utmost difficulty, in contact with magic and the supernatural. He has made of it something homely, comic, true; reminding us of what *bourgeois* nature really is. By showing us the type under abnormal conditions, he reminds us of the type under its best and most satisfactory conditions—

' Hamelin Town's in Brunswick,
    By famous Hanover city;
The river Weser, deep and wide,
Washes its walls on the southern side;
A pleasanter spot you never spied;
    But, when begins my ditty,
Almost five hundred years ago,
To see the townsfolk suffer so
    From vermin, was a pity.

' Rats !
They fought the dogs, and killed the cats,
And bit the babies in the cradles,
And ate the cheeses out of the vats,
    And licked the soup from the cook's own ladles,
Split open the kegs of salted sprats,

Made nests inside men's Sunday hats,
And even spoiled the women's chats,
    By drowning their speaking
    With shrieking and squeaking
In fifty different sharps and flats.

' At last the people in a body
    To the Town Hall came flocking:
" 'Tis clear," cried they, " our Mayor's a noddy;
    And as for our Corporation—shocking
To think we buy gowns lined with ermine
For dolts that can't or won't determine
What's best to rid us of our vermin!
You hope, because you're old and obese,
To find in the furry civic robe ease?
Rouse up, Sirs! Give your brains a racking
To find the remedy we're lacking,
Or, sure as fate, we'll send you packing! "
At this the Mayor and Corporation
Quaked with a mighty consternation.'

A person of musical abilities proposes to extricate the
civic dignitaries from the difficulty, and they promise him a
thousand guilders if he does.

' Into the street the Piper stept,
    Smiling first a little smile,
As if he knew what magic slept
    In his quiet pipe the while;
Then, like a musical adept,
To blow the pipe his lips he wrinkled,
And green and blue his sharp eye twinkled
Like a candle-flame when salt is sprinkled;
And ere three shrill notes the pipe uttered
You heard as if an army muttered;
And the muttering grew to a grumbling;
And the grumbling grew to a mighty rumbling:
And out of the houses the rats came tumbling.
Great rats, small rats, lean rats, brawny rats,
Brown rats, black rats, grey rats, tawny rats,
Grave old plodders, gay young friskers,
    Fathers, mothers, uncles, cousins,

Cocking tails and pricking whiskers,
    Families by tens and dozens.
Brothers, sisters, husbands, wives—
Followed the Piper for their lives.
From street to street he piped advancing.
And step for step they followed dancing
Until they came to the river Weser,
Wherein all plunged and perished!
—Save one who, stout as Julius Cæsar,
Swam across and lived to carry
(As he, the manuscript he cherished)
To Rat-land home his commentary:
Which was, " At the first shrill notes of the pipe,
I heard a sound as of scraping tripe,
And putting apples, wondrous ripe,
Into a cider-press's gripe:
And a moving away of pickle-tub boards,
And a leaving ajar of conserve-cupboards,
And a drawing the corks of train-oil flasks,
And a breaking the hoops of butter casks;
And it seemed as if a voice
(Sweeter far than by harp or by psaltery
Is breathed) called out, Oh rats, rejoice!
The world is grown to one vast drysaltery!
So, munch on, crunch on, take your nuncheon,
Breakfast, supper, dinner, luncheon!
And just as a bulky sugar-puncheon,
All ready staved, like a great sun shone
Glorious scarce an inch before me,
Just as methought it said, Come, bore me!
—I found the Weser rolling o'er me."
You should have heard the Hamelin people
Ringing the bells till they rocked the steeple.
" Go," cried the Mayor, " and get long poles,
Poke out the nests and block up the holes!
Consult with carpenters and builders,
And leave in our town not even a trace
Of the rats!"—when suddenly, up the face
Of the Piper perked in the market-place,
With a " First, if you please, my thousand guilders!"

'A thousand guilders! The Mayor looked blue;
So did the Corporation too.
For council dinners made rare havoc
With Claret, Moselle, Vin-de-Grave, Hock;
And half the money would replenish
Their cellar's biggest butt with Rhenish.
To pay this sum to a wandering fellow
With a gipsy coat of red and yellow!
"Beside," quoth the Mayor with a knowing wink,
"Our business was done at the river's brink;
We saw with our eyes the vermin sink,
And what's dead can't come to life, I think.
So, friend, we're not the folks to shrink
From the duty of giving you something for drink,
And a matter of money to put in your poke;
But as for the guilders, what we spoke
Of them, as you very well know, was in joke.
Besides, our losses have made us thrifty.
A thousand guilders! Come, take fifty!

'The Piper's face fell, and he cried,
"No trifling! I can't wait, beside!
I've promised to visit by dinner time
Bagdat, and accept the prime
Of the Head-Cook's pottage, all he's rich in,
For having left, in the Caliph's kitchen,
Of a nest of scorpions no survivor—
With him I proved no bargain-driver.
With you, don't think I'll bate a stiver!
And folks who put me in a passion
May find me pipe to another fashion."

'"How?" cried the Mayor, "d'ye think I'll brook
Being worse treated than a Cook?
Insulted by a lazy ribald
With idle pipe and vesture piebald?
You threaten us, fellow? Do your worst,
Blow your pipe there till you burst!"

'Once more he stept into the street;
    And to his lips again
Laid his long pipe of smooth straight cane;
    And ere he blew three notes (such sweet,

Soft notes as yet musician's cunning
    Never gave the enraptured air)
There was a rustling, that seemed like a bustling
Of merry crowds justling at pitching and hustling,
Small feet were pattering, wooden shoes clattering,
Little hands clapping and little tongues chattering,
And, like fowls in a farm-yard when barley is scattering,
Out came the children running.

' All the little boys and girls,
With rosy cheeks and flaxen curls,
And sparkling eyes and teeth like pearls,
Tripping and skipping, ran merrily after
The wonderful music with shouting and laughter.

    *   *   *   *   *   *   *   *

And I must not omit to say
That in Transylvania there's a tribe
Of alien people that ascribe
The outlandish ways and dress
On which their neighbours lay such stress,
To their fathers and mothers having risen
Out of some subterraneous prison
Into which they were trepanned
Long time ago in a mighty band
Out of Hamelin town in Brunswick land,
But how or why they don't understand.'

Something more we had to say of Mr. Browning, but we
must stop. It is singularly characteristic of this age that the
poems which rise to the surface, should be examples of ornate
art, and grotesque art, not of pure art. We live in the realm
of the *half* educated. The number of readers grows daily, but
the quality of readers does not improve rapidly. The middle
class is scattered, headless; it is well-meaning but aimless;
wishing to be wise, but ignorant how to be wise. The aristocracy of England never was a literary aristocracy, never even
in the days of its full power—of its unquestioned predominance did it guide—did it even seriously try to guide—the
taste of England. Without guidance young men, and tired
men are thrown amongst a mass of books; they have to choose
which they like; many of them would much like to improve
their culture, to chasten their taste, if they knew how. But

eft to themselves they take, not pure art, but showy art; not
that which permanently relieves the eye and makes it happy
whenever it looks, and as long as it looks, but *glaring* art
which catches and arrests the eye for a moment, but which in
the end fatigues it. But before the wholesome remedy of
nature—the fatigue arrives—the hasty reader has passed on to
some new excitement, which in its turn stimulates for an
instant, and then is passed by for ever. These conditions are
not favourable to the due appreciation of pure art—of that art
which must be known before it is admired—which must have
fastened irrevocably on the brain before you appreciate it—
which you must love ere it will seem worthy of your love.
Women too, whose voice in literature counts as well as that of
men—and in a light literature counts for more than that of
men—women, such as we know them, such as they are likely
to be, ever prefer a delicate unreality to a true or firm art. A
dressy literature, an exaggerated literature seem to be fated to
us. These are our curses, as other times had theirs.

> ' And yet
> Think not the living times forget,
> Ages of heroes fought and fell,
> That Homer in the end might tell;
> O'er grovelling generations past
> Upstood the Gothic fane at last;
> And countless hearts in countless years
> Had wasted thoughts, and hopes, and fears
> Rude laughter and unmeaning tears;
> Ere England Shakespeare saw, or Rome
> The pure perfection of her dome.
> Others I doubt not, if not we,
> The issue of our toils shall see;
> And (they forgotten and unknown)
> Young children gather as their own
> The harvest that the dead had sown.'

APPENDIX
The Ignorance of Man*
(1862)

A BOLD man once said that religion and morality were inconsistent. He argued thus: The essence of religion—part of the essence, at any rate—is recompense; a belief in another life is only another name for the anticipation of a time when wickedness will be punished, and when goodness will be rewarded. If you admit a providence, you acknowledge the existence of an adjusting agency, of a power which is recompensing by its very definition, and of its very nature, which allots happiness to virtue and pain to vice. On the other hand, the essence of morality is disinterestedness: a man who does good for the sake of a future gain to himself is, in a moral point of view, altogether inferior to one who does good for the good's sake, who hopes for nothing again, who is not thinking of himself, who is not calculating his own futurity. Between a man who does good to the world because he takes an intelligent view of his real interest, and another who does harm to the world because he is blind to that interest, there is only an intellectual difference,—the one is mentally long-sighted, the other mentally short-sighted. By the admission of all mankind, a disinterested action is better than a selfish action; a disinterested man is higher than a selfish man. Yet how is it possible that a religious man can be disinterested? Heaven overarches him, hell yawns before him. How can he help having his eyes attracted by the one and terrified by the other? He boasts, indeed, that religion is useful to mankind by producing good actions; he extols the attractive influence of future reward,

* A notice of *Science in Theology*. Sermons preached before the University of Oxford. By the Rev. Adam S. Farrar. Longmans, n the *National Review*, Vol. XIV., April, 1862.

and the deterring efficacy of apprehended penalty. But his boast is absurd and premature; by holding forth these anticipated bribes, by menacing these pains, he extracts from virtue its *virtue;* he makes it selfishness like the rest; he constructs an edifying and hoping saint, but he spoils the disinterested and uncalculating man.

These thoughts are not often boldly expressed. Fundamental difficulties rarely are. They constantly confuse the mind, and they are always floating like a vague mist in the intellectual air; they distort and blur the outlines of everything else, but they have no distinct outline of their own. An obscure difficulty is a pervading evil; the first requisite for removing it is to make it clear; if you assign a limit, you notify the frontier at which it may be attacked.

The objection is, in most people's apprehensions, and in its common incomplete expressions, confined exclusively to the doctrine of a future life, but it is at least equally applicable to the belief in a God who rules and governs. We can of course conceive of supernatural beings who do not interfere with us, who do not care for us, who do not help us, who have no connection with our moral life, who do good to no one, who do evil to no one. Such were the gods of Lucretius, the most fascinating of pure inventions; but such gods are not the gods of religion. The ancient Epicurean, in times when obscure difficulties were discussed in plainer words than is now either possible or advisable, expressly defended them on that ground. He did not want his gods to interfere with him; he thought it would impair the ideal languor of their life, as well as the inapprehensive security of his own life. They lived ' self-scanned, self-centred, self-secure,' and he was, in so far as was possible, to do so also. He did not wish the voluptuaries of heaven to become the busybodies of earth. He liked to have a pleasant dream of the upper world, but he did not wish it to descend and rule him. But as soon as we abandon the natural fiction of the voluptuous imagination; as soon as we accept the idea of a God who is a providence in the universe, and not an idol in heaven; as soon as we allow that he loves good and hates evil; as soon as we are sure that he is our Father, and chastises us as children; as soon as we acknowledge a God such as the human heart and conscience crave for, the God of Christianity,—we at once reach the primitive difficulty.

Here is a Being whom *we know* will reward the good and punish the evil; how can we do good without reference to that supernatural recompense, or evil without shrinking from that apprehended penalty?

Nor is it for this purpose in the least material, though for many other purposes it is very material, whether we consider God as acting by irrevocable laws fixed once for all, or upon a system which (though foreseen and immutable to him, to whom all the future is as present as all the past) is, according to our view of it,—to our translation of it, so to speak, into our limited capacities,—capable of flexibility at his touch, and of modification at his pleasure. If we know that we are rewarded and punished, it matters little, as respects our hope and our apprehension, whether that punishment be inflicted by a machine or by a person; in one case we shall shun the contact with the lacerating wheel, in the other we shall dread a blow from the punitive hand. But in either case the pain will be the determining motive, the deterring thought. We shall act, as we do act, not from a disinterested intention to do our duty whatever be the consequences, but from a sincere wish to get off patent and proximate suffering. The difficulty of reconciling a true morality with a true religion is not confined to that part of religion which relates to the anticipated life of man hereafter, but extends to the very idea of a superintending providence and preadjusting creator, in whatever mode we conceive that superintendence to be exercised, and that adjustment to have been made.

The answer most commonly given to this difficulty is unquestionably fallacious. It is said that the desire of eternal life for ourselves is a motive far greater and far better than the desire of anything else, either for ourselves or for others. It is not conceived as a form of selfishness at all—at least, not when regarded in this connection, and employed to solve this problem. At other times, indeed, divines are ready enough to twist the argument the other way. They will expand at length the notion that there is a ' common sense ' in the Gospel; that it appeals to ' business-like motives;' that there is nothing 'high-flown' about it; that it aims to persuade sensible men of this world, on sufficient reasons of sound prudence, to sacrifice the present world in order to gain the invisible one; that, whatever sentimentalists may assert, it is reward which incites to achievement, and fear that restrains from misdoing. Sermons are written in consecrated paragraphs, each of which is sufficient to itself, and the connection between which is not intended to be precisely adjusted; each has an edifying tendency, and the writer and the hearer wish for no more. Otherwise it would not be possible, as it often is, to hear religion commended in the same discourse at one time as self-sacrificing, and at another as prudential; to have a eulogium on disinterestedness in the exordium, and an appeal to selfishness at the conclusion. A mode of composition which less disguised the true ideas of the composer, would show that many divines really believe a desire for a long pleasure in heaven to be not only more longsighted and sensible, but intrinsically higher, nobler, and better than a desire for a short happiness on earth. Yet, when stated in short sentences and plain English, the idea is palpably absurd. The ' wish to come into a good thing ' is of the same ethical order, whether the good thing be celestial or be terrestrial, be distantly future, or be close at hand.

A second mode of solving the difficulty, though more ingenious, and in every way far better, is erroneous also. It is said, ' men generally act from mixed motives, and they do so in this case. They are partly disinterested, and partly not disinterested. They are desirous of doing good because it is good, and they are desirous also of having the reward of goodness hereafter. They wish at the very same time to benefit their neighbour in this world, and also to benefit themselves in the world to come.' The reply is ingenious, but it overlooks the point of the difficulty; it mistakes the nature of mixed motives. The constitution of man is such that if you strengthen one or two coöperating motives, you weaken, other things being equal, the force of the other: the lesser impulse tends always to be absorbed in the stronger, and it may pass entirely out of thought if the stronger is strengthened, if the greater become more prominent. We see this in common life; it is undoubtedly possible for a statesman to act at the same moment both from the love of office and from the love of his country; from a wish to prolong his power and a wish to benefit his nation. But strengthen one of these motives, and *cæteris paribus*, you weaken the other. Make the statesman love office more, you thereby make him love his country less he will be readier to sacrifice what he will call a 'vague theory and an impracticable purpose' for the sake of the power which he loves; he will cease to care to do what he ought, from a wish to retain the capacity of doing something. Or, suppose a further case: there have been many times and countries where the loss of office was equivalent to the loss of liberty, perhaps to that of life. In one age of English history, one great historian says, 'There was but a single step from the throne to the scaffold.' In another age, another great historian says, 'It was as dangerous to be leader of opposition as to be a highwayman.' The possessors of power in those times, upon principle, destroyed or endeavoured to destroy their predecessors. Such a prospect would induce a statesman to love office for its own sake. It would absorb the whole of his attention; he could hardly be asked to think of his country. Extraordinary men would do so, but ordinary men would be overwhelmed by the 'violent motive' of personal fear; they would only be thinking of themselves even when they were doing what in truth and fact was beneficial to their country.

The case is similar to the 'violent motive,' as Paley calls it, of religion, when presented in the same manner in which Paley presents it. If you could extend before men the awful vision of everlasting perdition, if they could see it as they see the things of earth—as they see Fleet Street and St. Pau.'s; if you could show men likewise the inciting vision of an ever-lasting heaven, if they could see that too with undeniable certainty and invincible distinctness—who could say that they would have a thought for any other motive? The personal incentive to good action, and the personal dissuasion from bad action, would absorb all other considerations, whether deterrent or persuasive. We could no more break a divine law than we could commit a murder in the open street. The fact that men act from mixed motives is no explanation of the great difficulty with which we started; for the precise peculiarity of that difficulty is to raise one of those mixed motives to an intensity which seems likely to absorb, extinguish, and annihilate the other.

The true explanation is precisely the reverse. The moral part of religion—the belief in a moral state hereafter, dependent for its nature on our goodness or our wickedness, the belief in a moral providence, who apportions good to good, and evil to evil—does not annihilate the sense of the inherent nature of good and evil because it is itself the result of that sense. Our only ground for accepting an ethical and retributive religion is the inward consciousness that virtue being virtue must prosper, that vice being vice must fail. From these axioms we infer, not logically, but practically, that there is a continuous eternity, in which what we expect will be seen, that there is a providence who will apportion what is good, and punish what is evil. Of the mode in which we do so we will speak presently more at length; but granting that this description of our religion is true, it undeniably solves our difficulty. Our religion cannot by possibility swallow up morality because it is dependent for its origin—for its continuance—on that morality.

Suppose a person, say in a prison, to have no knowledge by the senses that there was such a thing as human law; suppose that he never saw either the judicial or the executive authorities, and that no one ever told him of their existence; suppose that, by a consciousness of the inherent nature of good and evil, the fact that such an institution *must* exist should dawn upon his mind,—of course it would not, but imagine that it should,—it is absurd to suppose that he would feel his power of doing what is right *because* it is right diminished. When he goes out into the world, when he hears his judge, when he sees the policeman, when he surveys the intrusive, the incessant, the pervading moral apparatus of human society,— *then* he would be able to disregard and to forget what is due to intrinsic goodness and what is to be feared from intrinsic evil. No one will or can say that he now abstains from stealing oranges under a policeman's eyes from any motive, good or bad, save fear of the policeman; that motive is so evident, so pressing, so irresistible, that it becomes the only motive. But if he only thought the policeman *must* exist because he believed stealing oranges to be wrong, he would feel it quite possible to abstain from stealing oranges out of pure and unselfish considerations.

Assume that a person only knows a particular fact from a certain informant, and suppose that on a sudden he doubts that informant, of course his confidence in the communicated fact ceases, or is diminished. So, *if* all our knowledge of the religious part of morality be derived from the intrinsic impression of morality, as soon as we question the accuracy of the informant, that instant we must be dubious of the information. The derivative cannot be stronger than the original; cannot overpower it; must grow when it grows, and wane when it wanes.

But is our knowledge of the moral part of religion thus derivative and dependent? Two classes of disputants will deny it entirely: one class will say they derive their knowledge from Natural Theology; another will say they derive it from Revelation; and until the arguments of both classes are examined, the subject must remain in partial darkness. Natural theology is the simplest of theologies; it contains only a single argument, and establishes but one conclusion. Observing persons have gone to and fro through the earth, and they have accumulated a million illustrations of a single analogy. They have accumulated indications of design from all parts of the universe. They have not, indeed, shown that *matter* was created; the substance of matter, if there be a substance, shows no structure, no evidence of design: according to all common belief, according to the admission of such scientific men as admit its existence, that matter is unorganised. By its nature it is a raw material; it is that to which manufacture, manipulation, design, call it what you like, is to be applied—necessarily, therefore, it shows no indication of design itself. The reasoners from the workmanship of man to that of God must always fail in this: man only adapts what he finds: God creates what he uses. But within its legitimate limits the argument from design has been most effectual for two thousand years. On a certain class of purely intellectual minds, who think more than they live, who reason more than they imagine, it has produced the strongest and most vivid conception of God which, with their experience and their mental limitation, they are capable of receiving. It has shown that *out of the causes we know*, none is so likely to have worked up the substance of matter into its present form as a designing and powerful mind. *Subject to this assumption,* it shows that this mind intended to erect that mixed, composite, involved human society which we see. These theologians prove, for example, that man has a structure of body which enables him to be what he is, which prevents his being in appearance, and in most real particularities, different from what he is. They

show that the physical world is constructed so as to enable man
to be what he is, and to show what he is, so as to limit his power
of being greatly different, or of seeming so. They show, in
fact, that, if the expression be allowed, we live, as far as *they*
can tell us, in a factory, the builder of which projected certain
results, contrived certain large plans, devised certain particular
machines, foresaw certain functions, which he meant for us,
which he made our interest, which he gave us wages to perform.   They show not, indeed, that an omnipotent Being
created the universe, but that an able being has been (so to
say) about it. They do not demonstrate that an infinite Being
created all things, but they *do* show, and show so that the mass
of ordinary men will comprehend and believe it, that a large
mind has been concerned in manufacturing most things.

But these results do not constitute the interior essence;
scarcely, indeed, begin the exterior outwork of a substantial
religion.   They touch neither that part of it which moves
men's hearts, nor that part which occasions our primary
difficulty. They do not show us an eternal state of man hereafter, in which the anomalies of this world may be rectified and
recompensed; they do not show us an infinite Perfection,
distributing just reward with an omniscient accuracy, according to a perfect law. It is not, indeed, to be expected that
natural philosophy should prove the immortality of man,
since it does not prove the immortality of God. It shows that
an artful and able designer has been concerned in the construction of the strange existing world; but may it not have been
the last work of the great artist? There is nothing in contriving
skill to evince immortality; nothing to prove that the 'great
artificer' has always been or is always going to be. Of his
moral views we collect from natural theology as much as
this.   There are certain laws of the physical universe which
cannot be broken without pain, which avenge themselves on
those who overlook, neglect, or violate them. These were
presumedly designed (according to the moral assumption of
natural theology) for the end which they effect; they were
doubtless meant to accomplish that which they conspicuously
do. On a disregard of such laws, natural theology shows that
the Providence of which it speaks has imposed a penalty; the
contriving God (so to speak, for it is necessary to speak
plainly) is opposed to recklessness. He does not wish his

devices to be impaired or his plans neglected. Every animal has in natural theology, if not a mission, at least a function. There are certain results which a polyp must produce or die; certain others which a horse must effect, or it will be first in pain and then die too; certain other and more complex results which man must produce, or he also will suffer and perish. But recklessness is only a single form of vice: a watchful, heedful selfishness is another form. For the latter there is no indication in natural theology of any divine disapprobation, or of any impending penalty. A heedful being contriving for himself, living in the framework of, adjusting himself with nice discernment and careful discretion to, the laws of the visible world, incurs no censure from the theology of design. On the contrary, he could justly say he had done what was required of him. He had studiously observed, he could say, the rules of the factory in which he lived; he had finished his own work; he had not hindered any others from accomplishing theirs; he had complied with the arrangements of the establishment: natural theology seems to require no more. Self-absorbed foresight and contriving discretion may not be great virtues according to a high morality, or according to a true religion; but they are profitable in the visible world. They are the virtues of men skilful in what they see. Accordingly they suit a theology which is exclusively based upon an analysis of the visible world, which computes physical profits and sensible results, which aims to show that Providence is prudent, that God is wise in his generation.

Natural theology, therefore, contains nothing to disturb the explanation we have given of our original difficulty. The most cursory examination of it would show as much. We have only to open the well-known volumes in which the munificence of a former generation has embalmed the most striking arguments of a theology which that generation valued at more than it is worth. We find there pictures of a bat's wing, of the human hand, of a calf's eye; and we are told how ingenious, how clever, so to say,—for it is the true word,—these contrivances are. But no one could learn, or expect to learn, from a calf's eye, that the Creator is pure, just, merciful; that he is eternal or omnipotent; that he rewards good, and punishes evil. Throughout all the physical world he sends rain upon the just and the unjust; and no refined analysis of that world will detect in it a preference of the former to the latter. As it is with the moral holiness of God, so it is with the immortality of man: no one could expect to discover by a minute inspection of the perishable body, what was the fate of the imperceptible soul. Physical science may examine the structure of the brain, but it cannot foresee the fortunes of the mind.

What, then, of Revelation? Does this informant disturb the solution of our problem? The change from the world of natural theology to that of any revelation is most striking. The most impressive characteristic of natural theology is its bareness. It accumulates facts and proves little; it has voluminous evidences and a short creed. Accordingly the reason why it does not disturb our philosophy is that its communications are insufficient. It does not impart to us *such* a knowledge of a divine rewarder and punisher, of future human punishment and future human reward, as would render it impossible to be disinterested and hardly possible not to be foreseeing and selfish, because it communicates *no* knowledge on the subject. It does not teach the divine characteristic which involves the difficulty; it does not tell, either, that part of man's future fate which involves it likewise. With revelation it is far otherwise. That informant is precise, full, and clear. It tells us plainly what God is; it warns us what may happen, and easily happen, to ourselves. We learn from it that God is the divine ruler; we learn from it that we are punishable creatures, whose fate depends on ourselves. The observations which have been justly made on natural theology are here entirely inapplicable. We have passed from a *vacuum* into a *plenum*.

The real reason *is* a different one. Revealed religion does not invalidate our preëxisting moral nature, because it is itself dependent on that nature. When we examine the evidence for revelation we alight at once on a great and fundamental postulate; we assume that God is veracious; we are so familiar with this great truth, that we hardly think of it save as an axiom; both the readers of the treatises on the evidences and the writers of them pass rapidly and easily over it. But putting aside for a moment the evidence of our inner consciousness, and regarding the subject with the pure intellect and bare eyes, the assumption is an audacious one. How do we know that it is true? We have proved by natural theology that a designing being, of great power, considerable age, ingenious habits, and benevolent motives, somewhere exists; but how do we know that Being to be ' veracious ' ? We see that among human beings, the class of intellectual beings of whom we know most, and whom we can observe best, veracity is a rare virtue. We know that some nations seem wholly destitute of it, and that one sex in all countries is deficient in it. We know that a human being may have great power, and not tell the truth; ingenious habits, and not tell the truth; kind intentions, and not tell the truth. Why may not a super-human being be constituted in the same way, possess a character similarly mixed, be remarkable not only for morals similar to man's, but also for defects analogous to his? Our inner nature revolts at the supposition; but we are not now concerned with our inner nature; we have, for the sake of distinctness, abstracted and left it on one side. We are dealing now not with the evidence of the heart, but with the evidence of the eyes; we are discussing not what really is, but what would seem to be—what is all we could know to be, if we had only five senses and a reasoning understanding. From these informants, how could we know enough of the ingenious unknown Being, who is so useful in the world, as to be confident he would tell us the truth in every case? How could we presume to guess his unexperienced speech, his latent motives, his imperceptible character? Our knowledge of the moral part of the Divine character,—of his veracity, as well as of his justice,—comes from our own moral nature. We feel that God is holy, just as we feel that holiness *is* holiness; just as we know by internal consciousness that goodness is good in itself, and by itself; just as we know that God in himself is pure and holy. We feel that God is true, for veracity is a part of holiness and a condition of purity. But if we did not think holiness to be excellent in itself, if we did not feel it to be a motive unaffected by consequences and independent of calculation, our belief in the divine holiness would fade away, and with it would fade our belief in the divine veracity also.

Revelation, therefore, cannot undermine the very principle upon which it is itself dependent. Our notion of the character of God being revealed to us by our moral nature, cannot impair or weaken the conclusion of that nature. This is the meaning of the profound saying of Coleridge, that ' *all* religion is revealed.' He meant that all knowledge of God's character which is worth naming or regarding, which excites any portion of the religious sentiment, which excites our love, our awe, or our fear, is communicated to us by our internal nature, by that spirit within us which is open to a higher world, by that spirit which is in some sense God's spirit. True religion of this sort does not impair the moral spirit which revealed it; it does not dare do so, for it knows that spirit to be its only evidence.

But all religion is not true. A superstitious mind permits a certain aspect of God's character, say its justice, to obtain an exclusive hold on it, to tyrannise over it, to absorb it. The soul becomes bound down by the weight of its own revelation. Conscience is overshadowed, weakened, and almost destroyed by the very idea which it originally suggested, and of which it is really the only reliable informant. Such minds are incapable of true virtue. The essential opposition which is alleged to exist between morality and *all* religion does exist between morality and *their* religion. They have a selfish fear of the future, which destroys their disinterestedness, and almost destroys their manhood.

The same effect is undeniably produced on many minds—not necessarily produced, but in fact produced—by a belief in revelation. They are fearful of future punishment, because some being in the air has threatened it. They have not the true belief in the divine holiness which arises from a love of holiness; they have not the true conception of God which was suggested by conscience, and is kept alive by the activity of conscience; but they have a vague persuasion that a great personage has asserted this, and why they should believe that personage they do not ask or know. While revelation remains connected in the mind with the spirituality on which it is based, it is as consistent with true morality as religion of any other sort; but if disconnected from that spirituality, if it has become an isolated terrific tenet, like any other superstition, it is inconsistent.

The original difficulty with which we started, and the true answer to that difficulty, may be summed up thus: The objection is, that the extrinsic motive to goodness (which religion reveals) must absorb the intrinsic motives to goodness (which morality reveals). The answer is, that the second revelation is contingent upon the first; that those only have a substantial ground for believing the extrinsic motive who retain a lively confidence in the intrinsic. Perhaps some may think this principle too plain; perhaps others may think it too unimportant to justify so long an exposition and such a strenuous inculcation. But if we dwell upon it and trace it to its attendant results and consequences, we shall find that it will account for more of the world than almost any other single principle—at any rate will explain much which puzzles us, and much which is important to us.

First, this principle will explain to us the use and the necessity of what we may call the *screen* of the physical world. Every one who has religious ideas must have been puzzled by what we may call the irrelevancy of creation to his religion. We find ourselves lodged in a vast theatre, in which a ceaseless action, a perpetual shifting of scenes, an unresting life, is going forward; and that life seems physical, unmoral, having no relation to what our souls tell us to be great and good, to what religion says is the design of all things. Especially when we see any new objects, or scenes, or countries, we feel this. Look at a great tropical plant, with large leaves stretching everywhere, and great stalks branching out on all sides; with a big beetle on a leaf, and a humming-bird on a branch, and an ugly lizard just below. What has such an object to do with *us*, with anything we can conceive, or hope, or imagine? What *could* it be created for, if creation has a moral end and object? Or go into a gravel-pit, or stone-quarry; you see there a vast accumulation of dull matter, yellow or grey, and you ask, involuntarily and of necessity, why is all this waste, and irrelevant production, as it would seem, of material? Can anything seem more stupid than a big stone *as* a big stone, than gravel for gravel's sake? What is the use of such cumbrous, inexpressive objects in a world where there are minds to be filled, and imaginations to be aroused, and souls to be saved? A clever sceptic once said on reading Paley, that *he* thought the universe was a furniture warehouse for unknown beings; he assented to the indications of design visible in many places, but what the end of most objects was, why *such* things were, what was the ultimate object contemplated by the whole, he could not understand. He thought ' divines are right in saying that much of the universe has an expression, but surely sceptics are right in saying that as much or more has no expression.' Some of the world seems designed to show a little of God; but much more seems also designed to hide him and keep him off. The reply is, that if morality is to be disinterested, some such irrelevant universe is essential. Life, moral life, the life of tempted beings capable of virtue and liable to vice, of necessity involves a theatre of some sort; it could not be carried on in a vast vacuum; *some* means of communication between mind and mind, *some* external motive to question inward impulses, *some* outward events as the result of past action and the stimulus to new action, seem essential to the life of a voluntary moral being, to a being tempted as a man is, living as a man lives. The only admissible question is the nature of that theatre. Is it to be in all its parts and objects expressive of God's character and communicative of man's fate? or is it, as many say, in most parts to express nothing and tell nothing? The reply is, *if* the universe were to be incessantly expressive and incessantly communicative, morality would be impossible; we should live under the unceasing pressure of a supernatural interference, which would give us selfish motives for doing everything, which would show us supernatural punishment if we did anything. We should be living in a *chastising* machine, of which the secret would be patent and the penalties apparent. We are startled to find a universe we did not expect. But if we lived in a universe we should expect, the life which we lead, and were meant to lead, would be impossible. We should expect a punitive world sanctioning moral laws, and the perpetual punishment of those laws would be so glaringly apparent that true virtue would become impossible. An 'unfeeling nature,' an unmoral universe, a sun that shines and a rain which falls equally on the evil and on the good, are essential to morality in a being free like man, and created as man was. A miscellaneous world is a suitable theatre for a single-minded life, and, so far as we can see, the only one.

The same sort of reasoning partly elucidates, even if it does not explain the brevity of, our apparent life. If visible life were eternal, future punishments must be visible. We should meet in our streets with old, old men enduring the consequences of offences which happened before we were born. We should not see, perhaps, old age as we now see it; decrepitude would be unknown to us. If there was immortal life on earth, there would probably also be immortal youth; at any rate, immortal activity. The perpetuity of existence would not be divided from the perpetuity of what makes life desirable, of what makes effective life possible. But if children saw their fathers, and their fathers' fathers, and their fathers' ancestors, in an unending chain, suffering penalties for certain acts, and obtaining rewards for certain deeds, how is it possible that they could act otherwise than according to those visible and evident examples? The consecutive tradition of self-interest would be so strong among a perpetual race of immortal men, that disinterested virtue would be not so much impracticable as unthought of and unknown. The exact line of real self-benefit would be chalked out so plainly, so conspicuously, so glaringly, that no other action would be conceivable, or possible. The evidence of *all* consequences would be like the evidences of legal consequences now, only infinitely more effective and infinitely more perceptible. In human law, the *detection* of the offence by man is a pre-requisite of all punishment by man. An offence not proved to the ' satisfaction of the court ' escapes the judgment of the court. But in a visible immortal life, this pre-requisite would not be needful. *If* there be a future punishment, and *if* man lived for all futurity upon earth, that future punishment would be on earth, and it would be inflicted by God. Undetected crime, that general bad character without specific proved offence, which now mocks all law and laughs at visible punishment, would then, under our very eyes, receive that punishment. Job's friends kindly argued with him, ' You are suffering, therefore you are guilty.' And the argument was bad, because they only saw an exceptional accident in the life of a good man, not his entire life through a subsequent eternity; but if that eternal life had been passed in continuous residence on this globe, if notorious bad fortune had pursued him through eternity in the nineteenth generation, his descendants might well have said, ' Oh, Job, there is something wrong in you, for you never come out right.' A great historian has observed, ' that honesty is the best policy, is a maxim which we firmly believe to be generally correct, even with respect to the temporal interest of individuals; but with respect to societies, the rule is subject to still fewer exceptions, and that for this reason, that the life of societies is larger than that of individuals. It is possible to mention men who have owed great worldly prosperity to breaches of private faith; but we doubt whether it be possible to mention a state which has, on the whole, been a gainer by a breach of public faith.' If the visible life of individuals were yet longer than the life of societies, the rule would be subject to still fewer exceptions; if that visible life were eternal, the rule would be subject to no exceptions; the staring evidence of conspicuous results would purge temptation out of the world.

The physical world now rewards what we may call the physical virtues, and punishes what we may call the physical vices. There is a certain state of the body which is a condition of physical well-being, and (as life is constituted) very much of all well-being. If by gross excess any man should impair that condition, physical law will punish him. The body is our schoolmaster to bring us to the soul; it enforces on us the preparatory merits, it scourges out of us the preparatory defect. The law of human government is similar; it enforces on us that adherence to obvious virtue, and that avoidance of obvious vice, which are the essential preliminaries of real virtue. There is no true virtue or vice, so long as physical law and human law are what they are in any such matters. The dread of the penalties is too powerful not to extinguish (speaking generally, and peculiar cases excepted) all other motives. But these teachers strengthen the mental instruments of real virtue. They strengthen our will; they hurt our vanity; they confirm our manhood. Physical law and human law train and build up, if the expression may be permitted, that good pagan, that sound-bodied, moderate, careful creature, out of which a good Christian may, if he will and by God's help, in the end be constructed. If visible life were eternal instead of temporary, the same intense discipline which so usefully creates the preparatory pre-requisites would likewise efface the possibility of disinterested virtue.

Again, the great scene of human life may be explained, or at least illustrated, in like manner: *we are souls in the disguise of animals*. We lead a life in great part neither good nor evil, neither wicked nor excellent. The greater part of men seem to an outside observer to walk through life in a torpid sort of sleep. They are decent in their morals, respectable in their manners, stupid in their conversation. The incentives of their life are outward; its penalties are outward too. The life of such people seems to some men always—to many men at times—inexplicable. But if such beings were not permitted in the world, perhaps a higher life might be impossible for any beings. They act like a living screen, just as we say matter acts like a dead screen. It is not desirable that the results of goodness should be distinctly apparent; and if all human life were intensely and exclusively moral; if all men were with all their strength pursuing good or pursuing evil, the isolated consequences of that isolated principle must be apparent; at least, could scarcely fail to be so. If one part of men were cooped up in the exclusive pursuit of virtue, and were very ardent and warm about it, and another part of men were eager in the pursuit of evil, and cared for nothing but evil, the world would fall asunder into two dissimilar halves. If goodness in the visible world had *any*, the least, tendency to produce visible happiness, then incessant goodness would be very happy. The accumulations of the slight tendency by perpetual renewal would amount of necessity to a vast sum-total. Incessant badness would produce awful misery. Those absorbed in vice would be warnings dangerous to disinterestedness; those absorbed in virtue, attractions and examples almost more dangerous. The mischief is prevented by those *unabsorbed*, purposeless, divided characters which seem to puzzle us. They complicate human life, and they do so the more effectually that they typify and represent so much of what every man feels and must feel within himself. In each man there is so much which is unmoral, so much which comes from an unknown origin, and passes forward to an unknown destination, which is of the earth, earthy; which has nothing to do with hell or heaven; which occupies a middle place not recognised in any theology; which is hateful both to the impetuous 'friends of God' and his most eager enemies. This pervading and potent element involves life as it were in confusion and hurry. We do not see distinctly whither we are going. Disinterestedness is possible, for calculation is confused. Doubtless, even on earth virtue of all kinds eventually must have, on a large average of cases, some slight tendency to produce virtue. This earth is an extract from the moral universe—partakes its nature. But that tendency is too slight to be a considerable motive to high action; it would not be discovered but for the inward principle which sets us to look for it; and even when we find it, it is transient, and small, and dubious. It is lost in the vast results of the unmoral universe, in the vague shows, the multiform spectacle of human life.

Again, we may understand why the convictions of what duty is, and what religion is, vary so much and so often among men. If all our convictions on these points, on these infinitely important points, were identical and alike, an accumulated public opinion would oppress us, would destroy the freedom of our action and the purity of our virtue. If every one said that certain penalties would be the consequences of certain actions, we should believe that the consequences would be so and so, not because we felt those actions to be intrinsically bad, but because we were told that such would be the consequences. We should believe upon report, and a vague impression would haunt us, not produced by our own conscience, or our own sense of right and wrong, and would impair both our manhood and our virtue. The extraordinary discrepancies of believed religion and believed morality have weighed on many and will weigh on many; but they have this use,—they enable men to be disinterested. As there is no sanctioned invincible firm custom, there are no customary penalties, there is nothing men must shun; as the world had not made up its mind, there is no executioner of the world ready to enforce that mind upon every one.

Lastly, the same essential argument may be applied to a problem yet more delicate and difficult, to one which it is difficult to treat in Reviewer's phraseology. Why is God so far from us? is the agonising question which has depressed so many hearts, as long as we knew there were hearts, has puzzled many intellects since intellects began to puzzle themselves. But the moral part of God's character could not be shown to us with sensible conspicuous evidence; it could not be shown to us as Fleet Street is shown to us without impairing the first pre-requisite of disinterestedness, and the primary condition of man's virtue. And if the moral aspect of God's character must of necessity be somewhat hidden from us, other aspects of it must be equally hidden. An infinite being may be viewed under innumerable aspects. God has many qualities in his essence which the word 'moral' does not exhaust, which it does not even hint at. Perhaps this essay has seemed to read too sternly; as if the moral side of the divine character, which is and must be to imperfect beings in some sense a terrible side,—as if the moral side of human life, which must be to mankind not always a pleasant side,—had been forced into an exclusive prominence which of right did not belong to it. But the *attractive* aspects of God's character must not be made more apparent to such a being as man than His chastening and severer aspects. We must not be invited to approach the Holy of holies without being made aware, painfully aware, what Holiness is. We must know our own unworthiness ere we are fit to approach or imagine an Infinite Perfection. The most nauseous of false religions is that which affects a fulsome fondness for a Being not to be thought of without awe, or spoken of without reluctance.

On the whole, therefore, the necessary ignorance of man explains to us much; it shows us that we could not be what we ought to be, if we lived in the sort of universe we should expect. It shows us that a latent Providence, a confused life, an odd material world, an existence broken short in the midst and on a sudden, are not real difficulties, but real helps; that they, or something like them, are essential conditions of a moral life to a subordinate being. If we steadily remember that we only know the ultimate fate, the extrinsic consequences of vice and virtue, because we know of their inherent nature and intrinsic qualities, and that any other evidence of the first would destroy the possibility of the second, *then* much which used to puzzle us may become clear to us.

But it may be said, What sort of evidence is this on which you base the future moral life of man, and the present existence of a moral providence? Is it not impalpable? It is so, and necessarily so. If a consecutive logical deduction, such as has often been sought between an immutable morality and a true religion, could in fact be found, we should be again met with our fundamental difficulty, though in a disguised and secondary form. Morality might fall out of sight because religion was obtruded upon us. Morality would be the axiom, religion the deduction; and as a geometer does not keep Euclid's axioms in his head when he is employed upon conic sections, as a student of the differential calculus may half forget the commencement of algebra,—so the great truths of religion, if rigorously and mathematically deduced from the beginnings of morality, might overshadow and destroy those 'beggarly elements.' No one who has proved important doctrines by rigorous reasoning always retains in his mind the primitive principles from which he set out. As the concrete deductions advance, the primary abstractions recede. Happily the connection between morality and religion is of a very different kind. Religion (in its moral part) is a secondary impression, produced and kept alive by the first impression of morality. The intensity of the second feeling depends on the continued intensity of the first feeling.

The highest part of human belief is based upon certain developable instincts. Not the most important, but the most obvious of these, is the instinct of beauty. Since the commencement of speculation ingenious thinkers, who delight in difficulties, have rejoiced to draw out at length the difficulties of the subject. It is said, How can you be certain that there is such an attribute as beauty, when no one is sure what it is, or to what it should be applied? A barbarian thinks one thing charming, the Greek another. Modern nations have a standard different most materially from the ancient standard—founded upon it in several important respects, no doubt, but differing from it in others as important, and almost equally striking. Even within the limits of modern nations this standard differs. The taste of the vulgar is one thing, the taste of the refined and cultivated is altogether at variance with it. The mass of mankind prefer a gaudy modern daub to a faded picture by Sir Joshua, or to the cartoons of Raphael. What certainty, the sceptic triumphantly asks, can there be in matters on which people differ so much, on which it seems so impossible to argue; which seem to depend on causes and relations simply personal; which are susceptible of no positive test or ascertained criterion? You talk of impalpability, he adds; here it is in perfection. But these recondite doubts impose on no one. Not a single educated person would sleep less soundly if he were told that his life depended on the correctness of his notion that the cartoons of Raphael are more sublime and beautiful than a common daub. He cannot prove it, and he cannot prove that Charles the First was beheaded; but he is quite as certain of one as of the other. This is an instance of an obvious, unmistakable instinct, which does produce effectual belief, though sceptics explain to us that it should not.

The nature of this instinct differs altogether from that of those intuitive and universal axioms which are borne in infallibly upon all the human race, in every age and every place. It is not like the assertion that 'two straight lines cannot enclose a space,' or the truth that two and two make four. These are believed by every one, and no one can dream of not believing them. But half of mankind would reject the idea that the cartoons were in any sense admirable; they would prefer the overgrown enormities of West, which are side by side with them. The characteristic peculiarity of this instinct is, not that it is irresistible, but that it is *developable*. The higher students of the subject, the more cultivated, meditate upon it, acquire a new sense, which conveys truth to them, though others are ignorant of it, and though they themselves cannot impart it to those others. The appeal is not to the many, as with axioms of Euclid, but to those few,—the exceptional few,—at whom the many scoff.

The case is similar with the yet higher instincts of morality and of religion. It is idle to pretend that much of them can be found among bloody savages, or simple and remote islanders, or a degraded populace. It is still idler to fancy that because they cannot be discovered there full-grown, and complete, and paramount, there is no evidence for them, and no basis for relying upon them. They resemble the instinct of beauty precisely. The evidence of the few—of the small, high-minded minority, who are the exception of ages, and the salt of the earth—outweighs the evidence of countless myriads who live as their fathers lived, think as they thought, die as they died; who would have lived and died in the very contrary impressions, if by chance they had inherited these instead of the others. The criterion of true beauty is with those (and they are not many) who have a sense of true beauty; the criterion of true morality is with those who have a sense of true morality; the criterion of true religion is with those who have a sense of true religion.

Nor can this defect of an absolute criterion throw the world into confusion. We see it does not, and there was no reason to expect it would. We all of us feel an analogous fluctuation and variation in ourselves. We all of us feel that there are times in which first principles seem borne in upon us by evidence as bright as noonday, and that there are also times in which that evidence is much less, in which it seems to fade away, in which we reckon up the number of persons who differ from us, who reject our principles; times at which we ask, who are *we*, that we should be right and other men wrong? The unbelieving moods of each mind are as certain as the unbelieving state of much of the world. But no sound mind permits itself to be permanently disturbed, though it may be transiently distracted, by these variations in its own state. We have a *criterion* faculty within us, which tells us which are lower moods and which are higher. This faculty is a phase of conscience, and if at its bidding we struggle *with* the good moods, and *against* the bad moods, we shall find that great beliefs remain, and that mean beliefs pass away.

There is an analogous phenomenon in the history of the world. Beliefs altogether differ at the base of society, but they agree, or tend to agree, at its summit. As society goes on, the standard of beauty and of morality and of religion also tends to become fixed. The creeds of the higher classes throughout the world, though far from identical in these respects, are not entirely unlike, approach to similarity, approach to it more and more as cultivation augments, goodness improves, and disturbing agencies fall aside.

> ' The Ethiop gods have Ethiop lips,
>   Bronze cheeks, and woolly hair;
> The Grecian gods are like the Greeks,
>   As keen-eyed, cold, and fair.'

Such is the various and miscellaneous religion of barbarism; but the religion and the morality of all the best among all nations tend more and more to be the same with ' the progress of the suns,' and as society itself improves.

The instincts of morality and religion, though we have called them two for facility of speech, run into one another, and in practical human nature are not easily separated. The distinction, like so many others in mental philosophy, is not drawn where accurate science would have directed, but where the first notions of mankind, and the necessity of easy speaking, in a language shaped according to those notions, have suggested. In a refined analysis, the instinct of religion, as we have called it, is a complex aggregate of various instincts, not a single and homogeneous one. But to analyse these, or even to name them, would be far from our purpose now. Our business is with the relation between the instinct of morality and that of religion, and with no other perplexities or difficulties. The instinct of morality is the basis, and the instinct of moral religion is based upon it, and arises out of it. We feel first the intrinsic qualities of good actions and bad actions; then, as the Greek proverb expressed it, ' Where there is shame there is fear;' we expect consequences apportioned to our actions, good and evil; lastly, for within the limits of purely moral ideas there is no higher stage, we rise to the conception of Him who in His wisdom adjusts and allots those far-off consequences to those conspicuous actions. The higher instinct is based on the lower; would fade in the mind should the lower fade. The coalescence of instincts effects what no other contrivance known to us could effect; it enables us to be disinterested, although we know the consequences of evil actions, because conscience is the revealing sensation, and we only know those consequences so long as we are disinterested.

These fundamental difficulties of life and morals are little discussed. Few think of them clearly, and still fewer speak of them much. But they cloud the brain and confuse the hopes of many who never stated them explicitly to themselves, and never heard them stated explicitly by others. Meanwhile superficial difficulties are in every one's mouth; we are deafened with controversies on remote matters which do not concern us; we are confused with ' Aids to Faith ' which neither harm nor help us. A tumult of irrelevant theology is in the air which oppresses men's heads, and darkens their future, and scatters their hopes. For such a calamity there is no thorough cure; it belongs to the confused epoch of an age of transition, and is inseparable from it. But the best palliative is a steady attention to primary difficulties—if possible, a clear mastery over them; if not, a distinct knowledge how we stand respecting them. The shrewdest man of the world who ever lived tells us, ' That he who begins in certainties shall end in doubts; but he who begins in doubts shall end in certainties;' and the maxim is even more applicable to matters which are not of this world than to those which are.

THE END.

INDEX